The Psychology of Working

A New Perspective for Career Development, Counseling, and Public Policy

Counseling and Psychotherapy

Investigating Practice from Scientific, Historical, and Cultural Perspectives

A Lawrence Erlbaum Associates, Inc. Series
Series Editor, Bruce E. Wampold, University of Wisconsin

This innovative new series is devoted to grasping the vast complexities of the practice of counseling and psychotherapy. As a set of healing practices delivered in a context shaped by the health delivery systems and the attitudes and values of consumers, practitioners, and researchers, counseling and psychotherapy must be examined critically. By understanding the historical and cultural context of counseling and psychotherapy and by examining the extant research, these critical inquiries seek a deeper, richer understanding of what is a remarkably effective endeavor.

Published

- *Counseling and Therapy with Clients Who Abuse Alcohol or Other Drugs*
  Cynthia E. Glidden-Tracy

- *The Great Psychotherapy Debate*
  Bruce Wampold

- *The Psychology of Working: A New Perspective for Career Development, Counseling and Public Policy*
  David L. Blustein

Forthcoming

- *The Pharmacology and Treatment of Substance Abuse: Evidence and Outcomes Based Perspectives*
  Lee Cohen, Frank Collins, Alice Young, Dennis McChargue

- *In Our Client's Shoes: Theory and Techniques of Therapeutic Assessment*
  Stephen Finn

- *Making Treatment Count: Using Outcomes to Inform and Manage Therapy*
  Michael Lambert, Jeb Brown, Scott Miller, Bruce Wampold

- *Assessment in Counseling Psychology*
  Karen Marsh

- *IDM Supervision: An Integrated Developmental Model for Supervising Counselors and Therapists, Third Edition*
  Cal Stoltenberg and Brian McNeill

- *The Great Psychotherapy Debate, Revised Edition*
  Bruce Wampold

The Psychology of Working

A New Perspective for Career Development, Counseling, and Public Policy

David L. Blustein
Boston College

 LAWRENCE ERLBAUM ASSOCIATES, PUBLISHERS

2006   Mahwah, New Jersey   London

Lawrence Erlbaum Associates, Inc., Publishers
10 Industrial Avenue
Mahwah, New Jersey 07430
www.erlbaum.com

Cover design by Kathryn Houghtaling Lacey

Library of Congress Cataloging-in-Publication Data
Blustein, David Larry.
    The psychology of working : a new perspective for career development, counseling, and public policy / David L. Blustein.
        p. cm. — (The LEA series in counseling and psychotherapy)
Includes bibliographical references and index.
ISBN 0-8058-4376-0 (cloth : alk. paper)
ISBN 0-8058-5879-2 (pbk. : alk. paper)
1. Work—Psychological aspects. 2. Work—Social aspects. 3. Vocational guidance. 4. Psychotherapy—Social aspects. 5. Social policy. I. Title. II. Series.
BF481.B57 2006
158.7—dc22

                                                                 2005054162
                                                                        CIP

CONTENTS

SERIES FOREWORD

This innovative new series is devoted to grasping the vast complexities of the practice of counseling and psychotherapy. As a set of healing practices delivered in a context shaped by health delivery systems and the attitudes and values of consumers, practitioners, and researchers, counseling and psychotherapy must be examined critically. By understanding the historical and cultural context of counseling and psychotherapy and by examining the extant research, these critical inquiries seek a deeper, richer understanding of what is a remarkably effective endeavor.

David L. Blustein, in *The Psychology of Working: A New Perspective for Career Development, Counseling, and Public Policy*, has elevated work to a position as a primary factor in the well-being of people. He shows how across cultures the meaning derived from work plays a central role in the lives of individuals and how the world of work can either promote well being or lead to distress, depending on the nature of the work and the interaction between the individual and the work environment. The implications for public policy and psychological intervention are immense. This book establishes the poverty of models that assume a fixed environment and attempt to assist the individual to locate within that environment. Instead, Blustein challenges the field to consider the individual and the world of work as a system and expands the notion of career psychology and vocational counseling.

—*Bruce E. Wampold, PhD, ABPP, Series Editor*
University of Wisconsin–Madison

FOREWORD

Most American adults spend a third to a half of their waking hours at work. Yet work finds relatively little place in the ways that we think about our lives. When it comes to psychological theory about the influences that shape our personalities or contribute to our happiness or unhappiness, the primary focus tends to be on human beings as the product of their childhoods. Thousands and thousands of pages have been published on the impact of early childhood experiences. Far less has been written on how the context of work shapes our lives. Yet, by the time most of us breathe our last, we will have spent far more hours being workers than being children.

This is not to disparage the importance of childhood. The habits, perceptions, and inclinations that characterize our lives are clearly powerfully shaped by the experiences of our early years. Moreover, those experiences have, we might say, a double impact in that they skew the kinds of later experiences we have, so that the later experiences are not random but are themselves a function of what the earlier experiences were (Wachtel, 1987, 1997). It is also the case, nonetheless, that the very meaning of being alive is that we live in response to events. The psychological structures that evolve over the course of development are not rigid structures that simply inhere in some "internal" realm. They are structures of response, ways we learn to respond to and make sense of what actually happens to us—and what actually happens matters!

One of the most important things that happens to most of us is that we get a job. Although some people stay in one job for many years, some change jobs frequently, and many spend at least a portion of their lives—often an especially painful portion—looking for work, work tends to be a common denominator for almost all of us. Yet we tend to view our time at work almost purely in functional terms: Do we "have" a job? How much money do we make? Are we "getting ahead?"

If we are to truly understand our lives, however, we need to understand both the experience of working and the meaning of working in our lives. Ours is a consumer society, and that fact has distorted our perception of work to an extraordinary degree. We measure our success as a society in terms of what we consume, and we give surprisingly little attention to how what we consume is produced. Recently, the sheer depravity of the working conditions associated with some of our "outsourced" production in Third World countries has led to heightened awareness and protests. But the nature of work in our own society is much less attended to. Domestically, we worry about the loss of jobs that the "race to the bottom" of global capitalism has unleashed, but we are far less attentive to the quality of work in our own society. By *quality of work* I mean more than just decent pay or possibilities for advancement. I mean, rather, that the daily experience of being at work is one of the most important contexts of our entire lives, and that a "good" job is not the same as a job that pays enough to let us buy things.

So consumed are we with consumerism, as it were, that we fail to think very deeply or thoughtfully about our role as the producers of all those things we consume. Elsewhere I have referred to our work lives as "the consumer's forty hours in purgatory," referring to the conditions we create for ourselves in the pursuit of more "efficient" production, and pointed out that (with the exception of those who lose their jobs altogether in the search for the most goods at the cheapest price), "The workers from whom we are always trying to extract greater productivity are none other than ourselves" (Wachtel, 1983).

Work, as David Blustein incisively describes, is more than just a way to produce things, and it is more than just something we have to get done in order to enjoy our "real" lives. Work is a very central part of our "real" lives, and if we do not attend to it with sufficient respect—and even compassion—then we will continue to create lives for ourselves that do not satisfy. The tensions we bring home from a day in "purgatory" spill over into family life, friendship, and community, affecting those central contexts of our lives as well. Blustein helps us to redirect our focus—to understand that work is a central part of how we give meaning to our lives, a central feature of our identity, a central part of how we are cruel or kind or are treated cruelly or kindly. Work is also a central way in which race, class, gender, sexuality, and health or disability are played out in our society and take on meanings that often become self-fulfilling prophecies. Often, these crucial dimensions and distinctions are obscured in our society's discourse, and it is only those in the privileged classes who are viewed as pursuing meaning or identity in work. For everyone else, the assumption is that TGIF and a paycheck are all that matters. Blustein tells us—and shows us—that that is not the case. He illuminates the role of work in every sector of the social system, and he does so with psychological as well as social perspicuity. This is a major contribution; I hope it gets the attention it deserves.

—*Paul L. Wachtel, PhD*
City College of CUNY

PREFACE

In the Bible Cain slew Abel
and East of Eden he was cast
You're born into this life paying
For the sins of somebody else's past
Daddy worked his whole life for nothing but the pain
Now he walks these empty rooms looking for something to blame
You inherit the sins, you inherit the flames

—Bruce Springsteen, "Adam Raised a Cain" (1978/1998)

Too many people live in barren houses like those of the father of Springsteen's protagonist. My intent in this book is to examine the ways in which those wandering in the empty rooms like the one described above can find meaning and pleasure in their work. More broadly, I seek to construct a new perspective for the psychological exploration of working that will give voice to the protagonist in Springsteen's lyrics, whose anguish speaks for so many others who have not had an opportunity for a rewarding work life.

Current Views and Challenges

The study of work and working has not been neglected by psychologists. For example, counseling psychologists have produced a very rich literature on selected aspects of vocational behavior (e.g., career exploration, career planning, and career decision making; see, for example, Brown & Lent, 2005; Walsh & Savickas, 2005). Industrial-organizational psychologists have produced an equally extensive literature on work-related behavior in modern organizations (e.g., Aamodt, 1991; Anderson, Ones, Sinangil, & Viswesveran, 2002; Hall, 1996; Landy, 1989).

The primary issues that are explored by traditional counseling and organizational psychologists (e.g., career decision making, career commitment, turnover, congruence) tend to assume a level of choice or volition that is not typical for most workers. For example, consider the following two examples of people struggling with work-related issues:

■ The first case is an immigrant from South Asia who worked as an engineer in her home country. Upon arriving to her new home in London, England, she learns that she does not have the appropriate credentials to continue in her chosen field. How does she face the task of moving into the work force? How does her view of working and of life itself become transformed as her hopes to work in a field that suits her interests are suddenly dashed and she must look for whatever will help her to survive?

■ The second example is an African American woman who owns a printing shop in an urban community. Her business has helped her to make a decent living and has given her a sense of autonomy that was not available to her parents and grandparents. However, an office-supplies chain moves into her area with a cheaper printing department, forcing her income to drop precipitously. Her dreams for self-sufficiency and economic empowerment fade as she confronts the lower prices and greater efficiency of her competition.

These two vignettes, when considered collectively, provide a vivid counterpoint to the prevailing view within vocational psychology and organizational psychology that people exercise choices in selecting and implementing their aspirations about the sort of work they will do. The need to work for survival, regrettably, has been relatively neglected in contemporary discourse on working and careers. This book seeks to redress this gap (along with several others) in the literature.

In addition, the study of working has been split off from other domains of human experience, resulting in artificial schisms between the knowledge of vocational and organizational psychologists, that of other behavioral and social scientists, and that of psychotherapists and career counselors. With the publication of this book, I seek to bridge the critical gaps and outline the features of a more overarching and, ultimately, more inclusive psychology of working.

I seek to place *working* at the same level of attention for social and behavioral scientists and psychotherapists as other major life concerns, like intimate relationships, physical and mental health, and socioeconomic inequities. I also seek to provide readers with an expanded conceptual framework within which to think about working in human development and human experience. Furthermore, I seek to construct a coherent metaperspective about working that will enrich the discourse across the broad spectrum of psychology's concerns and agendas.

I hope that this book will stimulate the development of richly explanatory theoretical statements in the years to come. I also hope that the body of knowledge emerging from the psychology of working will inform clinical practice and public policy about the full range of working experiences in contemporary life. I would like readers to emerge from this book with a more refined understanding of how work functions in our lives. Ideally, the psychology-of-working perspective will provide a foundation upon which therapists and counselors can develop greater sensitivity and skill about the complexities of work-related issues that arise in counseling individuals, groups, and families.

I also hope that the psychology-of-working perspective will generate new knowledge leading to greater engagement in public policy about education, training, labor policy, and employment issues. Using a more expansive lens with which to explore the nature of working, I believe that social and behavioral scientists as well as counselors can develop more compelling arguments for the creation of equitable policies about education, training, unemployment, family/work policies, occupational health, and other related issues.

My Personal Journey
Into the Psychology of Working

The actual process of writing this book was a labor of love, but was not without its struggles. My reasons for writing the book have remained constant across the 4-year span from its inception to its completion. As a counseling psychologist with a passionate interest in career development, I have experienced considerable conflict in my own work, which historically has focused on the traditional themes of career decision making, exploration, and identity development. I have felt very privileged to contribute to the literature and provide direct services to clients who were confronting career decision-making and other work-related struggles. In addition, the research, practice, and teaching were all quite rewarding and in turn rewarded me with a steady and upwardly mobile career.

Something, however, was not right in my work. Naturally, I realized that the career development enterprise (entailing vocational assessment, career counseling, career development courses, and structured career exploration activities) was quite effective and well established. My thinking about careers and working was transformed gradually and profoundly as I spoke with inner city youth with few opportunities for education and training, and interviewed research participants working in car washes and supermarkets with no prospects for advancement. My thinking also was transformed by my experiences as a therapist, working with clients whose work-related struggles often were quite pronounced, but who had little idea that these concerns had a legitimate place in their treatment. Furthermore, my evolving concern with the full scope of working in psychology has been inspired by social justice movements within the social and behavioral sciences and within the broader body politic. In short, I realized that the field of career development and related discourse on work in psychology needed more than minor tinkering around the edges. I have become convinced that the study of work and careers in psychology needs a reasoned critique and a new perspective. (I want to underscore that the critique detailed in this book includes my own work and my earlier assumptions about work and careers.) This book, therefore, represents my attempt at both the critique and the construction of an intellectual framework for a cogent, inclusive, and ultimately more comprehensive psychology of working.

The Mission and Audience

My intention with the publication of this book is to integrate our thinking about working into the broader fabric of psychological theory and practice. Moreover, I believe that it is critical for behavioral and social scientists and practitioners to confront the vast inequities in life circumstances that are typically most evident in education and work. Thus, this book seeks to develop a language and a way of thinking about working that will more closely resemble the reality of our lives.

Another critical point that inspired this book is the fact that working is changing rapidly for many, if not all, citizens of the Western world (e.g., Arthur & Rousseau, 1996; Wilson, 1996). I review the more important features of these changes in an attempt to develop a conceptual infrastructure for understanding how these changes affect and are affected by the ever-expanding array of roles and responsibilities emerging in the 21st century.

The audience for the book includes many potential readers encompassing the interested layperson, counselors and other therapists, scholars from career development and organizational behavior, and policy analysts who are concerned with work and access to opportunity. I am speaking to all who seek to intervene in the lives of others—the counselors and counseling psychologists who have historically provided direct services to clients who present with work-related issues, but also psychotherapists, social workers, and psychiatrists. In general, I believe that all clinicians will find the material presented in this book to be central in developing an inclusive and more effective mode of psychological treatment. I also am confident that organizational consultants and management specialists will find this book useful. Additionally, I am speaking to social and behavioral scientists and readers interested in public policy who think about work, education, social justice, and human development.

The Knowledge Base and Structure of the Book

A major source of knowledge for the psychology of working is grounded in existing research and theory by psychologists; however, I also include relevant input from sociologists, anthropologists, and economists. In addition, I believe the voices of workers, speaking on behalf of their own experience, can teach us a great deal. Accordingly, I rely on published case material, qualitative vignettes, and narratives from other books and journal articles, as well as on poems, fiction, memoirs and song lyrics, as a means of obtaining a deeper connection to the *experience* of working in the human condition (e.g., Bowe, Bowe, & Streeter, 2000; Thomas, 1999). Finally, I intersperse some counseling cases representing amalgams of themes and issues presented by former clients to illustrate some of the issues. Such material conveys the emotional richness that work evokes, and informs the development of new ideas that can be explored further in subsequent research.

I realize that my approach is novel, representing a synthesis of intellectual currents that falls outside of the purview of the traditional social and behavioral sciences. The need to include a broad spectrum of views and voices is critical if we are to develop a meaningful body of knowledge that is useful in shaping counseling practice and public policy. Indeed, the stakes have never been higher. We are entering a period of great uncertainty in which the lives of all workers, not just the unskilled, are facing substantive changes. To create knowledge without a close connection to the internal constructions and emotional experiences of people grappling with work would yield only part of the picture. As such, I have sought to connect to readers both intellectually and emotionally in order to create a fully engaging and compelling perspective of the psychology of working. Naturally, my social science training suggests the need for caution, but I hope that the synthesis of these elements leads to a transformed discourse about working that is multidisciplinary, affirming of diversity, and informative in developing maximally effective practices and policies.

In order to achieve these objectives, I begin the book with an overview of the general terrain of work within psychological research, theory, and practice. I then explore how the world of work is shifting across the globe, with implications for all workers and individuals who seek work. I devote space in the early part of the book to detailing how work fulfills various core human needs, including the need for survival, relational connection, and self-determination. The impact of social barriers in our ability to fulfill these needs is then assessed, followed by an analysis of the theoretical and research implications of the psychology of working. I close the book with a detailed exploration of the clinical implications of the psychology of working followed by an assessment of how this new perspective can inform public policy.

In sum, I hope that the new ideas in this book create an enthusiastic and passionate dedication to exploring the full gamut of working experiences. Ideally, readers will come away from this book with a broader vision, one that affirms working as a central ingredient in life. By advancing a new perspective, I clearly have created a challenging agenda. However, as the opening vignette of this preface suggests, the pain and anguish of people without means to a dignified working life is palpable. To ignore it risks further marginalization of people without much hope. By opening readers' eyes and hearts to a fuller scope of working, I hope to stimulate a movement to reshape psychology's approach to working. The expanded focus I propose here is not without its challenges; but, in my view, the only hope for psychology to reach its potential in our society is for it to include an engaged and thoughtful discourse about working. This book is a first step; I hope that readers will join me as we move forward to create a fully inclusive psychology of working.

Acknowledgments

I have been influenced by many colleagues, friends, artists, writers, poets, musicians, and family members in overt and more covert ways as I developed the ideas that are presented in this book. To list all of the influences would be nearly impossible as many of these influences have become so embedded into my thinking and value system that the etiology of the influence is now hard to discern. Throughout the book, I have sought to reference ideas that are derived from my colleagues and peers. However, I take full responsibility for the content, positions, and arguments detailed in this book.

This caveat notwithstanding, I would like to acknowledge a number of people who have helped to shape the ideas presented herein or who have inspired me to think broadly, outside of the purview of our professional and intellectual training. As I propose in this book, relational influences are closely embedded with our work lives; as such, the people who I am acknowledging here have often influenced both my sense of feeling supported as well as the development of my thinking.

My graduate school professors from Teachers College, Columbia University, were critical in helping me to understand the role of work within psychology. In this context, I have appreciated the spirited input of Jean Pierre Jordaan, Peter Cairo, Patricia Raskin, and Roger Myers. My dear friends from the University at Albany, State University of New York, will no doubt see their influences in my work. I have appreciated the mentorship and colleagueship of Monte Bruch, Doug Strohmer, Mike Ellis, Marilyn Stern, Don Blocher, Sheldon Grand, and Micki Friedlander, who provided me with the rigorous way of thinking that characterizes the best of our field. I particularly owe a debt to Susan Phillips and Richard Haase, two beloved colleagues who strongly believed in my ability to write, think, and, ultimately, create new ideas. Their influence is evident throughout these pages.

In my current home at Boston College, I have many colleagues who continue to nourish my intellectual development. I would like to acknowledge Mary Brabeck, Jim Mahalik, and Maureen Kenny for making a compelling case for me to join the faculty at Boston College. Furthermore, the input from Janet Helms, Mary Walsh, Guerda Nicolas, Lisa Goodman, Belle Liang, Etiony Aldarondo, Sandy Morse, Bob Romano, and Liz Sparks has been very important in helping me to shape the social justice, multicultural, feminist, and public policy agenda in my work. I also have been supported by the outstanding professionals who administer the Lynch School of Education; in this context, I would like to acknowledge the assistance of Joseph O'Keefe, S. J., Brinton Lykes, Dennis Shirley, and Mary Ellen Fulton, who provided me with the resources and support to work on this book over the past few years. Furthermore, I am grateful to the administrative staff of my department at Boston College who helped to manage my often over-committed life with grace and humor. Without the help of Dottie Cochran, Marguerite Tierney, and Diane Beaulieu, the book would have taken considerably longer.

From the broader world of vocational psychology, many colleagues have entertained my ideas and provided critically needed feedback. I especially owe a debt to Mary Sue Richardson, whose 1993 article in the *Journal of Counseling Psychology* on the role of work as a focal point for counseling psychology helped to inspire many of the ideas outlined in this book. I also am grateful to Mark Savickas, whose friendship has now moved into its third decade. We have both come a long way from our hesitant forays at American Psychological Association conventions in the mid 1980s. Mark's intellectual breadth and depth of knowledge in vocational psychology is impressive and has been instrumental in helping to shape my thinking. The input of Hanoch Flum can also been discerned in these pages. His friendship and his colleagueship are very special and have helped to give me the confidence to tackle this project. I also would like to thank the broader world of the Society for Vocational Psychology, which has provided a wonderfully supportive network of friends and colleagues. The following individuals were particularly influential in this venture: Nadya Fouad, Ruth Fassinger, Bruce Walsh, Tom Krieshok, Ellen McWhirter, Saba Rasheed Ali, Scott Solberg, Kimberly Howard, Graham Stead, Michael Brown, Mary Heppner, Joaquim Armando Ferreira, Eduardo Santos, Jane Swanson, Lisa Flores, Daryl Luzzo, Mark Pope, Nancy Betz, Gail Hackett, Cindy Juntunen, Dan Mahoney, and Donna Schultheiss.

My students have also helped to shape my thinking. In particular, I would like to acknowledge Justin Perry, David DeWine, Alexandra Kenna, Matt Diemer, Anna Chaves McDonald, Julia DeVoy, Ravi Gatha, Bianca Schaefer, Michelle Friedman, Tim Ketterson, Shanna Dullen, and Kerri Murphy for their intellectual input and logistical support in developing the ideas presented in this book. I also appreciate the valuable assistance of Katie Benoit, Stephanie Glassburn, Nadia Gill, Yanhong Li, Anthony Issaco, Susan Taylor, and Marie Land, who deserve special thanks for the onerous job of obtaining the permissions and in searching for references needed for this book. I particularly appreciate the long-standing contributions of Alexandra Kenna, who worked so hard on the seemingly endless references and citations.

The staff of Lawrence Erlbaum Associates has been truly supportive throughout this project. Beginning with the encouragement of Susan Milmoe and continuing with Steve Rutter, I have felt empowered to pursue my vision with this book. Moreover, both Susan and Steve helped to edit the text and provided valuable input throughout the writing of the manuscript. In addition, Bruce Wampold was critical in helping me to think about this project; I am very humbled by his gracious support of this work and his role in helping me to realize that LEA would be the ideal publisher for this book. I appreciate the support of Nichole Buchmann and Providence Rao, who have helped to steer the manuscript through the production process. The text has been carefully copyedited by Debbie Ruel, who has helped to improve the quality of the presentation considerably. In addition, I thank Paul Wachtel for sharing his insights and observations in the essay he prepared for the Foreword of this book. I also appreciate the input of Bruce Wampold and Lenore Harmon, who read the entire manuscript and provided thoughtful and helpful advice. Additional feedback was provided by Hanoch Flum, Donna Schultheiss, and

Camille DeBelle, who each reviewed a few chapters in their respective areas of expertise. The collective infusion of ideas from the LEA editorial team and the aforementioned colleagues has been critically important in refining my writing and in clarifying the logic and coherence of my positions. I very much appreciate the time, energy, and intellectual rigor that each of these talented individuals devoted to this project.

Given the unique approach that I employed in developing the knowledge base for the psychology of working, I have had a wonderful opportunity to explore contributions from a wide array of writers, novelists, poets, playwrights, songwriters, and other artists who have shared their insights about working. The excerpts that I have included here represent the tip of the iceberg of the material that I read in preparing this book. I would like to acknowledge the debt that we all owe to the various artists and musicians who have given voice to the experiences of working. I particularly thank the individuals who granted permission for me to reprint their work in this book.

Finally, I would like to thank the people in my life who have loved and supported me so that I could put my ideas into words in this book. I would like to acknowledge the support of my brother, Richard, whose own journey in his work life has demonstrated a deep sense of resilience in the face of considerable obstacles. I thank Babo Kamel, who stood by me as I worked on this book, and also helped to edit the text. I would also like to thank Sally Weylman, whose own commitment to work and relationships has been an inspiration to me and to all those who know her. In addition, I thank my daughters, Larissa and Michelle. They were always patient with me as I struggled to get one last sentence down before our next engagement. Last, but not least, I dedicate this book to my parents: Harry and Janet Blustein. My parents taught me about work, the dignity of work, and the importance of relationships as a means of coping with and relishing both the struggles and joys of work. My parents toiled hard and long to make their living in this world; often they came home from work exhausted and worn out. Yet, they were never too tired to parent, to love, and to laugh. Their presence is on each page of this book.

—*David L. Blustein*

CHAPTER 1

Psychology and the Experience of Working: A Blurred Focus That is Sharpening

Work influences us throughout our lives as few activities do. No other choice we make—with the possible exception of our spouse—influences each of us, our families, our children, our values, or our status as much as our choice of a job or occupation. Throughout our lives, but especially from our late teens and early 20s to our 60s, we spend more time engaged in work activities than any other single pursuit (except for sleep, which does not seem to be a pursuit or activity).

—Hulin (2002, p. 8)

We take the position that career choice will be salient only for individuals who believe that their choices are or can be effective (thus self-esteem, locus of control, and attributional concepts are all important), who live in an environment in which their choices truly can be effective, and who are free from survival needs for food, shelter, and safety (Maslow, 1970).

—Harmon and Farmer (1983, p. 64)

Entering the new century of psychology's contributions to the social sciences and to human welfare, we are in a unique position to reappraise our relationship to the study of working. As reflected by the quotes that begin this chapter, the relationship between working and psychology has been complex and somewhat ambivalent within the first century of psychological discourse. In this chapter, I explore the strengths and limitations of existing formulations of working, vocational behavior, and career development. In reviewing the diverse streams of ideas generated from existing psychological discourse, I initiate a critique of traditional perspectives on working, which are often discussed under the rubric of vocational psychology and organizational development. The chapter concludes with a call for a new psychology of working, encompassing a fuller array of relevant issues facing individuals in the 21st century.

Defining the Scope of the Psychology of Working

The psychology-of-working perspective that I advance here is constructed with a deep appreciation of the rich contributions from various sources in the social and behavioral sciences. My position is that working is central to understanding human behavior and the context that frames life experience. In this section, I present many of the intellectual currents that have contributed to my position, culminating in a definition of the meaning and scope of the psychology of working.

In my opinion, the psychological study of working has enormous potential to inform public policy on labor issues, educational reform as well as counseling practice. In this book, I seek to create the scaffolding for subsequent investigations of working. Prior to delineating my definition of the psychology of working, I first describe some historical contributions from outside of psychology that have influenced my formulations.

In the 19th century, Marx (1867) articulated a view of work as a means of self-definition; however, he also critiqued the way in which most workers were exploited, underscoring the divisive disconnection between modes of production and consequent feelings of alienation that characterized the industrial era (and still, unfortunately, is evident in contemporary times). Freud (1930) observed that working helped to provide a sense of regularity to life and a connection to the broader social and cultural community. For both Marx and Freud, working was not a means of achieving personal satisfaction or feelings of achievement. To the contrary, their respective positions were manifestations of the modal experience of 19th-century workers, whose labors were physically arduous and whose connection to the means of production and results of labor were often distant, at best.

Within philosophy, Heideigger (1962) viewed work as a means by which human beings engage in projects, which furnish people with a means of connecting to their world and to establishing continuity in their existence. Gini and Sullivan (1989) also based their definition on a broad philosophical framework by noting that "work is the means by which we become and complete ourselves as persons; we create ourselves in our work" (p. 3). The philosophical positions of Heideigger and Gini and Sullivan, taken together, underscore a sense of self-determination that work entails, which has clearly influenced contemporary psychological considerations of careers and organizational behavior. An economic definition of work can be culled from a landmark report by a special task force to the Secretary of Health, Education, and Welfare in the United States (1973) in which work was defined as activities that result in valuable services and products for others.

From a psychological perspective, O'Brien (1986) defined work as "the expenditure of effort in the performance of a task" (p. 1); this view captures a rather common view of work that has characterized significant scholarship and research, particularly within organizational psychology. Wilson's (1996) sociological definition limits the notion of work to labor that is exerted within the formal economy, which would be characterized by regular schedules and commitments.

When considering these perspectives in tandem, a number of common elements emerge, which have contributed to my multidimensional view of working. My definition of working seeks to embrace the wide scope of work-related activities, with a focus on the psychological meaning that we attach to working:

1. Working functions to provide people with a way to establish an identity and a sense of coherence in their social interactions. In other words, work furnishes at least part of our external identity in the world.
2. Working has very personal meaning that is influenced to a great extent by individual constructions and by socially mediated interactions with others. Working also has unique meaning that is derived from and embedded within specific cultural contexts, which shape and are shaped by individual experiences of working.
3. Working involves effort, activity, and human energy in given tasks that contribute to the overall social and economic welfare of a given culture. This includes paid employment as well as work that one does in caring for others within one's family and community.
4. Working has been one of the constants in our lives; the experience of working unifies human beings across time frames and cultures.

In this book, I focus on the psychological experience of working, embedded within an explicitly contextual framework. My thinking, which is consistent to a great extent with M. S. Richardson's (1993) position and with the recent framework offered by N. Peterson and González (2005), is that the notion of career (reflecting a hierarchical and planned series of jobs that are thoughtfully selected) is deeply embedded in a sociocultural framework that is relevant to only a minority of individuals around the globe. The vast changes in the concept of career, which is reflected in countless articles and books on the rapid changes in the notion of "career" (e.g., Arthur & Rousseau, 1996; Collin & Young, 2000; Hall, 1996) certainly suggest that very significant shifts are occurring across the globe for many relatively well educated workers. As I argue in this book, I believe that the psychology of working offers the best conceptual tools with which to frame new policy initiatives, practice interventions, and research goals required to address the dramatic changes in the world of work in the 21st century.

The conceptual framework of working described here seeks to embrace work that is engaged in for survival and work that is engaged in as a means of expressing one's interests in the world. (Ideally, these two motivational aspects of working are intertwined.) I am deliberately constructing a framework that is maximally inclusive, entailing working that occurs in the economic market place as well as work required in caring for loved ones and family members. By drawing the boundaries wide, I hope to create the intellectual space for overarching perspectives, theories, and research findings that will be maximally informative to counseling practice and public policy.

A Sociocultural History of Working

Pre-Industrial Trends

Earliest mentions of working can be traced to the Judeo-Christian Bible, with its graphic and compelling narratives about power, spirituality, conviction, and, of course, work. Work as a form of human expression dates back to our ancient history as hunters and gatherers (Goldschmidt, 1990; Wallman, 1979). Naturally, one of the primary tasks of life then (as it is now, albeit with a few more layers of complexity added) is survival. Indeed, anthropological analyses of contemporary hunting and gathering tribes reveal complex patterns of work that contain many of the foundational elements of current work experiences (Donkin, 2001; Goldschmidt, 1990). One of the major transitions that occurred in many human communities was the development of agriculture, which tended to locate people in stable environments. An outcome of this transition was the increasingly hierarchical nature of work in which men began increasingly to own property and women tended to work in caregiving tasks (Donkin, 2001).

Some of the earliest writings about work can be found in the Bible, which reflects work as the curse of human existence, "… 'a punishment for Adam's disobedience.' Work now involved fatigue and suffering, for nature had ceased to yield her fruits without the application of strenuous human effort"

(Thomas, 1999, p. 4). The view of men and women as lazy and without initiative is in fact reflected in numerous writings in pre-historic and medieval periods (Bettenson, 1947; Donkin, 2001; Ehmer, 2001; Neff, 1985; Thomas, 1999). One of the themes apparent in very early historical contributions is that working was often viewed as being undesirable because of the tediousness, physical exertion, and often inhumane conditions that surrounded many jobs, particularly for the vast majority of individuals who did not own land or own businesses (Firth, 1979; Goldshmidt, 1990; Neff, 1985). As I propose in this book, the pain of many jobs, including considerable physical effort, and the sense of alienation that exists for many individuals in contemporary times, are still major issues and are not solely artifacts of previous historic eras.

The extensive amount of time that people devote to working, coupled with the often challenging and even life-threatening conditions of many jobs, has led to a diverse array of explanations about the nature of working. Prior to the industrial revolution, the number of possible occupations was limited to agriculture, semi-skilled work (e.g., carpentry; masonry), small businesses (e.g., shopkeeper), and a small number of professions (religious callings; medicine; law) (Donkin, 2001; Ehmer, 2001; Neff, 1985). For the most part, the professions were reserved for wealthy individuals or people with powerful and connected families. Similarly, in many countries, owning land and businesses was not open to all individuals, with restrictions often stemming from religious, racial, gender, and ethnic backgrounds as well as the social connections of one's family (Fischer, 2001; Neff, 1985). For this reason, the entire enterprise of working was determined to a significant extent by social position for the vast majority of people in most societies. In general, people worked in farming or in other labor-intensive jobs that were motivated primarily by the need to make a living (Ehmer, 2001; Neff, 1985; Heilbroner & Singer, 1984). The major psychological manifestations of working focused on ways to survive such arduous conditions, with far less attention devoted to finding meaning in one's livelihood (Donkin, 2001). For example, consider the plight of many recent and more remote ancestors of individuals who migrated to the United States or similar places (e.g., Canada, Australia) with the hope of obtaining a better life. As many of us have read and learned in our family histories, working was a major burden, often characterized by significant pain and despair. The sweatshop workers of the urban centers and the sharecroppers of the southern part of the United States shared many common experiences, including very long hours, little financial reward, dangerous working conditions, and often humiliating treatment by one's supervisors (Donkin, 2001; Heilbroner & Singer, 1984; Neff, 1985).

Excerpts from the narratives of these workers are remarkably evocative, as they convey a special aspect of our collective history that is often neglected or lost in our high-technology, information-rich world. Consider the following narrative from Booker T. Washington (1901), who recalled some of his early childhood spent as a slave:

> I was asked not long ago to tell something about the sports and pastimes that I engaged in during my youth. Until that question was asked it had never occurred to me that there was no period of my life that was devoted to play. From the time that I can remember anything, almost every day of my life has been occupied in some kind of labour; though I think I would now be a more useful man if I had time for sports. During the period that I spent in slavery I was not large enough to be of much service, still I was occupied most of the time in cleaning the yards, carrying water to the men in the fields, or going to the mill, to which I used to take corn, once a week, to be ground. The mill was about three miles from the plantation. This work I always dreaded. The heavy bag of corn would be thrown across the back of the horse, and the corn divided about evenly on each side; but in some way, almost without exception, on these trips, the corn would so shift as to become unbalanced and would fall off the horse, and often I would fall with it. As I was not strong enough to reload the corn upon the horse, I would have to wait, sometimes for many hours, till a chance passer-by came along who would help me out of my trouble. The hours while waiting for some one were usually spent in crying. The time consumed in this way made me late in reaching the mill, and by the time I got my corn ground and reached home it would be far into the night. The road was a lonely one, and often led through dense forests. I was always frightened. The woods were said to be full of soldiers who had deserted from the army, and I had been told that the first thing a deserter did to a Negro boy when he found him alone was to cut off his ears. Besides, when I was late in getting home I knew I would always get a severe scolding or a flogging. (cited in Thomas, 1999, p. 19)

The description of Booker T. Washington's recollections of life as a slave attests to an intermingled set of memories about working and childhood. That Washington recalled his youth as embedded in such an onerous set of tasks is reflective of slavery, which is, thankfully, far less evident around the globe (although not completely eradicated). However, the inner experience that Washington recalls underscores a sense of working that is characterized by feelings of helplessness and fear, which is still common at different points in the lives of many individuals. Thus, this vignette conveys an emotional depth about working that I believe is necessary in understanding the meaning that working can have for individuals and communities.

Pre-industrial musings about working were not entirely filled with despair and sadness. Even among the working classes and farmers, working had the potential to be rewarding and satisfying, particularly for those who enjoyed the challenges and completion of tasks involved in deriving one's source of sustenance. In addition, working was seen as a means of helping to advance one's unique social position as well as provide connections to one's larger reference group. The following excerpt illustrates an early description of the broader social consequences of work:

> Man's industry ... brings impossible things to pass. This industry, oh, it can almost do anything. It has (as it were) removed mountains, or at least made ways through them: so did Caesar over the Alps, and Alexander in his voyage to the Indies. It has dried up and diverted seas and navigable torrents. It has erected hetacombs and pyramids from little atoms of principal materials. It has made glass malleable, instructed in all arts, languages, sciences, professions, found out the use of simples and their compositions, of metals and their digestion, of minerals and their use, of peace, war, justice, religion; nothing has been too hard for the industry of man to cope with and conquer ....

> Now, though I do not believe industry can do all that is boasted of it, yet I do advisedly conclude that in the industry of man there is such a latent power and life of actuation that it comes near the verge of miraculous.
> (Waterhouse, 1663, cited in Thomas, 1999, p. 78)

The passage from Waterhouse describes the vibrant sense of agency and achievement that working in a given community can attain. As this passage suggests, working can move from survival to producing substantial changes in our environment, often resulting in beautiful artistic endeavors and adaptive transformations of the environment.

Another view of work has been developed by scholars who have sought to understand the broader or more macro-aspects of working in pre-industrial and early industrial societies. Some of these ideas formed the basis for contemporary economic systems, including both capitalism (Locke, 1690/1975) and socialism (Marx, 1867). The degree to which these economic systems provide equitable and fair means of production and distribution of wealth is beyond the scope of this book. (However, the challenges of determining ways of more effectively distributing *access* to the resources to obtain dignified and meaningful work are relevant to the psychology of working and are discussed in the final chapter.) It is important, though, to note that both of these economic systems, developed by wealthy aristocrats, did not involve the input of the vast majority of workers who would be profoundly influenced by these economic systems, particularly when they were implemented in extremely rigid ways. Questions about the extent to which workers have volition in their lives are still prominent in contemporary discourse (e.g., Gini, 2000; Peterson

& González, 2005; M. S. Richardson, 1993; Rubin, 1994). In this book, I seek to use a psychological perspective to explore issues of power, self-determination, and interpersonal relationships, which reflect themes that have been evident throughout the history of human work (e.g., Goldschmidt, 1990; Herriott, 2001; Thomas, 1999).

Industrial Trends

By the advent of the industrial revolution, the entire structure of working began to change dramatically. One of the most important factors contributing to the transformation of working was the growing need for more skilled individuals to work in the increasingly complex factories that were developed to produce goods (Gini & Sullivan, 1989; Marshall & Tucker, 1992). In order to obtain the workforce needed for this newly emerging labor market, enormous social shifts had to take place. Most prominent among these social changes was the need for greater education for workers to fill the factory openings and the industrialized occupational settings that expanded throughout the world. Rather than considering literacy and numeracy skills as unnecessary (or even dangerous) for poor and working class people, education was viewed as a critical component of the industrial revolution (Brownlee, 1974; Fischer, 2001; Neff, 1985; Reich, 1991). Indeed, an educated populace has been a significant predictor of wealth within industrial societies (Hession & Sardy, 1969; Marshall & Tucker, 1992). However, the nature of the educational world was clearly circumscribed by the specific demands of the workplace. During the height of the industrial revolution in the 19th century, schools increasingly focused on training workers who would be able to learn by rote memory and who could follow orders clearly and without resistance. These characteristics were also the hallmarks of the ideal worker in a 19th-century factory (Gini & Sullivan, 1989).

A by-product of the need for more education was the development of a new period of life, known as adolescence (Blos, 1962). In contrast to the earlier family system wherein children were sent off to work and/or married when they were relatively young, older boys and girls were more likely to stay at home and obtain further education so that they could obtain the higher paying jobs that existed in the factories of many industrialized cities. Adolescence gave rise to a period of time when individuals could devote time and energy to the consideration of their vocational future and explore their options. The entire notion of people actually having choices about what sort of work they like to pursue is a very recent phenomenon in human history. Aside from the gentry classes and wealthy, the idea of volitional choices about work only became a reality for a sizable proportion of people in Western cultures during the 20th century. Prior to that time period, most poor and working class individuals took whatever work they could find, with the decision about what field to enter often determined by the social class and position of one's family of origin (Donkin, 2001; Gini, 2000; Thomas, 1999).

The industrial revolution did not necessarily mean great improvements for ordinary workers in factories and on farms. Quite to the contrary, the industrial revolution often led to greater hardship as ownership of the product of one's work was generally diminished (Gini & Sullivan, 1989; Hareven & Langenbach, 1978). At the same time, the industrial revolution did result in an exponential expansion of possible jobs for people to pursue, thereby offering far greater opportunities for people to experience satisfaction from their work. However, the industrial revolution also increased the distance of many working people from the fruits of their labor (Brownlee, 1974; Heilbroner & Singer, 1984). During this time, the trade union movement emerged, which helped to reduce tendencies on the part of employers to exploit working people (Aronowitz & Cutler, 1998; Clawson & Clawson, 1999; Edwards, 1993). However, the industrial age resulted in conditions that did not reduce inequities in the world of work. The gaps between rich and poor did not disappear in the industrial era as cycles of employment and unemployment became endemic for many working class adults (Reich, 1991; Wilson, 1996). In a brief vignette shared by one of the participants in Rubin's (1994) evocative study of working class families in the United States, a 34-year-old wife of an African American factory worker comments as follows: "I leave to go to work in the morning and he's (her unemployed husband) sitting there doing nothing, and when I come home at night, it's the same thing. It's like he didn't move the whole day" (p. 113). Understanding the experience of this unemployed individual is one of the goals of this book and I believe ought to be one of the moral challenges of the social and behavioral sciences given that highly inequitable economies continue to exist in most regions of the world. Moreover, I argue that it is critical for all psychologists and psychotherapists who seek to study and intervene in the working lives of clients to fully understand the complex and multidimensional nature of working in the 21st century.

The Psychological Study of Work and Working

The study of working within psychology has a number of well-established homes. Initially, I consider the role of vocational psychology and career counseling in articulating a discourse about the psychological aspects of working. Following that material, I explore the contributions that industrial/ organizational psychology has made to our understanding of working.

Vocational Psychology and Career Counseling

As industrialization became more pervasive, the number and diversity of occupational options grew geometrically (Herr, Cramer, & Niles, 2004; Savickas & Baker, 2005). At the same time, educational options increased, leading to a sense of confusion among adolescents and adults about their optimal vocational direction (Keller & Viteles, 1937). Growing out of the rapid set of social changes that occurred throughout the later part of the 19th century, a group of social reformers and educators began to develop various systems to help young people choose their careers. One of these individuals, Frank Parsons, a social activist and former mayoral candidate in Boston, is often credited with founding vocational guidance (Hartung & Blustein, 2002). Indeed, Parsons' contributions are noteworthy and merit some attention in our discussion. Parsons (1909) had strong progressive or populist leanings (Savickas & Baker, 2005; Zytowski, 2001) and believed in activist interventions in the lives of people, especially poor immigrants. One of his most important ideas was that people would be happier if they made "wise choices" about their work lives. While Parsons was not educated in psychology per se, his own diverse vocational experiences (which included college teaching, politics, social service work, and administration) gave him a particularly expansive view of the challenges that people faced in the world of work.

Initially, Parsons' Vocational Guidance Bureau was housed in a social service facility in Boston's North End, then a bastion of immigrants from Southern and Eastern Europe. The agency served as a sort of settlement house for immigrants, linking vocational guidance to a broad array of services, including adult education, vocational training, and the like (H. V. Davis, 1969). (In fact, one of the goals of this book is to bring psychology back to its very admirable roots of studying and intervening in the lives of all people, particularly the poor and working classes.

The history of vocational guidance has been documented extensively in the literature (Herr et al., 2004; Keller & Viteles, 1937; Savickas & Baker, 2005). Hence, this review will focus on the issues of central importance to this discussion, notably, the way in which the vocational guidance movement understood and made sense of working. Early in the history of vocational guidance, the major focus of attention was on helping individuals to find the best match between their interests and abilities and the requirements of a given position or job. This approach, known as the trait-factor (or later as the Person–Environment fit) model, was based to a large extent on the growing sophistication in psychometrics and testing. After World War I, large-scale test development projects were initiated in both North America and Europe to find the best ways to assess intelligence, vocational interests, and personality characteristics (Cohen & Swerdlik, 2002). The advent of these increasingly more sophisticated tests formed a large proportion of the tools used by vocational counselors and applied psychologists who were interested in helping their clients and students find the most adaptive fit in their career choices. This early study of tests and measurements was supplemented by the work of industrial and organizational psychologists (formerly known as personnel psychologists) who sought ways to assess person–environment fit from the perspective of the organization (Landy, 1989; Miner, 1969; Neff, 1985). In doing so, personnel psychologists developed a clearer understanding of the world of work, at least within the industrial and post-industrial context, thereby providing psychologists with a language and means of understanding the characteristics of diverse job settings and an organizational perspective with which to understand work.

An interesting paradox of the history of career development is that one of the most important advances theoretically also may have had the unfortunate effect of diminishing vocational counseling's historic commitment to the poor and working classes and other marginalized people. Specifically, perhaps the most eminent theorist in 20th-century career development, Donald Super, established a compelling and very creative set of theoretical ideas, generally known as life span, life space theory (Super, 1957, 1980; Super, Savickas, & Super, 1996). In short, this theoretical contribution sought to move the field of career counseling beyond the restricted range of the Person–Environment fit model. Rather than considering vocational choice out of the context of other life experiences, Super embedded the role of work into a more coherent and expansive set of assumptions about human development. (See Jordaan & Super, 1974; Super, 1957, Super, Starishevsky, Matlin, & Jordan, 1963; Super et al., 1996, for detailed and authoritative overviews of Super's critically important contributions.) In moving the field away from the notion that each individual has an ideal set of possible matches with the world of work that need to be assessed and identified, Super constructed a creative and far-reaching set of ideas about the notion of *career*. For Super, career represented "a sequence of positions held during the course of a lifetime" (Super, 1980). A similar definition has been advanced by Sennett (1998), who indicated that the term *career* had its roots in the English word for carriages, referring to "... a lifelong channel for one's economic pursuits" (p. 9).

In using the term *career*, Super (1957) inadvertently placed the notion of work into a context that was embedded deeply in a lifestyle that was, for the most part, characteristic of relatively well-educated and often affluent people within advanced Western countries. Super's objective in replacing the notion of occupation or work with the notion of career was to construct a perspective that would encompass work-related issues across the life span and not simply around the adolescent and young adulthood period of life. In addition, Super sought to create a discourse that would embed the study of work across the life space, thereby capturing the complex texture of contemporary life, replete with shifting roles. I believe that Super's important efforts to apply a developmental life span perspective to vocational psychology were not directed intentionally toward reducing the focus on working class and poor individuals. In fact, his major longitudinal study included primarily working class students from a modest town in New York, around 60 miles to the northwest of Manhattan (Super & Overstreet, 1960). (It is important to note as well that other scholars after World War II began to focus on careers as opposed to work, including most of the trait-factor theorists, such as Holland.) However, one of the *latent* effects of focusing on careers as opposed to work is that vocational psychology became a study of the work lives of people with status and achievement (M. S. Richardson, 1993).

It is important to note that the decline of the term *career* is not without some cost. As Sennett (1998) noted, the notion of career also was advanced by Walter Lippmann in the early part of the 20th century and was viewed as playing a major function in modern life. In Lippmann's book (1914) entitled *"Drift and Mastery,"* the goal of building a meaningful work life, which would take form in a career (as in Super's definition), was proposed as an antidote to the sense of rootlessness and alienation that many immigrants experienced as they began life in North America. For Lippmann, engaging a life-long career that had some meaning offered a means of inoculating individuals from the feeling of personal failure while also developing an enhanced sense of character. The adaptive aspects of work, as detailed in the career notions advanced by Lippmann and Super, are not lost in this book. Indeed, a primary objective of this contribution is to develop a perspective that will include as many people as possible in a world where they can increasingly seek out, obtain, and sustain meaningful work that satisfies their fundamental psychological, financial, and social needs.

As I have suggested, the field of career counseling has struggled in its focus and in its appreciation of the full array of work roles. However, it is important to note that voices advocating for the poor and marginalized have always been evident in this field, albeit somewhat muted at times (e.g., E. J. Smith, 1983;

Warnath, 1975). More recently, perspectives highlighting the complex and challenging lives of those who do not fit the typical white-collar career pattern have been profoundly influential within career development (e.g., Carter & Cook, 1992; Helms & Cook, 1999; M. S. Richardson, 1993; Worthington & Juntunen, 1997), and certainly are facilitating a major reappraisal of our efforts, as reflected in this book. Most notably, Super's (1980) revisions of his theory expanded the purview in career development to the lives of women and to ethnic minority group members. In addition, many of the most effective and articulate calls for equality for women in North American culture have come from vocational psychologists, led by Harmon (1972), Betz and Hackett (1981), Fassinger (2000), and Fitzgerald (1993). These advances in feminist thinking predated many of the inroads that feminism has made in applied psychology, evoked in part by the glaring inequities that exist in the world of work in relation to differential opportunities and unequal earnings for men and women.

Furthermore, a compelling discourse on the complex and challenging lives of people of color has taken shape in vocational psychology, led initially by E. J. Smith (1983) and later by Helms (Helms & Piper, 1994; Helms & Cook, 1999), Carter (e.g., Carter & Cook, 1992), Fouad and Bingham (1995), and others (e.g., Walsh, Bingham, Brown, & Ward, 2001). Finally, a few vocational psychologists stepping outside of traditional theoretical boundaries have gradually started to appreciate the potential that our field has for the full gamut of individuals across social class, race, and gender. In this context, scholars such as Savickas (1993, 1995), M. S. Richardson (1993, 1996), Fassinger (2000), Fouad and Bingham (1995), and N. Peterson and González (2005) have explored the meaning and consequences of a truly inclusive view of work in the lives of people across the life span and across the huge economic and political spaces that continue to afford individuals such vastly diverse work lives.

Thus, my perspective is clearly constructed on some noteworthy precedents. Like these important influences, I hope to expand the scope of our inquiry and practice by widening the circle of vocational psychology to an even greater degree. In order to fully expand this horizon, I now explore the historical precedent contributed by industrial/organizational psychology, which represents the second major specialty within psychology that has sought to study work.

Industrial/Organizational Psychology

The history of industrial/organizational psychology (I/O psychology) parallels many of the pathways of career counseling and vocational psychology. For example, in historical overviews (e.g., Landy, 1989; Miner, 1969; Zickar, 2003), I/O psychology also was initiated as a discipline in the later part of the 19th century and early part of the 20th century. Similar to vocational psychology, the vast changes in the labor market coupled with advances in the social sciences contributed to the development of an applied perspective to the problems that individuals and organizations faced in the world of work. In contrast to vocational psychology, I/O psychology focused on workers and employers as they implemented and adjusted to their work roles. Also, I/O psychology generally adopted the perspective of employers as opposed to the individual perspective of students, clients, and workers, which underpins the orientation of counseling psychology and vocational guidance practitioners.

Like early vocational guidance (Parsons, 1909), I/O psychology was initially interested in fostering optimal person–environment fits (P-E fit), with the focus primarily on the organization's needs as opposed to the needs of the individual (Landy, 1989). The movement to maximize P-E fit grew during World War I when the military forces needed to ensure that lengthy training could be provided to recruits who would likely benefit from such experiences (e.g., training recruits to be pilots and navigators). Another stimulus to the development of I/O psychology was the increasing sophistication that was evident in the measurement of abilities, personality attributes, and other work-related characteristics. Thus, early I/O psychology was very much a circumscribed "personnel psychology" that focused on issues pertaining to selection and training of new employees.

Beginning with the famous Hawthorne studies in the mid-1930s, applied psychology began to focus on organizational issues such as the quality of working environments (Neff, 1985). The Hawthorne studies demonstrated that enhancing the working conditions of a given organization could lead to notable improvements in productivity and in job satisfaction. The pronounced impact of these findings led many applied psychologists to study the nature of the work context, with the intention of developing a scientific framework for understanding how organizational commitment, job satisfaction, and productivity could be enhanced while also lowering employee turnover and worker alienation.

After the horrific war crimes of World War II, many I/O psychologists also turned their attention to group dynamics and leadership, both of which were solid lines of inquiry since the early 20th century (Landy, 1989; Miner, 1969). The failure of many individuals living in fascist countries to rise above the corrupting influence of dictatorial leaders led to a great deal of confusion and anxiety among social and organizational psychologists. As a result, a very rich body of knowledge has developed pertaining to the structure and function of groups and leaders in organizations (Cartwright & Zander, 1968). The impetus to the group dynamics movement can be traced to the action research efforts of Lewin and his colleagues, who after World War II began to apply their scholarship to the pressing problems of racism in federal housing programs (Shaffer & Galinsky, 1989). Thus, many branches of I/O psychology, like its sister field of vocational psychology, have considerable potential to improve the lives of all individuals who work, not just the middle and upper-middle classes.

Like vocational psychology, I/O psychology has become a rich and mature specialty with a vibrant professional community and a highly productive scholarly community. Without question, I/O psychology has made significant and long-standing contributions to the lives of many workers and to the productivity of many corporations (e.g., Arthur, Hall, & Lawrence, 1989; Hall, 1996; Herriott, 2001; Landy, 1989). However, much of I/O psychology, has, with few exceptions (see, e.g., Bailyn, 1989; Thomas, 1989; Zickar, 2004), ignored the experiences of working class and poor individuals; in narrowing its scope, I/O psychology has neglected the vast diversity of work roles that people occupy in contemporary society. This position does not seek to diminish the contributions of I/O psychology, but locates these contributions within a social stratum that is unique to modern and post-modern life in market-based economies. The social strata of I/O psychology's discourse generally ranges from the pink-collar jobs that many women occupy within organizations (e.g., nurses, secretaries, administrative assistants) to the white-collar jobs of men and women who work within the complex structures of modern profit and non-profit organizations within Western cultures. I/O psychology was born out of the developing bureaucracies of 20th century Western culture and has addressed these concerns with great creativity and with significant innovative theory and research. The resultant body of knowledge in I/O psychology is clearly robust and vibrant, providing a sound basis for the practice of organizational development in contemporary corporate and bureaucratic organizations. However, despite the push toward producing a knowledge base that will be of relevance to contemporary organizations, some notable voices within I/O psychology are advancing an agenda that is similar to the one that I am advocating in this book.

Within the organizational study of careers, a number of scholars have moved toward a more inclusive perspective that seeks to encompass the experiences of working-class and poor individuals. For example, the emphasis on the psychological experience of working that I am advocating is consistent with Bailyn's (1989) call for the examination of the individual subjective meaning of career and working. Similarly, Thomas (1989) adopted a macro-level perspective using sociological theory to explore the paths of blue-collar workers. In addition, several recent lines of work in organizational psychology have explored the experiences of blue- and pink-collar workers' relationships with labor unions (Drenth, Thierry, & Wolff, 1998; Howell & Dorfman, 1986). The questions raised in this body of work have focused on identifying the determinants of union participation (e.g., Howell & Dorfman, 1986; Johnson & Johnson, 1997; Tan & Aryee, 2002) and how union instrumentality is connected to workplace justice and citizenship behavior (Aryee & Chay, 2001).

The fact that so few studies in I/O psychology have explored the labor union movement and the experiences of nonmanagerial workers has recently attracted the attention of Zickar (2003, 2004), who has examined the lack of interest in labor unions on the part of I/O psychologists. His analysis also identifies some of the reasons for I/O psychology's focus on management personnel and management-based issues. Zickar argued that early I/O psychologists were generally offered greater employment opportunities with management; the financial insecurity of labor unions made such financially lucrative offers less likely. In addition, Zickar noted that some labor unions did not trust psychologists and that many I/O psychologists in general allied themselves with the goals and mission of management. However, Zickar (2003) pointed out that there were some exceptions in the history of I/O psychology, most notably Arthur Kornhauser. Kornhauser, who worked primarily in the early and middle part of the 20th century, explored the sort of issues that are consistent with some of the ideas I advance in this book. For example, Kornhauser devoted extensive effort to studying labor unions early in his career and worker mental health later in his career (see Zickar, 2003, for an excellent overview). Zickar highlighted the insightful and prescient contributions of Kornhauser by concluding that "his research in all four areas (selection, opinion surveying, unions, and worker mental health) was guided by his concern for improving the lives of working people" (2003, p. 368). Another important point raised by Zickar is that the relative lack of attention devoted to workers and unions seems unique to I/O psychology of the United States.

When considered collectively, research and scholarship on the broader array of working-related issues has attracted attention of a few I/O psychologists. A line can be extended from Kornhauser to Zickar (see, e.g., Zickar, 2001), albeit often a thin line, which maps issues of relevance to an inclusive psychology of working. One of the current manifestations of this line can be found in the current scholarship on occupational health psychology (e.g., Barling & Griffiths, 2003; Quick & Tetrick, 2002; Schaufeli, 2004). Occupational health psychology has emerged as a vibrant specialty that has elements from various fields, including I/O psychology, health psychology, and social/personality psychology (Quick & Tetrick, 2003). The mission of occupational health psychology is to enhance the overall physical and mental health of workers across the occupational spectrum (Quick & Tetrick, 2003; Schaufeli, 2004). Some of the thematic elements in occupational health psychology include the study of ways to reduce worker injury and health-related problems at the workplace (Quick & Tetrick, 2002; Schaufeli, 2004). Additional research has explored the interface of job strain and worker performance (e.g., Rau, 2004). The impact of working conditions on the mental and physical health of employees also has attracted considerable attention (e.g., Greiner, Krause, Ragland, & Fisher, 1998; Lamberg, 2004).

Of particular relevance to the psychology of working is the focus within occupational health psychology on the work/home interface (e.g., Cinnamon & Rich, 2002; Frone, Yardley, & Markel, 1997; Voydanoff, 2004). This line of work, which has been explored within both vocational (e.g., Betz & Fitzgerald, 1987) and I/O psychology (e.g., Greenhaus & Beutell, 1985), has considerable potential for an inclusive psychology of working. Another line of work within occupational health psychology that is important to our discussion is the research on impact of layoffs and threats of layoffs on the lives of workers (e.g., Ferrie, 2001; Grayson, 1989; Grunberg, Moore, & Greenberg, 2001). Thus, occupational health psychology seems to be exploring some areas that are serving to expand the rather narrow purview of both vocational and I/O psychology.

In my view, the conceptual scaffolding of the psychology of working may help to shape the language and theoretical umbrella that will integrate the disparate studies in vocational psychology, I/O psychology, and occupational health psychology. As I have noted, many of the contributions from both vocational psychology and I/O psychology have been remarkably articulate about the need for greater inclusiveness and equity in psychological considerations of working (e.g., Carter & Cook, 1992; M. S. Richardson, 1993; E. J. Smith, 1983; Thomas, 1989; Zickar, 2004). The next section of this chapter seeks to follow the leads of the courageous and thoughtful scholars by offering readers a blueprint for an inclusive and vibrant study of working in the lives of human beings in the 21st century.

A Psychological Analysis of Working

In addition to advocating for the central position of working in psychological discourse, I seek to map the terrain for subsequent explorations of the psychological nature of work and working. The guideposts that I plant in this landscape are centered on my interpretation of three core needs that may ideally be fulfilled by work and working. A number of scholars have explored this question, both within and outside of the traditional purview of vocational psychology and I/O psychology (e.g., Axelrod, 1999; Freud, 1930; Neff, 1985; O'Brien, 1986; Super, 1957; Vroom, 1964). Taken together, these perspectives form the basis for the three core functions of work that are presented in this book (and are summarized at the end of this section).

Existing Perspectives of the Psychological Attributes of Working

Psychoanalytic Perspectives. Freud (e.g., 1930) helped to place the study of work into a psychological framework, although he tended to consider work-related issues as derivatives of intrapsychic human characteristics. As Axelrod (1999) noted, Freud explored the psychoanalytic meaning of work later in his career in his description of work as an economic necessity and not as a primary source of intrapsychic gratification. In short, Freud viewed work as a means of transforming instinctual energy into socially sanctioned functions. The classic feature of Freud's theory is the assumption that human behavior is a function of biological drives. For Freud, work provided a means of sublimating impulses into activities that drained instinctual energy, thereby allowing people to function in more socially acceptable ways. In addition, Freud tended to view work as a human necessity and as a source of tediousness and stress. At the same time, work was thought to provide an outlet for one's psychic energy, even though it represented the opposite of the pleasure principle. From an orthodox psychoanalytic perspective, some aspects of working provide people with an outlet for internalized drives, thereby enhancing psychic equilibrium.

More recent psychoanalytic considerations of work have moved away from the rigid assumptions of drive theory. Using a more contemporary psychoanalytic lens, Axelrod (1999) described how work has the potential to provide an outlet for natural talents, ambitions, and interests. In contrast to the biological essentialism of Freud's drive theory (1930), Axelrod cited a set of theoretical perspectives that views human beings as striving for connection, interpersonal intimacy, and affirmation from others. Using the theories of Kohut (1977), Erikson (1950), and others, Axelrod derived the following statement about the intrapsychic functions of work: "The synthesis of individual talents and skills with values and goals to create a guiding model of oneself at work is not only a major developmental achievement, it is also a source of pleasure and self-esteem residing in the deepest levels of the psyche" (p. 12). While this view is certainly more optimistic about the functions of work, Axelrod, like many vocational and I/O psychologists, tended to circumscribe his views of workers to those who have choices and volition in this part of their lives.

Self-Concept Perspectives.   Drawing upon humanistic theories that were gaining a strong foothold in North American psychology in the mid-part of the 20th century (e.g., Rogers, 1995), Super (1957) articulated a self-concept theory of career development. Super proposed that choices about work and careers ideally represented a natural manifestation of inherent interests, talents, and values within the world of work. The self-concept represents the internal "I" or "me" that one develops over the course of the life span. One of the functions of work, therefore, is to find an outlet for one's self-concept in the occupational world. From this vantage point, work is thought to provide individuals with a means of satisfaction, accomplishment, and achievement. As Neff (1985) noted in his criticism of Super's view of work and human behavior, the self-concept implementation notion is based on the assumption that people have choices to make with respect to their work lives, which is not the case for most workers in the world at the present time. Despite this limitation, Super's perspective, that work provided an outlet for one's self-concept, captures an element of work behavior that is certainly worth striving for as technology increasingly makes repetitive work less available.

Contextual Views.   Beginning with Marx (1844/1988), a more contextualized perspective was applied to the functional analysis of work. Marx argued that industrialization had resulted in a deep sense of alienation among workers who tended to perform routine functions in a rote fashion. Also, Marx discussed the widening gap between workers and the outcome of work, which resulted in a maldistribution of wealth, with investors and business owners becoming increasingly rich and many workers struggling to survive. In this scheme, working met only the most basic of psychological needs, primarily centering on survival. Thus, Marxist views focused on the way in which the economic, social, and workplace context influenced the experience of working. However, Marx did maintain a view that work, in its purest forms, did have the potential for helping people to feel connected to nature.

As O'Brien (1986) noted, many of the theories that emerged from I/O psychology have some common themes with Marx's (1844/1993) views. O'Brien used Maslow's (1943) self-actualization theory as a means of organizing the diverse functions that work can yield. According to O'Brien, work has the potential to become part of a self-actualizing experience if the individual's basic needs are met (i.e., safety, love, esteem) and if the work tasks offer a means of expressing one's core values, aspirations, and interests. The key element in the Maslowian approach is the acknowledgment that self-actualization is contingent upon the degree to which core physical and psychological needs have been met.

Within traditional I/O psychology, the functions of work are understood as being related, at least in part, to the actual task demands of a given job. Herzberg's (1966) contribution viewed work as offering people considerable opportunities for personal growth and productive careers providing that the task experiences offered opportunities for achievement, social recognition, and challenge.

Integrative Perspectives.　Neff (1985) offered an integrative analysis of the psychological functions of work. Building on psychoanalytic, self-concept, and contextual perspectives, Neff sought to respond to the question, "Why do different people mobilize their energies for work and focus their interests and attention on work in such varying degrees?" (p. 145). His discussion yielded the following factors:

- *Material needs:* As Neff noted, people obviously work out of necessity. The need to earn money to survive is viewed by Neff as a key component in a functional analysis of work.
- *Self-esteem:* Consistent with various perspectives within I/O psychology (e.g., Brockner, 1988), Neff proposes that work can enhance self-esteem. The primary ways in which work functions to influence self-esteem are through the self-perceptions that emerge in relation to one's work role and the connection between working in general and access to the rights and privileges of workers within a one's culture.
- *Activity:* According to Neff, work has the potential to furnish people with a source of daily activity, thereby alleviating boredom and lethargy. Neff also cites various psychoanalytic scholars who viewed work as

a means of warding off anxiety and aggressive impulses (e.g., Menninger, 1942).

■ *Respect by others:* For Neff, work provides people with a source of social affirmation and status. This factor, which is related, yet different from self-esteem, refers to the external status characteristics that a particular occupational role engenders in a given culture.

■ *Need for creativity:* Neff articulates that creative needs can be fulfilled by work, but he acknowledges that this factor is not as pervasive or universal as the first four needs. Neff's view is that some people have strong creative strivings that can be either met or frustrated by their jobs.

The contributions of Neff (1985) clearly furnished a meaningful taxonomy that was particularly relevant in the work context of the later part of the 20th century. Moreover, Neff's analysis, like the conceptualizations that emerged from I/O and vocational psychology as well as psychoanalytic theory, focused on the working experiences of relatively affluent, well-educated people who have some degree of input into how they engage in their working lives. Nevertheless, these perspectives inform the current discussion of the functional needs fulfilled by work.

Herr et al. (2004) offered another integrative perspective that is relevant to the present discussion. Using a broad-based conceptual framework, Herr et al. proposed that work has a number of meanings that shift in relation to cultural influences and historical time period. In the Herr et al. analysis, work serves several psychological functions, which provide individuals with a means of fulfilling needs for connection, achievement, structure, and purpose. In addition, work fulfills economic functions, which parallel the survival needs that have been noted earlier in this chapter. The third set of needs fall under the rubric of the sociological functions of work, which describes the broad array of differentiated relationships and social expectations that are associated with the working role.

An Integrative Taxonomy of Working

Building on the taxonomies described in the previous section, I propose an inclusive and comprehensive taxonomy that is constructed around three core functions that working has the potential to fulfill. The functional analysis that I advance here seeks to include the full gamut of working experiences, ranging from people with volition in their work lives to those who work in any task simply to survive for another day.

Working as a Means for Survival and Power. The first function of work is the role that work plays in providing people with a means of accessing survival and power. In this analysis, power refers to the actual exchange of work for money or goods and services, which then allows an individual to sustain his/her life. The function of work in obtaining money and power, which is typically the province of economists, also has considerable psychological implications, which I believe need to be clearly understood. In addition, work has the potential to confer social status, which may enhance prestige and power. Despite the importance of ensuring one's survival (and the attainment of economic power), these functional attributes of a psychological analysis of working have been woefully neglected in contemporary discussions of careers. In addition, an explicit focus on the role of working in sustaining individuals' capacity to survive and thrive facilitates a keen awareness of the obstacles that often keep people from obtaining the means to work. I explore these issues in greater depth in chapter 3.

Working as a Means of Social Connection. The second major function of work is the way in which working connects people to their social context and to interpersonal relationships. Two specific dimensions define this element: First, work furnishes us with a means of developing important social relationships and bonds. For many people, working serves as their major source of interpersonal connection. Second, working links people with a broader social milieu, thereby providing a structured means of relating to their proximal and distal social contexts. Emerging out of this discussion is the foundation of a relational approach to working, which is fully described in chapter 4.

Working as a Means of Self-Determination. The third major function of work that I examine in this book is the potential offered by work in fostering self-determination. In contrast with views of job satisfaction that do not capture the experience of the working lives of poor and working class individuals, I offer the self-determination theory of Deci and Ryan (1985; Ryan & Deci, 2000) as a potentially rich explanatory lens. This perspective, which is detailed in chapter 5, describes how extrinsically motivated activities may become internalized and part of a broader set of values, behaviors, and overall life goals. As such, I seek to examine the full gamut of motivational experiences in relation to working, including individuals who work out of intrinsic interest, as well as those who work to achieve the outcomes of work (money, status, etc.).

Mapping the Landscape
of the Psychology of Working

After more than a century of scientific study and practice within vocational psychology and I/O psychology, what, then, are our options as we enter the 21st century? One could argue that we ought to maintain the circumscribed focus of the aforementioned disciplines as they offer the most sophisticated conceptual and empirical tools for studying working. Indeed, this argument certainly has merit if we continue to focus on the work lives (or careers) of affluent, relatively well-educated individuals in Western cultures. However, I believe that this is neither sufficient nor morally justifiable. I do not believe that the relative neglect of the poor and working class represents an explicit collusion among intellectuals to oppress the disadvantaged cohorts of society. Rather, I think that the majority of scholars within vocational psychology and I/O psychology simply did not have the life experiences of poor and working class individuals or of persons of color on their collective radar screens, in part due to the tendency for most psychologists to have emerged from the middle class (or to have disavowed their working class origins). In addition, there have been no formal or informal inducements to study the experiences of people who had little, if any, volition in their working lives. The vocational counseling movement, while tracing its origins to working class, poor, and immigrant students and workers, moved gradually toward a focus on middle-class students and clients who were faced with complex choices. Similarly, I/O psychology maintained close linkages with the corporate world, which often funded the major studies that have informed this discipline's knowledge base. (The avoidance of race and class issues is not unique to psychologists who have been studying careers and work. The relative neglect of working class and poor individuals, as described by Lott, 2002, has been endemic throughout applied psychology and in many other fields within the social and behavioral sciences.)

The pressing social problems in many Western societies in many ways parallel the dilemmas faced by Marx (1867) and others in the 19th century. Society continues to be stratified by class and racial lines in many communities across the globe, with the disparities becoming increasingly more pronounced (Krugman, 1993; Shipler, 2004; Wilson, 1996). Means of reducing these growing gaps in wages, knowledge, and access to the opportunity structure have thus far eluded policy analysts and social activists as well as government leaders. While a psychology of working, broadly conceived, will not, in and of itself, solve these considerable social dilemmas, it is clear that the intellectual power of psychologists is going to be critical to the development of a meaningful set of solutions to the social crisis we face. I believe that this book presents the beginning of a needed discourse on the nature, attributes, and consequences of working in contemporary society. A clear objective of this initiative is to develop a knowledge base that will inform the development of policies and solutions to the problems faced by our society that are often located squarely at the focal point where people interact with the broader economic world—within our experiences in preparing for, locating, and adjusting to work.

Additionally, the neat and tidy distinctions between work and nonwork roles, which have been implicit in most of psychological theory and practice throughout the 20th century, are increasingly fading (Blustein, 2001b; Blustein & Spengler, 1995; Flum, 2001; Hackett & Lonborg, 1993). In addition to the obvious linkage of work and nonwork issues in psychotherapy and career counseling, the vast changes taking place in the work world are having a dramatic effect on the way in which we live our lives. For the middle class and educated workforce, the information age is transforming our entire experience of work (T. L. Friedman, 1999; Grantham, 2000; Sennett, 1998). With the advent of personal computers and other forms of information technology, we are no longer able to separate our work lives and home lives by occupying physically distinct spaces (i.e., office and home). As a result, we are witnessing a revolution as work and personal life become weaved together in a complex and not well understood synthesis. My view is that we need to understand more about the psychological nature of working, without the constraining limits of existing conceptual rubrics in order to develop maximally effective theory and practice to help people create meaningful order out of such highly disparate blending boundaries. I am not advocating that we discard entire schools of thought, which have developed over many decades and have demonstrated robustness in empirical research (e.g., Holland, 1997; Super, 1980). Rather, I believe that we need to think expansively to ensure that our efforts are maximally inclusive. We are relatively clear about the utility of person-environment fit models for individuals with some degree of choice in their work lives. However, we are far from clear about how individuals from inner city ghettos, Native reservations, shantytowns in South America, and the rest of humanity's complex mosaic approach their working lives. Moreover, the models that we have developed to date assume that boundaries exist to clearly demarcate domains of life experience. The actual nature of life experience suggests far more complexity and role diffusions than would be suggested from most scholarly and theoretical efforts in vocational and I/O psychology (e.g., Blustein, 2001b; Flum, 2001; Hall, 1996; M. S. Richardson, 1993; Savickas, 1993).

How will the psychology of working differ from vocational psychology and I/O psychology? It is difficult to respond to this question at this point. One important point, however, is clear. We have developed our previous psychologies of work from vastly different social conditions, at a time when the needs of society were very much rooted in an industrial era that fostered a great deal of regularity and constancy in work lives. Moreover, much of the literature that has been developed has not relied upon the inner lives of individuals who are coping with their work lives. There is no psychological formulation that can provide some meaning to the powerful lyrics in the Bruce Springsteen song that opened this book in the Preface or to many of the eloquent passages in Terkel's (1974) and the Bowe et al. (2000) volumes that have given voice to the inner experiences of workers. Therefore, I propose that we need an "experience-near" connection to the lives of workers in order to develop a true and useful psychology of working (cf. Blustein, 2001a; M. S. Richardson, 1993). (The terms *experience-distant* and *experience-near*, which are derived from relationally oriented psychoanalytic approaches, reflect variations in the degree of empathy between two individuals. In this book, I use these terms to refer to the "relationship" between readers and the material presented in this book.) This book intends to pave the way for this approach by using vignettes and stories from the experiences of poor and working class people along with traditional social scientific research and theory to explore the meaning and consequences of work in the 21st century.

Another objective of a psychology of working is to place work at the central place that it ought to occupy in contemporary psychological discourse. A review of contemporary psychotherapy theory and practice reveals that work is consistently neglected as a major theatre of human life. (See Bergin & Garfield, 1994; Bohart & Greenberg, 1997; Wachtel, 1993, for examples of well-regarded scholarship on psychotherapy with nearly no mention of work.) With some exceptions (see, e.g., Axelrod, 1999; Blustein, 1987; Lowman, 1993; M. S. Richardson, 1996), it seems that most psychotherapists have neglected one of the two major domains of human experience (i.e., work and love) that was presented by Freud and others (e.g., Smelser & Erikson, 1980). In most forms of psychological intervention, work is relegated to secondary or tertiary consideration, if it is considered at all. This book will seek to redress this critical lapse by providing a coherent framework with which to develop counseling and psychotherapeutic interventions that are fully inclusive of life's dreams and disappointments.

In my view, psychologists and other social scientists have no consistent theoretical perspective with which to guide theory development and practice efforts in the working realm of human experience. This book will seek to develop such a perspective. In closing, the perspective that I am offering in this book does not seek to supplant the robust and important findings and theories emanating from vocational psychology and I/O psychology. Rather,

I hope to provide a new trajectory for our study of work in people's lives; the direction that I am proposing is one that is inherently inclusive. The inclusiveness that I seek to create would establish space for poor, working class individuals as well as those who are marginalized due to their gender, sexual orientation, psychological and medical health issues, and racial or ethnic status. At the same time, I believe that the material presented here is of relevance to the middle class, where the struggle to work is often just as compelling and challenging as it is for poor and working class individuals. For example, the emerging role of immigrant workers in small businesses merits the attention of psychologists interested in working.

In addition, the inclusiveness refers to a broader infusion of theoretical perspectives, from fields ranging from relational psychology to human motivation. Furthermore, the inclusiveness refers to the methodology of this work; rather than relying exclusively on existing social scientific methods, I believe that we need to explore deeply and widely from human narratives, memoirs, poems, song lyrics, and clinical case material in order to understand how work has been and is experienced. (It is important to note that the narrative material will be used to generate new ideas and concepts as opposed to providing firm evidence of a given proposition or inference. In effect, the passages that are interspersed within the text of this book reflect a means of engaging in discovery-oriented scholarship.)

In this sort of intellectual enterprise, I have necessarily developed my thinking in a manner that clearly owes a debt to the many important scholars who have paved the way for a serious psychological study of working (e.g., Betz & Fitzgerald, 1987; Fassinger, 2000; Fouad & Brown, 2000; Harmon, 1972; Harmon & Farmer, 1983; Helms & Cook, 1999; Parsons, 1909; M. S. Richardson, 1993; Savickas, 1995, 2002; Super, 1957; Young & Collin, 1992; Zickar, 2004). In a sense, this book represents the logical next step in an emerging critique that has challenged the status quo within vocational and I/O psychology. One of my primary goals is to find the pain, courage, distress, pride, and dreams that working has evoked and continues to evoke in the human imagination. The framework I develop in the subsequent chapters will foster, I hope, a study of working that is pragmatic, fair, and facilitative of an equitable social justice that is the birthright of each human being. As I propose in this book, working is the battleground for social justice as working offers us the most direct access to the power structure and to greater equality in opportunities. In writing this book, I hope to bring this battlefield to the attention of psychologists, therapists, and other social and behavioral scientists who have dedicated their lives to improving the condition of human existence.

CHAPTER 2

The Changing Nature of Work
in the 21st Century

The minute you stepped out of the factory gates you thought of no more about your work. But the funniest thing was that neither did you think about your work when you were standing at your machine. You began the day by cutting and drilling steel cylinders with care, but gradually your actions became automatic and you forgot all about the machine and the quick working of your arms and hands and the fact that you were cutting and boring and rough-threading to within limits of only five-thousandths of an inch. The noise of motor-trolleys passing up and down the gangway and the excruciating din of flying and flapping belts slipped out of your consciousness after perhaps half an hour, without affecting the quality of the work you were turning out, and you forgot your past conflicts with the gaffer and turned to thinking of pleasant events that had at some time happened to you, or things that you hoped would happen to you in the future. If your machine was working well—the motor smooth, stops tight, jigs good—and you sprung your actions into a favourable rhythm you became happy. You went off into pipe dreams for the rest of the day. And in the evening, when admittedly you would be feeling as though your arms and legs had been stretched to breaking point on a torture rack, you stepped out into a cosy world of pubs and noisy tarts that would one day provide you with the raw material for more pipe dreams as you stood at your lathe.

—Sillitoe (1958, pp. 35–36)

At the River Winds Café, the "global economy" now appeared the source of their misfortunes, particularly in its use of foreign workers. IBM had begun "outsourcing" some of its programming work, paying people in India a fraction of the wages paid to the Americans .... The fear that foreigners undermine the efforts of hardworking native Americans is a deeply rooted one. In the nineteenth century, it was very poor, unskilled immigrant workers who seemed to take away jobs, by their willingness to work for less. Today, the global economy serves the function of arousing this ancient fear, but those threatened at home seem not just the unskilled, but also the middle classes and professionals caught up in the flux of the global labor market.

—Sennett (1998, pp. 126–127)

I was unemployed for about a month and a half or two months. I went insane. [What was that like for you?] I went insane. I couldn't sit around the house. My house was never that clean, I must have cleaned it about once a day. You know, it was really disappointing because I was really used to working and now I was unemployed. I was looking for a job but there wasn't anything out there at that point in time. [So that was rough on you?] That was real rough, yes.

—A participant in the Albany School-to-Work Project

The vignettes that are presented at the outset of this chapter convey some of the anguish, tedium, and pervasive worries about working, which have often been missing from psychologically oriented analyses of career development, vocational adjustment, and organizational life. With some exceptions (e.g., N. Peterson & González, 2005; Wilson, 1996), these experiences have often been on the margins of our collective consideration and therefore have not received the attention that they merit. One of the purposes of this chapter is to give voice to individuals whose work lives are not always rewarding or even available to them in a consistent fashion. In order to provide a context that would allow us to internalize the important messages that are being presented in the quotes at the outset of this chapter, many of the major features of the changing nature of the workplace are reviewed in this chapter. Of course, a critical message in this book is that we are not speaking about solely one workplace or even one set of workplaces within a particular place and time. Rather, workplaces vary nearly as dramatically as people do, thereby making it impossible to cover the entire landscape of work contexts and experiences of working. With this caveat, in this chapter, I seek to provide an overview of the major landmarks of the shifting nature of work in the 21st century.

That work is changing rapidly has become a reality within most cultures across the globe, often accompanied by rather dramatic claims about the future (e.g., T. L. Friedman, 2005; Hall, 1996; Rifkin, 1995). Indeed, a perusal of bestselling books, magazine articles, and newspapers reveals considerable interest in the changing nature of work in the 21st century (e.g., T. L. Friedman, 1999,

2005; Grantham, 2000; Rifkin, 1995; Sennett, 1998; Wilson, 1996). Within the management and I/O fields, the vast shifts in the workplace have become perhaps the most significant challenge facing scholars, consultants, and of course, workers who struggle to deal with these changes on a daily basis (e.g., Arthur et al., 1989; Hall, 1996). Simply reading some of the titles of popular books in recent years (such as Hall's *The Career Is Dead*; Rifkin's *The End of Work*; Wilson's *When Work Disappears*; and Friedman's *The World Is Flat*) conveys the scope of these dramatic changes.

This chapter begins with a review of the most overt shifts in the workplace, focusing on the transition from an industrial era to postindustrial age, and finally to the information age. However, unlike most other treatments of this enormous set of changes, I examine the shifts across a broad spectrum of workers, including unskilled, skilled, and professional workers. As we shall see, the prognostications have emerged with significant seriousness and often with well-argued positions, describing vast changes in the way in which corporations and modern organizations are restructuring in the face of automation and technological changes. However, with only a few exceptions (e.g., Hall, 1996; Rifkin, 1995; Savickas, 1993; Wilson, 1996), the significant changes in the nature and expression of work have occurred in an environment that has ignored or downplayed the effect on individuals who are not part of the grand career narrative. (The "grand career narrative" refers to the Super et al., 1996, description of the hierarchical, planful, and volitional work lives of educated, relatively affluent people in Western countries in the middle and late 20th century. The grand career narrative is perhaps best exemplified by the life stages that Super, 1957, proposed that evocatively captured a sense of stability in the labor market, which is no longer available to many workers.) Throughout the chapter, I seek to balance the "experience-distant" perspective of the workplace evident in scholarly statements and empirical studies, with an "experience-near" perspective, exemplified by the voices of workers facing the shifting sands of the workplace. The first major theme to be reviewed is the notion that the traditional concept of career is dead, or, at the very least, in the final throes of a fatal illness.

Is the Career Dead?

A number of emergent trends, when considered collectively, convey a view of the traditional grand career narrative as increasingly less viable due to wide-ranging changes in the nature of the work context and demands of the labor market (e.g., Hall, 1996; N. Peterson & González, 2005; Rifkin, 1995; Wilson,

1996). The reasons for this portrayal are complex and are rooted in some hard facts about major changes in the structure of the economy and equally substantive changes in organizational life in Western societies. In order to understand these changes, it is important initially to describe the organizational structure that emerged to support the grand career narrative.

The Birth of Career: An Historical Foundation

Prior to the industrial revolution, an agrarian economy primarily characterized work settings (Donkin, 2001; T. L. Friedman, 1999; Neff, 1985). For the most part, people did not select their line of work; they typically assumed the work roles of their families. There was, however, a small minority of individuals who did select jobs, which were generally known as "callings" or vocations. Many of these occupations reflected a spiritual, quasi-spiritual, or intuitive decision to leave one's family and/or prescribed work role and engage in a trade, profession, or religious work. Savickas further noted that the secular version of a calling was known as a craft. The number of available choices in the pre-industrial period was quite circumscribed; naturally, most of the workforce in this era was involved in farming and related activities. A considerable proportion of the male population often would be conscripted into military service or would elect to join the military due to the absence of other viable options. However, urban centers, which began as trading posts, harbors, or locations of farmer's markets, soon arose and housed workers with more specialized skills as well as a growing mercantile class. Yet the array of choices that workers had was highly limited and the lack of available education served to further constrain these options. Prior to the 20th century, education beyond primary school was typically not available, except for the wealthy and gentry, who typically pursued classical studies in secondary and post-secondary settings (Marshall & Tucker, 1992). It is important to note that many societies still exist around the globe that parallel the characteristics of the agrarian period (see, e.g., Diamond, 1999; Wallman, 1979) and are worthy of the attention of the psychology of working.

During the agrarian period, working was often embedded in a culture of connection and relatedness. Whether one was working on one's family farm or in a trade guild or religious order, the major quality of agrarian work was the deep sense of rootedness within relationships, nature, and structured social interactions. Moreover, for individuals who worked on family farms, the sense of ownership and investment in one's efforts was naturally clear and consistent. Without question, work was often arduous, painful, and exhausting, with no guarantee that such effort would actually result in survival for oneself and family members. Indeed, many people were not able to support themselves or their families; people often starved in droughts and famines, disease would kill others, and of course, constant warfare and feuds created yet further instability. In my view, this working context, while clearly not "the garden of Eden" and most definitively hard and risky, was an integrated aspect of human experience. People generally experienced work as a critical, albeit often painful and arduous, component of their lives. At the same time, working often took place within one's home or near one's home, thereby offering access to relational support.

The development of work groups to help distribute tasks related to hunting and gathering or farming was instrumental in advancing the survival potential of our species (Neff, 1985; Price & Brown, 1985). Some scholars have proposed that the use of social organizations to facilitate the tasks of feeding, clothing, and caring for one's tribe or kinship cohort was one of the building blocks of contemporary human civilization (e.g., Bowlby, 1988; Donkin, 2001). Going back into our early evolutionary history, one can speculate that work was essentially equivalent with the tasks necessary for survival for one more day or week. Diamond's (1999) analysis of human history describes the importance of work tools as powerful indicators of life within a given community of humans or proto-humans. In fact, he argues that the use of more advanced tools is associated with more diverse activities, such as ritualistic behaviors pertaining to early religious practices, artistic endeavors, and more complex social organizations. The movement from a hunter-gatherer existence, for example, to a farming existence, offered enormous advantages for human society, such as the ability to support a denser population and time to work on other tasks that helped to create the intellectual and cultural infrastructure of many contemporary civilizations. Thus, a look at our ancient roots reveals that work was integral to human functioning and was increasingly diversified as people developed more sophisticated tools and social organizations.

Following the agrarian economy, the modal work environment in Western countries changed in the 19th century to an urban economy, which was the context for the development of the career. As many scholars have noted (e.g., Drucker, 1999; Marshall & Tucker, 1992; Reich, 1991), the industrial revolution created a need for a complex hierarchical organizational structure in corporations. Line workers, who actually produced goods and products, typically needed careful supervision and monitoring, especially early in the industrial era when the educational opportunities available to poor and working class youth did not match the demands of the workplace. In turn, upper management required teams of relatively well-educated, but compliant workers who could supervise various office tasks, coordinate production, and handle complex inventory tasks. These individuals later became the middle management within many organizations, who carved out an important place in the corporate structure of the industrial era. One of the major tasks of these middle-level managers was to facilitate communication between upper management and line workers as well as to supervise the staff within a factory or production shop. (See Marshall & Tucker, 1992, and Statt, 1994, for further details on the structure of the workplace around the time of the industrial revolution.) The following vignette from an oral history project of a mill town in New England describes one particularly evocative recollection of life in the heart of the industrial revolution during the early part of the 20th century:

> I was brought up in the area of the mill. All of our people were mill people, and we didn't know anything else but mills .... I did not enjoy working in the mills. It was hot in the summer, cold in the winter. You had an eight-hour stretch, a half-hour dinner, and you couldn't smoke .... The millyard was fenced in and there was a watchman at the gate, so you couldn't run out of the building into the streets even if your particular building was situated near the street, which mine was .... I didn't like the fact that you were tied to that machine or to your job. It was as though you were in jail for eight hours, and you knew there was no escaping. Nothing good to look forward to when you go to work but eight hours of work. Fortunately, the people you worked for were in the same predicament, so they would try to get some pleasure out of it with joking; but I didn't like it, and I don't think too many people in there liked it either. It sounds funny, but the only thing I did like was my pay. It was good money at the time. (Hareven & Langenbach, 1978, pp. 152–153)

As this vignette suggests, working may have provided structure and predictability, but it did not always offer a path toward satisfaction and a meaningful life. The narrator describes a life that is highly organized and even ritualized within the community of mill workers who lived and worked together. However, his sense of despair is palpable. One of the outcomes of this type of work was an increasing level of disconnection between one's labors and the product of one's working life. Whereas in the agrarian age, workers generally were able to experience a deep sense of connection and ownership to their efforts, the industrial age resulted in highly regimented work roles, which often left people in a state of ambiguity and alienation. In fact, one can argue that Marx's (1891) critique about the dehumanizing characteristics of work was generated in part because of the increasing loss of connection between effort and outcome in the rapidly changing work context of the industrial age. In describing our evolutionary past, one can see that there has been historically a very clear connection between one's efforts and the outcomes of one's work. Indeed, many of the drawings and rudimentary writings from prehistoric times deal with work and survival (Diamond, 1999).

As working began to shift in the industrial era, a struggle emerged that created a complex dialectical dilemma for workers, particularly in urban communities. In the course of the industrialization of Western countries, urban dwellers were increasingly embedded in highly regimented work, which contrasted sharply with a pervasive sense of instability, which was a function of economic cycles that led to economic recessions and even depressions. Thus, while people often felt denigrated and disengaged from their efforts due to the highly tedious and repetitive nature of many jobs, they also had to deal with a sense of insecurity in that one's access to work was rarely, if ever, stable or constant. When economic cycles became depressed, workers in production-based factories were often the first ones to feel the pinch as they would lose hours, pay, or even their jobs. A significant body of work has developed in both literature and the social sciences that has sought to describe the dialectical struggle that many workers experienced during these periods of time (e.g., Riis, 1890; Sinclair, 1906; Steinbeck, 1939; Thomas, 1999). Indeed, this dialectic is resurfacing with greater prominence currently for many workers as people strive to adjust to the changes of the information age and globalization, often in jobs that offer little variety or challenge. Hareven and Langenbach (1978), who conducted an oral history of mill workers in Manchester, New Hampshire, described the overriding striving toward stability. The mill workers reported clear interests in job security, often above other aspirations (such as job satisfaction); at the same time, as the quote from the mill worker cited previously suggests, the security that was such a major motivation for workers in the industrial era was often achieved with a price. The price was manifested in the spirit and autonomy of many workers, which is conveyed eloquently in the following passage by Gissing (1889) in his description of life in an English town late in the 19th century:

> At noon to-day there was sunlight on the Surrey hills; the fields and lanes were fragrant with the first breath of spring, and from the shelter of budding copses many a primrose looked tremblingly up to the vision of blue sky. But of these things Clerkenwell takes no count; here it had been a day like any other, consisting of so many hours, each representing a fraction of the weekly wage. Go where you may in Clerkenwell, on every hand are multiform evidences of toil, intolerable as a nightmare. It is not as in those parts of London where the main thoroughfares consist of shops and warehouses and workrooms, whilst the streets that are hidden away on either hand are devoted in the main to dwellings. Here every alley is thronged with small industries; all but every door

and window exhibits the advertisement of a craft that is carried on within. Here you may see how men have multiplied toil for toil's sake, have wrought to devise work superfluous, have worn their lives away in imagining new forms of weariness. The energy, the ingenuity daily put forth in these grimy burrows task the brain's power of wondering. But that those who sit here through the livelong day, through every season, through all the years of the life that is granted to them, who strain their eyesight, who overtax their muscles, who nurse disease in their frames, who put resolutely from them the thought of what existence *might* be—that these do it all without prospect of hope or reward save the permission to eat and sleep and bring into the world other creatures to strive with them for bread, surely that thought is yet more marvelous. (Gissing, 1889, cited in Thomas, 1999, pp. 508–509)

In a similar vein, the lyrics to Springsteen's (1978/1998) song entitled "Factory" describes the dull routine of industrial-era work that had a tendency to chip away at one's sense of wholeness and cohesiveness as a person:

Early in the morning factory whistle blows,
Man rises from bed and puts on his clothes,
Man takes his lunch, walks out in the morning light,
It's the working, the working, just the working life.

Through the mansions of fear, through the mansions of pain,
I see my daddy walking through them factory gates in the rain,
Factory takes his hearing, factory gives him life,
The working, the working, just the working life.

End of the day, factory whistle cries,
Men walk through these gates with death in their eyes.
And you just better believe, boy,
somebody's gonna get hurt tonight,
It's the working, the working, just the working life.

One of the critical methods that I advocate using in the psychology of working is empathic introspection (Kohut, 1977). While originally developed as a tool of psychoanalytic therapy and psychoanalysis, I believe that empathic introspection provides a particularly rich means of understanding the inner experiences of working. Empathic introspection refers to the use of empathy as a means of enhancing understanding, both intellectually and emotionally, with the individuals and experiences of the phenomenon one is studying. By seeking to obtain a closer connection to the core experiences of people as they grapple with working, empathic introspection offers scholars and practitioners a valuable tool that can reduce the divide between scholarship on working and the real-life problems that people confront in their attempts to make a living. (A detailed examination of the role of empathy in research on the psychology of working is found in chapter 7.) Using empathic introspection is not simply a means of connecting to the emotional tone of a given passage; it also provides a potentially powerful method of enhancing our understanding of a given experience.

Thus, I believe that a major task for social and behavioral scientists as well as counselors and therapists who read Gissing's (1889) and Springsteen's (1978) passages is to seek a deeper sense of connection with the workers who inspired these passages and who devoted so much of their lives to their jobs. As we can sense from these passages, the goal for these characters was survival and not necessarily the accumulation of wealth for its own sake. The awareness of the need to work for survival is a key element of the psychology of working, and provides an important conceptual and clinical tool in developing effective individual treatment models as well as public policy recommendations about the nature of work in the 21st century.

When considering the observations of the British town Clerkenwell in conjunction with the bare terrain of Springsteen's portrayal of factory life, one can begin to speculate about how the notion of an orderly work life soon gave way to the notion of career. The workforce during the industrial era (which generally encompassed the time frame from the early to middle of the 19th century to the mid- to later part of the 20th century) generally required highly regimented, loyal, and committed workers at all levels, from factories to front offices. The concept of career, as described by Super et al. (1996), fit perfectly with the needs and characteristics of the industrial era, particularly within the expanding array of managerial positions and technology-based professions. Organizations tended to introduce change rather slowly in their production given that competition was not as keen as it is at the current time (Marshall & Tucker, 1992). The relative slowness of communication, in contrast with the current high-speed digitized world, made it far more difficult for the sort of intense competition that exists currently in the marketplace (Rifkin, 1995). In addition, technological advances were far less rapid, thereby leading to an era that was somewhat more stable. As a result, workers were able to consider jobs as having a forward time dimension, assuming that they functioned effectively on the job and that the employer was still viable and able to compete in a given market (Sennett, 1998). This forward time dimension allowed for the development of an internal narrative that placed career within a broader life story, with a past, present, and future (Savickas & Baker, 2005). For the most part, the notion of career, however, was assumed to encompass a degree of volition or choice in one's work life. As the passages presented previously suggest, the extent to which one could self-determine a work life depended greatly on education and access to opportunity. Thus, while many workers had stability (that often turned into tedium) in their work lives, only a small proportion actually assumed control of their work.

Sennett's (1998) analysis of the development of the notion of career is particularly informative in relation to the goals of this chapter. Sennett cites the contributions of Walter Lippmann (1914) as having a key role in the conceptualization of the notion of career within the 20th century. For Lippmann, the changes that were associated with the industrial revolution fostered dramatic ruptures in the structure of life for nearly all of the citizens in industrialized nations. The intensity of the transformation in life, which included considerable geographic mobility, led to a sense of drift or aimlessness that was of great concern to individuals who had to confront massive dislocations of their relationships, and often their sense of identity. The implicit solution for Lippmann was the development of a career, which offered individuals a connection to the important social structure of the working world. However, in contrast to the life-draining experiences characteristic of 18th-century factories, Lippmann argued that people would benefit greatly from work that had some sort of continuity and meaning in their lives. In Sennett's analysis, which was informed in part by Lippmann's contribution, work functioned as a strong antidote to the other losses that people faced in being cut off from their communities, families, and often, even from their loved ones. Sennett then proposed that the individual attributes of a career were the development of a long-term future orientation, standards of ethical behavior at work, and a commitment to responsibility for one's work-related behavior. Sennett described the evolution of career as providing individuals with a means of coping with a highly fluid world and of providing structure and continuity in their lives.

By the mid-part of the 20th century, the notion of career as a series of life-long positions with a hierarchical structure was in full bloom. Proponents of career were evident in counseling psychology (e.g., Super, 1957) and I/O psychology (e.g., Hall, 1996) and indeed throughout the world of middle-class and educated workers in many locales around the globe. In short, the concept of career came to represent the work lives of individuals with a coherent set of skills who generally made conscious choices about the sort of work they would pursue. In addition, careers represented the overarching vertical horizon that individuals could expect or aspire to in their work lives (Savickas, 2000; Super, 1957). In other words, an individual taking a position as an attorney with a law firm could look forward to a gradually increasing set of responsibilities that would be associated with rising pay and status within the organization and within the broader community. At the same time, scholars such as Super (1980) increasingly conceptualized the work role in relation to other life roles, thereby expanding the notion of career to include the work role, but not to be exclusively defined by work.

The mid 20th century saw the rise of the post-World War II economic boom for many in North America and in some Western countries, which was fueled in large measure by technological advances and by the relative absence of economic competition from countries that had been devastated in the war. Furthermore, this period of time was characterized by the increasing availability of post-secondary education, particularly in North America and Western Europe. The increasing expansion of post-secondary education certainly helped to facilitate the economic progress in many Western countries; here again, we witness considerable inequity as these opportunities expanded only in a minority of countries.

While many would have the view of this time period as relatively tranquil and full of opportunity, the reality is a far cry from the myth of the two-car garage, family of four, with a house in the suburbs. In actuality, much of the workforce did not have access to this sort of work life. Vast pockets of poverty, inadequate education, poor housing, and inconsistent health care still existed in the islands of prosperity that arose in the West after World War II (Kozol, 1991; Weis & Fine, 1993; Wilson, 1996). In effect, the career narrative was not even born for the modal worker who struggled to find jobs that would pay a livable wage; thus, discussions of the death of career serve to underscore distance and marginalization for those who never had access to a career in the first place.

Technology and the Information Age: The End of Job Security?

For those whose work lives took on the shape of a grand career narrative, the story line began to shift dramatically in the 1970s and 1980s. The current phase of major workplace transitions, known as the information age or the global economy, began as technology, particularly computer-based innovations, swept into the entire spectrum of the industrial economy. The changes that have been occurring are vast, complex, and still not entirely understood. Indeed, numerous books and journal articles have been written about how technology is changing our world (e.g., M. Fox, 1994; Gini, 2000; Grantham, 2000; Rafnsdottir & Gudmundsdottir, 2004; Rifkin, 1995; Russell, 2003; Sennett, 1998; Wilson, 1996). Rather than reviewing each of these contributions, I integrate some of the common observations that have particular relevance to the conceptual foundation needed for an inclusive psychology of working.

The information age, which has been characterized by the introduction of digital technology into nearly every aspect of contemporary life, has generated a very different work environment. Undoubtedly, the changes have affected the entire scope of the prototypical late-20th-century bureaucratic organization. The advent of the now common voice mail and answering systems that evolved in the 1970s and 1980s serves as a telling illustration about the way in which workplaces are changing. As many readers have experienced, calling a business or service or even a friend brings us into contact with machines and technology. The struggle to be in contact with a "live person" is occurring throughout the workplace and serves as an informative metaphor for many who are grappling with losses of human connection in the workplace. However, the actual depth of the changes goes deeper and is even more pervasive. Rifkin's (1995) analysis, which has received considerable attention from diverse quarters (e.g., Gini, 2000; Collin & Young, 2000), describes the gravity of the changes in a very compelling manner in the introduction to his book:

> From the beginning, civilization has been structured, in large part, around the concept of work. From Paleolithic hunter/gatherer and Neolithic farmer to the medieval craftsman and assembly line worker of the current century, work has been an integral part of daily existence. Now, for the first time, human labor is being systematically eliminated from the production process. Within less than a century, "mass" work in the market sector is likely to be phased out in virtually all of the industrialized nations of the world. A new generation of sophisticated information and communication technologies is being hurried into a wide variety of work situations. Intelligent machines are replacing human beings in countless tasks, forcing millions of blue and white collar workers into unemployment lines, or worse still, breadlines. (p. 3)

According to Rifkin (1995), digital technology is rapidly replacing skilled, unskilled, and service workers across the entire globe. Rifkin noted that about 75% of the labor market in most industrial nations work in jobs that require repetitive tasks and do not involve much problem solving or training. Many of these jobs can be replaced by machines and computers as technology becomes more sophisticated and accessible. Moreover, Gordon, Morgan, and Ponticell (1994) reported that the vast majority of workers in the United States are not adequately educated or trained to assume the sorts of jobs that will exist in the 21st century. Furthermore, the highly lauded economic boom of the 1990s in the United States resulted in a workforce wherein only 70% of the employed had jobs with conventional hours, standard pay, and health benefits. The other 30% of workers were able to obtain only temporary jobs or part-time employment. Taken together, these trends suggest a major upheaval in the nature of work, which, according to Rifkin's argument, will have equally dramatic effects on the social structure. What are the unique characteristics of technology that are thought to lead to a loss of working opportunities? In Rifkin's analysis, these factors can be summarized as follows:

■ Computers have allowed factories to increasingly turn work over to machines and robotic devices, thereby reducing jobs in numerous occupational fields and making other jobs completely obsolete. Many of these jobs have long served as a means of upward mobility for poor and working class people (Wilson, 1996). The computers and robotics are often more reliable than human workers and are far less expensive, thereby keeping production costs low. This naturally enhances the competitive posture of profit-making organizations, which is critical in the global economy.

■ Digital technology allows production to move to any part of the world and still be tightly controlled and managed from a central location. In addition, education has become far more rigorous throughout the world, therefore providing corporations with a "no-lose" situation. Corporate leaders could easily relocate manufacturing to a developing country and pay far less in wages while maintaining or even enhancing the quality of the products (Marshall & Tucker, 1992).

■ Automation has led to a vast decline in the need for middle-level managers, who are not as critical in managing unskilled and semi-skilled workers and in relaying information between various sectors of an organization. In addition, many companies have experimented with significant downsizing in the 1980s and early 1990s in order to remain competitive. This movement led to leaner organizations, which have used technology to help with communication that was heretofore handled by middle managers.

When considered collectively, these three factors have transformed the landscape of work within Western countries and increasingly throughout developing nations. Rifkin also highlighted that losses of employment opportunities will not be solely located within manufacturing. He presents evidence that workers in service sectors will be increasingly less necessary as various tasks are transformed into technological routines that are programmed for robots or computers. For example, Rifkin describes an emerging technology that will replace bartenders with an automated beverage control system. Rifkin cited numerous other illustrations of how various service sector jobs will be diminished in numbers by technology and by downsizing as companies strive for competitiveness and profitability. In addition to these notable losses is the reality that many workers from the manufacturing sector have moved into the service sector, as technology and the global work force have replaced the once stable factory jobs that dotted the Western economic scene. In Rifkin's views, this set of interrelated processes will soon lead to the demise of many occupational options that have long been critical for the working class and poor.

Rifkin then reprises an argument that Reich (1991) proposed about the social consequences of the diminished opportunities in manufacturing, and now, increasingly within the service sector. Reich described the evolution of an increasingly bifurcated society that is severely stratified by social class. On one side of this divide are "symbolic analytic services," whose ranks include highly educated workers who use their minds and their sophisticated educational training to contribute to the technological, entrepreneurial, and professional domains of the economic structure. On the other side of this widening gulf are "routine production services" and "in-person services," both of whom act out simple and repetitive tasks and have increasingly less access to shared wealth, opportunity, adequate schools, and decent housing. This division, if left unchecked, could lead to significant social strife as the poor and wealthy become juxtaposed with little shared experience to connect their lives. Rifkin takes this position even further by arguing that if our society does not deal assertively with this impending crisis, we will see dramatic rises in crime, drug abuse, violence, and other indices of social alienation.

While Rifkin's work has attracted attention from scholars interested in work (e.g., Gini, 2000; Gorz, 1999) and career development (e.g., Herr et al., 2004), it is important to examine his assumptions in light of traditional economics research and theory. A group of economists (e.g., Gottschalk & Moffitt, 2000; Jaeger & Stevens, 2000; Neumark, 2000) have explored some of the assumptions that Rifkin and others (e.g., Reich, 1991; Wilson, 1996) advanced using national data sets derived primarily from employment statistics in the United States. The question that these economists pondered is: To what extent are changes in job stability and job security evidence of a long-term trend or reflective of short-term adjustments in labor force participation? Using the major data sources informing labor economics for the past few decades (nationwide labor statistics), the economists who contributed chapters to the Neumark volume identified a number of inconsistencies with some findings demonstrating considerable job stability and other results pointing to a decrease in stability. A chapter in the Neumark book by Levenson (2000) focused on part-time and temporary workers, observing that increases in job insecurity seem most pronounced for individuals without discernible employment skills.

When considering the contributions in the Neumark (2000) collection in tandem, it does seem clear that there are notable changes in job security and job stability. Neumark, who sought to integrate the findings of the economists who contributed to his book, concluded as follows:

> Overall, my reading of the evidence is that the 1990s have witnessed some changes in the employment relationships consistent with weakened bonds between workers and firms. Although the magnitude of these changes sometimes suggests sharp breaks with the recent past, they nonetheless indicate that these bonds have only weakened, not broken. Furthermore, the changes that occurred in the 1990s have not persisted long enough even to earn the label "trends." This makes it least as plausible, based on what we know at this point, to conclude that these changes are the unique product of changes in the corporate world in the 1990s rather than longer-term developments that will necessarily persist or accelerate in the near future. It is therefore premature to infer longer-term trends toward declines in long-term employment relationships, and even more so to infer anything like the disappearance of long-term, secure jobs. (Neumark, 2000, p. 23)

While Neumark is fairly confident in his concluding statement, it should be noted that elsewhere in his book, a number of economists presented data indicating that greater job insecurity has been found with African American workers than with workers from European American backgrounds (e.g., Jaeger & Stevens, 2000; Neumark, Polsky, & Hansen, 2000). In addition, Levenson (2000) presented data reflective.of greater instability for workers without high levels of employment skills. Thus, while the Neumark contribution represents a major statement from the labor economics world, many of its authors tend to view the experiences of middle-class, educated workers as the "figure" with the rest of the working world as the "ground." Furthermore, the studies in Neumark's book focused exclusively on the United States, which naturally limits generalizability. These points notwithstanding, the data and corresponding inferences that were detailed in this book provide a sober counterpoint to the more dramatic conclusions of Rifkin (1995).

An interesting observation in the Neumark (2000) contribution is the attempt by economists to infer human motivational factors in response to aggregate data sets. For example, Levenson (2000) proposed that perhaps the declines in labor force participation represent a response to lower wages among unskilled and semi-skilled workers. While this inference makes intuitive sense, one wonders what investigations conducted from a psychology-of-working perspective might add to this debate. In my view, without explicit input from low-wage and semi-skilled workers, whose lives are affected daily by macroeconomic trends, we will remain at a very distant level from the experiences of working class people, and hence, greatly disadvantaged in developing individual and policy interventions that are meaningful and maximally inclusive.

In effect, the arguments that are outlined by Rifkin (1995) and others (e.g., Drucker, 1999; Marshall & Tucker, 1992; Neumark, 2000; Reich, 1991) provide further support for the need for an inclusive psychology of working. The solutions offered by Rifkin, Reich, and others occur at the broad policy level and are not necessarily attentive to individual psychological concerns and needs. For example, Rifkin offers a number of options based on the development of structured volunteer experiences that would help to resolve outstanding social problems (such as inadequate housing, schools, etc.). He suggests the use of "third-sector" organizations that do not represent either government or the private sector, but rather reflect growing non-profit groups that are directed toward ameliorating social inequities and other outstanding problems. Rifkin also recommends tax-based proposals that would result in a social wage for workers who contributed their labor and work efforts to non-profit organizations. In addition, he argues in favor of a shorter work week, which would allow for work efforts to be more adequately shared across the population. I concur that major policy initiatives are needed to address the full gamut of challenges that technology is bringing into working lives across the globe. However, we need a far better understanding of how work functions in human life in order to construct meaningful and effective solutions to these problems. It may be that the solutions offered by Rifkin, Reich, Marshall and Tucker, and others are premature in that they do not consider the critical player in this whole process—the worker, that is the man or woman who must somehow react with grace and flexibility to the impending loss of one of the most important aspects of human life. In my view, we need to have a clearer understanding of how work functions psychologically in order to develop policy initiatives to address the changes that are transforming the workplace. For example, the suggestion to move work-related efforts to the sector of volunteering, with compensation being offered via government allowances, assumes a considerable degree of knowledge about human motivation for work. Psychologists and other behavioral scientists need to be actively and assertively involved in this debate in order to ensure that the individual experience is not lost amidst the macro-level policy changes that are being considered.

Globalization

Another critical factor in reshaping the work place is globalization. T. L. Friedman's (1999, 2005) contributions on globalization provide a comprehensive overview of the various trends, which when considered collectively, have led to changes in the nature of not just the economic structure, but the entire array of political and social forces that influence and shape human development. In this section, I focus on defining globalization and offering an analysis of how this process is changing the experience of working.

Friedman argues that the economic foundations of our current social structure are being completely rearranged by globalization. His introductory comments about globalization, which are outlined in the following passage, convey some of the salient attributes of this movement:

> To begin with, the globalization system, unlike the Cold War system, is not static, but a dynamic ongoing process: globalization involves the inexorable integration of markets, nation states and technologies to a degree never witnessed before—in a way that is enabling individuals, corporations and nation states to reach around the world farther, faster, deeper and cheaper than even before, and in a way that is also producing a powerful backlash from those brutalized or left behind by this new system.

> The driving idea behind globalization is free-market capitalism—the more you let market forces rule and the more you open up your economy to free trade and competition, the more efficient and flourishing your economy will be. Globalization means the spread of free-market capitalism to virtually every country in the world. Globalization also has its own set of economic rules— rules that revolve around opening, deregulating and privatizing your economy. (T. L. Friedman, 1999, pp. 7–8)

One of the major implications emerging from this definition of globalization is the pervasive spread of free market capitalism. Despite one's views about free market capitalism, the predominance of this economic system in the world's economy seems incontrovertible according to Friedman. The manifestations of a global free market economy for working life are extensive and far-reaching. First, the competitiveness of economies at the level of nations and larger corporate entities has a profound impact within the workplace of the 21st century. The lack of job security, which is a growing trend across diverse workplaces (Grantham, 2000; Hall, 1996), has become a major theme in the work narrative of the new economy. The old loyalty between worker and organization is giving way to a loyalty to the bottom line with respect to a company's viability in a very competitive marketplace. The keen competitive nature of the workplace has served to enhance the payoff that a strong high school and post-secondary education yields in the labor market (Rifkin, 1995; Statt, 1994).

Second, the integration of technology with globalization has created a labor market that is no longer bounded by national or linguistic lines. Instead, employers are able to shift production and even service jobs to locations where the workforce is able to produce high-quality labor at a competitive cost. The use of technology allows organizations to maintain control over great distances, while the move to free market economies globally has allowed highly educated workers from previously state-run economies to take on production and service work for multinational corporations. This movement, of course, has engendered significant reactions from workers around the world. T. L. Friedman (1999, 2005) describes the backlash that globalization has stirred up, which is certainly evident in the demonstrations that occur when world leaders congregate in summits and other meetings to discuss trade and other related economic issues. On a more individual level, globalization has created vast pockets of despair and social disengagement. The workers that were described at the outset of this chapter in Sennett's book (1998) certainly were giving voice to their frustration after their layoffs from IBM.

Another interviewee working in management within a modern corporate context, who is cited in Kahn's (1996) chapter on the need for secure relationships at work, noted the following:

> The message we're getting now is that the company doesn't owe you anything. Consultants have told us that the company is not there for your emotional support, that they don't owe you raises or job security, just honesty. And that a day's pay for a day's work is honest. Everyone is shocked. The drones are panicking and looking for someone to tell them what to do. The better ones are looking for opportunity. (p. 160)

Like the technological changes described earlier, globalization is still an active phenomenon yielding processes and transitions that are difficult to ascertain fully. However, based on what has transpired to date, it is possible to make some logical inferences about the impact of globalization in relation to the psychological experiences of working. One of the most prominent implications is that the work place is becoming far more competitive because the range of workers who can fill available jobs now has few if any local or even national boundaries. In Sennett's (1998) book, which describes the layoffs in IBM in the late 1980s and early 1990s, programmers from India were hired to replace Americans, where their contributions were immediately available due to the rapid speed of technological transfers of information. Thus, the picture that emerges is one wherein workers need to be highly trained and highly productive in order to obtain and maintain their jobs. As a seminal report from the W. T. Grant Foundation noted in 1988, we have entered a period wherein high wage jobs will only be available to workers with high skills. As such, considerable effort has been devoted to enhancing the rigor of educational systems in many nations in order to train a workforce that will be able to compete effectively in the global marketplace. Marshall and Tucker (1992) described the emergence of highly competitive schools and job training programs in parts of Europe and Asia, which they argued were largely responsible for the redistribution of jobs and production into these parts of the globe. Following the Marshall and Tucker analysis, I believe that educational excellence and high standards have become another key aspect of globalization. With a work force that has high skills in literacy, numeracy, technology, problem solving, and interpersonal relationships, one can very quickly compete for jobs that had heretofore been primarily found in Western Europe and North America.

Another critical implication is that the workplace for many has become more stressful and frenetic. Increasingly, workers are facing the need to juggle multiple tasks and to perform well beyond a level that may have been acceptable a decade or so ago. The inherent competitiveness of work has clearly been felt by many who now report that they are working very hard, both in their paid employment as well as in caregiving. For example, the vignette from Wolfe's (1998) study of the changing values of middle-class communities in the United States provides a voice for an experience that is becoming common across the globe:

> (People) are so pressed for time that they're always looking for a shortcut. I mean, everyone does. You look for a quick way to be able to juggle, you know, because you've got a lot of things you need to do. You need to go home and clean your house, you need to get groceries, or need to stop by the doctor's .... People are always trying to kind of shortcut the system. And society has encouraged that. I mean, you no longer have to wait in line for a bank teller. So we're getting to the point where we're always looking for a shortcut. Everybody, everybody is. (pp. 244–245)

This quote strikes at the core of a critical aspect of globalization. For some, the global marketplace is creating a loss of paid employment with far-reaching consequences such as deterioration in physical and mental health as well as the overall functioning of a given community (Statt, 1994; Wilson, 1996; Winefield, 2002). However, for others, the competitiveness of globalization has led to an expansion of one's work responsibilities. The growth in the number of hours that professionals and entrepreneurs are devoting to their jobs has been another major by-product of globalization and the technological boom (Schor, 1991). Consequently, for the less well educated and poor, Rifkin's predictions may lead to long periods of unemployment or underemployment, while for others, the problem is that work never ends. In effect, what exists now is a significant maldistribution of both work and wealth. While Rifkin's suggestions offer some plausible solutions, we require a deeper understanding of the actual experience of working in order to construct and implement effective solutions to this growing disparity. Another way to view globalization is that the distribution of work around the globe is consistent with the key tenets of market-based economics. As such, one may argue that the recent movement of information technology jobs to Asia and South America in fact reflects a redistribution of opportunities that may reduce income disparities across the globe.

In effect, globalization and the technological boom have worked in tandem to rearrange the workplace for a large proportion of the world (T. L. Friedman, 1999, 2005; Rifkin, 1995; Wilson, 1996). A key observation of many scholars is that work is no longer secure and predictable (e.g., Collin & Young, 2000; Gelatt, 1989). Moreover, the downsizing adopted by many organizations has had a considerable effect on the nature of work. While the economic boom of the 1990s may have given an illusory impression that work opportunities were not fading, recent events in the early 21st century seem to support at least some of the concerns voiced by Rifkin. Whether Rifkin's predictions will become reality, of course, is impossible to discern at this point. Moreover, the degree to which public policy can influence the factors that Rifkin and others have identified as eliminating vast numbers of jobs, is also hard to predict. But what is clear is that for many people in the 21st century, access to work is no longer a given in life. And for those who are working, the nature of the "contract" between worker and employer is being rewritten, as is outlined in the next section.

The Changing "Contract"

One of the hallmarks of the industrial era was the deep connection between an employer and a worker. At nearly all levels of employment within medium and large organizations, workers and employers generally held onto a view of a psychological contract that defined and structured a stable and predictable relationship. The notion of a psychological contract existing between employer and worker has long interested organizational psychologists, who have been motivated to understand how such a contract could be enhanced to bolster employee commitment and productivity (e.g., Hall & Mirvis, 1996; Schein, 1965). A psychological contract represents the overt and covert expectations that exist between worker and employer; these expectations focus on the nature of the relationship as opposed to the actual legal arrangements, which are typically found in "employment contracts." During the industrial era and the early phases of the information era, the psychological contract was essentially premised on the assumption that sustained effort, adequate productivity, honesty, punctuality, and an overall responsible attitude toward one's work tasks would result in a sense of belonging and connection. A significant consequence of a psychological contract is that one would feel part of a larger organization. Indeed, people often felt pride in working with a given company or organization. However, the psychological contract that has emerged in recent years is not based on a long-term relationship; rather, workers are now learning that their commitment needs to be directed toward their own skills, experience, and personal work trajectories. The reality of contemporary corporations and many non-profit organizations is that long-term psychological contracts are not necessarily consistent with the need for highly competitive, lean organizational structures that can be cost-effective, and highly responsive to change. Even in government jobs in North America, long the most stable places to work during the industrial era, downsizing has become a norm. Similarly, Japan, which has historically had the most structured and stable psychological contracts, has had to change its modal approach in establishing relationships between organizations and employees (Rifkin, 1995). Workers throughout the industrialized nations have had to reorient themselves in a manner that is illustrated in an interview that Sennett had with an AT&T executive: "In AT&T we have to promote the whole concept of the work force being contingent, though most of the contingent workers are inside our wall. 'Jobs' are being replaced by 'projects' and 'fields of work'" (1998, p. 22).

The advent of the information era, which is characterized by the twin change engines of technology and globalization, has completely recast the psychological contract that exists between workers and employers (Arthur & Rousseau, 1996; Hall, 1996). In relation to the psychological connection between employers and workers, Hall and Mirvis (1996) proposed a major shift from organizational careers to protean careers. The organizational career, which is based on the psychological contract of the industrial era, implied a long-term relationship of an employee to an organization. The employee could hope for an upwardly mobile series of jobs, often within the same organization or within the same field, in which responsibilities and pay increased over time, assuming, of course, that the worker was effective, productive, and reasonably committed. However, this type of contract is no longer possible for most workers, creating the foundation for what Hall and Mirvis call the protean career. As Hall and Mirvis proposed, "the protean concept encompasses any kind of flexible, idiosyncratic career course, with peaks and valleys, left turns, moves from one line of work to another, and so forth. Rather than focusing outward on some ideal generalized career 'path,' the protean career is unique to each person—a sort of career fingerprint" (1996, p. 21). The protean career, therefore, seems to be the modal pattern for the information age for many highly educated workers. As outlined in chapter 1, many individuals are no longer able to construct a career narrative that can be framed within an expected set of work tasks and work settings. The changes that are inherent in the information era are rapidly making the predictability of coherent career paths a vestige of an earlier era.

Hall and Mirvis (1996), however, have offered a means of creating opportunity out of crisis. First, for workers who have the educational advantages that allow them access to the "symbolic analyst" jobs of the 21st century (Reich, 1991), a protean career can be constructed on individual goals, aspirations, and talents, thereby allowing for greater autonomy and control. Instead of using external criteria to assess one's success, a protean career allows for the development of internal criteria. Hall and Mirvis (1996), however, pointed out the downsides of a protean career. They noted, for example, that the protean career often is characterized by an absence of a long-term employment contract, resulting in work without health benefits. (In the United States, health benefits are not provided to all citizens by the government; hence, stable employment is one of the major means of obtaining adequate health coverage as most health insurance is furnished in large measure by employers.) Second, one's sense of identity, which for many within Western nations is tied to a stable work life and a linkage to a larger organization or mission (e.g., Schein, 1965; Sennett, 1998), is increasingly becoming diffuse and unstable. Third, for workers who are in mid-life or older, moving from an organizational career to a protean career is very challenging. Furthermore, Hall and Mirvis noted that for workers who are not located within a stable organizational context (e.g., working from home), the new protean career does not offer the social connections that work had provided in the past. The lack of social connection and relational support has engendered an illuminating discussion about the changing nature of work, which is summarized in the next section.

Contemporary Work and Isolation

A number of scholars have voiced deep concerns about the social and relational consequences of the rapid changes in the nature of work (e.g., Grantham, 2000; Hall, 1996; Sennett, 1998). Sennett's contribution describes a sense of longing for connection in the face of what he calls the "new capitalism." For Sennett, the consequences of the information era and globalization are the pronounced allegiance to flexibility and the need for rapid change, which he believes have become the hallmarks of the economic structure that defines 21st century work life. As Sennett detailed, the changing nature of work is leaving people with a deep longing for a sense of "we," which he argues is being diminished as the workplace moves toward increasing competition, flexibility, and risk-taking. One of the most prominent consequences of the new capitalism is the loss of stability at work, which is having a corresponding impact on our capacity to derive meaning from work and to forge stable relationships in the workplace. In Sennett's view, the shifting landscape of work has left many feeling quite disengaged and even shameful in their desire for a sense of mutual interdependence. When the overriding norm is one of autonomy and success at any cost, the sense of shared community values and people caring about others has become increasingly less viable. The implications of these changes for the work context are quite extensive in Sennett's view. For example, when workers who have devoted such effort and time to their work lives are told that they are no longer needed, or that they are needed only when the employer deems it so, the experience may be akin to a major emotional betrayal. The consequence of the new capitalism, therefore in Sennett's view, is what he calls the corrosion of personal character—the gradual, but pervasive chipping away of a sense of completeness, relational connection, and inner sense of cohesion. Indeed, Sennett ends his book with the following cautionary comment, which provides a major theme in this book as well: "... I do know that a regime which provides human beings no deep reasons to care about one another cannot long preserve its legitimacy" (p. 148).

In a somewhat similar vein, Hall (1996) entitled a landmark collection of essays "*The Career Is Dead—Long Live the Career: A Relational Approach to Careers.*" In a sense, this title describes one of the major trends in the grand career narrative along with a potential solution. As noted earlier, Hall and Mirvis (1996) argued that the organizational career is being replaced by the protean career, which may result in greater isolation and instability. A critical characteristic of the protean career is that relationships can serve multiple functions in the new working climate of the 21st century. One of the most innovative chapters in the Hall volume by Fletcher (1996) focused on an elegant integration of theories from feminist scholars from Wellesley College's Stone Center (e.g., Jordan et al., 1991) as well as the work of Gilligan (e.g.,

1982) to articulate a relational approach to the protean career. The key premises of Fletcher's contribution pertain to the fundamental assumptions that are made about human development. In contrast to models of development that have viewed autonomy as the ideal goal, which has been associated with masculine-based notions of autonomous and independent modes of functioning, the relationally oriented theorists have sought to infuse a more affirming feminism into existing conceptualizations of development and adaptive human functioning (e.g., Josselson, 1992; J. B. Miller, 1986). The inclusion of feminist thinking has helped to reframe the goal of development; rather than suggesting that human beings attain the most mature state when they can function alone, the relational scholars have developed compelling arguments and credible evidence suggesting that people need and thrive on relational connections to others (Gilligan, 1982; S. A. Mitchell, 1988). The relational perspectives, which have emerged from contributions in developmental psychology (e.g., Ainsworth, 1989; Bowlby, 1982), feminist thought (e.g., Gilligan, 1982), and psychoanalytic theory (e.g., Kohut, 1977; Mitchell, 1988), have painted a very different picture of human functioning. The picture that emerges is a richly peopled context in which natural strivings for connection are affirmed and not shamed. In relation to the changing nature of work and career, the emergence of globalization and technology has made it difficult to generate and sustain the connections that are so integral to human behavior. Fletcher argues that organizations need to value relational skills and contributions more assertively and in concrete ways. In addition, Fletcher as well as others in the Hall volume (e.g., W. A. Kahn, 1996; Kram, 1996) proposed that individuals who are negotiating protean careers need to work harder in nurturing their relational support systems, particularly in light of the difficulties that are presented in maintaining stable relationships at work.

When considered collectively, the contributions by Sennett (1998) and Hall (1996) have suggested that the major upheaval in the structure of careers in the 21st century is having a significant impact upon the sense of connection that work ideally could bring to one's life. By changing the nature of the contract that exists between workers and employers, people are often left feeling significantly disconnected and even isolated. Indeed, much of what has been described thus far is analogous to what Kohut (1977) and others in relationally oriented psychotherapy have called relational lapses. These relational lapses are leaving an increasing number of people who can obtain jobs feeling alienated, frightened, and often confused about their own identities. (These issues, which I think are critical in an inclusive psychology of working, are pursued in greater depth in chapter 4.)

Changes in Caregiving Work

As noted in chapter 1, I consider caregiving to be a form of work as well as a critical relational function. As such, a discussion of changes in caregiving in light of the technological and globalization trends cited earlier is warranted. In addition to the changes noted previously on the nature of working, we are witnessing vast shifts in health care and gender norms that are contributing to both challenges and opportunities with respect to caregiving. Naturally, it is difficult to document the wide diversity of values that exist with respect to caregiving around the globe. Within traditional communities, families have tended to stay close to each other with caregiving roles being distributed throughout the multiple generations that may inhabit a given family space (Boyd & Stevens, 2002). However, in most cultures, women have generally been socialized to assume caregiving tasks. Like other authors, I concur that there is no biological or social imperative for women to provide more caregiving then men (e.g., Betz & Fitzgerald, 1987; Hesse-Biber & Carter, 2000; Yoder, 1999). Indeed, I believe that a major agenda for a truly inclusive psychology of working is to continue to advocate at all levels for greater gender equity with respect to childcare, housework, and other caregiving tasks.

The review by Barnett and Hyde (2001) summarized numerous studies that assessed gender differences in caregiving across cultures. They concluded that men are equally equipped from a social and psychological standpoint to provide care to children. In addition, they observed that multiple roles, including caregiving as well as paid employment, are beneficial across a wide array of psychological and social domains. Despite these findings, considerable evidence exists suggesting that an unequal distribution of caregiving continues to occur within Western countries (Barnett & Hyde; see chapter 4 for further details). In my view, there are competing trends that may conflict as people struggle to find ways of integrating caregiving into an increasingly complex set of roles and responsibilities. The expanding life span is creating a growing cohort of elderly, who are now living longer than ever (Boyd & Stevens, 2002). In fact, the most rapidly growing group of people in the United States are those who are in their 80s (Boyd & Stevens, 2002). This group will require many individuals, including a significant proportion who are actively caring for their children and working outside of the home, to take on additional caregiving responsibilities. I envision that far greater demands will be placed on middle-aged adults to care for aging parents and relatives.

Yet at the same time, the decreasing earning power of wages and salaries coupled with the important inroads that women have made in the last few decades in attaining a greater role in paid employment is creating a greater push toward dual working couples (Cooper & Lewis, 1999; Davidson & Fielden, 1999; Statt, 1994). In addition, single mothers, who represent a growing group due to the increased acceptance of divorce and the advent of alternative family arrangements, have emerged as an increasingly significant proportion of the family structure in North America in recent years (Betz & Fitzgerald, 1987; Malley & Stewart, 1988). These factors have functioned to create situations wherein little choice exists over whether to work or devote more time to caregiving. For many people in Western countries, and of course for many across the globe, working both at home and at paid employment does not represent a conscious decision, but rather reflects the reality of survival (Rubin, 1994; Shirk, Bennett, & Aber, 1999). To add to the complexity, national governments vary considerably in the extent to which adequate, safe, and affordable child care and elder care are offered. This is a major problem, especially in the United States and in developing countries, where safe, nurturing child care is generally a prerogative of the wealthy and middle-class. The poor and working classes are often left to fend for themselves. In the past, many people could rely on extended family members, who would pitch in for each other in caring for children, disabled adults, and the elderly. However, another trend of the post-modern age, notably the increasing rate of geographic mobility, has left many working class and poor adults with few options with respect to integrating family work and paid work (Rifkin, 1995; Wilson, 1996). Moreover, the increased use of contract work, part-time jobs, and outsourcing has further exacerbated the challenges that workers face in attempting to care for their families and loved ones.

Another complication that adds further difficulty is that caregiving has unfortunately become associated with less prestige and with minimal external rewards (Neff, 1985; M. S. Richardson, 1993). Obviously, the inherent rewards are potentially significant, as are the challenges. Moreover, the extent to which caregiving is valued varies considerably across cultures and time frames. However, the current situation, especially in the United States, is that caregiving, whether offered for pay or provided by loved ones and family members, remains a low-status endeavor.

Taken together, these trends suggest that easy solutions will continue to be very difficult to develop. On one hand, we are witnessing substantial growth of elderly people in many Western countries as improving health standards are leading to longer life expectancy. In addition, many governments continue to express ambivalence about the extent to which caregiving is considered "work," which seriously detracts from efforts to provide economic rewards, health insurance, and pensions for individuals who care for others as part of their livelihoods. Yet, if we take Rifkin and others (e.g., Arthur & Rousseau, 1996; Sennett, 1998) seriously, we may be faced with an interesting conundrum that may also offer some solutions. What seems to be occurring in many sectors of societies across the globe is that some people have too much to do, including paid employment and caregiving, while others are not as actively engaged in their social and occupational responsibilities. As such, it may be that public policy efforts to train interested candidates to assist with caregiving may yield two positive outcomes in one fell swoop. Even without such structural changes, it seems clear that the findings from Barnett and Hyde (2001) should be presented clearly to the popular media. People need to understand that there are no biological, economic, or social reasons for men to avoid caregiving or other household duties. Much of the evidence presented by Barnett and Hyde suggests that men and women who are involved in multiple roles, including caregiving work as well as paid work, fare quite well with respect to mental and physical health indices as well as subjective reports of well-being. In addition, families need to take in the recommendations of various scholars (Bergman, 1995; Mahalik & Morrison, in press) who have advised parents to help boys feel more comfortable in nurturing and relating in a mutual fashion as they are socialized into adulthood.

The trends noted herein with respect to caregiving have a potentially powerful interaction with the other major shifts in the nature of work. The sense of unpredictability is certainly palpable when one considers globalization, technological changes, and vast shifts in the types of jobs that are likely to be available in relation to greater caregiving demands. Yet caregiving has been a constant in human experience. Moreover, many aspects of caregiving are not easily transformed into technological routines, suggesting that this part of our lives may provide some sense of stability amidst the sea of changes that are reshaping working around the globe.

Changes in Labor Unions

A discussion of the changing nature of working in the 21st century would not be complete without attention to the shifting role of labor unions. In the United States, the percentage of workers who were members of labor unions declined from 39% in 1954 to 13.2% currently (Clawson, & Clawson, 1999; Shipler, 2004). This decline has had an enormous impact on the world of work in the U.S. Similar declines have been observed in Europe, with France in particular experiencing significant losses in labor membership (Lamont, 2000). Other nations that have linked labor unions to major political parties, however, have faced somewhat less of a loss in union presence and political influence.

The reasons for the decline are multifaceted, yet revealing about the changes taking place in the world of work. One of the primary reasons for the decline in the U.S., according to Clawson and Clawson (1999), can be understood as emerging from demographic shifts. For example, the movement of workers in the U.S. from northern cities (where union activity is extensive) to the Sunbelt cities in the South and West, which had a far less extensive network of unions, contributed significantly to the decline in union membership. Additionally, the growing proportion of professional and managerial workers coupled with the loss of manufacturing jobs changed the nature of the labor market, making unions less compelling for many workers.

Another prominent reason for the decline in union membership, according to Clawson and Clawson analysis, is the fact that unions experienced considerable pressure to protect gains achieved in previous contracts and therefore focused less on recruiting new members and expanding their base and impact. In addition, Clawson and Clawson argued that the advent of globalization led to intensive attacks on unions and existing labor contracts, with the intention of creating leaner and more competitive organizations that could compete internationally. Clawson and Clawson did note that the hostility toward unions became particularly pervasive in the United States, which has experienced substantive changes in how unions are understood and perceived.

The reduction in labor union presence in many workforces has created an even greater sense of instability for many individuals as they confront a rapidly shifting work environment. Earlier in the 20th century, labor unions represented a viable means of giving workers a voice via collective bargaining and negotiation with management. The loss of that voice for many workers and potential workers has created a growing sense of uneasiness and powerlessness, particularly for workers who do not have highly marketable skills.

The Current Status of Career and Working

The material presented thus far does indeed offer a rather fluid and, at times, stark picture of the changing nature of work and working. However, many other sectors of human experience are not well represented in this discussion. We shall now turn to people who are generally not part of the scholarly and policy debates about the transformation of work in the 21st century.

Beyond the Dying Career: Work Among the Poor and Working Classes

While the poor and working class have been included in many notable discussions of the changing nature of work (e.g., N. Peterson & González, 2005; Reich, 1991; Rifkin, 1995; Wilson, 1996), issues pertaining to the death of career, naturally, have not focused on those who never had access to the grand career narrative. As Hall (1996) mentioned in the conclusion of his book of essays about the future of career, there are considerable areas of darkness where little light has been shed. He mentions the sausage maker and others who may not have even had a glimpse of a career in the sense that Hall and others have written about in the later half of the 20th century. As has been noted in this chapter, a number of important scholarly statements have been advanced about the implications of the changing nature of work on a broad spectrum of individuals (e.g., T. L. Friedman, 2005; Marshall & Tucker, 1992; Reich, 1991; Wilson, 1996). However, the vast majority of this literature has focused on the work lives of relatively well educated and affluent workers in Western countries (e.g., M. Fox, 1994; Grantham, 2000). Moreover, with a few notable exceptions (e.g., Wilson, 1996), very little of this body of material has furnished insights into the inner experience of the workers who are grappling with forces that are taking place well outside of the purview of their lives and proximal communities.

Consistent with the position that I have adopted in this book, I believe that exploring the narratives of workers and others who are struggling with work may provide important insights that complement and extend the observations of social scientists. Within the United States, Wilson's (1996) book describes one man's struggles as he confronts the reality that his job does not offer the sort of financial rewards that are available in a life of criminal work:

> My husband, he's worked in the community. He's 33. He's worked at One Stop since he was 15. And right now, he's one of the highest paid—he's a butcher—he's one of the highest paid butchers in One Stop. For the 15—almost 18—years that he's been there, he's only making nine dollars an hour. And he's begged and fought and scrapped and sued and everything else for the low pay he gets. And he takes so much. Sometimes he comes home and he'd sit home and he'd just cry. And he'd say, "If it weren't for my kids and my family, I'd quit." You know, it's bad, 'cuz he won't get into drugs, selling it, you know, he ain't into drug using. He's the kind of man, he wants to work hard and feel good about that he came home. He say that it feels bad sometime to see this 15-year-old boy drivin' down the street with a new car. He

saying, "I can't even pay my car note. And I worry about them comin' to get my car. (p. 69)

Similarly, Shirk et al. (1999) observed families who are struggling against enormous odds to make a living and support themselves. One such family of Latino background, living in Oakland, California, is presented as facing considerable obstacles in moving out of poverty. The following excerpt describes the struggles that the mother, who is a single parent, faces in securing employment:

> "For two weeks, I went down to the office every morning and asked whether there was work," Magda said.
> "The man asked me, 'Do you have experience?'"
> "I said, 'No, but you can show me. Just give me a chance.'"
> "He said, 'No, I can't afford to take the time to teach you. Time is money.'"
> "And I told him, 'Please, I really need a job. I got two kids and no husband, and I have to support them.'" ...
> "Scott [the janitorial supervisor] would say when he saw me coming, 'Here's that lady again. She must really want to work.' And I'd tell him, 'I really need work. My babies need to eat.'" (p. 43)

This vignette and the previous excerpt convey a sense of desperation that has not been part of the discourse in traditional psychological examinations about career and working. As we consider working in contexts outside of Western nations, which have been the object of the vast majority of scholarly attention to date, the notion of career or meaningful work seems about as distant as possible. Kurian (1982) describes a stark day of a woman who works in tea plantations in Sri Lanka. The day begins typically at 3:00 am when plantation workers need to prepare meals for their families. They then help their children to get to school and begin their paid employment at 6:00 or 7:00 am. The major job task on the tea plantations is to pluck tea leaves and their buds. The work is very carefully supervised, and women who make any mistakes are severely castigated. When the need to attend to the crops is not that high, the women can leave work at 4:00 pm, but when the demands are urgent, the women may have to work until 5:30. Like most of their counterparts in the West, the plantation workers then have to go home and perform the vast majority of household tasks, resulting in a day that ends at about 10:00 pm.

Some of the stories found in the literature are not as gloomy as the one cited previously about the plantation workers from Sri Lanka. In T. L. Friedman's (1999) book about globalization, he recounts a narrative of Liliane, a social worker from Brazil. The following text provides a more optimistic view of the changing nature of work:

... Liliane, a thirty-two year-old Brazilian social worker who lived in the Rocinha favela [favelas are the make-shift shanties that poor Brazilians have set up adjacent to large cities in their search for work] and [now] works for the municipal government. She gave [Friedman] a tour of a day-care center in the favela and along the way explained that she had saved for years to finally be able to move her family out. Now that they were out of the favela and into the Fast World, the last thing that she wanted was for that world to fold up, even if it was a struggle to get in. She said to [Friedman]: 'When I was young everyone in the neighborhood in the favela had to watch TV in one house. I am now moving to a place that is one hour and twenty minutes from my work, instead of twenty minutes, but it is not the favela and it is away from crime. I am moving there for my children because there are no drug dealers. I make 900 reels a month. [Now] I can buy a telephone. Now our house is made of bricks, not wood, and at the end of the month I still have some money left. (p. 289)

Returning to the United States, we once again approach a situation that is analogous to the favela, which has evoked such a sense of sadness and concern in Brazil. The U.S. version of a favela, an inner-city ghetto, has a somewhat different set of etiologies and dynamics, but also contains a great number of similarities. The following passage depicts the economic factors that many people living in U.S. ghettos face as they struggle to makes a living:

Like when I moved I got behind. The telephone and moving expenses. Like one month's [rent for a] security [deposit], the telephone company eat your tail out and all the other little bills I have. I have to take it more slowly to get back on my feet. I never liked public aid. I'm on public aid now. I've been on and off for eleven years with [my daughter], I had to go on with her. I was tryin' to collect some of my unemployment. I was tryin' to get a job where I could get off completely, but you just don't know. 'Cause you may lose your job. I have to do something to keep these kids going through, otherwise if I was by myself, I could do other little things like, you know, 'cause I cannot see myself workin' the streets. I cannot see myself doin' that. I can't see it at all. (Wilson, 1996, p. 79)

One of the most obvious areas of congruence across the settings in these vignettes is the lack of work, which tends to reduce the level of structure and continuity in a given community. The following excerpt from a member of Wilson's (1996) research team captures an image which speaks volumes about some of the most obvious consequences of disappearing jobs in inner-city communities in the United States:

The once-lively streets [of the urban African American community in Chicago]—residents remember a time, not so long ago, when crowds were so dense at rush hour that one had to elbow one's way to the train station—now have the appearance of an empty, bombed-out war zone. The commercial strip has been reduced to a long tunnel of charred stores, vacant lots littered with broken glass and garbage, dilapidated buildings left to rot in the shadow of the elevated train line. At the corner of Sixty-third Street and Cottage Grove Avenue, the handful of remaining establishments that struggle to survive are huddled behind wrought-iron bars .... (p. 5)

The material presented in this section captures the tip of the iceberg in the vast diversity of contexts and cultures within which people work around the globe. The vignettes presented here, when considered in light of the argument by Wilson (1996) and Rifkin (1995), portray a dynamic set of social forces that, while still not completely understood, may be quite powerful in reshaping social and cultural institutions. As the narrator in the passage from Wilson's study states, the loss of stable and accessible work in a given community is often associated with a domino-like transformation that tends to strip away a sense of order and structure in people's lives. Both Wilson and Rifkin describe this process in detail. Bruce Springsteen's song (1980/1998) entitled "*The River*," which follows, conveys this sense of anomie in a particularly vivid fashion:

I come from down in the valley
where mister when you're young
They bring you up to do like your daddy done
Me and Mary we met in high school
when she was just seventeen
We'd ride out of that valley down to where the fields were green

We'd go down to the river
And into the river we'd dive
Oh down to the river we'd ride

Then I got Mary pregnant
and man that was all she wrote
And for my nineteenth birthday I got a union card and a wedding coat
We went down to the courthouse
and the judge put it all to rest
No wedding day smiles no walk down the aisle
No flowers no wedding dress

That night we went down to the river
And into the river we'd dive
Oh down to the river we did ride

I got a job working construction for the Johnstown Company
But lately there ain't been much work on account of the economy
Now all them things that seemed so important
Well mister they vanished right into the air

Now I just act like I don't remember
Mary acts like she don't care

But I remember us riding in my brother's car
Her body tan and wet down at the reservoir
At night on them banks I'd lie awake
And pull her close just to feel each breath she'd take
Now those memories come back to haunt me
they haunt me like a curse
Is a dream a lie if it don't come true
Or is it something worse
that sends me down to the river
though I know the river is dry
That sends me down to the river tonight
Down to the river
my baby and I
Oh down to the river we ride

The narrator in this song describes a sense of longing for a time and a place that may no longer be available. The sense of loss is palpable, with the narrator describing how life seemed so open when work was available. The loss of access to work renders the protagonist on a downward spiral of pain and sadness with corresponding despair in his relational life. (The overlap of relationships and work is a major theme in this book and is discussed in greater depth in chapter 4.) The consequences of the disappearance of work from people's lives are still hard to imagine. However, the glimpses that we have obtained in these powerful narratives speak to feelings of despair that cannot be ignored as policymakers and government leaders struggle to find ways to cope with the immense changes that are taking place in the nature and availability of work.

One of the gaps in the literature about working is that many of the narratives and vignettes have been gathered via modern methods of books, journals, music, and other published media. Yet vast pockets of human beings live and work in communities where few, if any, written accounts of their experiences are available. For example, it is difficult to obtain information about workers living in townships of South Africa, hunters living in the jungles of South America, and farmers in India and China. Thanks to the efforts of creative anthropologists (e.g., Goldschmidt, 1990; Wallman, 1979), we have some useful insights into the nature of working in some of the diverse settings around the globe. Indeed, this knowledge base has been especially useful in creating the intellectual scaffolding for the psychology of working. However, the experience-near understanding of working, which is a clear attribute of psychological analyses, offers a critically needed perspective that can serve to enrich existing social scientific analyses of working.

A major thread that weaves throughout the literature on the work lives of people without grand career narratives is that work is pursued to a great extent as a means of survival. The degree to which work is satisfying or meaningful, naturally, is still a major consideration, but it is often of secondary or tertiary interest for people who are striving to earn enough money to locate decent housing and to feed themselves and their families. Often, feelings of satisfaction are based on the secondary gains of work, such as the income that fulfills basic human needs. Another theme that emerges in this discussion is the role of work in providing structure for individuals and for communities. As Wilson (1996) noted, this structure is perhaps most evident when jobs disappear from a community or from a family. In addition, the nature of work in the 21st century seems to be rendering enormous changes across the globe, not just in regions where information and technology are prominent cultural and social characteristics. Aside from a modest growing interest in the work lives of working class and poor people in Western countries (e.g., Juntunen et al., 2001; N. Peterson & González, 2005; Phillips, Blustein, Jobin-Davis, & White, 2002), psychologists have not devoted much attention to the working lives of the vast majority of people. The material presented in this section suggests that we have much to learn about the psychological experience of working that does not necessarily fall into the tidy boundaries of careers.

The Knowledge Gap

Another growing trend that is very much integral to the changing nature of work is the need for greater levels of skills and knowledge in the workforce of the 21st century. As the literature presented thus far has suggested, many of the jobs that had been occupied by unskilled or semi-skilled workers are now being replaced by technology and automation. At the same time, a number of scholars have recognized that new jobs will very likely involve high levels of skills (e.g., Hunt, 1995; Marshall & Tucker, 1992; Reich, 1991; Rifkin, 1995). Indeed, one of the reasons that many jobs have left traditional pockets of industrial production (e.g., North America; Europe) is that the growing skills and knowledge of workers in other countries has made it far more economical for production operations to relocate. In short, a potentially substantial disjuncture has emerged in which the needs of the workforce often involve far more complex skill sets than are available in the labor market; for example, within some communities in the United States, employers have had difficulty in locating workers with sufficient skills and knowledge to fill available positions (Bladassarri & Paganetto, 1996; Marshall & Tucker, 1992; O'Brien, 1986.). As a result, employers have sought to locate their production and service centers in regions of the world where skilled workers are more available, often at lower wages. One of the outcomes of this disjuncture is the compelling need to enhance standards in schools; indeed, this trend is particularly pronounced in the United States and many other technologically enriched nations, which are seeking to enhance the quality of education and to reduce achievement gaps between rich and poor (R. Johnson, 2002; Levine, Lowe, Peterson, & Tenorio, 1995; Tucker & Codding, 1998). The question raised in many thoughtful analyses is whether workers across the globe are sufficiently knowledgeable for the available jobs that exist and that will be created in the coming decades (Hunt, 1995). A corollary concern is the growing divide between those who are educated and those who have insufficient or inadequate educational backgrounds.

Based on the material presented thus far in this chapter, the knowledge gap seems to be a highly intuitive outcome in a macro-level analysis of the workforce of the 21st century. As we consider the twin engines of globalization and the information age, it is becoming increasingly apparent that knowledge will be a critical factor in filling jobs that will involve skills in computers, literacy, problem solving, and quantitative reasoning (T. L. Friedman, 1999; Marshall & Tucker, 1992; Reich, 1991). Moreover, knowledge is going to be necessary for people to engage in the sorts of entrepreneurial activities that are becoming one of the major job-creating engines in the era of globalization and the technological transformations. (I am not suggesting that governments should not be involved in job creation; see chapter 10 for some initial policy proposals on the role of government as a major player in the changing nature of the opportunity structure.)

In Hunt's (1995) analysis, he identified the cognitive and intellectual characteristics that will increasingly define the 21st-century workplace. After a careful synthesis of the impact of technology on work, coupled with an overview of human cognition, Hunt's summary included the following forecasts:

- Work organizations will change from highly regimented organizations to small groups that often will work in localized settings producing specialized products.
- The social structures of workplaces will change rapidly, with workers increasingly having to master different tasks.
- In the face of these rapidly shifting workplaces, a premium will be placed on cognitive flexibility as well as social flexibility. People who can adjust and thrive in changing situations will be the most valued.

■ The cognitive attributes that will be needed in the workplace include sophisticated technological skills, high-level problem-solving skills, and a capacity to engage in interpersonally effective communication with others.

One of the conclusions that emerges from Hunt's (1995) analysis in conjunction with other discussions of the knowledge gap (e.g., Marshall & Tucker, 1992; Reich, 1991; Wilson, 1996) is that we cannot afford to conduct educational practice that continues to rely heavily upon the assumptions of the late 19th century and early 20th century. Workers who cannot handle the cognitive and intellectual demands of an information-rich workplace will very likely be deprived of the opportunity of obtaining a production or service job that will be stable and adequately remunerative.

An unfortunate attribute of the knowledge gap is that access to sources of knowledge is not fair or equitable in many nations or across nations. Within the United States, the vast discrepancies between school systems represent a powerful means by which social class and racial barriers are entrenched across generations (Kozol, 1991). The inequalities in the distribution of resources to schools in the United States provide a powerful case in point of how the social system reproduces itself. However, what is clear is that a comprehensive psychology of working will necessitate a careful analysis of this knowledge gap and its effect on individual experiences of working.

Point-Counterpoint: The Changing Nature of Work and the Experience of Working

The material presented in this chapter has attempted to weave a tapestry despite the lack of a fully developed design, with the effect of presenting a picture that seems half finished. Throughout the chapter, I have sought to bring clear conclusions in light of highly complex trends. The challenge would be great enough if our concern was with those who typically have access to the grand career narrative. However, the dilemma is far more challenging when we factor in the objective of constructing a psychology of working that will be inclusive and comprehensive. Given the complexity of this task, it is naturally impossible to derive inferences that will have immediate relevance to workers across the globe, whose experiences vary so sharply. However, a number of emergent dialectical themes are useful marker points on the unfinished tapestry that has been created thus far.

Too Much Work Versus Not Enough Jobs

Perhaps the most painful dialectic in this analysis is that many people are left without consistent or stable work in their lives, as exemplified by Wilson's (1996) account of inner city America, which contrasts notably with Schor's (1993) analysis of the overworked American. Are these authors describing two completely different worlds? In many ways, the answer to this question is an affirmative one. One of the goals of an inclusive psychology of working is the systematic exploration of the boundaries between the haves and the have-nots, who are increasingly facing a bifurcation of income, jobs, lifestyles, and educational affordances. As recent economic trends have indicated, the distance between the wealthy and working classes and poor has become far more pronounced in the United States in recent decades (e.g., Keister, 2000).

One of the major concerns that has not been adequately dealt with in the literature is that of identifying the consequences of not working. To what extent are humans evolutionarily wired to work for their survival and a sense of meaning in their lives? I believe that the knowledge that develops from the psychology-of-working perspective is critically needed to respond to this question. Obviously, a key factor in responding to this question is the status of one's concern with survival. If society can provide food and shelter for all (which, of course, is a complex question in of itself), will people feel satisfied in their lives without projects to work on which will engage them with others, fulfill their curiosity, and provide an outlet for their natural strivings to express their talents and interests? In order to respond to this question, it is important to initiate an examination of the various psychological needs that are met by working and to understand how these needs and aspirations are socially constructed and individually understood.

Needs for Connection Versus the Increasing Isolation of Technology

For many, the new workplace is gradually leading to a loss of feelings of connection, social engagement, and investment in a greater social entity. Furthermore, technology, which allows for greater physical distance between workers and others within their organizations and work groups, is contributing to more pronounced feelings of isolation. Thus, it is not unusual to hear reports from educated individuals in Western countries who work from home, who describe feelings of isolation as they struggle to make meaningful connections via e-mail and phone meetings (Sennett, 1998).

The growing sense of isolation is further complicated by the reality that people in many Western countries are increasingly moving away from familial supports. This geographic mobility, which seems to be a function of industrialization and post-industrial trends, may also transform less affluent countries that are forced to accept the challenges offered by globalization. The difficulty for individual workers facing the movement toward greater isolation is that this characteristic of contemporary work is inherently inconsistent with natural human strivings for connection and relationship (e.g., Jordan et al., 1991; Josselson, 1992; S. A. Mitchell, 1988). In fact, one of the major psychological movements in the past few decades, known as the relational perspectives (Blustein, 2001b; Flum, 2001; Gilligan, 1982; Schultheiss, 2003), has highlighted the importance of human relationships for positive well-being. In contrast to traditional notions of adaptive and mature behavior as a manifestation of strivings for independence and autonomy, the relational perspectives are based on the notion that people have an inherent striving for connection (Josselson, 1992; S. A. Mitchell, 1988). As such, we have, on one hand, a tendency within workplaces for greater distance, both physically and emotionally, between worker and other workers as well as the products of one's work. Yet, on the other hand, we have a growing awareness that perhaps human beings are not ideally suited for isolated and independent functioning. The implications of this dialectical struggle are difficult to estimate and most certainly merit further attention in psychological studies of working.

Work as a Means of Self-Expression and Spiritual Growth Versus Work as a Means to an End

In recent years, a number of books have appeared that have explored the spiritual meanings of work and working (e.g., M. Fox, 1994; Bloch & Richmond, 1997). These books follow logically from the extensive literature in Western countries on finding meaning in work and in deriving maximal satisfaction from one's vocational efforts (e.g., Bolles & Bolles, 2005). At the same time, we have the vast majority of the people on this planet who probably give little to any thought about the spiritual meaning of their work. Their concerns are far different, reflecting an almost Maslowian developmental process wherein the poor and working classes are concerned with survival and the educated elites are concerned with self-actualization. Are these folks actually experiencing the same phenomenon? Is the work of the well-educated even remotely within the same family of activities as the work of the poor and working classes that make up the vast majority of this planet's adult population?

The answers to these questions are highly complex and speak to one of the fundamental challenges in contemporary times. One of the inferences that can be derived from many of the passages presented in this chapter, as well as the extensive vignettes found in the literature (e.g., Terkel, 1974; Thomas, 1999), is that there seem to be some common bonds in the nature of the working experience. Of course, major distinctions exist, most of which pertain to the reality that only a small proportion of the earth's population actually has much volition in its working life. In my view, the dialectical energy derived from the complexities of describing working across the spectrum of humanity can be used to remind us that much effort needs to be expended in order to reduce the glaring inequities that still exist as we move into the 21st century.

Conclusion

An oft-repeated phrase in recent years that has become cliché is "the rapidly changing nature of work." The discussion that has been presented in this chapter gives some shape to these changes, although there are still many areas of uncertainty and confusion. For example, the twin engines of globalization and the information era seem to auger in a very different period of time. How this period will actually differ from previous eras is hard to discern. For example, while Rifkin (1995) argued that traditional jobs will soon give way to technology, the economic forecasts of Neumark (2000) and his colleagues led to a less drastic prognosis. In addition, while the traditional notion of career (as reflected in the grand career narrative) seems to be dying, it was evidently clear in this chapter that most people across the globe never had this sort of career trajectory in the first place.

Thus, the most confident conclusion that we can reach is that work is very much influenced by a host of contextual factors. Included in this context are economic trends, cultural beliefs about work and wealth, relationship factors, historical issues, and political frameworks. While this observation might suggest that the study of working should be left to macro-level social scientists (such as sociologists and economists), my perspective is quite different. What we know about the psychological dimensions of working has been derived to a great extent from a circumscribed literature on careers among middle-class workers or from macro-level analyses conducted by social scientists without the input of psychologists. Although this literature has been highly informative, it leaves vast gaps in our knowledge base. For example, to what extent are the changes in the workplace that have been detailed in this chapter influencing how people across the globe think about and experience their working lives? Moreover, there has been a notable lack of attention to the inner motivations, personal constructions, and the way in which people make meaning of working in the literature. Without the voices of workers from all sectors of life, developing a clear understanding of working seems nearly impossible. The remaining chapters of this book seek to create a foundation for an inclusive psychology of working that may help to create a perspective that will be maximally informative for the vast majority of people who struggle to earn their daily bread.

CHAPTER 3

Working as a Means of Survival and Power

If any one should not work, neither should he eat.

—St. Paul, as found in Donkin (2001, p. 23)

During the early part of the winter the family had had enough money to live and a little over to pay debts with, but when the earnings of Jurgis fell from nine or ten dollars a week to five or six, there was no longer anything to spare. The winter went, and the spring came, and found them still living thus from hand to mouth, hanging on day by day, with literally not a month's wages between them and starvation ....

Such were the cruel terms upon which their life was possible, that they might never have nor expect a single instant of respite from worry, a single instant in which they were not haunted by the thought of money. They would no sooner escape, as by a miracle, from one difficulty, than a new one would come into view. In addition to all their physical hardships, there was thus a constant strain upon their minds; they were harried all day and nearly all night by worry and fear. This was in truth not living; it was scarcely even existing, and they felt that it was too little for the price they paid. They were willing to work all the time; and when people did their best, ought they not be able to keep alive?

—Sinclair (1906, pp. 102–103)

Arthur reached his capstain lathe and took off his jacket, hanging it on a nearby nail so that he could keep an eye on his belongings. He pressed the starter button, and his motor came to life with a gentle thump. Looking around, it did not seem, despite the infernal noise of hurrying machinery, that anyone was working with particular speed. He smiled to himself, and picked up a glittering steel cylinder from the top box of a pile beside him, and fixed it into the spindle. He jettisoned his cigarette into the sud-pan, drew back the capstain, and swung the turret into its broadest drill. Two minutes had passed while he contem-

plated the precise position of tools and cylinder; finally he spat onto both hands and rubbed them together, then switched on the sud-tap from the movable brass pipe, pressed a button that set the spindle running, and ran in the drill to a neat chamber. Monday morning had lost its terror.

—Sillitoe (1958, p. 26)

When I think about the way this society forced men in my father's generation to be completely responsible for their families, it makes me furious. I've been in the professional world for a while now and I know how much pressure is involved. It isn't something anyone can handle easily by themselves. To hold your whole family's fate in your hands just isn't fair. My father took that on himself because that is what other fathers did then. As a result, my mother didn't really know much about the working world. She had to find out the hard way. It wasn't her fault, but the whole situation was terrible. It was a bad way to organize a family's survival.

—Newman (1988, p. 119)

The narratives that begin this chapter capture a wide spectrum of emotions and conceptions of working that people have articulated in various contexts and within diverse cultures. For the most part, these quotes tell a story in which working is closely and inexorably linked to the need to survive. In this chapter, I seek to describe the complex relationships among working, survival, and power in contemporary life. A key assumption of this discussion is that working provides people with a means of obtaining the necessary goods and services to survive and to enhance their social and economic status. Embedded in this analysis is the reality that access to work throughout the world is far from equal. Indeed, numerous complex and interrelated filters, many of which are socially sanctioned, function to limit the ability of people to obtain the requisite education, social connections, and related opportunities that may facilitate a meaningful and empowering work life. (These barriers, which are foreshadowed throughout this chapter, are discussed in greater depth in chapter 6.)

The chapter begins with a theoretical presentation of the psychological meaning of survival and power. Using diverse conceptual threads, a view of survival and power emerges that is closely intertwined with the experience of working. The chapter concludes with a case vignette and a discussion of the clinical implications of the connection between working and strivings for survival and power.

Psychological Analyses of Survival and Power

Generally, discussions about financial survival and power are rooted in political or economic discourse, although a growing literature is beginning to grapple with the psychological meaning of power (e.g., Martín-Baro, 1989; Prilleltensky, 1997). In this chapter, I explore the psychological meaning of one of the most fundamental functions of working: to afford people with the resources necessary for survival. Consistent with both scholarly literature and narratives of human experience across time frames and cultures (e.g., Gini & Sullivan, 1989; O'Brien, 1986; Terkel, 1974; Thomas, 1999), a key psychological function of working is to help people to survive and flourish in the economic sphere of their lives. As human affairs has increased in complexity throughout the evolutionary process from primitive hunting and gathering to more organized social orders, the process of working for survival also has become more complex. With this complexity, human beings then developed intricate psychological and social mechanisms that functioned to stratify the distribution of resources needed for survival. Perhaps the most central of these mechanisms is the striving for power, which also is discussed in the present chapter. Prior to delineating this conceptual framework, I first review the foundations for a psychological analysis of survival and power.

Psychological Formulations: Historical Perspectives

With Freud's evident evolutionary influences, it would seem logical that his extensive contributions also would seek to explore the fundamental needs of working. However, Freud did not devote a great deal of attention to the functions of work, except for his 1930 contribution entitled *Civilization and Its Discontents*. In this book, Freud focused on the role of work as a means of survival, noting that work was generally not a pleasant endeavor. As in other Freudian interpretations of human behavior, an assumption about human beings as inherently driven by sexual and aggressive urges underlies the conceptualization of working. For Freud, people worked primarily to maintain their means of survival. Although he did acknowledge that working could lead to personal satisfaction, the primary focus of his formulation was on the way in which work functioned to provide access to the means of survival and to a socially sanctioned means of expressing libidinal and aggressive urges.

Axelrod's (1999) recent analysis of the Freudian view of work is particularly illuminating in relation to the goals of the present discussion. Axelrod noted that "Freud's perspective on work life reflected the realities of work in his society and conceptions of mental functioning that made sense in that culture. His jaundiced view of work grew out of an era in which most of the world's economies were based on manual labor [and] brute strength ..." (1999, p. 3). It is important, though, to note that the context that framed Freud's conceptualizations is actually still a reality for the majority of the world's workers. When considering Freud's views about the stark reality of life for most of humankind (in which the struggle to eat and obtain shelter have been consistent challenges), his thinking about the critical importance of work for survival strikes a familiar chord.

Later psychoanalytic thinkers continued the focus, to some extent, on the role of work as ensuring survival, but also considered its impact on enhancing psychological power and well-being. For example, Fromm (1947) argued that work could foster experiences of autonomy and self-expression. He also noted that job tasks could be designed in a way to enhance one's potential and one's creativity. However, the survival needs of working, initially advanced by Freud, are still evident in Fromm's writing. As we shall see in subsequent chapters, more recent psychoanalytic conceptualizations of working have incorporated a focus on relationships and self-expression (Axelrod, 1999). Yet Freud's pessimistic view of working in the early part of the 20th century still seems to have relevance as we examine the lives of the vast majority of people who do not have many choices about the direction or expression of their work lives. For most adults around the world, working represents a necessary means to an end. As Freud argued, the intrinsic reward of the tasks that one does to earn money for food, shelter, and clothing is not generally salient to most people who work. For the purposes of the present discussion, the extent to which work functions as a means of sublimating libidinal desires is secondary to Freud's resonant psychological analysis of the economic necessity of work.

Maslow's Contributions

Another way to frame a psychologically informed discussion of power and its relation to work is via the lens of Maslow's (1968) still timely theory of human motivation. Although many scholars tend to focus on the self-actualization aspect of Maslow's theory, the core of this theoretical model revolves around the primary human striving to satisfy physiological and safety needs. Maslow's theory postulates that human beings are driven to meet specific needs that fall into a hierarchical pattern, beginning with physiological needs and then progressing to safety, love, esteem, and finally self-actualization. In order for an individual to have an opportunity for self-actualization, one needs to have access to food, water, and shelter in an environment that feels safe and secure. Maslow described the experience of work that was self-actualizing as a calling or a mission, which is consistent with many aspects of the vocational psychology landscape. Yet, without the fulfillment of the basic human needs, notions about self-actualization appear far less relevant, especially for the vast majority of workers who do not have access to education and training opportunities.

As we review these historic, yet still prevalent theories, the need for survival emerges in bold relief. Despite the external layers of social and cultural meaning that exist in human behavior, Freud and Maslow, respectively, acknowledged a core reality that resonates deeply with the psychology of working outlined in this book. As noted earlier, much of the existing psychological research on working (i.e., traditional career development; e.g., D. Brown, 2002a) occurred in a culture of affluence and relatively free choices. This perspective, unfortunately, overshadows the fundamental need that work serves in providing people with a means of feeding and housing themselves and their loved ones. Once we explore the psychological aspects of working from a global and truly inclusive perspective, it becomes obvious that one of the basic functions of work is to provide people with the means to support themselves.

The View of Working Outside of Psychology: Anthropological and Sociological Perspectives

The need to work in order to survive has been transformed symbolically into a wide array of social and cultural interactions. From an anthropological perspective, Goldschmidt (1990) describes the inherently human process of using symbols to help construct physical reality. As human beings moved from hunter-gatherers to farming and the domestication of animals, the tasks involved in ensuring survival became more complex and more differentiated (A. W. Johnson & Earle, 1987). Anthropological studies of various indigenous peoples around the globe, who remain relatively untouched by industrialization, have suggested that work has taken on a more symbolic nature as cultures sought to structure and ritualize social discourse (e.g., Applebaum, 1984; Wallman, 1979). Inherent in this construction of working tasks is the striving to maximize one's access to the attributes that can help to ensure survival. Thus, people living in small tribes or villages would likely seek out means of becoming adept at hunting, gathering, creating clothes, performing important rituals, and other social and economic tasks that would enhance their role and status within their community (Wallman). Anthropological research has cast an informative net on the complex cultural rituals that help to ensure that working will yield access to the resources of a given community (Applebaum; Goldschmidt).

Following the anthropological framework, Wallman (1979) describes the fundamental need of work as the striving to control nature with the intention of deriving sustenance from nature. Wallman outlines a number of dimensions of work, many of which would fit under the current rubric of fulfilling needs for survival and power. In Wallman's introduction to a volume of anthropological essays about work across cultures, she noted that work involves the expenditure of energy to meet some specified goal and to yield some resources (both economic and social). Here again, we see the striving for survival at the core of Wallman's integrative conceptualization of working across highly diverse cultures.

By exploring the experience of working in societies that are transitioning into market-based economies, anthropological research furnishes another open window into the evolving psychological meaning of working. For example, Applebaum (1984) described transitional societies (which refer to cultures in which the basic economy includes both market and non-market features) in which people move outside of their communal groups in order to work. This process necessitates the adoption of more complex social roles (Neff, 1985). The overt striving to work in order to survive, however, is still maintained in cultures that are moving toward market economies and industrialization as well as in contemporary industrial and post-industrial societies. Applebaum noted that in more market-oriented societies, the distance between one's tasks and one's community becomes greater, thereby creating less connection to one's daily life tasks.

Similar views have emerged in sociological analyses of working, as reflected in the observation that the increasingly differentiated division of labor that characterized the industrial revolution has been associated with greater disconnection between the efforts of workers and the outcomes of their labor (e.g., Heilbroner & Singer, 1984). The sociological line of inquiry about survival and working is manifested in Wilson's (1996) thoughtful analysis of the impact of the absence of working on individuals and community within urban communities in the U.S. In short, Wilson's qualitative and quantitative studies document the domino-like effect of the loss of work on individuals' inner psychological functioning as well as on the stability and cohesiveness of their communities. (See chapter 2 for further details on Wilson's landmark study.)

Moving From Survival to Power

One of the outcomes of working, following logically on the need for survival, is the accrual of economic, social, and psychological power. By developing systematic access to the resources necessary for survival, one can ideally consolidate greater power within a given community or culture. A particularly rich analysis of psychological power can be found in the work of Martín-Baro, a psychologist and social activist in Central America before his untimely death in a politically motivated murder in 1989. Martín-Baro advocated for the inclusion of all citizens in psychological discourse with the goal of developing ideas and practices that would function to reduce structural barriers to equality and social justice. Given Martín-Baro's mission, he naturally gravitated toward analyses that explicitly incorporated social and political factors. The discussion of psychological power, which follows, is characterized by Martín-Baro's thematic focus on sociopolitical contexts.

Working for Survival and Power: A Conceptual Analysis

Beginning with the assumption that an explicit discussion of power is inherent to any comprehensive analysis of human relations, Martín-Baro defines power as "the condition that makes it possible for one of the actors to make his or her will or objectives prevail ..." (1989, p. 62). He then differentiates between the resources that make power possible and the psychological construction of power. For Martín-Baro, access to resources (including physical strength, knowledge, money, etc.) provides the means for the development, consolidation, and expression of power. Following this conceptual framework, therefore, the existence of disparities in access to resources creates the conditions for disparities in power. In the current discussion of working, power is a notable by-product of obtaining access to resources, such as education, knowledge, money, social status, and prestige.

The literature on the anthropology of work (e.g., Goldschmidt, 1990; A. W. Johnson & Earle, 1987; Wallman, 1979) furnishes an illuminating lens with which to explore how strivings for survival have become transformed to social status, privilege, and power as societies became more market-oriented and less insulated. Goldschmidt's analysis of the human career provides a framework to consider how working for survival can be transformed into strivings for power and social status. Goldschmidt detailed the complex layers of social and cultural mores that informed the experience of working in tribal and transitional societies. One of the primary means of social stratification historically in human communities depended on the quality and productivity of one's work efforts. Individuals most effective in generating food supplies, housing, and other resources tended to gain higher social status in comparison to those who were less efficient and productive. Thus, people who were able to master tasks that were valued by one's community were able to generate enhanced levels of social status, which facilitated the accrual of power.

In the current analysis, work functions as one of the primary means for human beings to access power, via obtaining money for food, shelter, and ultimately for social status and privilege. As societies became more complex and layered with symbolic and socially constructed meaning, it became important for cultures to find ways to designate that certain people had greater access to the necessities of life. Initially, societies would grant selected individuals a greater sense of prestige based on their work efforts and accomplishments (Goldschmidt, 1990). Once these rewards became known, they helped to establish cultural norms that promoted working as a pro-social activity that would benefit the greater community as well as the worker and his or her family.

Over time, people who were particularly adept at survival attracted the attention of other members of their community, who naturally would be impressed with the skill and effort that yielded such a rich set of resources. Therefore, those who were successful enjoyed two basic elements that enhanced their sense of power in relation to others. One of the elements was access to the material resources that ensure survival—food, water, clothing, and housing. In addition, a related element evolved that is best described as enhanced social status. Just as many people currently admire successful figures in our own cultures, a tendency exists within various social contexts in which individuals attach a positive value to those who are adept in their work tasks and in the process of consolidating the means of survival (Tesser, 1995). Thus, even in human communities that are still in the hunting/gathering mode, the natural inclination is for people to look up to selected members of a cohort for their ability to function effectively in the environment (Wallman, 1979). The result of this process is that certain people would develop socially sanctioned power that influences their relationships with others in their community. (I am not suggesting that working is the sole means by which power is accrued within social groups. As we shall see in chapter 6, power is also based on access to resources that are, regrettably, based on irrelevant aspects of human appearance and functioning, such as skin color, sex, ethnicity, and sexual orientation).

A careful examination of this process reveals that working is integral to the development of power. While not all workers are necessarily focused consciously on becoming powerful, in a more subtle fashion, working functions to help people establish the means for empowerment. Working hard often will yield greater income and benefits, thereby giving people more power to survive and possibly even purchase other consumer goods. Furthermore, working provides people with a sense of social status, which enhances prestige and confers additional resources onto an individual and his or her family (such as access to important social groups and decision makers of a community, the admiration of people within one's social milieu). Thus, the increasingly differentiated array of roles and responsibilities that have characterized contemporary life have yielded cultures in which the needs for survival and power are closely intertwined.

Working for Survival and Power: An Experience-Near Analysis

Although the function of working to enhance survival is not a particularly novel notion in the social sciences (e.g., Gini & Sullivan, 1989; Goldschmidt, 1990; Marx, 1891), this notion has generated very little interest on the part of psychologists who conduct vocational research and who practice psychotherapy and vocational counseling. One notable exception is E. J. Smith's (1983) contribution in which she articulates a compelling position with respect to existing theories of career development and career education. The passage that follows details her position, which resonates strongly with the views advocated in this volume:

> Most career theories and current career education philosophy have assumed that dignity exists in all work (K. Hoyt, 1974; L. B. Hoyt, 1978). This concept, although attractive to vocational psychologists, neither reflects the reality of many individuals' work lives nor the career literature that shows there is in

American society (and most societies in the world) a clear hierarchy by which jobs are ranked from very high to very low in desirability. Often when vocational psychologists speak about the dignity of work they are confusing issues. People may have or experience dignity because they are able to provide for themselves economically; they may or may not believe that their occupation is rejected by society. Vocational psychologists need to reexamine the concept of dignity of all work and its corollary that work is central to the lives of all individuals. For both minority and majority Americans, work may simply help to mark the passage of time. (E. J. Smith, 1983, p. 187)

As Smith's passage conveys, working has not always been synonymous with the grand career narrative of the later part of the 20th century. In contrast to the image of the worker with a multitude of options is the stark reality that working for most people does not function to enhance one's self-esteem or provide an outlet for interests and values. Smith's contribution gives a scholarly voice to the passages that opened this chapter, which describe the experiences and consequences of considering the survival and power needs met by working.

Consistent with the thematic goals of Smith's contribution, concern with the lack of focus on the survival aspects of working has been most evident within multicultural critiques of vocational psychology. Carter and Cook (1992) described the limitations of the traditional choice-based theories in their critique of the existing career development theories in light of the challenges of visible racial and ethnic group populations within Western cultures. A few years later, Helms and Cook (1999) argued that sociocultural factors function to differentially provide access to education and work opportunities, with people of color typically experiencing the most pervasive obstacles in North America. They also described a number of internalized factors that are based on social constructions of race, ethnicity, and social class, which function to complicate a process already tainted by the existence of institutional racism. Clearly, within countries that have histories and current practices that privilege one group above another, racial, cultural, gender, sexual orientation, and other demographic or phenotypic considerations play a significant role in determining one's access to working, and consequently to survival. However, there exists little experience-near understanding of this perspective within traditional outlets of applied psychology. Despite the relative lack of attention within traditional psychology, poets, writers, and musicians have struggled to make sense of the essence of working, which is so inherently wrapped up in the need to survive. In the poem that follows by Langston Hughes (1942/1965), the life of the sharecropper is eloquently conveyed:

Just a herd of Negroes
Driven to the field,
Plowing, planting, and hoeing,
To make the cotton yield.

When the cotton's picked
And the work is done
Boss man takes the money
And we get none.

Leaves us hungry, ragged
As we were before.
Year by year goes by
And we are nothing more

Than a herd of Negroes
Driven to the field—
Plowing life away
To make the cotton the yield.

The Hughes poem describes some of the feelings and experiences of people who work at jobs that are not naturally interesting or fulfilling. The description is replete with images and words that pertain to the physical challenges of the work; moreover, the protagonists do not even keep the money that is earned when the crops are finally sold. While the relationship between sharecropper and landowner (which perhaps exemplifies the general relationship between the powerful and the disempowered) has received considerable attention in a variety of scholarly contexts, the focus on the internal experiences of working is not part of the psychological landscape within traditional scholarship and psychotherapeutic discourse.

Another very evocative narrative is evident in a brief story set to music by Bruce Springsteen (1995/1998). The song, entitled "Sinaloa Cowboys," describes the story of two brothers who travel to California to try to make a better living for themselves and their family.

Miguel came from a small town in northern Mexico.
He came north with his brother Luis to California three years ago
They crossed at the river levee, when Luis was just sixteen
And found work together in the fields of the San Joaquin

They left their homes and family
Their father said, "My sons one thing you will learn,
for everything the north gives, it exacts a price in return."
They worked side by side in the orchards
From morning till the day was through
Doing the work the hueros wouldn't do.

Word was out some men in from Sinaloa were looking for some hands
Well, deep in Fresno county there was a deserted chicken ranch
And there in a small tin shack on the edge of a ravine
Miguel and Luis stood cooking methamphetamine

You could spend a year in the orchards
Or make half as much in one ten-hour shift
Working for the men from Sinaloa
But if you slipped the hydriodic acid
Could burn right through your skin
They'd leave you spittin' up blood in the desert
If you breathed those fumes in

It was early one winter evening as Miguel stood watch outside
When the shack exploded, lighting up the valley night
Miguel carried Luis' body over his shoulder down a swale
To the creekside and there in the tall grass, Luis Rosales died
Miguel lifted Louis' body into his truck and then he drove
To where the morning sunlight fell on a eucalyptus grove
There in the dirt he dug up ten-thousand dollars. all that they'd saved
Kissed his brothers lips and placed him in his grave. (Springsteen, 1998)

On the surface, the story that Springsteen conveys describes important aspects of working life, including the migration of Mexican adolescents to the United States and the harsh conditions they face as they enter the labor market. However, this narrative describes some of the inner experiences of Miguel and Luis that are generally missing from contemporary social and behavioral science discourse. The connection between the two brothers is palpable as is their desire to enhance the living conditions of their family in Mexico. The decision to work in the drug production trade is made here for primarily financial reasons, thereby underscoring a sense of disempowerment that lack of access to work can engender. The fact that one of the brothers dies in a work-related accident adds a note of tragedy to the narrative that is unfortunately part of the working life for too many citizens throughout the world.

Another source of experience-near material on the survival and power dimensions of working can be found in the narratives in Wilson's (1996) book entitled *When Work Disappears*. The following passage describes one man's solution to the loss of available work within his inner-city community:

Four years I have been out here trying to find a steady job. Going back and forth all these temporary jobs and this 'n' that. Then you gotta give money at home, you know you gotta buy your clothes which cost especially for a big person. Then you're talking about my daughter, then you talking about food in the house too, you know, things like that .... Well, lately like I said I have been trying to make extra money and everything. I have been selling drugs lately on the side after I get off work and, ah, it has been going all right .... Like I was saying you can make more money dealing drugs than your job, anybody. Not just me but anybody, for the simple fact that if you have a nice clientele and some nice drugs, some nice 'caine or whatever you are selling then the money is going to come, the people are going to come .... (Wilson, 1996, pp. 58–59)

This passage provides a glimpse into a world in which people adapt to limited opportunities by engaging in working activities that are antisocial or criminal. Yet at the same time, this individual describes the struggles to make a living, thereby creating a context for a shift in values and behavior that has a host of consequences, both individually and from the perspective of this man's community. This narrative suggests a sort of dialectical struggle in the work lives of many people. On one hand, we observe the sense of despair and pain that is engendered by the lack of opportunity to work, even at a job that is not inherently interesting and meaningful. While it is difficult to make generalizable inferences from these vignettes, they do provide a window into the inner experiences of working that is not typically available via traditional quantitative and macro-level methodologies.

Concluding Comments

Given the despair evident in these narratives and in the material presented in chapter 2 about the changing nature of work, daunting challenges face psychologists, behavioral scientists, and therapists. The material presented in this section gives voice to aspects of working that have, for the most part, been excluded from traditional psychological discourse about work and careers. The vignettes convey the striving to work as a means of ensuring that one has the requisite physiological and safety needs met, an observation of Maslow's (1968), which has regrettably been forgotten or dismissed in existing psychological formulations about working. Moreover, a working context that requires far greater skills and knowledge than ever before currently confronts us (Marshall & Tucker, 1992). Yet, access to the skills and knowledge is far from open or equal, both within the United States and among many nations and regions around the world. As such, the exploration of work in light of the need for survival and power forces psychologists and other mental health professionals to confront the unequal social structure that characterizes most societies (Blustein, McWhirter, & Perry, 2005; M. S. Richardson, 2000). The implications of infusing the fundamental need of working as a means of survival and power have significant implications for psychology and for mental health treatments as well as public policy. The subsequent chapters explore these implications in a number of contexts and situations, each designed to fill the missing elements of psychology's rather narrow views of working to date. In the next section, I explore the clinical implications of infusing the very real notion that working functions, in part, as a means of survival and power.

Power and Working in Psychological Treatment

As noted earlier in this volume (and detailed further in chapters 8 and 9), issues related to working have not had a clear or explicit place within most theories of counseling and psychotherapy. Ironically, however, despite the lack of explicit attention to issues pertaining to work and power in clinical contexts, the process of psychotherapy encourages people to open themselves up to the deeply felt experiences that they may face as they struggle to obtain work and sustain themselves economically. As I have suggested earlier, the very process of preparing for, engaging in and negotiating one's work life often embeds people most saliently with the social forces that function to stratify opportunity. In the case that I summarize next, issues of work and power are presented in the context of psychotherapy with an exploration of the intense affect that these issues evoke within therapeutic relationships. (These cases are fictional, but are based on themes that have emerged in my own clinical work.)

Pedro

Pedro was a 33-year-old Latino man who sought me out to help work through problems he was facing in his marriage. He was born in Puerto Rico and moved to a northeastern city in the United States when he was 8. His parents migrated to find more stable employment and to enhance the opportunities for their four children. Pedro was the youngest of these children, and he grew up in an urban community that was working class (i.e., people tended to work in skilled or semi-skilled fields). His major presenting issues were related to the fact that he was on the verge of leaving his marriage because he stated that his wife was "tired of his temper and abusiveness." Pedro reported that he was still in love with his wife and his two children. He stated that he was very invested in keeping his marriage alive. Other clinical issues that emerged early in the treatment included a history of alcohol abuse, which was episodic. Pedro reported that he liked to drink on weekends, but that he tried to control himself now that he had children. Considerable drinking and some substance abuse (marijuana and cocaine) characterized his adolescence. He denied any current psychoactive substances during our work, except for the weekend drinking, which was no longer at the level of binging. (He indicated that he and his wife enjoyed having a few beers with dinner and a beer or two after dinner on Friday and Saturday nights.)

Pedro's major presenting issues were clearly in the relational domain, with the initial session focusing on his marriage, his frustrations with his wife, and his attempts to control his angry outbursts. The initial sessions also revealed no significant depression or thought disorder. However, Pedro did report some anxiety and insomnia which he indicated was a problem for him for most of his life. When I explored the sorts of things that made him angry at home, he was not able to clearly articulate what his wife and children did that would evoke angry responses. Pedro indicated that he had not physically hurt his wife and that he also did not abuse his children. He did acknowledge that he yelled at his wife, especially when he was tired. However, as I explored his working life, Pedro became much more animated. Rather than describing his anger as if someone else was somehow experiencing it, he became immersed in intensely enraged feelings.

Pedro was a technician for a cable television company; his job consisted of making house calls and either installing cable lines or repairing cable lines. His territory was an upper middle class community that had very few people of color and very few workers like Pedro, who made his living based on technical and psychomotor skills.

As Pedro and I explored his working life, it became clear that he was experiencing considerable racism and abuse from co-workers and from customers. He indicated that a few of his co-workers called him derogatory names to his face and that some of the customers also made nasty comments about his ethnicity. On one occasion, he actually had a fight with a co-worker who called him a "spic bastard." He nearly lost his job because of this incident, and he had vowed to himself that he would be like Jackie Robinson (the first African American to play baseball in the major leagues) and try to not to let his anger show upon hearing racist comments.

Pedro also indicated that he had considerable trouble throughout school and in his work life. During his years in school, he was placed in special education classes solely because he did not have adequate English skills. He was never able to catch up in school and as a result he bypassed college and joined the U.S. Marines. His military service was uneventful, but he did learn some technical skills that helped him to get a job with the cable television company. Pedro reported that he has had reasonably good relationships with his family-of-origin. He did indicate that there was some tension with his parents when he was a teenager, but in retrospect, he appreciated that his parents tried to keep him from getting too involved in street life in his community. His mother and father had a good marriage and were quite respectful to each other.

When I asked Pedro if he liked his job, he indicated that in fact he truly hated his job, because of both the abuse he experienced and his lack of satisfaction with the job itself. As I explored his feelings about his satisfaction with the actual tasks of cable repair and installation, he replied that he never really thought that he would be able to have a job or career that would be consistent with his interests. His interests were in the arts and film. He loved music of all sorts, including Latin-based genres, classical music, and jazz. Moreover, he loved film, including both popular movies as well as art films. Pedro did not feel like he had a future in his job; more importantly, he said that he felt humiliated by the treatment that he was receiving from people he called "country bumpkins," who had never had contact with Latino people. The anger became particularly intense when he described the telephone dispatcher, who had a history of being nasty and rude to him.

The course of the treatment, therefore, focused on exploring the complex space that existed in his relationship with his wife and the relationships that he had with his co-workers. As we examined these relationships, Pedro realized that he felt that his wife was not sufficiently respectful toward him when she asked him to help around the house or to help care for their children. This feeling state paralleled the experiences that he had with his co-workers. While his wife (who also was Latina) was not racist in her comments toward him, the subtle trigger was that he felt disempowered by her. At the same time, Pedro acknowledged that it was safer for him to get angry at his with wife than his co-workers. Within the first 6 months of the 18 months in which he was treated by me, we focused on two specific issues related to his anger. Using an approach that was derived from Wachtel's (1993) work, I integrated cognitive-behavioral with relationally oriented psychodynamic approaches in helping Pedro to take action on his new insights. In short, Wachtel's model posits that action-oriented interventions are not necessarily mutually exclusive from psychodynamic approaches. Wachtel also proposed a framework for integrating these approaches in a perspective that he called *cyclical psychodynamics*.

The first objective was to help Pedro understand, both intellectually and emotionally, that he was displacing anger from his workplace to his wife. This involved exploring with Pedro how to manage his anger at work, which included the use of specific anger management strategies (including the use of cognitive restructuring and mindfulness meditation. The mindfulness approach to dealing with intense affect is derived from meditation and from Zen perspectives; in brief, the notion is that intense feelings do not need to dominate one's psychological space or experience. Rather, we can choose to observe the feelings and take perspective on them, allowing them to inform us but not necessarily dictate our next set of decisions or choices. The core of mindfulness is that the self is more than any given momentary experience.)

The second and more complex aspect of this treatment focused on an exploration of the reality that Pedro had little clear choice in making his decisions about his working life. We also examined his feelings of anger and rage in relation to the racism that permeated the entire fabric of his work life. His feelings of anger toward his co-workers and customers, in my view, were natural reactions to a system that was denigrating and even dangerous to Pedro. Working in an environment where one's ethnicity, culture, and appearance become the brunt of discriminating and racist comments is incredibly stressful and disempowering. Thus, we focused some of our efforts on finding ways for Pedro to feel more empowered at work. Rather than muffling his feelings, we explored different strategies for him to engage the racist comments in ways that were adaptive and authentic. (For example, he was able to confront some co-workers when they made disparaging comments about people of color in ways that did not result in fights, but did allow him to feel greater comfort with his feelings and racial identity.) He increasingly began to set limits with his co-workers who responded by respecting these boundaries and behaving in a more civil fashion. Pedro realized, though, that he was not likely to develop close relationships with many of his co-workers due to their racist worldviews.

Another key issue that is a hallmark of a therapeutic intervention informed by a psychology of working is the exploration of the client's perceived and real levels of choice with respect to work tasks and contexts. As such, I brought up the question of how much volition Pedro felt he had in his work life. As indicated earlier, Pedro initially felt that he had no choice about what sort of work to obtain. He had a family and his wife did not have many viable skills that were needed in the community in which they lived. I then asked Pedro if he had thought of obtaining more training or education, which might enhance his options. He seemed ambivalent about this; part of him wanted to pursue his interests in the arts, but he was also daunted by his lack of confidence about his skills in school. By the end of treatment, Pedro had agreed to take a writing course at a community college. However, he completed therapy prior to enrolling in the course. While we did not fully resolve the lack of satisfaction he felt with his work life, his marriage improved markedly. He was calmer at home, drinking less, and was more engaged with his children. Pedro noted that he was less prone to anger toward his wife, who he realized was not the actual target of his rage.

Discussion

The case of Pedro is rich in a number of respects. For the cohort of clients who actually formed the essence of Pedro, the impact of living and working in the face of classism, racism, and unequal access to opportunity was often so pernicious that changing the inner psychological characteristics that motivate and sustain effort in an unfulfilling environment is extremely challenging. In addition, the case of Pedro offers an illuminating view of how the struggle for power and survival is compromised by social barriers such as racism and classism. Because of Pedro's ethnicity and social class, he faced considerable obstacles, including subpar schools, inadequate housing in an urban center, and continued stigma. (These issues are explored in greater depth in chapter 6.) Pedro's anger toward his wife, which was soon converted to its true target—his racist co-workers and denigrating customers, was not viewed as a pathological attribute that is located within the core of his psyche. Rather, I conceptualized Pedro's angry outbursts, while clearly unacceptable in the context of his family, as a natural outgrowth of an unfair and unjust social system. This observation, coupled with the new behavior management skills that he learned in therapy, served to fuel positive growth for Pedro and helped him to move forward in a productive way in his life.

The Psychology of Working and Power and Survival: Conclusion

The role of working in providing people with access to power and survival, while clearly an issue in most of our life experiences, has been notably missing from psychological discourse on careers and organizational behavior. In this chapter, I have sought to place this issue at the forefront of a discussion of working. As we harken back to the seminal contributions of Maslow (1968), the importance of survival is clearly evident. Yet as the post-World War II affluence spread throughout many sectors (although clearly not all sectors) of Western life, a myth evolved that somehow working was primarily about expressing one's interests or desires for self-actualization. The harsh reality, as we have seen in this chapter, is that this particular narrative is not the prevalent theme in humankind. Certainly, there are many workers who take the need for survival for granted, due to their access to education and reasonably secure jobs. However, as the working world shifts to a more unpredictable and insecure phase, the need for survival as a major need met by working will no doubt emerge more explicitly among the full spectrum of young adults and adults.

The material presented in this chapter has sought to give voice to the voiceless in our field—in doing so, we have been able to discern with greater clarity than via traditional social science accounts the important role of work as a means—indeed, for many, the sole means—of survival. The major themes that have emerged in this chapter are fairly clear. First, working provides people with access to power, initially by ensuring one's survival. As an individual becomes more entrenched in the labor market and develops more skills and access to the resources that are associated with marketable skills, the ability to survive is then transformed into social and economic power. Second, access to the opportunity structure is far from equal. Moreover, much of this inequality, as we shall examine further throughout this book, is due to phenotypic attributes that have no bearing on one's ability to profit from training, education, and other opportunities (Helms, Jernigan, & Mascher, 2005; Sternberg, Grigorenko, & Kidd, 2005). Third, the material presented here suggests that a thoughtful examination of the psychology of working will necessitate a critical view of the sociopolitical context that frames individual life experiences. This discussion may actually help psychologists engage in informed debates about employment/unemployment policies, training, education, and mental health policies. In each of these areas, knowledge of the fundamental needs that working fulfills forms a central foundation for thoughtful analyses of the many challenges that exist in developing more equitable societies.

Viewing working as one of the central theaters of life is no doubt a central theme of this book; moreover, the material presented here suggests that this particular theater conveys with vivid clarity the unequal playing field that exists as people seek to ensure their health, welfare, and security (M. S. Richardson, 2000). My hope is that this chapter will facilitate the development of a body of knowledge that will ultimately inform social policy efforts to enhance the opportunities that working offers for people to feel empowered and engaged in their communities and lives.

CHAPTER 4

Working as a Means
of Social Connection

When you get away from the hard, cold business ethos, that "Oh, we have to make money," we can just go with the flow and enjoy what we are doing. Then the job is fun, and you still make money. You make it fun for yourself. Most employees get together pretty often—we get along pretty good. People always have their cliques and remain in them. We do things for entertainment outside of the restaurant. I've gone out shopping with some of the girls from the job. We spend time together, maybe a movie, clubs.

—Newman (1999, p. 108)

The news goes from desk to desk
like a memo: Initial
and pass on. Each of us marks
surprised or Sorry.

The management came early
And buried her nameplate
deep in her desk. They have boxed up
The Midol and Lip-Ice,

the snapshots from home,
wherever it was—nephews
and nieces, a strange, blurred cat
with fiery, flashbulb eyes.

as if it grieved. But who grieves here?
We have her ballpoints back,
her bud vase. One of us tears
the scribbles from her calendar.

—Kooser (1980)

This is a business (styling hair) that is unlike most, there's something very nurturing about it. It is one of the few places in our society where you have permission to touch people. It's so intimate. We humans have a need for connection. Some salons have gone so far in the opposite direction, they're austere, so above it all. In the shop where I work, we've been through deaths, cancer, weddings. How can someone denigrate that?

—Rose (2004, pp. 47–48)

The quotes that start this chapter describe aspects of working that have often been overlooked or ignored to date—the intimate, complex, and challenging interactions between working and interpersonal life. In the three opening contributions, two diverse trajectories are conveyed about the interconnections between working and interpersonal relationships. In the first passage, which is from Newman's (1999) book about urban youth working in fast-food restaurants, jobs that initially may be viewed as dead-end with little to no positive benefit except for the pay are described as offering a valuable opportunity for connection. In contrast, the poem entitled "A Death at the Office" reveals a profound sense of alienation and disconnection among fellow workers, who treat a colleague's death with rituals that have been robbed of their emotional depth. The third vignette describes the potential for interpersonal connection in styling hair; the protagonist gives voice to the fundamental need for relatedness in an evocative way, reflecting aspects of working that are often not explicit in traditional scholarship and mental health practice. These three contributions describe an overlapping web of interconnections that exist within the shared space of working and interpersonal relationships. In this chapter, I expand this view by offering a multidimensional examination of working and relationships, with the objective of exploring the complex ways in which work and interpersonal life intersect. Moreover, the function of work in connecting people to the social world, both symbolically and experientially, is detailed in this chapter.

A review of the literature in vocational and organizational psychology indicates that, with a few notable exceptions (e.g., Flum, 2001; Greenhaus & Parasuraman, 1999; Hall, 1996; Lopez & Andrews, 1987; Luckey, 1974), working has been treated as a relatively discrete aspect of human experience, with little connection to the world of interpersonal relationships. Recent research and theory have considerably shifted this perspective (Blustein, 2001b; Blustein & Spengler, 1995; M. S. Richardson, 1993; Schultheiss, 2003;

Swanson, 1995). However, the majority of this work has been within the familiar "grand career narrative," with little attention devoted to those who have not had access to an orderly and planful work life. This chapter builds on this emerging perspective and the previous chapters to advance a relational perspective of working. As the chapter unfolds, I highlight the deep, subtle, and often complex interactions that place working within a web of social interactions.

Working as a Source of Social Connection

At this juncture in the development of psychological theory, an emerging position within vocational and organizational psychology can be framed as a relationally oriented perspective (e.g., Blustein, 2001b; Blustein & Noumair, 1996; Blustein, Prezioso, & Schultheiss, 1995; Blustein, Schultheiss, & Flum, 2004; Flum, 2001; Hall, 1996; Schultheiss, 2003). One of the major influences in the development of a relationally oriented perspective is in the increasing realization that working is inherently contextualized in the social fabric of human experience (Herriot, 2001; Powell, 1999; M. S. Richardson, 1993; Young & Collin, 1992). Emerging from various directions within both vocational and organizational psychology, research and theory have increasingly focused on the external context that frames working (e.g., Hall, 1996; Super, 1980; Vondracek, Lerner, & Schulenberg, 1986). A major theme that links these contextually informed perspectives is the explicit attempt to connect working to the world of intimate relationships and social support networks (Flum, 2001; M. S. Richardson, 1996; Schultheiss, 2003). As I propose in this chapter, the advancement of a contextual view of career offers important lessons for the psychology of working, which is explicitly embedded in a social, cultural, political, and historical context.

From ancient times, working has been deeply intertwined within social and relational contexts (Gini & Sullivan, 1989; Johnson & Earle, 1987; Wallman, 1979). On the most basic level, working generally took place within the framework of interpersonal relationships and complex social bonds. For example, early bands of hunters and gatherers often functioned in tandem, pooling talents and resources to enhance their effectiveness (Goldschmidt, 1990; Wallman, 1979). Even for ancient workers who functioned in relative isolation (e.g., the shepherd—perhaps the modal job in the Bible), working brought people into a social sphere based on the inherent need to share one's products and to barter and trade in order to ensure survival for oneself and one's family. In a very fundamental sense, working facilitates contact with the broader social fabric of our culture. Individuals who work (as well as individuals who consume the products of work) are contributing in some ways to the overall economic structure of the social order. Thus, the notion that work functions as a source of social contact actually contains two interrelated dimensions. Both historically and currently, work has functioned to foster direct contact and meaningful connections with others. Indeed, some scholars (e.g., Bowlby, 1982) have suggested that our need for survival in a challenging context against more powerful predators may have helped humans to develop communication and to facilitate the emergence of social communities. Moreover, working links us with the broader social context, often providing people with their major or even sole connection to their culture, political systems, and economy (Wallman, 1979). Indeed, Grantham's (2000) analysis of the shifting workplace within corporate cultures suggests that enhanced relational bonds and more complex social connections will characterize many work settings, especially in high-technology settings. Sennet (1998), however, articulated a contradictory position in which growing technological changes are viewed as creating more distance, and ultimately, greater isolation for workers. This dialectical debate forms a cornerstone of the fundamental question of understanding the nature of the intersection between human strivings for connection and working.

This chapter explores the intersections of working and relationships, which have been discussed in various ways in the social and behavioral sciences. Each of the major domains of the relationships/working context is reviewed with an initial focus on observations and research findings that are rooted in the "grand career narrative." I then highlight ideas about each domain, culled from recent social science research and/or narrative and literary analyses, which have emerged from a more inclusive exploration of the full range of working experiences, outside of the traditional bodies of knowledge. I conclude with a clinical case to illuminate how work and social connections function in a recursive and complex manner to paint a full picture of life experience.

Family Life and Working

The focus on the connections between family life and working has been a consistent and growing theme in both vocational and organizational psychology (e.g., Blustein, Walbridge, Friedlander, & Palladino, 1991; Cinnamon & Rich, 2002; Greenhaus & Parasuraman, 1999). The most heavily examined lines of inquiry in this area are the discussions of the complex boundaries that are shared by work and family life (e.g., Barnett & Hyde, 2001; Fletcher & Bailyn, 1996; Fredriksen-Goldsen & Scharlach, 2001; Greenhaus & Parasuraman, 1999; Parasuraman & Greenhaus, 1997), which are reviewed next.

The Interface Between Working and Family Life

Work and family issues have generally been examined in relation to the difficulty that workers experience in negotiating work and family responsibilities, which often occur in tandem and evoke considerable stress in individuals, families, and work contexts (Betz & Fitzgerald, 1987; Greenhaus & Parasuraman, 1999). From an historical perspective, much of the scholarly interest in the family/work interface initially was related to the fact that women have become increasingly active in the paid employment sector in middle-class Western cultures, particularly after World War II (Fredriksen-Goldsen & Scharlach, 2001). Historical analyses of work have pointed to World War II as the major cultural antecedent that facilitated the movement of women to the labor market (Barnett & Hyde, 2001; Hesse-Biber & Carter, 2000). The need for workers in factories due to the notable loss of men who were serving in the armed forces helped many Western cultures overcome an historical reluctance to allow women to have an active role in the paid workforce. Thus, after World War II, women entered the labor force in greater numbers, leading to many critically needed advances in gender equity that have emerged from feminist initiatives in the later half of the 20th century.

As a result of these gender-based changes in the workforce, the literature on work–family linkages has historically been examined within the rubric of "women's issues." In reality, the struggle to find ways of relating meaningfully to both work and family is a challenge for both men and women (Barnett & Hyde, 2001; Greenhaus & Parasuraman, 1999). Barnett and Hyde noted that "adding the worker role is beneficial to women, and adding or participating in family roles is beneficial for men" (2001, p. 784). The contribution by Barnett and Hyde outlined an expansionist theory of the work–family interface that seeks to bring this literature into the 21st century. In relation to existing perspectives of the work–family interrelationship that have been based on empirical research that is no longer credible, Barnett and Hyde have postulated four principles that can be used to guide scholarship and practice in the family–work domain. These postulates furnish useful perspectives with which to view the complex network of relations shared by men, women, and work:

- Men and women who have multiple roles (including active work and family responsibilities) benefit in a variety of domains, including mental health, physical health, and relationship functioning.
- A number of important psychosocial processes contribute to the enhancement of the balance of work and family in contemporary middle class cultures, including buffering (wherein stress in one domain is compensated by satisfaction in another domain), social support, success in life pursuits, and adaptive gender-role beliefs.
- There are specific conditions in which multiple roles are beneficial; however, the benefits of multiple roles actually depend on the time demands and commitments involved in each role.
- Consistent with conclusions reached by other scholars (e.g.,Wester, Vogel, Pressly, & Heesacker, 2002), "psychological gender differences are not, in general, large or immutable" (Barnett & Hyde, 2001, p. 784).

Although this expansionist theory offers a broader view of family–work interactions, the underlying assumptions of this literature continue to highlight the lives of relatively well-educated and affluent individuals in Western cultures. Indeed, the study of dual-career couples, which has emerged as a major scholarly initiative in recent years, has focused primarily on couples in which both individuals are making volitional choices about their lines of work (e.g., Gilbert, 1988). Attention to populations that are not part of the "grand career narrative" can be derived from diverse sources, primarily scholarship that examines the work–family conflicts of people of color and of individuals in different historical and cultural circumstances, which is examined next.

Unlike the relatively neat theoretical models that predominate the study of family–work linkages within middle-class populations (e.g., Barnett & Hyde, 2001; Fredriksen-Goldsen & Scharlach, 2001), the situation faced by workers who do not have volitional vocational options is far more complex and murky. The empirical research that has been conducted on working class and poor individuals has revealed a complex set of relationships that, in many ways, defy simple theoretical lines (Borman, 1991; Menaghan & Parcel, 1990; Perry-Jenkins & Gillman, 2000; Rubin, 1994). Indeed, the scholarship on work and family among poor and working class populations has primarily emerged from sociological research, which, while quite informative, does not capture the full range and depth of psychological experiences.

Vignettes that capture the rich and highly textured interactions that exist in the space shared by family life and working may not yield parsimonious theories, but they may provide a more experience-near understanding of working. The following passage is taken from a collection of essays and interviews of women working in mines (Moore, 1996); this vignette provides some insight into the highly connected interactions that occur in family and working experiences within a working-class context:

> With both of us [husband and wife] in the mines, we had an important part of our lives in common. We had the children, of course, and our day-to-day life together, but you get closer when you share work like coal mining. It gave Red [her husband] a new respect for me. And it gave me a much deeper understanding of what his years in the mines have meant to him. After I started in the mine, Red was even more gentle with me. He tried so hard to make things nice for me at home, because he knew what I'd been through during the day. We didn't have that much time together. I worked the graveyard shift, and he was on straight afternoons. But we had mornings and weekends, and it was what you would call quality time …. On the crew it's like the group becomes a single person. Some wives have trouble with their husbands' developing such a close relationship with women. It's not sexual, but a type of friendship that they can't share. (pp. 223–224)

The preceding vignette captures an experience of diverse social connections inherent in some of the working lives of people who have not had access to highly remunerative jobs. This passage conveys how work groups can function as family and how one's occupational life can have positive effects in intimate and familial relationships. While the relational perspectives have tended to portray a picture of a challenging work life that is compensated to some degree by a supportive network of relationships and connections, a close look at narratives and memoirs reveals a far more complex picture about the social roots of working.

In the following poem by Carl Sandburg, entitled "Mag," the relationship/working space engenders considerable anguish as the need to work for survival is unfulfilled, leaving a gaping hole in the protagonist's ability to derive benefit from relationships:

> I wish to God I never saw you, Mag.
> I wish you never quit your job and came along with me.
> I wish we never bought a license and a white dress
> For you to get married in the day we ran off to a minister
> And told him we would love each other and take care of
>   each other
> Always and always long as the sun and the rain lasts anywhere.
> Yes, I'm wishing now you lived somewhere away from here
> And I was a bum on the bumpers a thousand miles away
>   dead broke.
> I wish the kids had never come
>   And rent and coal and clothes to pay for

And a grocery man calling for cash,
Every day cash for beans and prunes.
I wish to God I never saw you, Mag.
I wish to God the kids had never come. (Sandburg, 1994, p. 11)

This poem attests to the pain of not being able to earn sufficient money to support one's family. The protagonist in this poem describes the feeling of wishing that he had never married Mag rather than face the intense disappointment and despair of not being able to sustain their most basic survival needs.

The capacity for working to fulfill needs for interpersonal connection is richly evident, in both traditional social and behavioral science literature as well in the voices of poets and workers. In a tangible sense, working allows people to support themselves and thereby facilitates the resources to create relationships and family lives. However, the fact that working is often inaccessible and/or psychologically or physically painful creates a complication in the family–work interface that requires greater understanding and study. One of the useful means of exploring the family within a broader framework is systems thinking, which is described next.

Family Systems Perspectives

Drawing on the innovative epistemology of systems theories (Patton & McMahon, 1999), a number of scholars have crafted perspectives of career that are rooted in a systems-based analysis of families and social structures (e.g., Chusid & Cochran, 1989; Lopez & Andrews, 1987; Ulrich & Dunne, 1986). The application of family systems theories to the traditional psychological study of careers has offered an illuminating perspective with which to view the interconnections between life roles. The family systems perspectives that have been used in this theoretical movement generally rely on some of the fundamental assumptions that characterize the diverse world of family therapy (e.g., Patton & McMahon, 1999). One of the core assumptions is that causality is not generally linear in complex human relationships; rather, causal connections are thought to be recursive and reciprocal in that a given action can be considered to shift an entire psychological system (Bowen, 1978; Patton & McMahon, 1999). Another assumption in this perspective is that individual behavior is best understood from the conceptual lens offered by family systems theory (Bowen, 1978). In other words, if an individual were having trouble making a decision about work and school well into adulthood, one would wonder what function this may serve not just for the individual, but also for the individual's entire family and relational system (Lopez & Andrews, 1987).

A particularly compelling observation in this line of work is that individuals have the potential to reenact aspects of their unresolved family issues in the workplace (Chusid & Chochran, 1989). In fact, an extensive line of clinically oriented scholarship has emerged that has attempted to reduce the artificial boundaries that social scientists have established around the complex threads of contemporary human existence (e.g., Blustein, 2001b; Lowman, 1993). In addition, the reenactment of unresolved issues can be manifested from work to home life. For example, an individual who is experiencing despair and shame at work may bring his or her anger to the home setting, where the expression of such affect may result in fewer social and economic consequences, albeit more pain for family members (Blustein & Spengler, 1995; Patton & McMahon, 1999).

Patton and McMahon (1999) have provided an excellent synthesis of the systems perspective of career development. Using a broad systems perspective (as opposed to a more focused family systems approach), Patton and McMahon advocated the use of a systems theory framework as a means of organizing thinking about the career development process. Specifically, Patton and McMahon have argued that career issues are best conceptualized from a broad systemic vantage point that affirms the circular and recursive nature of interactions between working and other life roles. In relation to the family–career connection, the Patton and McMahon contribution has sketched a set of concentric circles that frame the individual's career choices and adjustment to working. Included in this array of factors are community groups, peers, and family.

The family systems analyses have certainly sought to contextualize our understanding of career development. However, like most studies of career and organizational psychology, this line of inquiry has assumed that individuals have some volitional input into the nature of the work they choose and how they wish to express their interests in the world. Even with this limitation, the flexibility of this epistemological perspective does have relevance to the psychology of working. On one level, the attempt to integrate family systems thinking with vocational behavior has facilitated the creation of the intellectual foundation for a relational perspective of working. Thus, this line of inquiry has helped scholars and practitioners to consider the reality that work-related experiences are embedded in a relational matrix with complex interactions governing the nature and direction of relationships between family life and work life.

As in the literature on family–work interactions, this scholarship has tended to view working from the "career" lens. While the infusion of feminist thinking has helped family systems theories to consider nontraditional family structures, the reality that most people in the world are not making conscious, willful decisions about working has yet to be incorporated into this perspective. For example, one wonders what a family systems analysis would reveal about impoverished people for whom work represents the sole means of feeding themselves and their families. I suspect that some of the principles would be relevant; however, these questions require careful thought and empirical scholarship as we travel the road to a psychology of working that is constructed from the inner experiences of workers around the globe.

A Relational Approach to Working

A particularly promising new direction that has originated within both vocational psychology and organizational development has focused on the connection between natural human strivings for connection and various aspects of work life (e.g., Flum, 2001; Hall, 1996). As an introduction to a set of research articles on work and relationships (Blustein, 2001b), I proposed that psychology is presently undergoing a relational revolution. The perspective that is emerging from diverse lines of inquiry is based on the notion that human beings have a natural, inherent striving for connection, attachment, and intimate relationships (e.g., Bowlby, 1982; Jordan, Kaplan, Miller, Stiver, & Surrey, 1991; Josselson, 1992; Mitchell, 1988). In contrast to views of human behavior in which sexual and biological drives or learning contingencies are considered primary to human behavior, relational perspectives are based on assumptions that many aspects of our emotional and behavioral lives can be understood as manifestations of strivings for connection and closeness with important others. (See Josselson, 1992, and Mitchell, 1988, for more detailed analyses of these positions.) For the most part, the development of the relational perspectives has emerged from the crucible of therapy relationships, drawing from the discourse of clients who have tended to frame much of their lives in the language and affect of relationships (Josselson; Wachtel, 1993). For example, the relational perspectives suggest that feelings of anger or rage, which some theoreticians view as inherent to the human condition (e.g., Freud, 1930), are actually secondary or derivative experiences, emerging from relational lapses and disappointments (Mitchell, 1988).

In actuality, the relational perspectives represent a number of different theories, some of which have emerged from psychoanalysis (e.g., Mitchell, 1997), feminist theory (e.g., Jordan et al., 1991), and developmental psychology (e.g., Bowlby, 1988). When considered collectively, relational perspectives explore not just the nature of interpersonal and intimate human behavior, but also examine the *functions* of interpersonal life in relation to a wider array of human behaviors. As Bowlby (1988) stated, human beings are "hard-wired" to experience attachment bonds in early infancy, which enhances the survival chances of vulnerable infants and children. At the same time, adults are "programmed" to experience caregiving bonds to infants and children, thereby enhancing the likelihood of passing their genes along and ideally ensuring their viability as they grow old (Bowlby, 1988).

Relational theorists have presented compelling evidence supporting the fact that people seek connection with others, from their earliest days as babies well into their adult and elderly years (e.g., Flum, 2001; Josselson, 1992; Kohut, 1977). These strivings take the form of romantic attachments, close friendships, family connections, and work-based connections (Ainsworth, 1989; Bowlby, 1988; Feeney & Noller, 1990; Hall, 1996). Moreover, clinical wisdom coupled with extensive empirical research has increasingly pointed to the importance of relationships in providing a critical buffer in the face of stress, mental illness, unemployment, and other aversive life events (e.g., Aquino, Russell, Cutrona, & Altmaier, 1996; Cutrona, 1996; Greenhaus & Parasraman, 1999).

The Striving for Connection and Working

The connection between strivings for relational closeness and intimacy and working has been explored by Flum (2001), who applied the relational taxonomy developed by Josselson (1992) to the career development process. In Josselson's original study, eight dimensions of relatedness were identified by qualitative interviews and diagrams of the relational space. Flum selected seven of these dimensions including attachment, eye-to-eye validation, idealization/identification, mutuality, embeddedness, holding, and tending (or caregiving), and applied them to various aspects of vocational life. The compelling argument that Flum developed underscores the critically important shared space that exists between working and relational functioning.

How, then, does a relational perspective fit into our thinking about the psychological functions of working? In my view, the implications of the relational perspectives are dramatic and far-reaching. If we assume that human beings are oriented toward interpersonal and intimate connections with others, then we may have an opportunity to examine various aspects of work behavior in an informative light. The first issue that we need to address is the artificial boundary that has often existed around psychological and scientific examinations of work and interpersonal life. Consistent with a contextual analysis of working, it seems clear that one of the major sources of influence is the world of human relationships (Josselson, 1992; Schultheiss, 2003). More importantly, some of the functions of working may be understood as supporting the inherent striving for connection that is so critical in contemporary perspectives of human behavior.

Considerable scholarly research has supported the proposition that work is inherently relational, with highly complex and recursive relationships occurring throughout the work–relationship interface. For example, numerous studies have identified the role of close attachment relationships in negotiating various aspects of the career development process (see Blustein et al., 1995, and Schultheiss, 2003, for a review of this research). Similarly, positive findings have been identified in the study of unemployed adults, demonstrating that access to consistent and available social support is a major buffer against the aversive consequences of unemployment (Fineman, 1983; Gore, 1978; O'Brien, 1986). Recent efforts by Flum (2001), Schultheiss (2003), and others (e.g., Phillips, Christopher-Sisk, & Gravino, 2001) have explored various dimensions of the interface between work and relationships. These contributions have initiated a mapping process in which the space shared by work and relationships is being charted. A consistent finding in this scholarship is that the availability of close social supports and intimate relationships is highly advantageous in negotiating career development tasks and in effectively dealing with career crises and stresses (Blustein, Phillips, Jobin-Davis, Finkelberg, & Roarke, 1997; Blustein et al., 1991; Phillips et al., 2001).

One of the more important contributions emerging from a relational analysis of working has been articulated by Hall and his colleagues (1996), who used contemporary relational theory to expand our understanding of the career experiences of management-level and professional workers. Fletcher's (1996) chapter applied the self-in-relation model developed by scholars from the Stone Center at Wellesley College (Jordan et al., 1991; J. B. Miller, 1986) to the working experiences within large organizations. The chapters by Kram (1996) and W. A. Kahn (1996) integrated theories derived from Bowlby's (1982) attachment theory and other relational theories that have emerged in feminist thought (e.g., Jordan et al., 1991) to the traditionally masculine environment of the modern corporate work setting in North America and Europe. Taken together, the major conclusions of their contributions are summarized as follows:

- Psychological growth is not only contingent upon strivings for autonomy and independence, but is also rooted in strivings for connection, attachment, and intimacy.

■ Working life within organizations often generates important relational challenges, which, if resolved successfully, can help workers to advance their careers. Thus, conversations with others about career concerns along with developing mentors have the potential to furnish individuals with many of the tools to affect positive changes in their work lives.

■ Workers can enhance highly stressful organizational settings by striving to create safe relational havens, thereby replicating a key ingredient in the relational matrix.

Consistent with the position I advance in this chapter, Hall (1996) argued that relational connections and influences refer not just to the individual's proximal interpersonal context, but also to the entire social milieu. Moreover, Hall's contributions have been constructed in light of the rapid changes in the organizational career narrative. Interestingly, Hall concludes with a concern for older workers and for blue-collar workers who have been left out of much of the recent discourse on careers, foreshadowing the issues raised in this book.

In another relevant contribution, Herriot (2001) advanced a position in which the relationship between employees and employers in corporate settings is viewed as the major factor in helping individuals to engage effectively in their work lives. Moreover, given the heightened nature of competition among modern corporations, Herriot argues that the employment relationship ought to be far less conflictual than is currently the case in many settings. For Herriot, the key relationship at work is the connection between the individual and the organization; however, Herriot acknowledges that the organization consists of people who need to work out relationship struggles on a daily basis. The Herriot argument is that inherent dialectical struggles exist within many organizations in which positive attributes of an employment relationship are countered by a flip side that undercuts the potential assets of adaptive employee–employer relationships. One possible solution to these challenges is that dialogue needs to take place encompassing not just thoughts and ideas, but also emotions and feelings (cf. Payne & Cooper, 2001).

Also using an explicit relational framework is Sennett's work (1998), initially presented in chapter 2, which described the disturbing consequences that have transformed the lives of workers who face an increasingly dehumanizing market-based structure. For Sennett, the key characteristic of modern capitalism is flexibility, which influences the nature of worker specialization, production, and organizational structure. In the face of this pervasive lack of consistency, Sennett proposes that workers have lost a key element of inner stability and have also lost a profound sense of connection to their community. In this insightful analysis, Sennett describes the loss of a sense of "we" in the working lives of managers and other educated workers. Sennett argues that the social stigma of interdependence, which has been promoted in part by many corporate cultures, has led to a sense of shame about strivings for connection, which collude with the changes in organizational life to evoke feelings of mistrust and alienation.

In a similar vein, Fletcher and Bailyn (1996) advocated that modern organizations have increasingly diminished the capacity for workers to balance family and career. With the advent of downsizing and the growing competitiveness of the global economy, many corporate entities have reduced family benefits and have demanded (either explicitly or implicitly) that workers who want to get ahead need to devote themselves first and foremost to their work responsibilities. Fletcher and Bailyn argue that our social structure will suffer from the loss of available adults to care for others (such as children, the elderly, and our communities). Moreover, they suggest that organizations will ultimately suffer as people are forced to make unnatural choices between work and family.

In closing, various lines of research and theory development have linked vocational functioning to the world of relationships, social support, and intimacy (e.g., Blustein, 2001b; Flum, 2001). While some of the studies have employed relatively well-educated samples, an increasing number of investigations and theoretical innovations are involving participants who do not have access to rigorous education and upwardly mobile careers (e.g., Blustein et al., 2002; Phillips et al., 2001). These studies and conceptual initiatives, which are reviewed later in the chapter, form the basis for a relational perspective on working.

Relational Conflict and Working

As social and behavioral scientists as well as counselors increasingly attend to the interface of work-related issues and relational functioning, it becomes clear that the shared space can also contain patches of darkness and conflict. As an illustration, in a recent study by my research team (Blustein et al., 2001), we examined the "Getting Down to Cases" series from the *Career Development Quarterly*, which revealed that conflict in relationships does at times interface with working life. A number of career counseling vignettes in this series described individuals, many of whom experienced little to no volition in their work lives, as struggling considerably with interpersonal conflict that affected their work. Another observation, albeit based on a minority of cases from this series, revealed that social comparison (in which individuals compare their progress with others) had the potential to serve as a motivator in resolving difficult vocational tasks.

The next passage, coming from the classic play by Arthur Miller entitled "Death of a Salesman" (1949), describes the pain and disappointment in facing one's family after experiencing work disappointments:

> *Biff:* Hap, I've had twenty or thirty different kinds of jobs since I left home before the war, and it always turns out the same. I just realized it lately. In Nebraska when I herded cattle, and the Dakotas, and Arizona, and now Texas. It's why I came home now, I guess, because I realized it. This farm I work on, it's spring there now, see? And they've got about fifteen new colts. There's nothing more inspiring or—beautiful than the sight of a mare and a new colt. And it's cool there now, see? Texas is cool now and it's spring. And whenever spring comes to where I am, I suddenly get the feeling, my God, I'm not gettin' anywhere! What the hell am I doing, playing around with horses, twenty-eight dollars a week! I'm thirty-four years old, I oughta be makin' my future. That's when I come running home. And now, I get here, and I don't know what to do with myself. *After a pause:* I've always made a point of not wasting my life, and everytime I come back here I know that all I've done is to waste my life. (p. 23)

This passage is complex in its nuances and feeling about the sense of experiencing oneself as a failure. What is particularly striking about it is that somehow Biff is exposed to a rather negatively tinged sort of mirroring wherein he feels empty and depleted in the face of his historic conflicts with his father, Willy. Indeed, the textual material from Miller's classic play suggests that, at times, family relationships may exert aversive influences on an individual's working life.

Research on Relationships and Working:
Empirical and Narrative Analyses

A handful of studies in recent years have foreshadowed the psychology of working with a particular focus on the role of relationships in the work lives of individuals who generally have not had access to the "grand career narrative." For example, my colleagues and I (Blustein et al., 1997) found that support from parents, teachers, and other important adults predicted job satisfaction and occupational congruence among non-college-bound young adults. Similar findings have been identified by Schultheiss, Kress, Manzi, and Jeffrey

(2001) as well as Way and Rossman (1996a, b), who have each concluded that relational support is of particular importance to working-class adolescents and young adults. In addition, a review that my colleagues and I (Blustein, Juntunen, & Worthington, 2000) conducted on the school-to-work transition for non-college-bound youth revealed that contact with adults and support from family members are significant factors in the negotiation of the difficult move from high school to the labor market. These studies suggest that the relational support is potentially quite relevant to a psychology of working. However, a closer look at a number of recent qualitative studies provides a more in-depth view of the nature and extent of the relational context of working.

Juntunen and her colleagues (Juntunen et al., 2001) focused on the work experiences of a sample of 18 Native Americans adults. Using in-depth interviews and a rigorous qualitative design, Juntunen et al. found that the working lives of Native Americans were explicitly nested within their social networks, particularly their families and communities. For example, decisions about schooling and work were generally made in collaboration with family members. As the following passage from one of the participants conveys, even thoughts and dreams of success are rooted in one's feelings for family and community:

> At basic levels, success means being able to feed and clothe my children. To send them to college. To buy a home. On a higher level, success is getting to a point where I can contribute to … Native Americans. I can't honestly say success for me would be an individual thing. I think my family would be involved. I would hope that success for me would mean success for them also. I think my success will definitely be shared with the rest of the family and the community. (Juntunen et al., 2001, p. 278)

This passage describes the interrelated needs that working fulfills in both ensuring survival and affirming relational and familial connections. The protagonist in this vignette conveys the deep sense of connection that exists between one's work life and one's relational life in a culture that fosters collectivist values.

One of the more impressive sets of findings from the growing research on the role of relationships among working class and poor populations is the research by Phillips and her colleagues (e.g., Phillips et al., 2001). In contrast to notions of career decision making that are made in an autonomous fashion, Phillips and her research group have found that working class and poor individuals generally approach decision points about work and school in a consultative fashion. In short, the working class young adults from these studies, who were typically in jobs that did not require college training, tended to make decisions explicitly in a social context, often obtaining input from their families and other responsible adults in their lives. The following excerpt from a participant in the Phillips et al. (2001) study underscores the relational context of decision making among working class adults who have not completed a 4-year college:

> I don't make decisions alone. I make them with my family. And if it meets everybody's needs then I know it's O.K. So I mean my family has a big part in a lot of decisions I make and what goes on. I don't just have the power to make decisions by myself, because I have to check everybody's agenda and to make sure that everything fits, and then I can go, O.K. (p. 203)

This vignette describes the embedded nature of decision making for a student who is able to articulate a web of relational connections that have often been overlooked in traditional career development theory and research. Moreover, the Phillips et al. (2001) research has effectively raised questions about the reification of rational decision making in career development theory and practice and the corresponding denigration of relationally embedded decision-making styles. The Phillips et al. study identified an adaptive mode of decision making known as "consultative," offering a glimpse of the potential for the psychology of working to transform some of the conventional wisdom of traditional career development and organizational psychology theory.

In addition to the support of others in decision making, recent research has identified the role of significant family members and friends in preparing for work-based transitions. Phillips et al. (2002) interviewed work-bound eleventh-grade students in two high schools, one urban and one in a working-class suburb, with the intention of exploring their views of their lives after high school. A number of the participants focused on their social supports and attachments as critical factors in how they felt about their futures and how they were able to handle the responsibilities and challenges of high school. The following participant's comments describe the relational climate that seems to support an optimistic and planful approach to the school-to-work transition:

> My mother, she's been helpful. It's like a lot of things. If it wasn't for my mother .... Like cause everybody needs someone to motivate them. Like have somebody talk to you about good things in life, and if you don't have nobody to talk to then it's like you be straight. You don't know what's going on out there ....

As the previous vignette suggests, when close, supportive and consistent relational connections are available, the struggles of working may be somewhat less painful. However, the existence of close relationships does not, in of itself, confer positive attributes to a client, student, or worker. In contrast, it seems that close connections provide the soil for effective work-based transitions, providing, of course, that opportunities are available and individuals are able to access these opportunities in a relatively equitable fashion.

A relatively unexplored aspect of the relationship–working interface is the role of intimate connections in warding off the psychic pain of numbing work tasks. A conceptual framework for understanding how intense intimate connections can function in life is found in Kohut's (1977) self psychology. In Kohut's formulations, the self is the major organizing structure for human behavior and development. The full theoretical richness of Kohut's work in describing the psychological antecedents and consequences of variations in self experience is beyond the scope of this book. (I refer interested readers to A. Kahn, 1993; Strozier, 2001; Wolfe, 1988, for more detailed descriptions of Kohut's work.) In self psychology, human beings are viewed as striving for self-cohesion, which is characterized by feelings of confidence, healthy self-regard, and the ability to tolerate the emotional ups and downs of life. The opposite of self-cohesion is self-fragmentation, wherein one experiences feelings of depletion, sadness, needs for constant affirmation, and incoherence. One way of warding off self-fragmentation feelings is to use alcohol or drugs, or to engage in intense sexual relationships, often with little emotional commitment. The function of such interpersonal experiences has been detailed quite evocatively in novels and other forms of human narrative. The following excerpt from Sillitoe's (1958) novel entitled *Saturday Night and Sunday Morning* gives voice to the feelings of despair and alienation at work, which is dealt with by drinking binges and sexual liaisons with the wife of a co-worker:

> Arthur sweated at his lathe, working at the same fast pace as in winter to keep the graph-line of his earnings level. Life went on like as assegai into the blue, with dim memories of the dole and schooldays behind, and a dimmer feeling of death in front, a present life punctuated by meetings with Brenda on certain beautiful evenings when the streets were warm and noisy and the clouds did a moonlight-flit over the rooftops. They made love in the parlour or bedroom and felt the ocean of suburb falling asleep outside of their minuscular coracle of untouchable hope and bliss. (p. 136)

The protagonist in Sillitoe's novel is cognizant of his feelings of disengagement and despair about his job. He realizes, though, that without this work, despite its tediousness and danger, he would have no work at all. As such, he sees a life of greyness around him, coloring his views of the past, present, and future. To ward off these feelings and to reach for some meaning in life, he has initiated an affair with a co-worker's wife, who offers him some solace, at least when they are together. However, Arthur describes elsewhere in the book his fear of marriage, which he views as creating even more burdens in his life. While it is obvious that Arthur's despair is very likely due to more than his struggles with work, Sillitoe's novel conveys the way in which the affair with Brenda, despite its moral compromises, offers at least a brief respite from the dullness of his factory job.

Concluding Comments

In sum, the various studies and theoretical statements on relational strivings and working point to a fundamental connection between our relational lives and our working lives. The precise nature of the linkage is difficult to discern and is clearly rooted in a cultural and historical context that belies parsimonious theoretical propositions. However, the framework that this material has established provides firm scaffolding for a relational approach to working, which is described further at the conclusion of this chapter.

Caregiving and Working

One of the important contributions of M. S. Richardson's (1993) seminal article on work was her clear endorsement of caregiving as a specific aspect of work. In this book, caregiving refers to efforts that are devoted to caring for children, elderly relatives, and other significant people in one's life (cf. Fredriksen-Goldsen & Scharlach, 2001). Indeed, consistent with recent findings suggesting far fewer inherent sex differences due to biological disposition than had originally been considered in the past (e.g., Hesse-Biber & Carter, 2000; Wester, Vogel, Page, & Heesacker, 2002), there is little biological evidence to support a bifurcation of caregiving roles based on gender. While few would argue that caregiving is a form of work, some debate exists as to how this aspect of our lives is understood. (Although I advocate that caregiving be considered a form of working, I also believe that helping others, whether they be our children, family members, or elderly, represents an inherent aspect of being human that includes, but is clearly not limited to the psychological experience of working.)

The existence of notable gender differences in the division of caregiving labor is a reality that continues to plague many women in Western cultures (Fredriksen-Goldsen & Scharlach, 2001; Greenhaus & Parasuraman, 1999).

In the psychology of working, one of the goals of scholarly and policy initiatives needs to be continued changes toward equalization of gender-based commitments to caregiving. The growing psychological study of masculinity and men's issues (e.g., Levant & Brooks, 1997; Mahalik, 1999) is providing an important knowledge base with which to develop social policies that will help to reduce the aversive impact of gender role socialization. As we understand the nature of men's socialization, it will be easier to affect change by enhancing opportunities for men to access, without shame, their natural relational strivings as boys (Pollack, 2000).

A critical perspective in understanding caregiving is the reality that this sort of work is not inherently valued (Fitzgerald & Weitzman, 1992; Fredriksen-Goldsen & Scharlach, 2001). In brief, caregiving work is generally not compensated with money or explicit access to economic or social power. As a result, caregivers struggle in many communities in Western cultures to care for themselves and their loved ones; moreover, working as a caregiver may leave an individual at a distinct disadvantage when attempting to locate paid employment. As an example of the way in which caregiving is viewed, the current situation in the United States offers a number of observations that underscore a lack of respect for caregiving. For instance, child care in the United States is not offered in a nationally governed or systematic fashion to parents. In addition, nursery school teachers in the United States are paid considerably less than their peers in elementary and secondary education, often earning only half of the salary of their peers at higher grade levels (U.S. Department of Labor, 2004). Moreover, there is considerable evidence suggesting that women continue to do the vast majority of caregiving work, even when they are working outside of the home full-time (Fredriksen-Goldsen & Scharlach, 2001).

A particularly evocative exploration of these issues is found in the comment from a husband in Rubin's (1994) analysis of working class families in the United States in the late 1980s and early 1990s, who remarked:

> I know that my wife works all day, just like I do ... but it's not the same. She doesn't *have* (italics in original) to do it. I mean, she *has* (italics in original) to because we need the money, but it's different. It's not really her job to have to be working; it's mine .... I do my share around the house, only she doesn't see it that way. Maybe if you add it all up, I don't do as much as she does, but then she doesn't bring in as much money as I do. And she doesn't always have to be looking for overtime to make an extra buck. (p. 85)

While this one illustration certainly does not speak for an entire culture with respect to the gender differentiation that has occurred in caregiving roles, it does capture a time and place that resonates for many in Western countries. In my view, the first way to redress this considerable source of inequity is to dignify caregiving by considering it as a legitimate form of working. Obviously, caregiving is not solely a working activity in a psychological sense; caregiving also is a relational process in which considerable emotional and intellectual effort is expended. However, caregiving certainly satisfies many of the criteria of working that are advanced in this book. First, caregiving functions to enhance the social connection of both the giver of care as well as the recipient of care. Second, caregiving has the potential to foster self-determination in that it offers individuals a critical expression of inherent motivations and dreams, often related to family goals or to the intrinsic motivation to be helpful to others. Third, caregiving has the potential to enhance power in that one has legitimate and significant social responsibility for the development and adjustment of other individuals. However, in North America and to a lesser extent in Europe, caregiving does not confer the sort of power that is associated with financial rewards and access to power within organizational contexts (Fredriksen-Goldsen & Scharlach, 2001). As such, the psychological function of caregiving as offering people access to legitimate economic and political power actually represents an aspiration as opposed to a description of the status quo in most Western cultures.

In my view, a consideration of caregiving as working may help social and behavioral scientists to advocate for more humane and equitable policies for those who care for children, individuals with disabling conditions, and the elderly. Indeed, the lack of status associated with caregiving in the United States in comparison to the status that it has in other cultures suggests that social policies and shifting mores may help to change the status quo with respect to the work lives of caregivers.

Working as a Means of Connecting to the Broader Social World

In addition to providing people with a means of accessing relationships and social support, I propose that working helps people to connect to the broader social and economic world. Given that most adults work and that this collective effort yields considerable economic and social resources, I believe that the experience of working functions to connect people to the external world, including the economy, political structure, and culture. The process of working, regardless of the type of job one has, adds to the economic resources and overall social structure of a culture. Thus, while a business executive or other highly trained professional may have more status than an attendant at a car wash or migrant farm worker, the social and economic fabric theoretically needs each thread to create the current economic and social structure.

Considerable research has documented the benefits that working affords in helping people to feel more engaged with their communities. Wilson (1996), for example, described how the lack of working engendered feelings of alienation among inner-city African American residents in Chicago, leading to less family cohesion and to increases in self-destructive behavior. In addition, Shore (1998) argued that work functioned to help at-risk adolescents become more engaged in their lives. Similar arguments have been advanced in rehabilitation counseling in which the experience of working has been thought to help individuals with disabling conditions feel more connected to the broader social and economic world (e.g., Szymanski & Parker, 2003). Finally, Sennett's critique of the loss of a sense of "we" at the workplace underscores the consequences that lack of access to work creates in individuals who then struggle to fit into their communities.

The social connections described thus far, therefore, encompass the real relationships that exist at one's work setting, in the relational spaces surrounding work, and the more symbolic relationships that exist between individuals and the social world. The symbolic connections that are established, naturally, are more elusive and subtle than are the real relationships that have been discussed throughout this chapter. However, I believe that working plays a valuable, and often understated, role in connecting people to their communities and to the overall social context. Clearly, more research is needed to explore the nature of this experience, to identify the extent of individual differences in one's sense of connection to society, and to develop policies that will maximize the sense of community that working can engender.

Relationships and Working in Psychological Treatment

Despite Freud's dictum that one needs to be able to love and work in order to live an effective life, relatively little clinical literature has focused on the role of working in psychotherapy. As I noted in the first chapter, the domain of work issues has been considered secondary to the world of relationships, which has assumed far more importance in most psychotherapeutic theories (cf. Axelrod, 1999; Blustein, 1987). Despite this trend to marginalize discussions of work in treatment, Blustein and Spengler (1995) observed at least some interest in the role of work issues in psychological treatment, with considerably more attention devoted to this interaction evident in recent years (e.g., Axelrod, 1999; Blustein, 2001b; Socarides & Kramer, 1997). Yet at the same time, evidence has been obtained that clinicians tend to overshadow work issues with relationship issues, even when these issues are relatively equal in their perceived severity (Spengler, Blustein, & Strohmer, 1990). Thus, despite the intentions of such important efforts as Axlerod's (1999) integration of work into psychoanalytic treatment and Lowman's analysis of work-related dysfunctions, the tendency still exists to view work issues as secondary to relationship issues in treatment.

From my perspective, one of the most important means of reducing this bias is to explore the interface of work and relationships within psychotherapeutic discourse. Once counselors think about working outside of the boundaries of the career development and organizational behavior perspective, we are in a much more inclusive position to help our clients who do not have "traditional" career trajectories attain a meaningful life that ideally includes more rewarding working experiences and an amelioration of psychological symptoms. In the section that follows, I describe a fictional client, whose narrative is based on an integration of several themes that emerged in my psychotherapeutic practice.

Florence

A client, named Florence, entered into individual psychotherapy with the presenting problems of depression, social isolation, and chronic physical pain. Florence was a 54-year-old European American woman who lived by herself in a trailer about 40 miles away from a medium-sized city. Her life at the time she entered treatment was characterized by considerable pain related to rheumatoid arthritis, which kept her from being able to work. (Her working life had included caregiving when her children were younger, followed by work in a department store as a clerk, a job that she had held for about 10 years prior to the recent progression of her illness 3 years ago.) Florence also had been divorced, leaving her husband 10 years prior to initiating therapy after a 21-year marriage. Her three children continued to reside at her home after the divorce, but soon moved out as they began to work full-time or attend college. After the divorce settlement, Florence had to sell her home and then moved into the trailer, where she resided during the treatment. Her relationship with her ex-husband was still conflictual; the relationships with her children seemed solid, but were growing increasingly distant as Florence became more depressed and isolated.

I initially engaged Florence in a relationally oriented approach wherein I attempted to help her explore her feelings of loss, while also affirming her still-disavowed strivings for connection (e.g., Jordan et al., 1991; Josselson, 1992; Mitchell, 1988). In the course of treatment that consisted of 5 months of weekly therapy followed by 10 months of every-other-week treatment, Florence focused extensively on her feelings of loneliness. She spoke longingly about her job, which offered her a source of connection in her community and feelings of support from her colleagues. Her physical pain, however, was most pronounced when she had to stand for a period of hours, which was the case in her job, thereby forcing her to leave and go on disability. As the treatment progressed, we were able to deal with her feelings of anger and betrayal with respect to her ex-husband, who had left the marriage after starting an affair with a younger woman from his job (which was in a local factory). She also was able to confront her feelings of sadness about her "empty nest feelings" and the resulting sense of aimlessness that filled her days, as she had neither her caregiving nor her clerk responsibilities to fulfill. At that point, we seemed to reach an impasse, as her sense of isolation was palpable and pervasive; we then focused on the loss of paid employment.

Although she was able to support herself, albeit modestly, on her disability payments, she reported that she missed contact with others on a daily basis. We then engaged in the exploration of her interests and hopes for her life, which certainly embraced the work domain. Florence acknowledged that she had always wanted to learn about computers and that she wanted to consider returning to work as a programmer. She found a certificate program at a local community college that offered training for adult learners (including those without any college background, which was the case with Florence) in computer programming. When she entered this program, her mood became markedly less depressed; she met other adults in similar situations and began to feel connected again to her community. In a letter that I received from her a year after she terminated treatment, she informed me that she obtained a part-time job at a bank doing computer programming and word processing. While she still reported considerable physical pain, she was able to work because she could sit down and because the focused activity of working allowed her to take her mind off of her discomfort and pain in her joints. She continued to feel better and reported starting some new friendships with colleagues from the bank.

Discussion

This case vignette underscores the linkages between social connection and working. While it is certainly impossible to derive generalizable inferences from one clinical vignette, the process of treatment parallels a growing literature on the importance of working in the development and maintenance of integrated psychological functioning (e.g., Axelrod, 1999; Shore & Massimo, 1979). In the case of Florence, we observe how the loss of work begins a spiraling process of disengagement from one's social world. Obviously, Florence's physical ailments played a major role in her depression; however, to examine this case without taking the critical role of working into account is to miss a major aspect of the treatment picture. The role that work played in Florence's life is evident throughout the case presentation; indeed, one of the goals of therapy was to help Florence find a meaningful way to re-engage in her working life. In addition, the function of work in furnishing Florence with important social connections was a major factor in the progress that she made in her treatment.

The findings from Blustein and Spengler's (1995) review of the literature on the relationships between personal adjustment and vocational functioning support the sort of therapy described in this case in which a work-based intervention was integrated seamlessly into the treatment. Moreover, the empirical literature on recovery from psychiatric disorders strongly supports the social-connection functions of working (Shore, 1998; Shore & Massimo, 1979). For example, Caplan, Vinokur, and Price (1997) performed a literature review of job loss and found a number of negative mental health consequences that resulted from the diminishment of an active working life. In fact, Shore and Massimo (1979) developed a vocationally oriented mode of psychotherapy as a means of helping psychiatrically disabled clients move toward a more active engagement in their lives.

The importance of work in people's lives has been well articulated by Shore (1998), who detailed an agenda for professional psychology that is constructed in large measure around the distribution of meaningful work to people across the social spectrum. As Shore noted, the employment figures tend to belie "the cynicism, insecurity, and fear (about work) that psychologists pick up in their everyday social relations and clinical settings" (p. 477). Moreover, he noted that work is often viewed as a source of punishment, as exemplified by the movement from welfare to what has euphemistically been called "workfare." Rather than helping individuals who had been on welfare receive training and education that would give them a sense of volition in their lives, the legislation ended up mandating work in ways that did not consistently enhance skills and self-determination.

While it is typical for vocationally oriented practitioners and researchers to criticize psychotherapists for relegating work to a secondary or tertiary level of importance, the reality is that the practice of career counseling has historically not been very effective in understanding the space shared by work and relationships. A telling example of the relative absence of integrative thinking with respect to work and relationships in career counseling can be found in the previously mentioned study by my research group (Blustein et al., 2001) of the 19 "Getting Down to Cases" articles in the *Career Development Quarterly* from 1986–1993. This series included a case description followed by recommendations for counseling intervention by notable practitioners and counselor educators. The most common response in this qualitative study was a call for more information on social connections and relationships on the part of the discussants. The case descriptions were striking in their focus on work and career, although a careful reading revealed that it was impossible to consider many of these cases without attention to the client's inner relational life and broader interpersonal life. A more recent collection of cases edited by Niles, Goodman, and Pope (2002) reflects greater sensitivity to the work–relationships interface, perhaps reflecting some positive growth in professional training in the past few decades.

The lack of understanding about the psychological meaning of work continues to hamper individual treatment and broader intervention strategies. Without acknowledging the intense feelings (both positive and negative) that work can engender, we risk invalidating a very real aspect of human functioning. As we expand our thinking from the narrow lens of the "grand career narrative" to the more inclusive notion of working, it is possible to include a far greater array of experiences in counseling and psychotherapy that would encompass all of the domains of human existence. Recent efforts such as the books by Axelrod (1999), Socarides and Kramer (1997), and Lowman (1993) have started to fill a gap in our knowledge about the psychotherapeutic aspects of work. However, in order for psychotherapists to develop a meaningful framework with which to consider work-related issues in counseling, an integrative conceptual perspective is needed on the interface of interpersonal life and working. (See chapters 8 and 9 for further thoughts on this challenge.)

The Psychology of Working and Social Connections: Conclusion

The material presented in this chapter is rich in its description of the social embeddedness of working. The literature initially pertaining to the growing study of family and relational influences in traditional career and organizational psychology certainly points a psychology of working in an explicitly relational direction. As the growing scholarship in this area suggests, the nature of work and interpersonal life in modern and post-modern middle-class cultures is closely intertwined (cf. Flum, 2001; Schultheiss, 2003). In creating the theoretical scaffolding for a psychology of working, it is important to initially start with the foundation offered by the traditional areas of vocational psychology and organizational development. When considered collectively, the literature on the familial and relational linkages to the development and expression of career interests and plans suggests that relationships and working share some important areas of overlap. It is important, however, to acknowledge that the working and relationship life spaces are not completely congruent and that life is generally not predictable across these domains of human experience.

Building on the career development and organizational psychology literatures, I then explored social connections to the working lives of poor, working-class and otherwise marginalized populations. Although this literature is still in its infancy, the early phases of this psychological research, coupled with the passages that were presented from narrative studies, poems, and memoirs, suggest a pronounced connection between relationships and working. Perhaps the most overriding theme of these social scientific and literary contributions is that working functions as a means of connecting people to their social contexts. Taken together, the studies and passages presented in this chapter point to psychological functions of working that are rooted in the social milieu of contemporary life. Whether the social context is framed within a highly structured organization or within a small family farm or business, working is one of the most social activities that we can engage in. As people engage in work activities, they are connecting to people in a consistent and often intimate manner, thereby linking themselves to the social fabric and economic assets of their communities.

As noted earlier, even work that is isolated by nature (e.g., lighthouse keeper; solitary fishing; writing; "Maytag" repairperson), while perhaps reflecting a desire for aloneness, does immerse people into a network of social exchanges and interactions, even if some of the interactions are symbolic rather than truly relational. As suggested in anthropological studies of work around the globe (e.g., Goldschmidt, 1990), coupled with theoretical contributions from career and organizational psychology (Blustein, 1994; Schein, 1990), working confers upon an individual an identity within one's social context. As we attend carefully to the voices of workers, a broader view becomes apparent wherein the nature of one's work is closely linked to the construction of identity (Gini, 2000; Thomas, 1999). Consistent with extensive scholarship in career development and organizational psychology, a critical aspect of identity is thought to be one's work role (Blustein, 1994; Schein, 1990). Indeed, work-based or vocational identity represents a major visible and socially sanctioned expression of one's inner psychological identity (e.g., Erikson, 1968; Grotevant, 1987; Holland, 1997).

The material presented in this chapter, when considered collectively, yields some coherent inferences about the nature of working and relationships. First, the working context and relational world do seem to share considerable overlap, although the nature and extent of these interconnections are difficult to identify or generalize (Blustein & Spengler, 1995; Schultheiss, 2003). The natural fabric of life does not typically differentiate between life domains; the lived experiences of people across contexts indicates that issues, challenges, and supports are mutually influential in the working and relational domains. Second, supportive relationships are very likely helpful to people as they negotiate with the complexities of work life in two interrelated ways. Relationships provide emotional support and nurturance, which helps people to feel safe, secure, loved, and resilient (Josselson, 1992; Schultheiss et al., 2001). Furthermore, relationships can help people by providing instrumental assistance in negotiating work-related tasks, such as locating employment, furnishing people with role models and connections for jobs, and providing people with funding for education and training. Third, the nature of working connects people to the broader social context. In doing so, the process of working becomes an explicit way for people to feel connected with the greater social and cultural context of their lives.

Given the powerful relational connections evident in the diverse literatures reviewed in this chapter, it seems critical to infuse a psychology of working with an explicit relational focus. The nature of this theoretical framework requires considerably more discovery-oriented and hypothesis-testing research as well as integrative theoretical analyses in order to effectively map the working–relationships life space. However, what does seem clear is that working links human beings in a highly complex yet critically important fashion with others, offering opportunities for a sense of community and for the social support that provides us with the emotional sustenance needed for a satisfying and meaningful life journey.

CHAPTER 5

Working as a Means of Self-Determination

The causes lie deep and simply—the causes are a hunger in a stomach, multiplied a million times, a hunger in a single soul, hunger for joy and some security, multiplied a million times; muscles aching to work, minds aching to create beyond the single need—this is man. To build a wall, to build a house, a dam, and in the wall and house and dam to put something of Manself, and to Manself take back something of the wall, the house, the dam; to take hard muscles from the lifting, to take the clear lines and form from conceiving. For man, unlike any other thing organic or inorganic in the universe, grows beyond his work, walks up the stairs of his concepts, emerges ahead of his accomplishments. This you may say of man—when theories change and crash, when schools, philosophies, when narrow dark alleys of thought, national, religious, economic, grow and disintegrate, man reaches, stumbles forward, painfully, mistakenly sometimes. Having stepped forward, he may slip back, but only half a step, never the full step back ....

—Steinbeck (1939, pp. 204–205)

Without realizing it, some two-thirds of the workforce would become the unwitting guinea pigs in perhaps the most extensive investigation into human motivation the world has known. The studies didn't start that way. Production rates and General Electric's insatiable desire to sell more lighting across manufacturing industry were at the heart of the first experiments. Tests were run in several places, including General Electric's Bridgeport Works and the Massachusetts Institute of Technology. The most rigorous experiments, however, appear to have been conducted at Western Electric's Hawthorne works, and it was these tests—three sets of experiments run at intervals between November 1924 and April 1927 that caused the biggest fuss. The first experiments, run by MIT engineers, appeared promising; lighting was improved in some departments and productivity went up. The problem was that productivity also went up among workers in a control group where lighting was not improved. One team managed to maintain output even when lighting was dimmed to the level of moonlight.

—Donkin (2001, p. 168)

All I ever wanted to do was write for a newspaper .... I just always knew what I wanted to do. And it's always been sort of two things that have drawn me to it—first of all, I love writing. I love the whole exercise of writing. I love the challenge of putting thoughts to paper, finding just the right word, the right rhythm, the structure in which that rhythm flows.

—Bowe et al. (2000, p. 300)

The passages that begin this chapter attest to the rich variation of motivational experiences that occur in relation to working. The first two functions of working that I have detailed thus far (in chapters 3 and 4) have gently circumvented one of the central tenets of the "grand career narrative" of Western nations pertaining to the implementation of the self-concept or identity in one's working life (e.g., Holland, 1997; Super, 1957). The notion that people can find an outlet for their interests in the world of work has a rich and historic tradition in psychology in industrial and post-industrial societies (e.g., Landy, 1989; Parsons, 1909; Savickas & Spokane, 1999). Underlying many career choice and development theories is the assumption that part of the motivation for people at work is that they have an opportunity to manifest or express their interests in the world of work. Indeed, this premise has formed the essence of vocational psychology, and to a somewhat lesser extent, organizational psychology. The question that I pose here is how does this hopeful picture of volitional self-concept implementation or interest expression relate to the vast majority of people who do not have significant or extensive choices in their working lives? Building on the premises that have been presented in chapters 3 and 4, I seek to chart a new conceptual foundation for the psychology of working that is centered on the self-determination theory of Deci and Ryan (1985, 2000; Ryan & Deci, 2000). Using this innovative motivational perspective as a foundation, I describe how working for extrinsic reasons may become a valued and perhaps even meaningful endeavor, provided that a set of supportive conditions are in place within one's proximal and more distal contexts. Moreover, this chapter seeks to give voice to the wide array of motivational experiences that occur as people grapple with labor markets and working conditions that are often beyond their control.

As I have stated throughout this book, the psychology-of-working perspective that I am advocating does not seek to distance itself from the very commonly accepted notion that people strive to express their interests and selected aspects of their identity in the world of work (Holland, 1997; Lapan, 2004; Lent, Brown, & Hackett, 2002; Super et al., 1996). Indeed, this aspect of the "grand career narrative" is a major motivating factor for those people who have the opportunity to seek work that is consistent with their interests. Ideally, the notion of searching for work that allows for the expression of one's interests and values is an attractive goal that one would hope would be available to increasing proportions of our global population. In addition, as I detail in forthcoming chapters, my position is that the goal of expanding options so that greater numbers of people can exercise volition in their working lives is critical and merits the attention of policymakers and government leaders as well as social and behavioral scientists. However, when we consider the experiences of the vast majority of workers, as reflected in the next passage, it is hard to imagine that interest expression universally drives the motivation to work:

> When I was eight years old, I worked in the cotton fields in the El Paso area. I used to chop weeds and pick chiles and onions. I averaged ten or twelve dollars a day. It all depended on how much I would pick. Even though the child labor laws prohibit kids from working all day long like I was doing, it was common for parents to take *all* the family to the field. (Martinez, 1994, p. 169)

Based on this vignette, it seems likely that the character in this passage is working primarily to satisfy the need to survive. The primary motivation in this context is likely related to the notion articulated by Maslow (1968) in which the need for survival functions as the baseline of our motivational system. While the need for survival is certainly underscored in recent theoretical statements (e.g., Lent et al., 2002; M. S. Richardson, 1993), the prevailing notion in the more traditional theories has tended to assume that people could choose work based on their interests and values (e.g., Dawis, 2002; Holland, 1997). In order to understand the motivational aspects of working more fully, I now explore how traditional theories within vocational psychology and I/O psychology have addressed motivation. I then present a self-determination view that seeks to carve out a more inclusive vision for the psychology of working.

The Motivational Aspects of Traditional Career Choice and Development Theories

Embedded within the historic core of the traditional theories of career choice and development is the notion that people have options and choices in their lives about the sorts of work that they could pursue. Indeed, when we consider the contextual influences of Parsons' (1909) contributions, the labor market in early 20th century North America and other Westernized nations was characterized by the growing presence of the industrial era, which increasingly required workers with greater levels of training and education (Hartung & Blustein, 2002). During this period of time, an increasing proportion of young people had the option of a more extended adolescence, which allowed for greater deliberation and choice with respect to one's vocational options. It is important to note, however, that the extent of one's choices had been (and is still) circumscribed by factors relating to one's social class, racial and ethnic status, and access to the opportunity structure. (These factors are explored in greater depth in chapter 6.) However, the thrust of Parsons' contributions was that people would be more satisfied if they were able to make informed decisions about the sort of work that they chose. Indeed, the title of Parsons' (1909) book, *Choosing a Vocation*, underscores the notion that one has an active role to play in the direction of one's working life. The resulting emphasis on helping people to choose their line of work then began to define vocational counseling theory and practice, with far less of a focus on the nature of working lives for people who had little if any input into how they earned their living. By mid-century, the notion that people worked in large measure to satisfy personal goals and interests became prevalent (Holland, 1958). Fast-forwarding to the current era certainly underscores the growing complexity of career choice and development theories (e.g., Dawis, 2002; Lent et al., 2002; Savickas, 2002). Yet remaining at the core of many of the most common theories is the explicit attention provided to people who can develop and implement their plans about their working lives with little attention devoted to people who have little or no volition in their choice of occupation.

Person–Environment Fit Theories

Forming the motivational core of person–environment fit theories is the fundamental idea that people strive for work settings that are consistent with their skills, abilities, interests, and values (Dawis, 2002; Holland, 1997). Once an individual is able to locate a reasonably good fit within the occupational world, there is an assumption that he or she will be motivated to engage in these activities because the tasks would tend to be self-reinforcing and intrinsically interesting. Moreover, a parallel assumption exists that posits that young people with goals and plans that are consistent with their interests will be more engaged with school and will be motivated to extend effort to reach their goals (Blustein et al., 2000). In other words, people who work at tasks that are congruent with their psychological and cognitive attributes will have a much greater likelihood of being satisfied with their work and will also be more likely to be intrinsically interested in their job. The school-to-work movement of the 1990s and similar initiatives in career and vocational education have sought to help youth become more motivated in their educational tasks by helping them to realize that greater levels of education will yield more choice and satisfaction in their adult working lives (Blustein et al., 2000).

In the theory of work adjustment (Dawis, 2002), a comprehensive theoretical system was developed that seeks to explain the motivational aspects of career-choice behavior. Dawis elaborated on the notion of needs, which refers to underlying physiological and/or psychological attributes that can be deficits or may, if the need is fulfilled, promote one's well-being. The central striving among people interacting within the occupational context, according to Dawis, is to seek out satisfaction and ideally correspondence in the satisfaction experienced by both the person and the work context.

Developmental Theories

A similar set of notions underlies the life-span, life-space developmental theories of Super (1957; Super et al., 1996). In Super's classic text (1957), he noted that "opportunity to use skills and knowledge helps to make work activities interesting" (p. 10). Moreover, Super observed that "opportunity for self-expression seems to be more important at higher than lower occupational levels" (p. 9). These statements create the conceptual infrastructure for the view that work has the potential to allow for expression of one's inner attributes, beliefs, interests, and abilities in a work context. However, Super foreshadowed many of the premises of my position in this book by noting that this sort of work life generally is not equally available to people across the socioeconomic spectrum. One of Super's core propositions, which is reiterated in the more recent extension of Super's work by Savickas (2002), is that the degree of job satisfaction that an individual may experience is proportionate to the extent to which the job provides an outlet for one's self-concept. Embedded in the self-concept is the unique configuration of attributes, such as interests, values, skills, and attitudes related to self and work. Yet, the developmental position, in the original version by Super and the updated version by Savickas, does acknowledge that the good life of a satisfying career is not available to all workers. The question of how to formally and inclusively construct a psychology of working, however, has not been answered to date, thereby leaving traditional vocational psychological theory and practice in a moral and intellectual quandary. In effect, the challenge that is embedded in career choice and development theories is that we have neglected the modal worker in our world—the worker who has little access to adequate schools and supportive contexts that would allow for the development of skills, knowledge, and talents that might facilitate a working life that can, in fact, satisfy one's goals and dreams.

Social Cognitive Career Theory

Recent theoretical contributions by Lent et al. (2002) have sought to incorporate the context of the individual more explicitly into the motivational explanations of various aspects of career choice and development. In describing the career choice process, Lent et al. affirmed the central view that has characterized many theories to date—namely, that people will seek out jobs that are consistent with their interests. However, they noted that contextual influences may constrain or facilitate one's capacity to find work that is consistent with one's interests. Lent and his colleagues also delved into the realm of task performance, which has generally been an issue of interest primarily for I/O psychologists. Deriving some of their core ideas from the work motivation literature by Vroom (1964), Lent et al. argued that performance attainments, which are related to one's self-efficacy beliefs and outcome expectations, affect a worker's capacity to perform on the job. As such, the Lent et al. social cognitive theory has explored the motivational dimension of vocational behavior. Unfortunately, this theoretical framework has not yet effectively explored the lives of individuals whose motivation to work is primarily externally derived and not related to interests or self-perceived abilities.

Social Constructionist Perspectives

The infusion of social constructionist theories has been a welcome addition to the intellectual framework of vocational psychology. For example, Young and his colleagues (e.g., Young, Valach, & Collin, 2002) have articulated a contextual approach to the understanding of career choice and development that has been instrumental in expanding the conceptual horizons of vocational psychology. In relation to the motivational questions raised at the outset of this chapter, Young et al. have developed a contextualist action theory of career that contains a number of relevant assumptions about the nature of motivational processes in vocational behavior. One of the core elements of the social constructionist position advanced by Young and his colleagues is that behavior is rooted in a social context that relies on language to furnish meaning to events. In general, Young et al. proposed that a complete understanding of career behavior must incorporate the notion of goal-directed action, which is defined as "the construct that allows us to keep all the pertinent information together so that we can understand the meaning of our own and others' behavior" (2002, p. 214). Another relevant feature of the Young et al. theory is the inclusion of an explicit role for emotion within the career development process. Following Kidd's (1998) contribution, Young and his colleagues suggested that emotion is actually quite interpersonal and deeply rooted in one's context. While the precise role that emotion plays in the motivational aspects of work has not been explored in depth, the inclusion of emotions is an important contribution, one that will be critical in creating a rich perspective within the psychology of working.

Given the assumptions of the social constructionist position (e.g., Gergen, 1999), which so eloquently grounds our understanding of career theory into an explicitly contextual framework (e.g., Blustein et al., 2004; Stead, 2004), it seems clear that issues of motivation and the meaning derived from work are complex and multidetermined. (For further details on social constructionist thinking and the psychology of working, please see chapter 7.) For example, one of the hallmark attributes of the social constructionist position is that reality is co-constructed in relationships and within the broader framework of culture and history. Following the social constructionist position, I suggest that caution be used in making inferences about such issues as the meaning that one derives about work. In this context, the notion that people work in order to express their interests or their self-concepts needs to be understood within the context of the inner experiences of individuals and their cultural and social milieu. Moreover, the assumption that jobs that require less complex skills and knowledge are inherently disinteresting merits careful scrutiny. Indeed, one of my hopes is that the psychology of working will stimulate the needed research on the meaning of work and the motivational aspects of work experiences.

Conclusion

When considered collectively, the prominent trend that emerges in the existing bodies of theory in career choice and development is that people who can find a good fit for their interests and personal attributes are more likely to be satisfied and ultimately more intrinsically interested in their work. In contrast, people who are not able to find a good match more likely work for extrinsic reasons; in other words, they work to survive and to connect to the broader fabric of social and economic relations that give structure to many aspects of contemporary life (Wilson, 1996). However, people who are involved in tasks that are not intrinsically interesting or rewarding are less likely to engage in their work tasks without the external rewards of money and the value of engaging in regular, structured work experiences. The major career theories that have provided the conceptual infrastructure for vocational counseling and career development have devoted little attention to the motivational processes of workers who have not been able to follow the grand career narrative with its trajectory of increasingly more responsible and more satisfying jobs. In effect, the net result of the nearly exclusive focus on choosing work based on one's interests and self-concept is that our field has, for the most part, ignored the experiences of workers who do not have this option. However, selected aspects of the motivational experiences of people who are not able to seek out work that is consistent with their interests have been examined to a somewhat greater extent within the industrial/organizational literature, which is explored in the next section.

The Motivational Aspects of Traditional Industrial/Organizational Theories

Given the focus on selecting personnel who will be dedicated and committed to their jobs, I/O psychology has developed a number of conceptual frameworks that may help to delineate the complex nature of motivation within the workplace (e.g., Landy, 1989; Vroom, 1964). Landy's view is that the basic principles of human motivation, which have been developed for the most part within experimental and theoretical psychology, would be relevant in the work context. In his text, he describes four basic motivational theories that have dominated I/O psychology in recent decades.

Need-Based Theories

The first of these models is need theory, which is best represented by Maslow's (1943) need hierarchy. This hierarchy, which was reviewed in chapter 3, posits that people are initially motivated to satisfy their needs for survival (physiological and safety needs), which, if fulfilled, provide people with an opportunity to satisfy needs for love, esteem, and self-actualization, re-spectively. Landy reported that empirical research does not generally con-form to the overall hierarchy outlined by Maslow (e.g., Hall & Nougaim, 1968). Another need-based theory presented by Landy is Herzberg's (1966) motivator-hygiene or two-factor theory. In contrast to Maslow, who proposed a detailed hierarchy that has been difficult to document in research, Herzberg argued that two primary levels of human functioning exist—motivation-seek-ing and hygiene-seeking. The motivation-seeking component refers to activi-ties that are higher order or more intrinsic to the individual. The hygiene-seeking component refers to the maintenance needs, which capture such ele-ments within the workplace as pay, job security, safety, and the like.

Instrumentality Theory

The second set of motivational theories summarized by Landy (1989) falls un-der the rubric of instrumentality models. Perhaps the best known of these the-ories within both vocational and I/O psychology is Vroom's (1964) VIE theory. In Vroom's model, the "V" stands for valence, which refers to the psy-chological attraction or repulsion that a given activity evokes in an individual. The "I" refers to instrumentality, which is defined as the extent to which a given activity is instrumental in obtaining an outcome of relevance to an indi-vidual. The "E" defines the expectancy component, which refers to the degree to which an individual expects that a particular activity will yield a specific and expected outcome. As indicated earlier, Vroom's work has been quite influ-ential in both I/O psychology and now in vocational psychology as exemplified by its most recent application to social cognitive career theory (Lent et al., 1994). In short, Vroom's model suggests that motivation at work is deter-mined by the individual's perception of the extent to which a given effort has a high probability of leading to a desired outcome. This outcome would, in turn, result in yet other outcomes, which the individual values. The Vroom model is relevant in understanding why people might expend more effort in a given job context as compared with another job context. In that context, the VIE theory is instructive to organizational psychologists and managers who are seeking to maximize employee output and reduce turnover.

Balance Theory

The third cluster of motivational theories reviewed by Landy (1989) is repre-sented by balance theories. These perspectives are based on the assumption that people are motivated to maintain a balance in their psychological functioning. Originally derived from cognitive dissonance research (e.g., Festinger, 1957), balance theories propose that people strive to reduce tension. The most prominent of these perspectives in the domain of work motivation is the contribution by Adams (1965). Using complex statistical analyses, Adams argued that people create ratios in which their inputs and outputs are compared with perceived input–output ratios for others. If the individual perceives equality in these ratios, then no tension is thought to exist; however, if inequality is perceived, the resulting situation is thought to be inequitable, hence evoking tension.

Reinforcement Theory

The fourth cluster of theories summarized by Landy (1989) is the reinforcement perspective, which is derived from behavioral or learning theories. This model has not engendered as much scholarly research within I/O psychology, but it has generated some applications within work settings. The use of differential reinforcement schedules has been applied to organizations to enhance productivity (e.g., Pritchard, Hollenback, & DeLeo, 1980). The relative dearth of research using strictly behavioral models, coupled with the plethora of cognitive models, underscores the need for complex perspectives that incorporate cognitive components of psychological functioning within the I/O approach to work motivation.

Conclusion

When considered collectively, the major motivational models within I/O psychology share the overall objectives of their discipline, which is to understand the behavior of workers within the organizational context. From this vantage point, these theories are both informative and useful. However, they do not address the broader macro-level issues of how people find meaning in their work and how work that is inherently denigrating or disinteresting can become more meaningful. A major theme that has been conveyed thus far in this book is that an inclusive perspective of working necessitates a broad examination of the social, economic, and cultural context of the life experiences of workers. One way of exploring the context is to place the culture of the worker into the figure of our perceptional field as opposed to the ground.

Culturally Informed Views of Motivation

A culturally informed view of work motivation has been articulated by Triandis, who has sought to differentiate between individualist and collectivist cultures. The following passage by Triandis (2002) summarizes how the cultural context likely influences the nature of work motivation:

> Individualism and collectivism are reflected in the goals of members of the culture. People in individualist cultures tend to have self-actualizing goals; those from collectivist cultures are oriented in achieving for the sake of others. As goals have important implications for work motivation, culture too has implications for work motivation. (p. 110)

The distinction that Triandis highlights with respect to the individualism-collectivism dimension of a culture has broad implications for our consideration of work motivation. For individuals with an orientation toward greater collectivism, such as people in Asian and African contexts, working takes on a more social tone, with greater emphasis on "cooperation, endurance, persistence, obedience, duty, in-group harmony, personalized relationships, order, and self-control" (Triandis, 2002, p. 112). In contrast, people who are from individualist cultures (such as those found in North America and Europe), the emphasis on working is placed on "self-realization, self-glory, pleasure, competition, and fair exchange" (Triandis, p. 112). Reviewing these cultural attributes reveals that many of the existing models within I/O psychology have been constructed around individualist assumptions about life. With some notable exceptions (see Hall, 1996, for an overview of a relational approach to careers), I/O psychologists have tended to assume that the individualist framework is perhaps the most adaptive, albeit not entirely universal. Yet, as we have seen in recent innovations in the organizational world (e.g., Grantham, 2000; Hall, 1996), the more effective and productive work contexts are increasingly relying on collectivist assumptions about human behavior. For example, in the positive vision of the future of work detailed by Grantham, one of the keys to a successful organization is an affirmation of many of the attributes of the collectivist culture detailed by Triandis. Thus, the workplace envisioned by Grantham is one in which the focus on individualism is replaced by a focus on collective values and relational connections. One of the goals of this approach is to restore an important sense of motivation for working that has been diminished as the workplace of the 20th century moves into a different shape and form in the 21st century.

The contributions of Triandis (2002) certainly help to advance our thinking about the motivational aspects of working within an organizational context.

However, many of the same problems inherent in the vocational psychological analyses of working are also evident in the I/O perspectives. Even with the infusion of Triandis' cultural perspective, we are still left wondering how workers can feel connected to their tasks if their tasks are not intrinsically interesting or fulfilling. One of the conceptual tools that can help to fill this gap is the motivational model by Deci and Ryan (1985), which has the potential to explicate the motivational elements for workers across the spectrum, including those with hierarchical careers and those who work primarily to make a living for themselves and their families.

A Self-Determination View of Working

In contrast to the motivational theories that have been detailed thus far, Deci and Ryan (1985; Ryan & Deci, 2000) have developed a theoretical framework for motivation that is constructed with careful attention to both human agency and the critical importance of social, cultural, and relational contexts. The work by Deci and Ryan, which is generally known as self-determination theory (SDT), began initially as a counterpoint to the deterministic views of the radical behavioral theories that were prevalent a number of decades ago. Rather than viewing behavior as an outcome of external events or inner drives (which were reflected in learning theory and psychoanalytic theory, respectively), Deci and Ryan argued that many (but certainly not all) aspects of human behavior are potentially motivated from an intrinsic or internalized position. For example, some of the early research by Deci (e.g., 1975) found that extrinsic rewards often diminished intrinsic motivation.

Assumptions of Self-Determination Theory

Building on these findings, Deci and Ryan (1985) articulated a comprehensive theory of self-determination. SDT has a direct allegiance to the movements in the 1960s and 1970s, often falling under the rubric of humanistic psychology, which sought to understand the full scope of human functioning without the constraining lens of determinism that had characterized major psychological theories of the era. The contribution of Sheldon, Williams, and Joiner (2003) provides an informative and illuminating understanding of the striving for self-determination:

> Self-determination theory is particularly interested in what humanistically and existentially oriented theorists might call "authenticity." The theory proposes

that people sometimes act out of their deepest, most wholehearted and growth oriented motives and needs, while at other times they act out of feelings of pressure, coercion, or bad faith .... (E)arly versions of SDT simply contrasted intrinsic (that is, authentic) motivation with extrinsic motivation (behavior undertaken to obtain anticipated rewards or avoid punishment). But this dichotomy proved to be too simple; obviously, people can still feel authentic even while engaging in nonintrinsically motivated behavior. For example, a man might feel considerable autonomy and sense of choice even as he changes his baby's (disgusting) diaper! (p. 20)

The points highlighted by Sheldon et al. underscore one of the clear attributes of SDT and its relevance to a psychology of working. As I have noted throughout this book, working often can be quite disinteresting, physically arduous, and even painful as well as psychologically denigrating. (Work is not, however, unidimensional. Work also has the potential to satisfy and indeed, when supportive conditions are in place, work can create the context for genuine self-expression.) Naturally, many people work in order to pay their bills with little or no hope of any more pleasure, satisfaction, or meaning. The question that SDT raises, however, is to what extent our knowledge about the motivational processes inherent in human behavior can help psychologists, educators, social scientists, and policymakers to create working environments that are more conducive to authentic and self-determined functioning. Prior to exploring this issue in depth, some additional assumptions of SDT are reviewed in the following points:

■ Intrinsic motivation is thought to be an evolved attribute of human development. In other words, human beings are naturally curious and seek out new activities, tasks, and experiences.
■ Intrinsic motivation is best sustained in a context that facilitates autonomy, competence, and relational support.
■ Intrinsically motivating activities can be undermined if they are linked to external contingencies.
■ Individuals use specific self-regulation processes to integrate extrinsically motivated activities into their psychological structures.

As reflected in these points, SDT seeks to describe a wide array of behaviors that range from highly intrinsically motivating to behaviors that are far less interesting and compelling. In effect, SDT furnishes a conceptual framework for understanding how extrinsically motivated behavior can become part of a self-determination motivational system. Thus, self-determination does not refer exclusively to those behaviors that are regulated by intrinsic motivation. In reality, many activities that people initiate are done primarily to fulfill some external need or influence, including, naturally, many aspects of working. The SDT framework includes a broad spectrum of differences in motivation ranging from amotivation to the highly intrinsically motivated state that is characteristic of activities that we engage in solely out of interest and curiosity. In the work domain, the "grand career narrative" view of career choice and development assumed that people had access to working activities that could be intrinsically motivating. Indeed, this aspiration is still evident in various literatures, ranging from self-help books (Bolles & Bolles, 2005), to traditional vocational psychological theories (e.g., Holland, 1997; Lent et al., 2002), and to the prevalent perspectives within I/O psychology (e.g., Landy, 1989). Yet, the material that has been covered thus far in this book, coupled with a growing literature in the social sciences and popular press (e.g., Bowe et al., 2000; Gini, 2000; Harmon, 1994; M. S. Richardson, 1993; Sennett, 1998; Wilson, 1996), suggests that work is far from intrinsically motivating for many people around the globe. Although it would be ideal if the world could provide opportunities for self-expression and interesting tasks for all contemporary workers, this vision is far from realization. (As I detail further in chapter 10, I believe that more can be done by government officials, educators, business leaders, policy analysts, and social scientists to expand the proportion of people who have access to work that is rewarding and meaningful.)

Applications of Self-Determination Theory

Recent research and theoretical efforts have applied SDT to the understanding of success in organizational contexts (e.g., Baard, 2002) and educational efforts (e.g., Reeve, 2001), underscoring the potential of SDT in applied, real-life contexts. The contribution by Baard, for example, described the use of SDT in a study conducted at a major investment banking firm. Using a post-hoc, cross-sectional methodology, Baard found that workers who were primarily motivated by intrinsic needs and who reported autonomy reported higher levels of work performance and adjustment. This finding has been corroborated in numerous other studies in which variations in motivational orientations, using the SDT rubric, have been associated in predictable ways with work-related attitudes and behaviors (Deci & Ryan, 2001). However, for the most part, these investigations have been conducted from the macro-level perspective of I/O psychology in which the focus has been on the overall functioning of an organization (see Baard, 2002, for further details).

In the educational context, Reeve (2002) reviewed an extensive literature that has documented the impact of SDT in teaching and learning. The major themes of the research on educational applications of SDT are that teachers benefit from autonomy-based instruction, which seems to motivate students in their academic tasks. In addition, Reeve observed that the research and theory in this area has indicated that students who are placed in autonomy-based learning environments do, in fact, perform better in educational environments. These findings, when considered collectively, do suggest that SDT has significant implications in understanding motivation in applied contexts. In fact, the Deci and Ryan (2000) collection documents extensive examples of how SDT can be used in a host of settings. Moreover, SDT has been found to be instrumental in facilitating growth in people within specific contexts. In the section that follows, I review the processes that facilitate greater internalization of extrinsically motivated activities so that they can help to promote self-determination.

The Internalization Process

In SDT, internalization refers to a process whereby individuals seek to transform external expectations or demands into internally consistent values, beliefs, and self-regulating processes (Deci & Ryan, 2000). The internalization process does not transform an extrinsically motivating experience into an intrinsically motivating experience; rather, assuming that certain conditions are fulfilled, extrinsically motivating experiences may become less onerous and, indeed, may become more meaningful as they are internalized into one's psychological and cognitive structures. Ryan and Deci (2000) charted a process of four stages of internalization, which are summarized in the following sections.

External Regulation. The most externally oriented mode of extrinsic motivation in the SDT model is known as external regulation. Relying primarily on an external locus of causality, the external regulation mode is the dialectical opposite of intrinsically motivated behavior. Individuals who are motivated by external regulation essentially behave because of external rewards; if they do not, aversive consequences may result and/or the individual may not obtain the resources needed to survive (Ryan & Deci, 2000). External regulation would describe many working people who obtain no inherent satisfaction or rewards from their tasks. Rather, they work primarily because they are obligated to, by circumstances such as the need to earn money to survive, or by authorities who may punish them if they do not work. The following passage by a Mexican immigrant to the southwestern part of the United States captures some of the sense of external regulation that is characterized by this motivational status:

> The silver mine where I worked was about 900 meters deep. It had fourteen or fifteen levels. It was very hot down there, and we would work half naked, carrying sacks all day long. At times there was no air. The water would run though the ditches, and it was so hot that it would vaporize. It was dangerous work. My father ruined his life working in the copper mines of Arizona .... (Martínez, 1994, p. 151)

As this narrative suggests, some jobs exist that are purely unpleasant and even painful. Working in a hot mine in the hot dessert of Arizona clearly sounds like the sort of activity that one would have trouble ever experiencing as an authentic, self-determined task. Yet people do jobs like this each and every day. The Deci and Ryan (1985) theory, while clearly contextual in its assumptions and manifestations, does not offer easy answers to this man and to his countless peers throughout the world. However, the SDT perspective does underscore the challenges that exist for people who are working in jobs that are primarily externally regulated. As we shall see shortly, there are some options, suggested by SDT, for providing greater support for a worker like the one in this vignette. The reality, though, is that work that is this arduous may be difficult to internalize into a self-regulating system without access to external rewards.

Introjected Regulation. The next phase of the internalization process, known as introjected regulation, also is based on an external locus of causality, albeit it is somewhat less extrinsic than the external regulation phase. Individuals who are functioning from an introjected regulation position are motivated by psychological dimensions such as self-esteem and the avoidance of guilt and anxiety (Ryan & Deci, 2000). Moreover, the tasks are still not yet integrated into a self-regulating system in that people are motivated to avoid painful feelings or to enhance vulnerable aspects of their sense of self.

A number of unemployed clients I have worked with would comment on how they often enjoyed the freedom that came with the loss of an especially tedious or arduous job. However, given the social press to work and the sense of guilt for using their savings or relying on family members for their sustenance, they would often reflect on feelings of shame and despair about not working, despite the pleasure of pursuing some of their hobbies and social activities.

Identified Regulation. The third phase in the internalization process is known as identified regulation, which is characterized by an increasingly more internalized locus of causality. The essence of this phase is that the individual engages in a given activity because of the outcomes of the activity. For example, an individual who is engaged in work that allows her to support her family and to receive medical benefits may in fact begin to identify with her goals in a manner that will become more self-regulated. The following vignette reflects comments from a participant in Newman's (1999) book entitled *No Shame in My Game.* This book, which was described earlier in chapter 3, describes the adaptive features of inner-city youth who work in fast-food restaurants. Latoya's comments reflect some degree of identification with her job, which is framed to a large extent by her awareness of the challenges of her current life circumstances:

> This was my first real job .... I take it seriously, you know .... It means a lot to me. It give you—what's the word I'm lookin' for? Security blanket. 'Cuz, a lot of married women, like when I was married to my husband, when he left on me. If [Jason] leave now, I can deal with the load because I work. [Jason] help me—we split the bills half and half. But if he leaves, I'm not gonna be, well, "Oh my God, I have no money." No, I have a little bank account; I got my little nest egg. You know, so it does mean a lot to me. I wouldn't just up and leave my job. (Newman, 1999, pp. 69–70)

As Latoya recounts in this vignette, she has identified with the security aspects of her job, which have helped her to feel safer in her world. While she does not necessarily enjoy all of her tasks at work, there is an aspect of her narrative that suggests that she is deriving some inherent structure for her life via her work. However, it is important to note that her job is very likely not intrinsically interesting to her and may not ever be intrinsically interesting.

Although I am exploring some of the ways in which Latoya's work life can be part of her self-regulation system, I am not suggesting that SDT be used to placate poor and working class people with limited vocational choices that will be inherently unrewarding with only the most modest of financial rewards. In contrast, my position is that our society needs to do more to consider the overall life experiences of all workers and potential workers, not just the privileged and affluent. The use of SDT theory, as is detailed later in this chapter, requires careful attention to the development and maintenance of supportive contextual factors. As such, SDT theory provides valuable knowledge for the development and implementation of systems and policies that can enhance working experiences.

Integrated Regulation.   Integrated regulation reflects the most autonomous and regulated of the phases of the internalization process. Characterized by an internal locus of causality, integrated regulation describes behaviors and efforts that are fully integrated into one's self-regulating systems. These behaviors are generally enacted because the individual has integrated the values and outcomes into one's motivational processes. However, the actual tasks are still not intrinsically interesting, although they are autonomously initiated. The following excerpt from a hat saleswoman, recounted in the Bowe et al. (2000) collection, conveys important aspects of integrated regulation:

> Surprisingly, though, I kind of like it [working in a hat shop]. I like being busy, I like helping people—if they are nice—and I like the excitement of the sale. I'd never had a sales job before, but I think that I am kind of a natural .... I don't know how to explain how I ended up here. I just don't know. When I was young, I thought that I was going to be a dancer. But realistically, I can't be a dancer. I was a fabric designer for a long time, but I hated that industry. I think that, unfortunately, the fact that I have been here as long as I have is a testament to the quality of the job as it is to my complacency. I mean, this job is only meaningful to someone who needs my assistance. I don't think that being a salesperson has any meaning at all .... If I really figure out what I want to do, I can do it. I've learned that from working here. (pp. 163, 166–167)

This vignette describes a woman whose job is not inherently interesting; at the same time, her experience at work is not terrible or disdainful. Rather, her working experience lies in the netherworld between the positive valence that we all hope to experience in our work and the sheer pain of tedious activity or exposure to aversive conditions or people that many people dread in their working lives. The hat saleswoman describes some internalized aspects of her working life that are satisfying, such as making a sale. Yet, she is able to reflect on her own questions of the meaning of her job, which is reflective of the lack of intrinsic motivation that she experiences. Although the hat saleswoman describes her interest in style and fashion, she claims that she is not a "hat person." In some sense, one might suggest that this individual is ambivalent about her job, which indeed may be the case. However, in relation to the motivational questions that are raised in this chapter, the hat saleswoman has internalized many important features of her job, including a commitment to her role as a competent saleswoman and her dedication to being helpful to her customers. The locus of her regulation at work, therefore, seems to be primarily located within herself, although it is clear that she is engaging in these tasks in order to make a living. At this point in the internalization process, individuals are motivated increasingly out of interest in the activity itself. Although the activity may not have originally evoked intrinsic interest, integrated regulation results in an experience wherein the external rewards are far less prominent and the activity or task becomes internally motivating.

Implications of Internalization. Ryan and Deci (2000) are clear in stating that the phases of internalization are not a hierarchical developmental process in which individuals pass through each stage on their way to a more autonomous and self-regulating life. Rather, they view the internalization process as a way of describing variations in the extrinsic motivation process, thereby avoiding simplistic dichotomous distinctions among motivational orientations. The internalization process offers a heuristically and conceptually solid foundation for considering how humans manage to engage in the wide array of tasks that are necessary to earn a living, with the acknowledgment that many of these tasks are not intrinsically interesting.

The implications of the internalization process for the psychology of working are extensive. As reflected in the material presented thus far, some aspects of extrinsically motivating experiences may, in fact, be internalized into one's overall value and belief system. For example, workers who have been engaged in activities or tasks that result in actions that contradict one's own value system may be less likely to experience rewards and satisfaction in their working lives. Moreover, the SDT framework has detailed specific contextual elements that need to be in place in order for an experience to become more self-determined and self-regulating. By applying these contextual factors to our analysis of the psychology of working, it may be possible to develop ideas about how to construct working experiences that may be more rewarding and satisfying.

The Contextual Frame of Self-Determination Theory

A central tenet of SDT is that individuals who are able to engage in activities that are self-regulated are more likely to experience greater satisfaction and are also more likely to relate these activities to their broader life goals (Ryan & Deci, 2000). In the research that has emerged from SDT, greater internalization has been associated with "more behavioral effectiveness, greater volitional persistence, enhanced subjective well-being, and better assimilation of the individual within his or her social group" (Ryan & Deci, 2000, p. 73). Ryan and Deci are clear, however, that internalized externally motivating activities are still very distinct from intrinsically motivating activities. Intrinsically motivating activities are characterized by the experience of authenticity and an internalized sense of commitment to the given task.

Ryan and Deci have developed an empirically supported model of specific contextual attributes that facilitate the internalization of motivational orientations. In short, they have proposed that individuals are more likely to internalize externally regulated behaviors, provided that three specific needs are fulfilled: autonomy, relatedness, and competence. SDT offers the psychology of working a potentially viable means of thinking about the lives of people who have not had opportunities to seek out jobs that are intrinsically interesting. Moreover, I believe that an exploration of the three contextual attributes of internalization may furnish scholars and policymakers with the conceptual tools to improve the conditions of working, which may in turn enhance the overall quality of life for many workers across the globe.

Motivation, therefore, is contingent upon the array of resources from one's social, familial, and psychological contexts. In effect, the internalization process is dependent on the context and how the individual interprets it. Moreover, I contend that the availability of these contextual factors may be a positive attribute for many individuals who are confined to jobs that are not intrinsically interesting, provided that the supportive needs outlined by SDT are in place and that the job tasks and goals of the organization are consistent with the worker's values. However, I want to caution that internalization, in of itself, cannot change many of the realities that exist in the world of work currently, including harsh and unsafe environments, lack of sufficient work for people, abusive supervisors, and inadequate pay and benefits. Still, exploring the relevant aspects of SDT has the potential to help many workers find ways of making their working lives somewhat more relevant in their lives. As we shall explore later in this chapter and in subsequent chapters, many of the contextual factors involve considerable social and economic reforms. In the sections that follow, I review these contextual attributes in greater depth and relate them to the working lives of people who have not had an opportunity to seek out intrinsically interesting jobs.

Need for Autonomy. Ryan and Deci (2000) proposed that the need for autonomy is important for an individual to experience a sense of authenticity in a given task. The essence of the Ryan and Deci's position is detailed in the following quote:

The experience of autonomy facilitates internalization and, in particular, is a critical element for a regulation to be integrated. Contexts can yield external regulation if there are salient rewards or threats and the person feels competent enough to comply; contexts can yield introjected regulation if a relevant reference group endorses the activity and the person feels competent and related; but contexts can yield autonomous regulation only if they are autonomy supportive, thus allowing the person to feel competent, related, and autonomous. To integrate a regulation, people must grasp its meaning and synthesize that meaning with respect to their other goals and values. Such deep, holistic processing (Kuhl & Fuhrmann, 1998) is facilitated by a sense of choice, volition, and freedom from excessive external pressure toward behaving or thinking a certain way. In this sense, support for autonomy allows individuals to actively transform values into their own. (Ryan & Deci, 2000, pp. 73–74)

As reflected in this description, the experience of autonomy in the internalization process has the potential to transform an externally regulated experience into a far more self-determined experience. Perhaps the best example of autonomy at work can be found by those whose responsibilities are very much linked to their intellect and creativity. In the study by Gardner, Csikszentimihalyi, and Damon (2001), the lives of geneticists and journalists are explored to discern the meaning of "good work." According to Gardner et al., good work reflects high-quality contributions that result in positive improvements in society. Both geneticists and journalists, naturally, would be likely to have access to the "grand career narrative," thereby offering them an opportunity to develop meaningful and rewarding work lives. In an excerpt from the Gardner et al. volume, James D. Watson, the famous geneticist, was one of the participants in their narrative analysis of the meaning of good work. Watson's description of his working life, as follows, conveys autonomy in a very evocative manner:

> One of the great things about this job is that I can have a meeting about anything that interests me. Because we were given this estate nearby where we have sort of thirty person meetings ... so I think that I've got the best job .... The wonderful thing was that I was the boss and you didn't have to worry about whether the Dean felt the Department should have balance ....
> (Gardner et al., 2001, p. 82)

In relation to many other passages in this book, the comments from Watson provide a sharp contrast to the passages from workers who do not experience such extensive and pervasive feelings of control and autonomy in their work lives. Yet Watson and other scientists, scholars, writers, and artists also form part of the complex tapestry of workers and merit our attention in an inclusive psychology of working. Indeed, the type of autonomy reflected in Watson's passage suggests intrinsic motivation, representing the "gold standard" of motivational experiences. It is important to note that Watson's experience conveys the vast potential for self-determination and inner satisfaction that working can provide. And indeed, Watson's voice and others with his talents and knowledge clearly belong in the complex mosaic of workers' voices that is presented in this book. Yet, the level of privilege that Watson has in his job is certainly not common, as is conveyed in the following passage from an automobile parts specialist in the Bowe et al. (2000) collection:

> I sell Honda auto parts. That's my job, and I've been working with automobiles in one way or another for twenty years, but I don't consider it my life. Not by a long shot. It keeps my family fed, but it interferes with what I'd like to be doing, which is painting, drawing, sculpting, making little airplanes.
>
> I wanted to be an artist. And I did pursue that for a while, but I became disillusioned with it in college …. So I gave it up and moved to Dallas, came here and got married …. What I do is sit behind a counter and I sell parts, just Honda parts for Honda cars. I get a salary and a little commission on each sale.
>
> It's a good job. There's problems, but it's not a perfect world. There's problems with everything. I've done enough different things to know what works for me. And what's good about this job is, first of all, I make a good income. Second, it's honest—I know my parts and I know Honda makes them well …. And third—and this is very important to me—I have a lot of downtime, lots of slow time that I can devote to my projects—just little things to keep my creativity alive. Lately, I've been making little airplanes. I make the wings out of plastic from warranty bags …. I build 'em then take 'em home, and put 'em up in the cabinets around the house …. We've [my boss and I] reached a point where he doesn't usually bother me as long as I do everything I'm supposed to do, all my duties ….
>
> You don't need to work yourself to death to be happy. I've got a good retirement package. I'm looking forward to that. I'll have more free time to do my projects and be myself. It'll be sweet. (pp. 79–84)

This example contrasts sharply with the Watson vignette, yet the comparison also offers insights into the complexities of motivation at work. In Watson's case, the interest is intrinsic and is clearly a major driving force in his work life. The Honda employee represents a more internalized pattern of motivation in which the actual tasks are not particularly interesting. However, the autonomy provided to him in his job has given him a great opportunity to pursue intrinsic interests. This passage from the Honda employee eloquently describes the experiences of an individual who was able to create a sense of autonomy in his work life literally out of material that is considered "waste" in his job. He is not very interested in the actual tasks of this job, but he has managed to find a position that allows him to engage in activities that he finds more intrinsically interesting. The fact that this worker has an opportunity to engage in tasks that he is curious about is not always possible, but it does suggest some of the ways that extrinsically motivating jobs may become more self-regulating for people. This individual has managed to create a combination of leisure and work that is subtly woven together and tolerated by his supervisor, provided that he is able to complete his tasks in the auto parts office.

In both of these examples, the opportunity for autonomy at work has the potential to engage the worker in a profound and meaningful manner. Both James Watson and the auto parts specialist have been able to manifest their own career interests at work, in effect, enacting their own version of the grand career narrative. It is important to note that the possibility of expressing one's own interests at work is not always necessary for one to experience autonomy at work. The following example from a steel worker describes the role of her union in helping her to feel autonomous at work:

> I'm a Heister operator. That's really just a generic name for steel hauling .... When I started it was just a job, and it paid well. I'd never really had too much experience with unions. I knew you got jobs; I didn't know what unions really had to do with them. But when '95 hit [a strike], that was it. I saw what the union meant to my job. Since then, it's been part of my job.
>
> You have to organize to have a good work environment. You make it a good place to work. You make it a place without rumors, but with information ....
>
> Whatever you do, I've always taught my kids, you're not doing it for them, you're doing it for yourself. You have to respect your work, not who you're doing it for. This job is no more meaningful than any other job except it means something to me. (Bowe et al., 2000, pp. 37, 41–43)

This passage describes the development of autonomy in perhaps a more traditional fashion within industrial and post-industrial nations. The development of labor unions certainly has played a major role in furnishing workers with a context that values and ideally manifests autonomy (MacDonald & Sirianni, 1996). The degree to which labor unions are still able to provide this critical role in the lives of unskilled and semi-skilled workers has increasingly diminished over the past few decades within the United States, Britain, Australia, Korea, and Japan along with other countries (Bamber & Lansbury, 1998). However, in other parts of the world (e.g., Norway, Sweden, and Austria), labor unions have maintained their strength (Bamber & Lansbury, 1998) and offer opportunities for not only autonomy, but for safer and perhaps even more stable working conditions. The three preceding passages suggest the complex pathways that individuals and organizations can take to foster autonomy at work. Furthermore, these vignettes convey the central role that autonomy plays in the process of developing a self-determined level of motivation at work.

Need for Relatedness.   Similar to the need for social connection that forms one of the three pillars of the psychology of working (Blustein, 2001a, 2001b; Flum, 2001; Schultheiss, 2003), Ryan and Deci (2000) proposed that internalization can be facilitated when individuals feel connected to others in a meaningful way within their specific context. Based on considerable empirical research both within the SDT tradition (e.g., Deci & Ryan, 2000; Ryan, Stiller, & Lynch, 1994) and within career development and organizational psychology (e.g., Blustein et al., 1995; Hall, 1996; Schultheiss et al., 2001), the experience of relatedness and interpersonal connection has been associated with positive outcomes in work-oriented contexts. With respect to the internalization process, Ryan and Deci follow the tradition of Bowlby (1988) in arguing that our need for relatedness is an outgrowth of our evolution, which has blossomed in large measure due to our success as social organisms. The need for relatedness, which was detailed in chapter 4, provides one of the building blocks of a context that supports the development of internalization.

Ryan and Deci believe that people have an inherent need for connection and that the availability of this connection helps to create the conditions for the internalization of self-regulation. A clear and discernible sense of relatedness functions to provide individuals with the emotional support that is needed to feel connected within a given context. Individuals who are working in a particular environment in which their needs for interpersonal relatedness are affirmed and fulfilled have a greater likelihood of experiencing greater self-regulation. For example, a worker from a Pacific Rim nation who is involved in the manufacturing of textiles in her home country may find her job to be quite dull when considered without attention to her context. However, if she enjoys her colleagues and has supportive and caring supervisors, one would think that this worker would have an easier time internalizing the external regulation that functions to modulate her motivation. Thus, the factory worker with greater emotional support at work may feel fulfilled in a psychological sense and may be better able to engage in work tasks that are not inherently rewarding. It is not uncommon to hear workers describe their satisfaction in seeing friends and co-workers as being one of the only joys in their otherwise meaningless tasks. The following vignette from the Bowe et al.

(2000) collection describes what the experience of lack of relatedness feels like to a public utilities specialist who conveys the experiences of a contemporary federal government worker:

> There's something lacking. I don't think that people know how to make lasting friendships, or to put the work in, you know, to follow up or see how people are doing, to keep the friendship going and things of that nature. And it's probably society-wide, because there's no excuse for it where we work. You know, a lot of us live in the same area. And we won't get together at all. I guess we don't want to be friends with each other. I don't know. It's just all strange to me. The way we have it, people just chitchat at work and then go their separate ways .... I just don't want my tombstone to read, 'Here lies a lifelong bureaucrat.' (pp. 587–588)

This passage conveys the sense of isolation and lack of interpersonal connection that increasingly characterizes many occupational settings, which was described in previous chapters. While the lack of relatedness is very likely not entirely responsible for this individual's sense of alienation and disconnection, the absence of relational support may be contributing to the protagonist's difficulty in developing a level of internalized self-regulation that might add greater meaning at work. Consistent with the emerging relational perspectives in the psychology of working (Blustein, 2001b; Flum, 2001; Schultheiss, 2003), the presence or absence of meaningful interpersonal connections is important to the process of internalizing selected aspects of one's motivational context.

Need for Competence. Ryan and Deci (2000) also have described the important role that competence serves in fostering internalization. Consistent with social learning models of human motivation (e.g., Bandura, 1986; Lent et al., 2002), the experience of competence in a given task is associated with greater internalization of self-regulating functions. Support for this inference also has been demonstrated in considerable research within the motivation literature (e.g., White, 1959) and within vocational psychology (Lent et al., 2002). From an intuitive and logical sense, the experience of competence would seem to promote internalization. People who are able to learn the relevant tasks involved in a given work setting are more likely to experience success and feelings of mastery, which have been associated with a number of positive outcomes, such as greater effort in a task (e.g., greater levels of exploratory behavior; Blustein, 1989) and persistence in the face of obstacles (Lent et al., 2002). For example, let us consider a woman who takes a job as a bus driver and reports feeling very disconnected from the job, with particular difficulty in negotiating the large vehicle within relatively crowded city streets. As she becomes more familiar with the tasks involved in operating the bus, managing the passengers, and negotiating urban traffic, the job may become more internalized, less stressful, and less alienating. I should note that improved competence, in of itself, would not necessarily lead to a highly satisfying job, one that is congruent with one's personality, or one that allows for expression of one's self-concept. Rather, the experience of competence may be associated with a greater sense of self-regulation, which may help the job to become somewhat more comfortable.

Some of the more prominent aspects of a context that provides opportunities for the development of competence can be found in the Bowe et al. collection, in which an adhesive company sales representative describes a sale in a vivid and passionate manner:

> [After four and a half years of working in technical services, the protagonist finally lands a sales job in her firm.] I just badgered the hell out of my district manager and finally after a year and a half of continually asking, the company put me into a sales territory in Kansas City .... I love it. What's hard is convincing them [the clients] that you know what you are talking about. Whereas a salesguy in this has more of a tough time getting in to see the person, once they get in, they really do not have to prove their credibility as much as a female does.
>
> But this doesn't bug me—I enjoy the challenge, absolutely, absolutely enjoy the challenge .... I've been very successful at convincing people to go with us. Generally, if I can get into a plant, and do a trial ..., I've won the account. And I've been even more successful—and this is really my forte, I think—at getting them to stay with us once they're on board. My technical background definitely helps me because I know the products really well. But, what's more important, I think, is that I know what to do to service the client .... (Bowe et al., 2000, pp. 141–143)

This vignette describes a job (i.e., sales) in which interpersonal skills are generally viewed as the key to success. And, while this individual presents herself in a way that suggests a comfort in working with and influencing others, she also conveys a level of competence about the product that is well integrated into her knowledge base. Indeed, as this individual progresses in her narrative, her sense of enthusiasm about her working life is clearly evident and compelling. Whether this sense of joy and excitement is entirely due to her competence in sales and in the product she is selling is impossible to discern. Consistent with the tenets of internalization that have been articulated by Deci and Ryan (1985, 2000), this narrative gives voice to the importance that competence plays in the development of adaptive self-regulating mechanisms at work.

Interface of the Contextual Conditions.   Deci and Ryan (2000) have commented on an observation about the potential conflict inherent in a simultaneous need for autonomy and the need for relatedness. Ideally, the need for relatedness and the need for autonomy can complement each other in a manner that is similar in some ways to the attachment paradigm. As Bowlby (1988) described, children who are securely attached will actually be more likely to venture out into the world, thereby enhancing their competence and their sense of autonomy. In fact, the connection between attachment theory and SDT was explored in a series of studies by LaGuardia, Ryan, Couchman, and Deci (2000), who confirmed the notion that the need for autonomy and relatedness can function in tandem to promote adaptive behavior. Adding the need for competence to the mix is also consistent with mainstream models of motivation (e.g., White, 1959) as well as social learning theory (e.g., Bandura, 1986). However, it is important to note that SDT has considerable conceptual differences with social learning theory. In particular, SDT focuses strongly on the role of the individual as the agent in his or her life. The environment is viewed as containing the nutrients to promote a natural striving for self-determination. This position contrasts with social learning theory in that SDT is constructed upon humanistic assumptions about human behavior, which lie in sharp distinction with the learning assumptions of social learning theory. More specifically, individuals are viewed as having the innate striving for self-regulation and ultimately for self-determination. Their motivation for these states is not contingent upon direct or vicarious learning; rather, the context is viewed as furnishing the necessary psychological and relational elements that can nourish the individual's innate motivation to maximize opportunities for self-determination.

Self-Determination in the Working Context

When considered collectively, SDT provides the psychology of working with a conceptually rich foundation to enhance the quality of working experiences. However, several other conceptual elements are necessary for a more complete understanding of the motivational complexities of working. One of the key elements that is needed for a more thorough understanding of working is a consideration of the consistency between an individual's values and the values of one's work organization (cf. Brown, 2002a, 2002b; Mitchell & Krumboltz, 1990). A second element is a clear understanding of the realities of the broader social, economic, and political environment, which has a considerable impact on the availability of work that is even remotely facilitative of self-determined functioning.

Need for Value Congruence.   Another factor that I would add to the contextual framework of the SDT view of working is value congruence. Brown (2002a, 2002b) has articulated a theoretical framework that is based on the critical importance of values in the career choice and development process. In a similar vein, I believe that individuals who share values with their work organization or employers will be more likely to become self-determined in their working lives. Brown (2002a) has defined values in an integrative manner that is linked to the broader discussion of values in psychological research. For Brown, values represent one's beliefs about the optimal means of functioning in society. Values emerge as cognitive structures that have implications for behavior and emotions. In addition, values often are manifested overtly via conscious choices or may be manifested covertly as embedded beliefs that subtly guide behavior and attitudes.

In addition to the need for relatedness, competence, and autonomy, I would add value congruence to the list of factors that ideally may foster internalization and lead to greater self-regulation in the working context. Whereas Brown (2002a) views values within the context of traditional career choice and decision-making questions in vocational psychology, my concern is more circumscribed; that is, I am interested in exploring how value congruence may enhance or detract from one's ability to work in a self-determined fashion. The striving for value congruence, naturally, is a complex, individualistic process that is shaped by the broader context. As Brown highlighted, values vary based on culture, socioeconomic status, individual life experiences, and a host of other variables. The social learning theory by Mitchell and Krumboltz (1990) also described the importance of values in career decision making. Despite the recent interest in understanding the role of values in vocational psychology, Brown (2002b) noted that very little direct research has been conducted to assess the precise role that values play in various aspects of the career choice and development processes. As such, the role of values in career development and, more specifically, the function of value congruence in the motivational experiences of workers needs to be examined in future research.

In relation to understanding motivation in the working context, I propose that workers ideally would prefer to connect to organizations that have values that are consistent with their own. Indeed, the search for value congruence may offer more of a viable opportunity for people who do not have extensive choice in their educational opportunities or vocational choices than the traditional focus on interest congruence. As an example, consider the working experiences of farmers who work in the cultivation of tobacco as opposed to farmers who are cultivating wheat. I would argue that the former might have greater difficulty in experiencing self-regulation because the values of their activities may be inconsistent with their own values (assuming that one values working in the production of life-enhancing products as opposed to products that have been associated with illness and premature death). A similar argument may be developed for a given psychologist who does not value the role and impact of intelligence testing in society. I would argue that if this psychologist worked for an organization, such as a school, that placed a strong value on the predictive role of intelligence testing, he or she would be less prone to experience intrinsic motivation or even self-regulating mechanisms at work.

Another way in which individuals can attain value congruence is when their values about working are consistent with the affirmed attributes within their occupational context. For example, value congruence can be attained when a worker values the process of exerting effort in his or her job and this effort is valued by that person's employers and co-workers. In reviewing narratives of workers, one of the common themes is the value that people hold in relation to putting forth maximum effort and energy in their job tasks (Bowe et al., 2000). If a work context is able to manifest its values about effort and initiative in an explicit and coherent way, it would seem more likely that people would be able to internalize self-regulating processes, thereby yielding greater levels of motivation. The comments and writing from workers across the socioeconomic spectrum are rich with narratives that convey the importance of having their work ethic or work values affirmed by their employer. For example, the following passage from the Bowe et al. (2000) volume describes the experiences of a construction foreman whose values about working are affirmed in his daily life and within his more immediate circle of co-workers and supervisors:

> I never say no to work. I've always had a fear that if you say no, and it slows down, you're not going to get the chance to say yes .... So, I find myself working a lot. But I like it. I find it very rewarding. Just building something, creating something, and actually seeing your work. I've never had an office job or anything, but I don't think everybody gets the same gratification. You start

with a bare, empty lot with the grass growing up and then you build a house. A lot of times you'll build a house for a family, and you see them move in, that's pretty gratifying. (p. 36)

This vignette describes the satisfaction that the foreman has in seeing the product of his efforts. Yet, prior to this statement, he indicated that his work "was not necessarily an attractive job" (Bowe et al., 2000, p. 33). In fact, he described several challenges and problems with his work; nevertheless, he seemed to value the product of his efforts, creating housing for people, and also the value of experiencing the connection between his efforts and his output. This vignette, coupled with the literature reviewed in this section, suggests that the infusion of a values perspective in the working context would seem potentially informative for subsequent research.

Need for Access to the Opportunity Structure.   Consistent with the movement in psychology to incorporate the broader context more fully into conceptualizations about working (cf. Helms & Cook, 1999; Martín-Baro, 1994; Prilleltensky, 1997; Wilson, 1996), a complete understanding of the motivational experiences of people at work needs to include a discussion of the opportunity structure. The opportunity structure reflects one's access to the resources and supports that frame the process of planning, training, locating, and adjusting to work. Included in the opportunity structure, therefore, is one's access to adequate housing, supportive family members, safe neighborhoods, effective education, and financial support for post-high school education and training.

In mapping the contextual framework of self-determined functioning at work, I propose that we also need to consider the degree to which access to the opportunity structure is available. People who have greater access are more likely to find jobs that offer greater opportunities for rewarding work. For example, the participants in the Albany school-to-work studies who had greater access to the opportunity structure, as indexed by their socioeconomic status, were more likely to view work in a positive light (Blustein et al., 2002). Indeed, similar findings are evident throughout the social and behavioral science literature (e.g., M. T. Brown, Fukunaga, Umemoto, & Wicker, 1996; Fouad & Brown, 2000; Riverin-Simard, 1991). In effect, the three attributes of internalization that Deci and Ryan (1985) have articulated may be more available in situations where people have greater access to other fundamental resources, such as the basic needs cited earlier (i.e., housing, good schools, etc.). Thus, I am arguing that the contextual framework of SDT needs the same sort of explicit infusion of contextual factors that I am seeking to provide for the psychology of working.

Conclusion

The addition of the need for value congruence and access to the opportunity structure to the Deci and Ryan (2000) model regarding the contextual qualities needed for internalization and self-determination continues the move that social and behavioral scientists are making in holding the context or environment accountable for some of the variations that we observe in psychological functioning (e.g., Helms & Cook, 1999; Helms et al., 2005; Prilleltensky, 1997). The value congruence notion provides an additional dimension of person–environment fit that seeks to include the match between the values of the employer and of the individual worker in the mix of elements that play a role in motivation and self-determination. The discussion about the broader social, economic, and educational context follows one of the core tenets of the psychology of working. In effect, the infusion of these ideas into the SDT work helps to move the question of motivation and self-determination to a location in which aspects of individuals, their proximal contexts, and their more distal contexts all interact in a complex, recursive way. Mapping the precise nature of these interactions, naturally, awaits further research. However, it is hoped that these initial ideas provide future scholars of working with some pivotal notions about how to understand motivational processes.

Motivational Issues and Working in Psychological Treatment

The discussion of motivational issues at work has typically occurred in relation to questions about productivity and turnover, generally within an I/O psychology framework (Landy, 1989). In the psychology-of-working framework that I am proposing in this book, I believe that the motivational framework that I have presented thus far would be informative to counseling and psychological treatment. Prior to presenting a case, I first explore the potential of SDT to inform our thinking about work-related issues in clinical practice.

One of the common hallmarks of psychological functioning has been one's ability to effectively handle the tasks of working, including locating a job, adjusting to the interpersonal and cognitive demands, and balancing work with other life roles (Blustein & Spengler, 1995; Neff, 1985; Shore & Massimo,

1979). Yet, little attention within the counseling and psychotherapy literature has been devoted to the individual experience of motivation at work that people experience. Counseling clients and others receiving mental health treatment often face daunting challenges in confronting and resolving some of the pressing problems that may be evoking psychological discomfort or pain. A key challenge in all sorts of treatments, including psychotherapy and even medical care, is motivating people to engage in activities that may not be intrinsically interesting or compelling. Sheldon and colleagues have addressed these challenges in their book (Sheldon et al., 2003), in which they have sought to describe how SDT can be used to enhance effectiveness of clinical treatments in both psychological and health-related contexts. (They did not address work-related issues in any way, a trend that continues to plague most contributions in clinical psychology and other mental health fields.) Sheldon et al. argued that promoting autonomy support is the most critical aspect of infusing SDT into treatment venues.

Autonomy support is a mode of interaction in which individuals have freedom to determine their own course of action. Autonomy support is context-free in that it can be applied to any social interaction, regardless of what type of information or persuasive communication is being exchanged, as conveyed in the following passage by Sheldon et al. (2003):

> Deci and Ryan conceptualize autonomy support as having *three* distinct components. First, the authority should take and acknowledge the perspective of the subordinate. That is, as much as possible within the limits of their empathic ability, authorities should address and honor their subordinate's worldview .... Second, the authority should provide choice whenever he or she can. That is, as much as possible within the limits of the situation, the authority should allow the subordinate to determine what to do .... Third, the authority should provide a meaningful rationale when choice cannot be provided. (p. 30)

These recommendations are certainly consistent with most of the tenets of effective counseling and psychotherapy. Indeed, Sheldon et al. (2003) actually believe that these guidelines are congruent with good manners. However, they note that many medical treatments—and, increasingly, many psychotherapeutic treatments (as reflected, for example, in some of the manualized treatments for circumscribed disorders that have appeared in recent years)—do not adhere to these elements of autonomy support. In my adaptation of SDT to the world of counseling and psychotherapy, I am also emphasizing the other two supportive elements (competence and relatedness) as well as value congruence and access to opportunities to the clinical challenges of working therapeutically with clients. The following case, which is based on an amalgam of clients with whom I have worked in my clinical practice, describes the vast potential that can be attained by thinking more carefully about motivation and working.

Angelo

Angelo is a 45-year-old attorney who was born in Italy and migrated to the United States prior to attending college. He has just been laid off from his position in a non-profit agency and is also experiencing considerable marital distress. The loss of his job, which was caused by budgetary problems and was not due to his performance, was a very painful event for Angelo. He loved his job and he was always very motivated at work. He used to wake up early some days in order to get to work and begin his day. He was very committed to the values of the non-profit group (which was involved in consumer rights) and he also enjoyed the connection he developed with his co-workers. In fact, the joy he felt at work helped to compensate for his sense of aloneness in his marriage. He and his wife, Maria, had grown apart over the past few years and their relationship was characterized by growing apathy and even bitterness. They had talked about divorce, but they both felt that they should stay together to support their children. Angelo and Maria have two children (both boys), ages 12 and 14, who are doing reasonably well in their own development, although they have been more anxious since Angelo lost his job.

Angelo sought treatment with me because of my skills in vocational counseling and psychotherapy. Indeed, in the first few sessions, we developed a treatment contract that included an integration of vocational counseling and psychotherapy. I was careful to offer Angelo choices about how to proceed, which is consistent with the tenets of SDT (Sheldon et al., 2003) and domain-sensitive treatment (Blustein & Spengler, 1995). After reviewing the nature of Angelo's depression, I determined that he was not experiencing a major depression, but that he was indeed dysphoric. I discussed with Angelo the utility of developing a timetable for his job search that simulated his work schedule, again underscoring his sense of choice and volition. We both concurred that he would be better off conducting his job search from an office provided by his state's Department of Labor (One-Stop Career Centers). In addition, he started a regimen of physical exercise, which offers clients a means of improving mood regulation along with enhanced levels of agency. The increased level of activity, both in his job search and his workouts, functioned in tandem to reduce his depressive moods and he soon regained feelings of hopefulness.

The sluggish job market in the region where Angelo lived, coupled with his lack of financial security, led him to apply for and receive a job in a small private law practice. The private practice involved a fair amount of family law as well as small business law, fields in which Angelo was not particularly interested. Also, Angelo's bosses in the law practice were clear that his evaluation and continued employment were contingent to some extent on his ability to generate business for the firm. So, rather than spending time with his children or engaging in his hobbies (which included painting and music), he had to move into social circles that would help him to develop leads for his firm. In addition, the lack of satisfaction at his new job changed the delicate balance that he and Maria had carved out of their troubled marriage. Angelo was no longer very satisfied at work and his lack of engagement at work made the pain of the marriage more salient to him. This, in turn, increased the level of conflict in the marriage, which was instrumental in helping Angelo and Maria initiate couples counseling.

Within 6 months after the start of counseling, Angelo was still struggling. While he had a new job, he was not particularly happy with his current position or his future career options. His marriage was rocky; however, he and Maria were now working on their issues rather than denying them or avoiding them. As we assessed his status at this juncture, I explored a number of issues with Angelo. First, with respect to his level of depression, Angelo was still somewhat dysphoric; however, each of the sources of despair were all rooted in specific issues that he was addressing. For example, the marriage counseling had resulted in a clearer level of awareness for him of how he was contributing to the distance with Maria. Second, the problems at work represented complex life choices that Angelo faced in an honest and open fashion. For Angelo to continue his work in the consumer rights area, he and his family would likely have to move out of the medium-sized northeastern city where they and their extended family lived. This option was not conceivable at this point, but might be as their children became older and moved onto college or post-secondary training. Therefore, we decided to focus on identifying ways for Angelo to find more satisfaction at work.

The ensuing treatment, which took place weekly and then once every other week for the next 10 months, focused on Angelo's working experiences and his marriage. One of the important observations from the counseling was Angelo's tendency to become overwhelmed by his emotionality. In both the work and family contexts, Angelo tended to reach very quick, often impulsive conclusions, generally after feeling hurt or bruised in a given interpersonal interaction. We explored the use of meditative and mindfulness interventions (Epstein, 1995), which were designed to help Angelo accept his feelings without necessarily acting on them. (For a review of these interventions, please see Epstein, 1995, and Safran, 2003.) In addition, Angelo realized that his intense reactions to challenging situations had left him feeling disconnected at his new job. Rather than viewing the comments of his bosses as helpful and instructive, he tended to experience them as denigrating and hurtful. In the same vein, the marital sessions revealed a similar pattern of over-reaction, which was a pattern that both Maria and Angelo used throughout their marriage.

While there was improvement in the marriage, Angelo continued to feel empty and disengaged at work. He longed for the non-profit organization that he worked for and he described feeling lonely and incompetent at work. The final stage of our work, therefore, focused on helping Angelo to feel more competent at work and to feel more connected to his colleagues. The issue of competence at the job was resolved to a great extent by the reality that he was gaining more skills and knowledge as he worked in these relatively new areas of family law and small business law. The issue of connectedness to his colleagues was more complex. Angelo did not share some of the core values of his colleagues, who were fairly conservative politically and who viewed law as a means of earning a good living as opposed to Angelo's idealistic views. However, he was able to make one solid friend at work who helped to create the sense of connectedness that had been missing. In addition, Angelo joined the local Democratic party to expand his social networks and explore other ways of contributing to the social good.

Discussion

The end of treatment for Angelo brought some improvement, but his working situation and his marriage were still not ideal. From the perspective of SDT, this case offers an illuminating opportunity to explore how motivational processes can intersect with the counseling process. One of the realities of Angelo's job loss is that he was forced out of a working environment that offered him intrinsic motivation and an almost idealized opportunity for optimal self-determination. However, as with many workers in the early part of the 21st century, the golden era of stable jobs that are hierarchically related and ever more challenging and satisfying is not always possible. Of course, Angelo and Maria had to make a difficult decision about family issues in their deliberations about moving to a new location so that he could pursue his dreams. The ending of the treatment for Angelo was not as rosy as it could be, but it was far more hopeful than it could have been.

One of the important characteristics of this case is that I was very cognizant of the importance of working for Angelo. Rather than viewing his work-related struggles exclusively or even primarily as a manifestation of biologically oriented depressive states or unresolved family dramas, I affirmed his concerns and sought to understand them from his perspective. (Of course, I did explore the other hypotheses, but I did so in a way that acknowledged the reality of Angelo's concerns about working.) The issues that emerged in examining Angelo's work life are very clearly illuminated by SDT. The new position for Angelo was not ideal for him; it was not very congruent with his socially minded interests and with his values. Therefore, Angelo was now faced with the task of adapting to an extrinsically motivating job. However, as Deci and Ryan (1985, 2001) have detailed, changes in the context can help people to become more self-regulating and ideally more content in extrinsically motivating situations. Consistent with the recommendations of Sheldon et al. (2003), I sought to enhance Angelo's autonomy support throughout the treatment. Angelo had felt disempowered by his job loss, a feeling that is, of course, very common among the unemployed. As such, his sense of autonomy in his life was notably diminished. I consistently offered Angelo choices about the next steps in his treatment. In addition, by having him adopt a "full-court" approach to the job search (involving 40-plus hours a week in the process of developing leads, writing letters and resumes, and going on informational interviews), Angelo naturally became more autonomous with respect to his vocational life. The improvements in his marriage also helped him to feel more in control of his life. Moreover, the development of tools that he employed to manage his emotional life also functioned to enhance his feelings of autonomy.

Furthermore, I worked with Angelo to enhance his relational supports, both at work and outside of work. The value differences between Angelo and his colleagues made this a difficult task, but it was not impossible. And, indeed, Angelo managed to develop a solid friendship at work that provided him with some of the relational resources needed for internalization. I also worked with Angelo to enhance his competence at work. We explored the possibility of his taking graduate level courses or advanced law courses to improve his skills in these new areas. Angelo became aware of the need to enhance his competence and, in effect, began to reframe his cases as opportunities for advanced training. He consulted with colleagues about his cases and also frequented the law library of the local law school to improve his knowledge.

In sum, Angelo's case reflects the potential that exists in using SDT in psychotherapy about working. As indicated earlier, the benefits of SDT in traditional psychotherapy have been detailed by Sheldon et al. (2003) with very similar approaches used to help people move forward. This case and the ensuing discussion extend the applicability of SDT to counseling and psychotherapy that is affirmatively inclusive of working. In some ways, adapting SDT to the work context offers counselors with a potentially valuable opportunity to help clients find ways to enhance their overall level of satisfaction with their lives. Naturally, the case of Angelo offered far more access to the opportunity structure than would a case involving a migrant farm worker or unskilled factory worker. These sorts of challenges involve attention to the individual (via activist and empathic counseling that will maximize one's autonomy and self-regulation) as well as attention to the social and economic context. Some of these issues, which are explored in depth in chapter 10, are foreshadowed in the next section.

The Psychology of Working and Motivation: Conclusion

The material presented here has vast potential to inform the psychological study of working. SDT has provided a powerful, empirically supported counterpoint to deterministic theories of motivation that have emerged from psychoanalytic theory and behaviorism. In contrast to these richly informative, yet dogmatic theoretical perspectives, Deci and Ryan have offered a means of thinking about human beings as active agents who exist in a fluid, dynamic, and complex environment. The implications of SDT for our purposes are that it may furnish counselors, scholars, and policy analysts with a means of enhancing the quality of life for an increasing proportion of workers who have little to no choice in what they do for their livelihoods.

Applying SDT to the psychology of working frames working in the broad array of activities in which human beings engage to survive. By exploring the extrinsic motivations that drive people to do things that they do not find intrinsically interesting, I am arguing that the psychology of working needs to consider the full spectrum of workers and potential workers. Naturally, SDT is relevant to those who do have choices about what they do to earn a living. People who engage in activities that they find intrinsically interesting have the opportunity for self-determination at work as well as all of the other positive outcomes that our research has identified over the years (congruence, job satisfaction, etc.). However, for the rest of humanity, SDT offers some potentially powerful means of enhancing self-regulation. If we follow the advice of

Deci and Ryan (1985, 2000), we may be able to identify ways of improving the quality of life for many workers across the globe. More precisely, the aforementioned supportive elements of internalization each provide useful guidelines for employers and government leaders who may wish to enhance working conditions. By designing work contexts such that they offer opportunities for autonomy, relatedness, and competence, it may be possible to create more satisfying work for people.

A more complete view of the conditions necessary for self-determined functioning at work, however, ought to include attention to values congruence and to access to the opportunity structure. In my application of SDT to the world of working, I have explicitly included attention to the importance of congruence of values between workers and their employers. While this sort of congruence may not always be feasible, especially for people with few options, it would seem important to explore the utility of this factor in future research on working. The second attribute that I added to the SDT perspective is access to the opportunity structure. In this case, I have attempted to sketch a more complete impression of human motivation at work, including the very real issues that are reflected in the complex array of economic, social, political, and historical factors that frame our lived experiences.

Detailing the full complement of implications of the SDT for the psychology of working awaits further research. However, the integration between the vibrant theoretical model offered by Deci and Ryan (1985; Ryan & Deci, 2000) with the nascent psychology of working reveals the potential for a viable long-term relationship. As I have argued, SDT offers a way of thinking about enhancing the meaning and satisfaction that working can yield, even in situations where the tasks in which one is engaged are not even remotely interesting. In addition, by providing a careful analysis of the contextual factors that support internal regulation and self-determined functioning, SDT has given us a valuable tool to map the policy implications of a psychology of working.

While these policy implications are examined in depth in chapter 10, I can foreshadow them briefly here as they provide a perfect coda to the material covered thus far.

In short, one of the most prominent implications of SDT for the psychology of working is its identification of contextual factors that support self-determination. Using these attributes as a foundation, it would seem important for scholars to delineate how self-regulation can be promoted, particularly for workers who do not have intrinsically interesting jobs. While the details of this scholarship are difficult to discern at this juncture, it does seem likely that the implications of transforming externally regulated working conditions to more self-regulated conditions would involve significant investments into education, training, and other contextual factors that support and nurture human development.

In the realm of working, investments in education would obviously yield greater levels of competence among workers, especially in the current era where such a vast premium is placed on knowledge. In addition, programs that foster greater relatedness at work and in one's communities are indicated, which would help to counter many of the isolating trends in contemporary society (Putnam, 2000; Sennett, 1998) as well as facilitating greater comfort and support at work. Autonomy support is far more complex, as it would entail a broad and far-reaching analysis of authority relations at work. However, if the payoffs of autonomy support are as robust as they appear (cf. Sheldon et al., 2003), it may be timely to rethink some of our assumptions about a well-organized work environment.

In closing, the motivational framework for the psychology of working provides the guideposts for sustained research, theoretical endeavors, and policy reform. The precise linkages among these guideposts have yet to be determined, but with the inclusion of SDT, future explorers of the psychology of working have the advantage of a theoretical framework that meshes with the humanistic objectives of an inclusive and affirming psychology of working.

CHAPTER 6

Social Barriers and Working: Exploring Race, Gender, Sexual Orientation, Disability Status, and Social Class at Work

Black teachers if they are in the school [a contemporary school in the South] at all are teaching for the most part remedial courses that are all black. Very few blacks are teaching courses that you would value, literature, history or social studies. They are teaching remedial reading for blacks or home ec. Schools are segregated within. In one high school that so-called has all the wealthy kids—the city high school as such, they've got one black teacher. She teaches home ec or gym or something like that .... Well, initially especially, they didn't want any black principals down there and they trumped up charges against a lot of them and that sort of thing. And then the coaches. And it's not too subtle.

—Foster (1993, p. 284)

Having experienced the surgeon's daily doses of racism and sexism during working hours, I had no desire to confront homophobia as well; I was more determined to keep my personal life private. I would have preferred working elsewhere on the UCLA campus, yet in 1982 I had accepted that job because it had been the only one available .... Meanwhile, in 1983, I began the equally difficult process of coming out to my family, at the same time as I was building a relationship, attending evening college classes, and attempting to find time to write fiction. I found myself caught between my Chicano-Catholic family and my closeted white lover. My family preferred to continue thinking of me as their celibate and unmarried daughter, not as sexual, certainly not as lesbian .... Exhausted from these conflicts, not to mention my long hours of work and school, I had little time to write fiction and even less to ponder the feasibility of being out in the workplace. On that point, I agreed with my family and my lover; in the already stressful environment of the medical center, I would not be safe being out.

—de la Peña (1995)

As I have noted in previous chapters and as further conveyed by the vignettes cited herein, access to the world of work is far from equal. Within the past few decades, psychologists and social scientists have described various social filters or barriers that function to inhibit equal access to the resources necessary for a satisfying work life (e.g., Arbona, 1995; Betz, 1989; Chung, 2003; Fassinger, 1996; Helms & Cook, 1999; Wilson, 1996). In this chapter, I explore these social filters, building on the advances of scholars who have investigated these difficult questions. The purpose of this chapter is to examine the impact that social barriers have in diverse working contexts. The argument that I seek to develop here is that the various means by which people are categorized in contemporary society functions to inhibit and even prevent the full expression of natural strivings to engage in meaningful and rewarding work. As I explore each of the major social filters, the unequal distribution of resources and barriers to people across the globe will become increasingly clarified. While this theme has been explored elsewhere (e.g., Helms et al., 2005; Lott, 2002; Sue, 2004), the focus of the present discussion is on the interface of these forms of social oppression in the working context.

The literature on social barriers has a rich tradition in psychology, with contributions emerging from various specialties. Given the wide array of social barriers that are reviewed in this chapter, I have elected to use social categorization theory (Devine, 1995) to help organize the material that follows. Social categorization theory provides a means of understanding how human beings establish various sorts of out-groups within their individual and collective social, economic, and political interactions. The functions of these out-groups vary considerably. On one level, social categorization helps people to organize vast amounts of stimuli, which facilitates our ability to process information in stimuli-rich social and interpersonal situations. However, Devine noted that human beings often tend to organize their perceptions of people into meaningless categories that have no inherent value. As Helms and Cook (1999) suggested, human beings use phenotypes (i.e., observable physical attributes) in many of their social perceptions, resulting in the development of categories with little or no inherent meaning.

One of the outcomes of social categorization is that people develop prejudices about others, based on observable differences in appearance or other irrelevant attributes (such as sexual orientation). These inferences or observations about others then affect judgments about individuals' capacity to function in the world (Devine, 1995), including the educational, work-based, and interpersonal contexts. For example, in the workplace, people of color have been (and continue to be) pre-judged in relation to their intelligence, work ethic, and linguistic skills, often with no corroborating evidence other than their appearance. As I detail in this chapter, the process of social categorization is pervasive and has functioned in both overt and covert ways in the occupational world. The development of social categories in our society has resulted in the evolution of groups that have greater social status and groups that have less social status. The implicit hierarchy in which groups are viewed has created social barriers in which some groups have greater advantages than others generally based on demographic characteristics. The existence of these social barriers functions to create inequity in education, access to the supportive conditions needed to achieve the full range of one's talents, and employment and advancement opportunities. My position is that an inclusive psychology of working needs to incorporate the full scope of these social barriers. Ideally, understanding the social barriers in relation to the natural human strivings to work may create the framework for effective psychological practice and public policy.

The choice to begin this chapter with a discussion of racism reflects the pervasive role that social constructions related to racial and ethnic characteristics have played in the maldistribution of wealth and resources in the United States and in other Western countries (Carter & Cook, 1992; Devine, 1995; Helms & Cook, 1999; Tatum, 1999; Thompson & Neville, 1999; Wilson, 1996). This discussion is followed by an exploration of other major forms of social and political oppression, including the role of sexism, classism, disability status, and heterosexism in relation to the psychological experience of working. The final section of the chapter presents a case vignette that seeks to capture some of the more challenging elements in understanding how these social filters impact on an inclusive counseling approach that integrates explicit attention to the experience of working.

Race and Racism

Recent psychological analyses have considered race to reflect a social construction as opposed to a biological or physiological characteristic (Clark, Anderson, Clark, & Williams, 1999; Helms & Cook, 1999; Helms et al., 2005). Following the Helms and Cook perspective, race is presented here as a phenotypic attribute that has the potential to evoke a host of social reactions and consequences. As Helms and Cook (1999) stated:

> When a person is perceived as being a member of a racial group, then the person's "racial" demographic identity typically obliterates his or her membership

in other demographic categories or social affiliations. That is, one's access to society's rewards and punishments is more often based on one's alleged racial characteristics than on any other real or fictive human characteristics. (p. 16)

This view, which is echoed by other scholars (e.g., Carter & Cook, 1992; Tatum, 1999), creates a situation in which people are judged based on the color of their skin. The use of skin color or other phenotypic attributes as a basis for making inferences about the internal characteristics of an individual has a long, and unfortunately, pernicious role in human history (Helms & Cook, 1999). That this cognitive bias still exists, even within some intellectual circles (cf. Rowe, 2005), is disconcerting and morally challenging for social and behavioral scientists who are interested in human welfare and the elimination of social and political oppression.

African American Experiences of Racism

The economic disadvantages that are associated with African attributes in the United States have been well documented in numerous other sources (e.g., M. T. Brown & Pinterits, 2001; Pope-Davis & Hargrove, 2001; Thompson & Neville, 1999; Wilson, 1996). In short, African Americans, Latino, Native Americans, Asian Americans and other people of color (also known as visible racial and ethnic groups; Helms & Cook, 1999), experience pronounced discrimination in nearly every aspect of their social and economic interactions. People of color in the United States earn less money for essentially the same work (Phelps & Constantine, 2001), are exposed to more violent and unhealthy housing (Wilson, 1996), are provided with less than adequate education (Arbona, 2000), and experience bias in nearly every aspect of their educational and vocational development (Helms & Cook, 1999; Walsh, Bingham, Brown, & Ward, 2001). The reality for people of color in the United States is that their working lives have been consistently characterized by a lack of volition in their working lives (Smith, 1983). Dating back to the slavery experience, African American people have faced a working life wherein the option of implementing one's self-concept has remained an elusive dream. In many ways, the interface of working and racism provides a vista into perhaps one of the most painful aspects of living in a society that stratifies access to opportunity based on skin color. For many visible racial and ethnic minority group members, the entire process of working, beginning with educational preparation and the job search process as well as the actual day-to-day working experience, forces a reckoning with the subtle and often overt sequelae of racism (Carter & Cook, 1992; Helms & Cook, 1999).

Despite the considerable obstacles that exist for people of color in Western cultures, relatively little attention has been devoted to these issues in the vocational psychology and organization psychology literatures. The earlier work in this area, as exemplified by E. J. Smith's (1983) contribution, began to chart the numerous ways in which traditional career development theory and research were of questionable relevance to the experiences of visible racial and ethnic minorities. Carter and Cook (1992) developed a conceptualization of the vocational lives of people of color by using systems theory as an organizing framework. Their analyses encouraged a wide-angle examination of existing and historic prejudices and barriers that function to inhibit the development of volitional and satisfying careers for African Americans, Latino/as, Asian Americans, and Native Americans. Helms and Cook (1999) expanded on the Carter and Cook contribution by articulating a means of integrating racial identity perspectives into our understanding of vocational behavior of visible racial and ethnic group peoples. The racial identity paradigm, as articulated by Helms and Cook, proposes that living in a multicultural context forces all of us to contend with the social construction of race, both individually and collectively. A key element in understanding racial identity theory in the vocational realm is the notion of racial salience, which is defined as "the extent to which a person conceives (correctly or incorrectly) of race as a significant definer of one's work options" (Helms & Piper, 1994, p. 129). For people of color, racial salience is exemplified by the awareness that selected vocational options are not easily accessible to people due to their skin color. For European Americans, racial salience might be manifested by the belief that African American people cannot perform high-level analytical work because of differences in intelligence or disposition.

Racial Identity Theory. Helms and Cook (1999) argued that the process of developing a racial identity intersects with pre-implementation and post-implementation working life. (Because Helms and Cook view race as a social construction, they have increasingly used the term "sociorace" as opposed to "race.") According to Helms and Cook, racial identity models "are descriptions of hypothetical intrapsychic pathways for overcoming internalized racism and achieving a healthy socioracial self-conception under varying conditions of racial oppression" (p. 81). The Helms (1990) model of racial identity, which actually represents one of a number of interrelated theoretical paradigms, has a rich empirical tradition and a great deal of relevance to the present discussion. In the Helms model, people of color ideally pass through the following racial identity ego statuses as they adjust to living in a racist society:

■ *Conformity:* This status is characterized by devaluing one's own racial and ethnic group, and affirming instead the standards of the oppressor and privileged group, typically the world of European American people.

■ *Dissonance:* This status is defined by ambivalence and confusion about one's own socioracial group.

■ *Immersion:* This status is characterized by an idealization of one's own socioracial group and a corresponding denigration of the White culture and community.

■ *Emersion:* This status is reflected by a sense of connection and identification with one's own socioracial group.

■ *Internalization:* As individuals move forward with their racial identity, they emerge into this status, which is typified by positive feelings and acceptance of one's own socioracial group and by a capacity to objectively evaluate people from the majority culture.

■ *Integrative awareness:* At this point, the individual is able to value his or her own collective identity, encompassing identity domains of other cultural groups, and to collaborate with members of other groups.

The racial identity paradigm also has been applied to the development of White people. One of the strongest aspects of Helms' work (e.g., Helms & Cook, 1999) is that she has argued convincingly that much of the important work on racial issues needs to be done by White people so that a more equitable society can be constructed. The stages of White racial identity focus primarily on the understanding of privilege and the processes by which people are able to give up their privilege in the hopes of developing more just attitudes toward others.

Racial identity theory, therefore, provides a means of reducing the human tendency to rely on social categories, many of which are irrelevant, in making judgments about others. Furthermore, Helms and Piper (1994) argued that the process of racial identity development would have meaningful interactions with the career development process. They have proposed that the attitudes and behaviors across the spectrum of human diversity would have a predictable impact on the way in which people approach their working lives. For example, individuals of color in the conformity status would approach their work tasks in dramatically different ways in comparison to individuals in the internalization status. Individuals in the conformity status might have a more difficult time in exploring themselves in an honest and open fashion; in contrast, individuals in the internalization status might be able to engage in extensive exploration and would likely have considerable confidence in approaching work-related tasks.

Additional insights about the impact of race in career development were detailed by Walsh et al. (2001). The authors of the chapters of this edited book confirmed the views of other scholars (e.g., Carter & Cook, 1992) in noting that the available literature is woefully inadequate to deal effectively with the complex problems faced by African Americans as they confront racism in so many sectors of the United States. Moreover, Walsh et al. noted the lack of coherent theoretical models to guide individual and systemic interventions. In my view, the problems that confront many African American citizens in the United States may mirror the modal working experiences of many people around the globe. Without access to the resources that support and nurture the development of a truly volitional work life, African Americans may continue to struggle to find their way in one of the richest societies in the world. By advancing the psychology of working perspective, I want to be clear that I am not suggesting in any way that African Americans will not or should not pursue volitional careers. In contrast, by attempting to get a closer connection to the lived experiences of people of color, we have a greater opportunity to understand the very real external obstacles that reduce opportunities. In fact, scholarship emerging from the psychology of working may allow for the development of systemic and public policy changes (see chapter 10) that ideally will contribute to reducing social barriers and obstacles so that people have greater equality as they embark on their life journeys.

Racism in the Working Context. The actual experience of working for people of color is perhaps best understood by reading the words of people who have had to face the unequal playing field of preparing for work. Wilson (1996) captured the existence of prejudice among employers in his research on the loss of jobs within urban communities. One respondent, who was the chairman of a car transport company, replied as follows when asked about his views on differences in the work ethic of different racial and ethnic groups:

> Definitely! I don't think, I know: I've seen it over a period of 30 years. I have it right in here. Basically, the Oriental is much more aggressive and intelligent and studious than the Hispanic. The Hispanics, except the Cubans of course, they have the work ethnic (sic) …
>
> **Interviewer:** You mentioned the case of native-born blacks.
>
> **Respondent:** They're the laziest of the bunch.
>
> **Interviewer:** That would relate to your earlier remarks about dependability. What is the reason for that?
>
> **Respondent:** The parents are that way so, what the hell, they didn't have a role model to copy, that's part of it. (p. 131)

This passage powerfully conveys one of the realities of the lived experiences of poor or working class African Americans. The remarks of this respondent give voice to the internalization of racist attitudes and the pervasive way that they are manifested in the employment process. Other respondents in Wilson's (1996) study, as exemplified by the following comment, attempted to contextualize their views of the issues faced of African Americans in the workplace:

> A lot of times I will interview applicants who are black, who are sort of lower class .... They'll come to me and I cannot hire them because their language skills are so poor. Their speaking voice one thing is poor ... they have no verbal facility with the language ... and these ... you know, they just don't know how to speak and they'll say "salesmens" instead of "salesmen," and that's a problem .... They don't know punctuation, they don't know how to use correct grammar, and they cannot spell. And I can't hire them. And I feel bad about that and I think that they're being very disadvantaged by the Chicago Public School system. (p. 138)

The overwhelming message that comes through in the preceding passages and in other passages in Wilson's (1996) book is the sense of fear, social distance, and at times pure antagonism, that is manifested by employers who are considering African American candidates. The brief review here, naturally, does not even begin to cover the broad array of issues that pervade the working experiences of African Americans. Indeed, far more research and theory is needed in this area. The material presented here, however, puts the inner experiences of African Americans at the center of the conversation, which has the potential to powerfully inform the social science literature and public policy pertaining to work and education.

Native American Experiences of Racism

The impact of racism, unfortunately, has not been exclusive to African peoples living in the United States. Considerable evidence exists that social categorization has been fairly widespread in human history (Devine, 1995; Helms & Cook, 1999). As we continue in our exploration of working and power, it is important to discuss the experiences of Native peoples in the Western Hemisphere who also have faced considerable racism as Europeans invaded their land and soon destroyed much of their culture. The story about the vast changes in the working experiences of Native peoples is too detailed for full explication here. However, the basic outlines merit some attention. Native peoples lived in the Western Hemisphere in a wide array of cultural contexts, ranging from elaborate urban societies to rural hunting and gathering or transitional contexts (Zinn, 1980). When Europeans introduced land ownership in the Americas and the Caribbean, Native peoples reacted in a number of ways, including courageous fighting, passive resistance, and then resignation, assimilation, or in some cases, continued struggle. In South America as in North America, Native peoples often were relegated to the lowest rungs on the socioeconomic ladder. In the following excerpt from Barrios de Chungara's (1978) powerful memoir about being married to a worker in the Bolivian mines, we move closer to the experience of working in a job that remains one's only option for earning a livelihood:

> When the worker is on the first shift [there are three shifts a day as the mine runs 24 hours a day], we women have to get up at four in the morning to prepare our compañero's breakfast. At three in the afternoon he gets back from the mine and he has not eaten anything yet. There's no way to take any food into the mine. It is not allowed .... With only breakfast in their stomachs, the miners go from five in the morning to three in the afternoon, when they get back home. The average life expectancy of a miner is 35 years. By then, he's totally sick with mine sickness. Since there are so many explosions to get the ore out, these dust particles are breathed into the lungs, through the mouth and nose. The dust consumes and finally destroys the lungs. (Barrios de Chungara, 1978, pp. 26–27)

This sort of experience of working is far from the "grand career narrative" that is described in the vocational psychology and organizational development literatures. In the sparse literature that exists on the working experiences of Native peoples (e.g., M. J. Johnson, Swartz, & Martin, 1995; Juntunen et al., 2001), little attention has been devoted to the indigenous ways in which work has been constructed within given tribes. Another challenge that confronts scholars and practitioners is the reality that Native tribes vary extensively in their cultural attributes (M. J. Johnson et al., 1995). Given the sparse literature on the working lives of Native peoples in the Western hemisphere, one of the most important directions for an inclusive psychology of working is to explore how indigenous cultural beliefs about working among native communities affect views of education, training, and working in general. By integrating knowledge of how work is constructed among Native peoples, public policy recommendations may be developed that are consistent with existing belief systems, perhaps providing new opportunities to reduce the pervasive existence of poverty and despair that continue to plague many native communities.

Asian-American Experiences of Racism

Within the United States, Asian American people also have suffered under the yoke of racism and discrimination (Leong & Serafica, 1995). Indeed, there is a considerable history of racist attacks directed toward Asian people that has been evident in nearly every region of the United States in which Asians interact with people from other racial and ethnic groups (Liang, Li, & Kim, 2004; Young & Takeuchi, 1998). Although a myth exists about Asian Americans being the model minority group (Chun & Sue, 1998), the reality of the situation is far from ideal. Recent research has indicated that people from Asian backgrounds face racism, prejudice, and stereotyping in their educational and working lives (Leong & Serafica, 1995). For example, Asian Americans often believe that they need to conform to stereotypes that suggest that they pursue technical or scientific careers. At the same time, the existing scholarship on Asian Americans does not embrace the highly diverse working experiences that Asian peoples manifest in their native countries. When we consider these diverse views in tandem, it is difficult to arrive at any generalizable ideas that would guide research and theory. As in the visible racial and ethnic groups that we have explored thus far, I advocate that we need to move closer to the lived experiences of Asian peoples in order to create a meaningful psychology of working. One relevant vignette from a Chinese American young adult recalling high school describes the vivid barriers that racism engenders:

> When I was growing up, in high school, people used to tease me all the time about being Chinese. I was the "Chink." So that kind of response gets a reflex in me, where I'm just kind of immune to it .... I guess it's because I grew up having people swear at me. Tell me that I was no good because I was Chinese .... (Cohn, 1997, p. 166)

The vignette from this Chinese American individual attests to experiences of being marginalized and made to feel the object of scorn and rejection. While these interactions are all too common for many people of color in Western cultures, the myth of Asian Americans is often that they do not experience such overt expressions of discrimination. By exploring the inner experience of students and workers as they reflect on their struggles to obtain access to adequate education, meaningful social connections, and rewarding work, it is far more likely that we will be able to identify the profoundly painful feelings of denigration that are evoked by cultures that are still immersed in racist practices.

Another narrative found in the Bowe et al. (2000) collection of American's responses to open-ended interviews about their working lives describes the experiences of an Asian American tofu manufacturer. This individual's story includes an evocative overview of how he approached the task of moving into the world of work as a young man.

> Me and my brothers were the first generation of our family born in America. And from when I was a kid, I knew we were expected to take over our father's business, because my father has this mentality which was justified in those days—not necessarily now—that we didn't have a "Chinaman's chance" in this country. In other words, you were Chinese, you couldn't do anything. Supposedly, the American government put shackles on you and you could only do certain work, like be a laundryman or work in Chinese restaurants, and we weren't allowed to do anything else. So we were expected to take over the business .... But I didn't have any choice in this matter. After college, I just went into the family business. And you know, that didn't bother me. That was just the way it was. Certain rules were accepted. (pp. 107–108)

In this case, the protagonist is reasonably successful in his working life. However, even for this individual, with access to education as evidenced by his attendance in college, racial barriers clearly limited his options. The most prominent theme in this vignette is the reality that this individual experienced virtually no volition in considering vocational options. The existence of "certain rules" in determining career trajectories represents a part of the picture of working among people of color and of others who face very real barriers in their working lives. These "rules" result in a complex array of influences, both overt and covert, that function to reduce access to the sources of survival and power that are one of the key hallmarks of contemporary working.

Latin American Experiences of Racism

People from Latin American countries living in North America also have faced considerable racism in obtaining access to the resources that facilitate entry to rewarding working lives (Arbona, 1990, 1995). Arbona's (1990) review cited the extensive network of barriers, including racism, language issues, and immigration histories, which have culminated in Latino/a peoples being on the outside of the American dream of equal access to opportunity. The following excerpt from a qualitative study by Farmer (1997) of a Latino high school student describes how racism is manifested in educational contexts:

> We didn't get treated very well by our fellow students and we didn't get treated very well by the administration [of the high school] ... Even our teach-

ers ... we didn't get treated very well by them either ... It was racial. I mean, it wasn't any lower expectations, it wasn't *anything* (italics in original) ... You weren't given the opportunity to do what they did. We were degraded the whole time we were there. (Cohn, 1997, p. 164)

This vignette conveys a pervasive quality of racial discrimination that seems to pervade the protagonist's inner experience in school. Given the strong connection between achievement in school and success at work (Blustein et al., 2000; Marshall & Tucker, 1992), the comments of this young man serve to inform our knowledge about the considerable barriers that differentially and arbitrarily inhibit one's access to rewarding work.

Another important aspect of the working experience within the United States is the plight of Mexicans who move north to find employment. The broad implications of this migration are too complex to detail here given the political, social, and economic ramifications of such dramatic shifts in population over the past decades (Arbona, 1995). However, the psychological aspects of this migration are clearly integral to an inclusive psychology of working. The following passage describes an individual's migration to the United States and then highlights his experiences in a chicken factory:

I'm from Mexico, Veracruz. I paid a "coyote" to bring me here—that's what we call the guides. It cost me one thousand and two hundred dollars. To come, you have to cross a desert, so it is pretty hard and it is dangerous. It takes four days and three nights and you can't get out of the truck. You can't stop. You are in these trucks, packed like sardines, very tight, and the trucks keep moving and turning around with us inside .... The coyote brought us straight to the work contractors who hire us and then the farmers hire us from them. A farmer brought me up to North Carolina from Texas .... I work very fast, and I am not always checking what I'm doing even while I'm doing dangerous work, like deboning with the disk saws. We are slaves. They don't care. If we are not done with the truck full of chickens, we cannot leave work at the end of our shift. Sometimes it's because of mechanical breakdown, machinery malfunction—nothing that we did, but it doesn't matter. We can't leave .... Another thing—racism. The large majority of the workers here are illegal Hispanics, like me. There's also some legal Hispanics, some Haitians, and black gringos. But most of us are illegal Hispanics. The bosses know we're illegal, and it's illegal for them to hire us, but we're the cheapest so they don't care .... And they always yell at us Hispanics. (Bowe et al., 2000, pp. 229–230)

The excerpt from this Mexican American worker in the chicken factory in North Carolina describes how many people of color live in impoverished conditions, often resulting in their need to leave their homes to look for work elsewhere. Moreover, the vignette describes how the intense deprivation associated with lack of work, culminating in chronic poverty, can lead to situations where people lose their dignity and freedom. As I have sought to convey throughout this book, access to work is one of the central strivings in our lives, and the absence of work leads to a chain of despair that affects entire communities.

In the next section of this chapter, I explore the impact of sexism, which has also evoked considerable creative and thoughtful research and policy innovations as well as powerful and compelling narratives from workers and potential workers.

Gender and Sexism

The study of sexism in vocational psychology and organizational psychology has a rich tradition of scholarship that has considerable implications for counseling practice and public policy (e.g., Betz & Fitzgerald, 1987; Fitzgerald & Weitzman, 1992; Gutek, 1987; Walsh & Osipow, 1994). In fact, the study of how women have prepared for and engaged in work has provided one of the most prominent means of infusing a social and contextual focus into the psychological study of working (Blustein, 2001a; M. S. Richardson, 1993). In this section, I focus on the role of sexism as a social barrier, which has functioned and continues to function to reduce the access that women have to a meaningful and financially secure working environment.

The prevalence of sexism in the workforce has been established in a number of broad and far-reaching analyses (see Betz & Fitzgerald, 1987; Phillips & Imhoff, 1997; Powell, 1999; Walsh & Osipow, 1994). Since the early 1970s, studies in vocational psychology (e.g., Harmon, 1972) have presented compelling evidence that women have faced considerable barriers in their educational preparation and in their ability to attain occupations that match their talents and interests. The early scholarship in this area tended to highlight the fact that women confronted more complex career decisions in large measure because they needed to make choices about their working lives in conjunction with decisions about their degree of involvement in family caregiving tasks (Betz & Fitzgerald, 1987; Harmon, 1972; Powell, 1999). (Of course, men also face family–work conflicts, but socialization within Western nations has typically placed the primary responsibility for the caregiving of children on the shoulders of women. However, shifts in the distribution of caregiving and housework responsibilities are finally changing, albeit slowly; Kikoski & Kikoski, 1996; Silverstein, Auerbach, & Levant, 2002.) Empirical research in vocational psychology has conveyed a picture of a world in which women have had to choose between having children and having a meaningful career (Betz & Fitzgerald, 1987; Ireland, 1993). Indeed, one of the most often cited studies in the literature on women's career development is the longitudinal investigation by Terman and Oden (1959) in which the lives of gifted men and women were followed over the course of much of their life spans. This study revealed that the decision to focus on marriage and child care emerged as the most important predictor of a woman's occupational attainment. Naturally, one may argue that gifted women who opt out of the labor market are, in fact, making a conscious life choice. However, a closer look at the socialization forces that have been functioning in Western cultures about women and work reveals that, for many women, the experience of free choice on this issue has not been the case (Betz & Fitzgerald, 1987). Rather, women very often faced hostility from their families and in the workplace if they did not conform to the rigid sex roles that governed life throughout Western cultures during much of the 20th century. Höpfl and Atkinson (2000) have argued that many of the broader public policy decisions that have led to such a dramatic bifurcation of gender roles have been made by men without much consideration of their impact on women.

Historically, social changes evoked by labor shortages during World War II are typically viewed as one of the primary causes of the shift in the labor market that allowed and, in fact, encouraged the involvement of women. Because men were needed for military service, women increasingly were needed to work in factories that were producing supplies for the war effort. Once the war ended, women were once again expected to return to their homes, subordinating any aspirations that they may have had about marketplace work to the aspirations of their husbands. However, women working outside of the home began to appreciate the benefits that working provided, particularly the independence and access to resources. It is important to note, however, that not all women in Western cultures have faced the same set of expectations. For example, African American women have historically worked outside of the home, which has been described by scholars as a logical outgrowth of women's work during slavery times (Carter & Cook, 1992). By the 1960s, feminist thought emerged as an important social movement throughout many Western nations, resulting in significant changes in the way in which women related to work both inside and outside of the home (e.g., Friedan, 1963).

The feminist movement, which actually has several different theoretical and ideological strands (see Brabeck & Ting, 2000, for a review of these lines of thought), has encouraged women and men to take a closer look at the socialization process that has resulted in such starkly distinct gender roles. Among the most obvious manifestations of gender role socialization is the way in which women and men perceive and confront their responsibilities to both work and family. Beginning in large measure during the 1960s, many of the tenets about how women and men should deal with work and career were reexamined. Like their colleagues in the multicultural arena, feminist scholars in counseling psychology in particular have had an enormous impact on the social landscape in the domains of educational and career development (e.g., Astin, 1984; Betz, 1989; Betz & Fitzgerald, 1987; Farmer, 1985; Gilbert, 1988; Hackett & Betz, 1981; Harmon, 1972). For example, one of the most important lines of work emerging from this intellectual current has been the focus on self-efficacy beliefs. In the early 1980s, Betz and Hackett (1981) demonstrated that self-efficacy beliefs (which reflect one's beliefs about one's ability to accomplish specific tasks) are a stronger predictor of female college students' aspirations to pursue careers in science and technology than are their abilities). The importance of self-efficacy beliefs in career development, which are determined primarily via interpersonal and contextual factors (Betz, 1992; Lent & Brown, 1996), underscores the powerful role of social filters as major factors in one's working life. Moreover, the literature on self-efficacy, which has stimulated the development of a social cognitive theory of career choice and development (Lent et al., 2002), has helped to explain the fact that women often disavowed their abilities and interests in seeking out options in the world of work.

By the 1980s, a fully formed literature emerged that addressed women's career development and organizational life (e.g., Betz & Fitzgerald, 1987; Gutek, 1987). This body of work clearly has acknowledged the pervasive impact of sexism in the social fabric of many cultures. This literature has been critically informative in understanding how gender influences the development of vocational interests (e.g., Betz & Fitzgerald, 1987; Hackett & Betz, 1981) as well as the career decision-making and vocational adjustment processes (Fitzgerald & Weitzman, 1992). One of the most important implications of the feminist infusion of new ideas and perspectives has been the argument that personal and psychological issues have broader political contexts and meanings (L. Brooks & Forrest, 1994). Indeed, the contribution by Brooks and Forrest has outlined a compelling set of assumptions about the sociopolitical factors that shape so many aspects of working life. Foremost among these assumptions is the observation that women face significant power differentials in many aspects of their lives, with substantial implications in the working context. Following this line of reasoning, the lack of access to the most productive and facilitative conditions that would promote satisfying and rewarding work lives is a function of a system that differentially distributes resources based on demographics and not on merit or effort. In relation to gender issues, women face various manifestations of sexism in their schooling, preparation for careers, and in the occupational context (cf. Betz & Fitzgerald, 1987; Fassinger, 2000). While this observation is fairly well accepted among many within the social sciences, the Brooks and Forrest analysis of career issues for women, with its explicit political and social arguments and its clear linkage of working to power, fits well with the conceptual foundation of an inclusive psychology of working.

Another aspect of women's experiences at work is sexual harassment. The existence of sexual harassment has continually emerged as a major social and personal crisis for women (Fitzgerald, 2003; Fitzgerald & Rounds, 1994; Russell, 1994). Fitzgerald and Weitzman (1992) noted that sexual harassment affects women psychologically, physically, and financially. The impact is typically quite intensive and pervasive, often reaching into families and cutting across generations (Riger, 1991). The following vignette describes some of the inner experiences of a woman who has faced sexual harassment; this vignette is also informative about the plight of workers without proper citizenship, who may have to engage in relationships that strike at the core of their values and identity:

> This man hinted that I could lose my job if I didn't agree. He also said that if I went out with him, I could get a better job and a higher wage. Finally, I agreed. I was with him until two months ago. He's the father of my two children. When my family realized what I did, they told me never to return home. A few months ago, he was transferred. I don't know how I'm going to maintain my children. (C. Richardson, 1999, p. 101)

The recent analysis by Höpfl and Atkinson (2000) assessing the future of work for women culminated in conclusions that are analogous to the positions that I present in this book about the psychology of working. Höpfl and Atkinson eloquently described how power lies at the root of many of the inequities found in the working context. Thus, men have typically been in the position of power to define work in a given culture and to distribute the resources that affect access to working. Moreover, Höpfl and Atkinson noted that the traditional career narrative, particularly for men, is based to a great extent on the exercise of volition or choice. Taking the work of Höpfl and Atkinson together with the seminal contributions of Betz and Fitzgerald (1987), Farmer (1997), Fassinger (2000), Harmon (1972) and others affirm the perspective outlined in this book about the centrality of work in people's lives and the inequitable distribution of access to meaningful, secure, and rewarding working experiences.

Outside of Western cultures, the impact of sexism has been differentially experienced, depending on a host of factors, including the way in which given cultures define work and gender roles. However, it is important to note that women, for the most part, have been exposed to sexism in various forms (e.g., Stockman, Bonney, & Xuewen, 1995). Furthermore, the vast majority of women around the globe still confront multiple demands from working within the home and working outside of the home (Andersen & Collins, 1992). For example, recent volumes on women's work in such diverse places as Russia, the Ukraine, and Sri Lanka (e.g., Andersen & Collins, 1992; Jain & Reddock, 1998) all point to the reality that women face significant obstacles with respect to their occupational attainment and treatment at work. The following vignette describes the experience of women in Afghanistan living under the Taliban's rule and their struggle to organize into a structured group (i.e., Revolutionary Association of the Women of Afghanistan; RAWA):

> Those days, not only in Afghanistan, but in other regions too, women were under great pressure, not only from social problems and other oppressions but also in their family. So women suffered multilayer oppressions. Obviously those who came together to establish RAWA were aware of the plight of women in Afghanistan .... We all had our own experiences, either personally in our family, or seeing our neighbors .... We were daily witnesses of rape, of domestic violence in families, and oppressions in work and all aspects of life. It was obvious that women always had the inferior role in family, society, and everywhere. And we thought that one woman cannot change all of this; there needed to be many women coming together, establishing a group movement to get rid of these inequalities. (Brodsky, 2003, p. 44)

As reflected in this vignette, the nature of totalitarian societies can have an enormous impact on the work lives of citizens, particularly individuals who may be easily categorized based on appearance and then targeted for oppression. In this case, the Taliban rulers effectively disempowered an entire cohort of the population by denying women the right to work. The preceding vignette underscores the importance of relational connections (Flum, 2001; Josselson, 1992) as a means of developing resilience in the face of social barriers, thereby fostering the very difficult and dangerous work of seeking to change oppressive social and political conditions.

As conveyed thus far, the social scientific literature highlights the role that sexism has played in women's career development (e.g., Brooks & Forrest, 1994; Fitzgerald & Weitzman, 1992). Because of sexism and because of other social filters, women often have had to consider work that involves their own sexuality as a commodity. (Men also have become sex workers throughout history, primarily within same-sex contexts, which has a different set of power issues.) Indeed, an inclusive psychology of working will need to come to terms with the sex industry, which has a global reach and has considerable implications for women's physical and psychological health, power, and welfare (Dalla, 2002; Sanders, 2001). (It is important to note that by including sexual work in this discussion, I am not implicitly or explicitly endorsing it as a viable source of work or income. Indeed, from moral and psychological perspectives, sexual work presents significant and very troublesome problems relating to power inequities and sexual abuse. Sexual work, however, is part of the landscape of the contemporary working world. The subordinate role that women face at work, particularly in sexual work, calls for a focus on women's experiences in this section.)

Called "the oldest profession," prostitution has been and continues to be a source of work for some women. Obviously, prostitution presents many problems for women, most of which revolve around the vast power differential that exists between women and men in these roles, the implied or explicit threats of violence, and the overall subjugation of women's bodies to the needs of men (Dalla, 2002; Sanders, 2001). In addition, men, who seek to disempower women to maintain their control, often manage prostitution, thereby further enhancing the power differential. Currently, the sex industry, most of which is underground, has expanded to include the Internet, video productions, and other technological venues. Nevertheless, the experience of working for women in the sex industry merits our attention as we strive to expand the scope of inquiry in the psychology of working. The following vignette from the Bowe et al. (2000) volume of a stripper's working life gives voice to at least some aspects of sex work:

> My office job didn't pay all of the bills—especially the $2,000 one that Visa kept sending me—I was already thinking about taking a second job waiting tables, which I had way too much experience at for my liking. So I thought about this stripper thing .... I took the bus to the Lusty Lady, a generic club near the financial district. I told the bouncer at the door that I was there to become a stripper, and asked to talk to the manager. He looked me over from head to toe .... I supposed I passed his test, because he brought me to the stage manager, Shannon, who took me into the dressing room .... There wasn't any kind of typical customer—I dealt with everyone from frat boys to a [fast-food chain] counterman to a school teacher to an ex-con to a lot of stockbrokers. And every one of them was capable of turning violent. It started to really warp my sense of men. Every guy I saw walking down the street turned into a customer in my eyes .... I quit stripping after about a year. It was a very smart decision. Certain people can't handle it—obviously I'm one of them. I think it really depressed and disturbed me. It was much more tiring than I had imagined. And much, much more sleazy that I had

imagined. When I first started, I felt in a sense, it was theater. I was made to feel like a performer when I walked into the dressing room. There were overstuffed couches, makeup lights. Toward the end, I walked into the same room and felt completely different about it. I saw dirt I hadn't seen before, grime I hadn't seen before—the place felt so slimy I just wanted to throw up. (pp. 449–454)

This vignette describes many aspects of sexual working that had previously been on the margins of discourse in social scientific analyses of working. The actual experience of working in the sex industry, as conveyed by this protagonist, is characterized by the implicit threat of violence and by the objectification of women. Rather than attempting to generalize from this one specific narrative, our task is to move closer to the inner experience that is evident in this vignette. In doing so, we gain access to a psychological world where work is linked inexorably with abuses of power. In this case, the function of work in providing access to the sources of survival and power is manifested in multiple levels. People engage in sex work, as in many other types of work, to earn a living—to obtain the resources needed to survive. This striving for power and resources, which is a core function of working across occupations, is then confounded with the power differentials in sex work, which are highly charged and tinged with implicit and explicit threats of violence (Sanders, 2001).

In moving closer to the broad array of inner experiences of women at work, the striving for power is evident in both the traditional research and theoretical literature as well as in women's narratives. One of the major themes within the career-psychology-of-women literature is the notion that working outside of the home represents a viable means of attaining power and equity in the world (Betz & Fitzgerald, 1987). A number of senior scholars in this area have openly advocated for women to engage in work outside of the home (e.g., Betz & Fitzgerald, 1987; Fitzgerald & Weitzman, 1992), noting that men who are caregivers at home are viewed as unemployed in Western contexts. The rationale for the argument raised by Betz, Fitzgerald, and others becomes even more compelling in light of the rapid changes in the world of work. Following Rifkin's (1995) argument (summarized in chapter 2), it would seem critically important for everyone to prepare for work and not to depend on others. Moreover, the dramatic changes in the structure of families (Hetherington, Bridges, & Insabella, 1998), with increases in divorce, single-parent families, and lesbian and gay parents, underscore the need for women and men to strive to work in the market economy. The core of the argument articulated by Fitzgerald and Weitzman (1992) is that work offers access to the resources that are needed to survive and flourish in society, a position that is similar to the one advocated in this book.

As we adopt the psychology-of-working perspective, the next step is to explore how female workers understand challenges that touch on the connection between work and power. The next vignette, taken from S. A. Friedman's (1996) contribution on women and working, describes a technical writer for a bank in the financial district of New York City:

> I can be a very timid person. I was in a convent as a novice. I've sat in a therapist's office for weeks on end, staring at the floor and not saying a word. I have let men walk all over me. But when it came to needing money, I always took risks. I was always very aggressive.

> The only way I could ever get anything I wanted was if I earned the money myself. I never wanted someone to come and rescue me. It never occurred to me. I would much rather take care of myself. I wouldn't have to depend on anyone else. I wouldn't owe anyone anything.

> My parents were hurt by the Depression. Money became a power tool. My mother had to ask my father for money every day, and they were married for forty years. She had to tell him what she was buying that day and he would give her what she needed. As a child I felt poor .... (p. 157)

This vignette describes the struggle to survive in a way that is often overlooked in academic contexts. In this woman's story, it is possible to discern how sexism can play such a pernicious role in the lives of women. Without access to work, women are clearly left in a subordinate position, one that maintains power hierarchies that privilege men. However, access to work and the consequent connections to social and economic power can radically shift the status quo, a point that has been a central tenet of feminism during the past few decades.

The vignettes presented here, coupled with the selected review of relevant empirical and theoretical literature on women and working, reveals that the struggle to survive and attain the socially sanctioned means of power in society (via working) has been significantly constrained by sexism. The literature on the career psychology of women has, in many ways, foreshadowed the inclusive psychology of working that I am advocating in this book (cf. Betz & Fitzgerald, 1987; Fassinger, 1996; Harmon, 1994; Harmon & Farmer, 1983; Höpfl & Atkinson, 2000). This literature has highlighted the vast inequities that impact differentially and aversively on the lives of girls and women as they prepare for work and as they seek to engage in meaningful working lives. The struggle for equality and the consequences of not attaining a level playing field have led to the feminization of poverty, in which women are very often disproportionately engulfed in economic circumstances that offer little hope and little access to upward mobility (Jain & Reddock, 1998; Höpfl &

Atkinson, 2000). In the section that follows, I explore poverty in further depth by exploring how social class functions to filter access to opportunity.

Social Class and Classism

Although social class has been discussed in the social sciences for generations, especially within sociology (e.g., Roberts, 1978; Willis, 1977), psychology has had an ambivalent relationship to exploring the role of social class in human behavior. On one hand, applied psychologists in the early part of the 20th century were quite aware of the impact of social stratification on individual behavior, including many thoughtful analyses of the influence of social class in relation to work (Bell, 1938; Dearborn & Rothney, 1938). Yet the infusion of thoughtful discussions of social class has only recently become part of the intellectual landscape in psychology (e.g., Kliman, 1998; Liu, 2001, 2004; Lott, 2002). In actuality, the impact of social class, both in intellectual discourse and in real life, is highly complex and embedded within other social filters and sources of discrimination.

Scholarly discussions of social class have historically been placed within a macro-level analysis of social systems (e.g., Giddens, 1983; Milner, 1999; Willis, 1977). Numerous definitions of social class have been advanced, ranging from strictly economic variables, such as parental income or educational level (e.g., Sewell & Hauser, 1975) to more complex definitions involving the broader array of influences that frame one's social and economic affordances (Fouad & Brown, 2000; Giddens, 1983; Liu, 2001; Willis, 1977). One particularly illuminating definition from a sociological perspective is offered by Milner (1999), who proposed that class "denote(s) a social group, conceived as located within a hierarchical order of unequal such groups, the identity and membership of which is primarily determined by 'economic' considerations such as occupation, income, and wealth" (p. 1).

A major debate within the social sciences has to do with how social class actually affects the course and trajectory of one's working life. On one side of this debate are scholars who argue that social class functions as a structural factor, determining access to resources and supports that would foster high levels of occupational attainment (e.g., Blustein et al., 2002; Rossides, 1990; Sewell & Hauser, 1975). In contrast, cultural production scholars (e.g., Willis, 1977) suggest that various aspects of a given social class are manifested in one's culture and are therefore internalized into one's beliefs and values system. The approach that I endorse is closer to the structural position, which I believe tends to underscore the vast impact that social and economic factors play in one's access to the antecedents of a rewarding and empowering working life. However, I am not adopting a dogmatic position that ignores the fact that various elements of social class are, in fact, transformed into cultural and psychological attributes and no doubt affect how one relates to school, education, and, indeed, to oneself. As is evident from these definitions and the corresponding debate about the meaning of social class, the function of working in giving people access to the means of survival and power clearly needs to incorporate an explicit focus on social class.

Another complication that needs to be included here is the reality that social class is confounded with race and gender (e.g., Helms & Cook, 1999; Höpfl & Atkinson, 2000; Liu, 2001). The distribution of resources within the United States has historically and currently been determined to a great extent by race and gender (Betz & Fitzgerald, 1987; Carter & Cook, 1992; Helms & Cook, 1999). That African Americans and women are disproportionately represented within poor and working class populations is a well-known attribute of American life (Helms & Cook, 1999; Loury, 2001). The complication that has arisen in public policy and intellectual circles has to do with unpacking racism, sexism, and social class. For example, some scholars have argued that racism is secondary in importance to social class (e.g., Lewis, 1966). Following this perspective, African Americans are thought to be struggling with a "culture of poverty" and therefore are primarily reacting to the historical influences of their impoverished social milieu and not to the impact of racism (Lewis, 1966). One of the problems with this position is that it functions to foster a treatment of racism as a minor annoyance or historical anachronism as opposed to a contemporary factor in life. Attempts to view race, social class, and gender without attention to their overlapping impact are unrealistic and obscure the reality of life in Western cultures. As such, I adopt a position in this book that considers the impact of race, gender, and social class as interrelated influences, which have complex and often enmeshed relationships. While some will argue that most of the poor in the United States are European American, the harsh reality is that the *proportion* of poor people increases dramatically for people of color (Helms & Cook, 1999; Danziger & Haveman, 2001).

The Impact of Social Class in the Working Context

Extensive research has been conducted on the impact of various elements of social class in relation to one's access to the resources needed to obtain work (e.g., M. T. Brown et al., 1996), educational transitions (McDonough, 1997), and occupational attainment (e.g., Sewell & Hauser, 1975). One of the most important findings in this body of work is that social class functions to facilitate or inhibit access to the resources and barriers that influence the options that people have in their lives (Sewell & Hauser, 1975). Taken together, these empirical reports reveal that access to the correlates of satisfying and empowering working experiences is powerfully framed by the circumstances of one's birth. If an individual is born into a wealthy family with access to good housing, adequate health care, and the sanctioned social attributes of a given culture, s/he is far more likely to negotiate a work life that will parallel the grand career narrative of the post-World War II period (Super, 1957). In contrast, people whose families of origin have not had access to jobs that offer lucrative or even sufficient salaries face far greater obstacles in their occupational attainment and fulfillment of their aspirations (M. T. Brown et al., 1996).

An interesting vista into the impact of social class in the transition from school to work can be found in a study that my colleagues and I conducted to explore how social class functions in a population of young people who were working in jobs that did not require college or specific skills (Blustein et al., 2002). Using a structured interview format, we examined the responses of 20 young adults; 10 of these individuals came from relatively lower socioeconomic backgrounds, and the other 10 came from middle-class backgrounds. The results of this investigation revealed that the individuals from the more affluent backgrounds had greater access to resources and supports within their families and schools. In contrast, the poorer youth who were at relatively similar jobs as the more affluent group tended to report far more barriers in their immediate familial and social contexts. The authors concluded that the relatively unskilled jobs may have been a resting point for the youth from the more affluent backgrounds, while these jobs may have been the final destination for the working class and poor youth. The experiences of the working class youth in their jobs tended to be characterized by a sense of hopelessness and frustration. The following comments from a few of the participants in our study give voice to the perceived functions of work that seemed to be evident within the cohort of young people from lower socioeconomic status:

> [T]he LSES [lower socioeconomic status] participants viewed reasons for working almost exclusively in terms of survival—receiving money and meeting basic needs. When Participant #38 was asked to describe the importance of money, he replied, "Very [important]. It's the only way you're going to survive. Can't go out and live off the land nowadays." This same participant viewed career success solely in terms of money. He stated, "I guess money, it's kind of shallow, but money had to be a big part of it." Participant #26 echoed these sentiments when he expressed, "Money is important …. It's just that's why I

want to get out of here and make some money. I don't care what it is. I'll do anything to make some money." (Blustein et al., 2002, p. 315)

The comments of these two participants convey a set of attitudes about the function of working that is often overlooked in contemporary analyses of career development. These observations from working class young adults underscore one of the core functions of working that is integral to the human experience—that is, the need for survival. The comments from the participants from more affluent families, illustrated next, tended to give voice to the "grand career narrative" that formed the essence of the career development movement of the second half of the 20th century:

> Another HSES [higher socioeconomic status] participant (#27) identified reasons for working in terms of satisfaction. He stated, "I think you could earn a lot of money in a job … and everything; you're not going to be happy so it's not like even worth it …. So as long as you're satisfied, that would be the main thing." HSES participant #33 defined reasons for working as "interest in what I do. I like to come to work and like what I'm doing. Um, that's what I get the most out of." (Blustein et al., 2002, p. 315)

These participants seem to be describing the function of working in a way that more closely resembles the views articulated in the vocational psychology and career development literatures; that is, they are motivated by the desire for self-expression in their work lives. In a general sense, the findings presented in this investigation suggest that social class does, in fact, influence access to opportunity, but it also affects how people construe their working experiences. These findings also underscore how social class intersects with the need for self-determination. As these results suggest, individuals from higher socioeconomic classes would likely have greater access to work that would be more intrinsically interesting. Although our study included a small sample from a circumscribed region of the United States, the findings were consistent with many other investigations and theoretical formulations regarding the pervasive role of social class in the attainment of meaningful and rewarding occupational goals (cf. M. T. Brown et al., 1996; Fouad & Brown, 2000).

Emerging from sociological studies of work, Halle's (1984) study of workers at an automated chemical plant in New Jersey provides an illuminating glimpse into the role of social class in working life. First, this 6-year ethnographic project furnished Halle with a clear sense of how jobs for the working class differ from jobs for the middle class. Halle's analysis revealed that working class jobs have the following characteristics:

■ Jobs for the working class tended to require only modest levels of formal education.

■ The class structure regenerates itself in the observation that working class men were most likely to engage in relationships with others from similar backgrounds.

■ Most working class jobs are relatively distant from the decision-making power within organizations.

The second and perhaps most noteworthy conclusion reached by Halle pertains to his notion of a class consciousness that he observed among the working class participants in his study. In short, Halle noticed that the men in his study seemed to maintain a clear sense of themselves as "working men," an aspect of their identities that transcended other identity domains. For Halle's participants, the fact that they worked and earned a living defined a core aspect of their lives. The following dialogue between a mechanic and a researcher, from Halle's study, attests to this notion:

Worker: Am I a working man. You bet! I'm standing here freezing and breathing in all of these fumes [a reference to the fumes crowding out of vents in the ground].

Researcher: Are big business working men?

Worker: No. They don't have to stand out here in the cold.

Researcher: How about lawyers and doctors?

Worker: No, they're not working men. They don't have to breathe in this shit [the fumes]. You're not a working man if you work in an office …. (Halle, 1984, p. 207)

Halle's (1984) analysis of this internalized identity takes on two standard views of working class life in contemporary life. One of the main explanatory means of understanding working class life is via the lens of Marxist theory (see Giddens, 1983, for a concise overview of this position). From this perspective, the experience of a coherent identity as a worker represents the natural outcome of a legacy of oppression and despair, which is the logical outcome of people being used as a cog in a capitalist system where profits are considered as the ultimate value. The alternative perspective is one in which the working class is viewed as content with their opportunities and their lives. Halle argues that neither of these two options entirely captures the inner experience of working men. Rather, he suggests that "the concept of the working man implies a moral critique of the distribution of income. But that is not the same as losing a belief in the possibility of attaining material benefits within the system" (Halle, 1984, p. 299).

Halle's study suggests that one viable means of explaining the pervasive loss of structure and coherence within urban communities may be related to the loss of the identity of the "worker." For people who have been poor and have had little, if any, access to the resources needed for a job that is an expression of one's interests, the choice of the sort of work to pursue is often made based on availability. Yet, an analysis of social class barriers would not be complete without examining the way in which work functions in contexts where access to traditional market-based jobs is severely restricted. When we compare the working lives of folks from lower socioeconomic backgrounds with more affluent people, the poorer workers seem to struggle to find meaning and psychological sustenance in their work. Yet, the picture looks a bit different when we explore the dialectic of working versus not working at all. The participants in Newman's (1999) evocative study of young workers in a fast-food restaurant in Harlem (in New York City) gives voice to a complexity of experience that is often missed in more traditional academic discussions of work and social class. The following participant, an adolescent living in an urban community and who has been working in a hamburger restaurant, describes how she deals with her job in public and social contexts:

> Regardless of what kind of work you do, you still can be respected. Ain't saying I'm ashamed of my job, but I wouldn't walk down the street wearing the uniform .... Guys [who] know you work there will say, "Hi, Burger Barn." I ain't gonna lie and say that I'm not ashamed, period. But, I'm proud that I'm working. You know, my daughter's father ... used to grab pigs and clean pigs all day. But he was respected for his job. I respected him because he worked, regardless of what kind of work it was. (Newman, 1999, pp. 99–100)

This narrative describes a sense of pride in work, despite the lack of prestige that is evoked by the well-known uniform of a fast-food worker. This one perspective provides one of the notes in a highly variegated song about working and social class. The impact of social class is further explicated in Wilson's (1996) book about the impact of the loss of employment in Chicago's urban core. For workers with few transferable skills, the diminished manufacturing base in the United States, particularly in urban centers, has led to a chain of events that is devastating. As detailed in chapter 2, Wilson argues that the loss of work for the adults in urban communities leaves people with little connection to their social worlds. The impact of social class is particularly noteworthy in Wilson's study in that the urban workers had few resources to cope with the loss of employment opportunities. From the most basic means of transportation to the social capital needed to obtain further education and training, the entire life space of the urban working class described in Wilson's study is filled with obstacles. These obstacles include the impact of classism, racism, and sexism, which function in tandem to create essentially two, unequal worlds in the urban/suburban landscape of the United States (cf. Reich, 1991, 1999).

Provided that one can obtain a job, people face continued struggles in negotiating the power dynamics of occupational contexts, which often reinforce rigid hierarchical patterns between workers and supervisors. This theme is evident in the following excerpt from a poem by Tom Wayman entitled "Boss":

> The boss who stands behind you
> watching you work.
> The boss who insists
> "I'm sure I told you to do that."
> The boss who, after you've made nine trips
> Carrying an extra-heavy load of boards,
> sees you walking with a light load
> and tells your foreman to order you to work harder
> The boss who commands you to look busy.
>
> The foreman who can't resist showing you a better way.
> The foreman who won't let you
> do something a better way.
> The one who is also head
> of the union's grievance committee.
> The foreman who is unable or forgot to
> requisition enough parts
> and orders you to "make do with what you have."
> (found in Oresick & Coles, 1990, p. 234)

The passage from Wayman's poem describes a power hierarchy at work that generally leaves people from lower social class origins in a subordinate position. Thus, the struggle for survival and power, which forms one of the core elements in the psychology of working, takes shape, often quite sharply, within the day-to-day experience of one's occupational context. In contrast to Halle's description of working class culture within a production plant in the 1980s, current occupational shifts are likely creating greater contact between workers from different backgrounds. The relatively circumscribed work contexts of the industrial era, in which factory workers and clerical workers maintained a sort of unique culture within larger organizations, are now being replaced by more horizontal settings. The advent of a service labor market within a global economy may result in less insulated occupational contexts that may result in a number of possible implications. On one level, people from different social classes may interact more freely, thereby reducing class boundaries. Alternately, the scenario conveyed in the Wayman poem may become more prominent as language, social and occupational position, and other indices of background create highly stratified and complex power dynamics in work settings. It is difficult to make an informed prediction about how social class will be manifested in the rapid waters of contemporary changes in working.

A recent set of contributions by Liu and his colleagues has helped to advance psychological treatments of social class (Liu, 2001; Liu, Soleck, Hopps, Dunston, & Pickett, 2004). Liu et al. noted appropriately that social class has not been defined in a careful or theoretically informed way in psychological research. Liu (2001) has proposed that the definition of social class revolves around the concept of worldview. The *social class worldview* (SCW) "is defined as the beliefs and attitudes that help the individual to understand the demands of one's economic culture, develop the behaviors necessary to meet the economic culture demands, and recognize how classism functions in one's life" (Liu et al., 2004, p. 9).

The Liu et al. (2004) social class worldview model offers some useful implications for the psychology of working. The social class worldview model (SCWM) is based on the assumption that strictly economic or sociological definitions of social class do not adequately capture the depth of inner experiences of social class. A key attribute of the SCWM is that it seeks to capture such emotional experiences as envy, guilt, and entitlement. In addition, Liu et al. developed a compelling case for considering the subjective experience of class differences as being central to psychological considerations of social class. As such, the Liu et al. model brings the study of social class closer to the psychological studies of race and racism, which have been significantly facilitated by the use of racial identity status models (Helms & Cook, 1999).

In defining the SCWM, Lui et al. (2004) described three specific attributes, which are detailed below:

> First, people are assumed to live in economic cultures, which are local environments (e.g., a neighborhood, a work environment) that place demands on them to survive and maintain their perceived position within that particular social class group (i.e., homeostasis). Hence, people attempt to live up to expectations placed on them by their economic culture. Meeting expectations successfully implies homeostasis both cognitively and affectively, but failure to meet the economic culture's expectations may lead to feelings of depression and anxiety, which we term *internalized classism.*

Second, the SCW is the intrapsychic framework (i.e., lens) through which people make sense of the economic cultural expectations and filter the demands into meaningful actions to meet expected economic culture goals. The worldview consists of a person's relationships to property (materialism), social class behaviors (e.g., manners and etiquette), lifestyle choices (e.g., vacation time), referent groups (family, peers, and a group of aspiration), and consciousness about social class. Consider the domains in the worldview to be apertures, and depending on the saliency of these various domains in the worldview, a person enacts and interprets classism in his or her life. That is, not everyone is classist in every possible way, but rather people tend to act out and experience classism in meaningful ways that are individualistic, related to their economic culture, and connected to their SCW.

[The third attribute is] *classism* [which] is defined as prejudice and discrimination directed at people engaged in behaviors not congruent with the values and expectations of one's economic culture. The types of classism described in the SCWM include upward (feelings against those perceived to be snobs and elitists), downward (feelings against those perceived worse off), lateral ("keeping up with the Joneses" because the Joneses keep reminding you that you are falling behind), and internalized. *Internalized classism* is defined as the negative emotional and cognitive consequences experienced by the individual resulting from that individual's inability to meet the demands of his or her economic culture. (p. 10)

The contributions from Liu and his colleagues have significant potential to reshape scholarship and theory development in relation to the psychology of working. The focus on understanding the subjective nature of class-related experiences is certainly consistent with the position that I have been outlining in this book. In addition, the SCWM identifies classism as a sister construct to social class, much as racism and sexism have been corollary concerns in the study of race and gender, respectively. By exploring the impact of classism, the burden of changing one's class-related worldviews to suit the superordinate group is potentially transformed. Much as Helms and Cook (1999) have so powerfully argued that the work of "change" needs to focus on those in power, a similar view can be inferred from the SCWM literature. That is, instead of efforts being devoted to diminish selected attributes of a given social class membership (such as a mode of dress, way of speaking), it may be more fruitful to explore how classism is perpetuated in overt and covert ways. Furthermore, the SCWM offers researchers in the working realm a viable conceptual tool that can help to standardize studies of social class and classism.

The literature on social class and working, like the other social barriers that I am exploring, is extensive, yet inconclusive. Without question, we know that social class functions as a major factor in creating an unequal playing field for people in their educational and working lives. We also know that social class, race, and gender all contribute in complex ways in tandem to the experience of working for individuals. And, while some authors have used intensive interviewing and other qualitative methods to obtain an experience-near sense of working (e.g., Newman, 1999; Rubin, 1994; Wilson, 1996), there is still much to be learned about how people understand and construct the relationship between social class and work. Moreover, scholars who work from a psychology-of-working perspective will need to understand the implications of classism (cf. Liu et al., 2004; Lott, 2002), which very likely functions in subtle yet powerful ways to maintain the structural attributes of society that privilege one group of people over others.

Disabling Conditions

Another highly complex social barrier that profoundly affects working life is ability/disability status. Following the insights of Wright (1983), later echoed by Neff (1985), the term "disabled" is considered inaccurate and even potentially stigmatizing in that it does not consider the reality that a disabling condition does not necessarily dominate a given person's life. For example, an individual who is paralyzed from the waist down may in fact be able to function quite well in a wide array of domains and will therefore not experience the sense that his or her condition is the sole focal point of identity or self-concept. Disabling conditions may impact on a wide array of biological, physical, and developmental contexts. Consistent with the views that are prevalent in rehabilitation counseling (e.g., Szymanski & Parker, 1996), I am adopting a definition of disabling conditions that includes individuals whose physical, psychological, or developmental functioning impairs their functioning in a consistent and maladaptive fashion.

The role of disabling conditions as a social barrier has a historic and disconcerting history in human evolution. As Neff (1985) observed, one of the major problems faced by individuals with disabling conditions is the sense of social stigma that has been part of human history throughout the millennia. Harkening back to the Middle Ages in Europe, Foucault (1965) described mentally ill people being sent up and down rivers in France, with the proscribed role of "fool" or "buffoon." More recently, social stigma theory has been applied to our understanding of individuals with disabling conditions. Following the work of Goffman (1961), the application of sociological and social psychological theory to our understanding of individuals with disabling conditions has proven to be quite fruitful. Specifically, Goffman observed that the existence of an overt disabling condition evokes social distance in the behavior of others within one's social space. In effect, the experience of a disabling condition often evokes a sense of distinctness in others. This feeling then becomes transformed into social stigma, which often leaves people with disabling conditions in an isolated or disconnected social space.

The literature in vocational rehabilitation (e.g., Szymanski, Hershenson, Ettinger, & Enright, 1996; Szymanski & Parker, 1996, 2003; Wright, 1983), which has an extensive tradition in counseling, provides important insights to understanding the impact of disabling conditions for the psychology of working. In contrast to the focus on "grand career narratives" that characterized much (but clearly not all) of the vocational psychology and organizational psychology traditions, rehabilitation counseling has maintained a focus on work and working as opposed to focusing solely on hierarchic careers. For many of the clients who confronted a work environment that was not particularly accepting of diversity in ability/disability, the goals were to obtain employment as a means of ensuring survival and not necessarily as a manifestation of one's interests or abilities. In the United States and other Western nations, people with very pronounced disabling conditions were generally supported by government payments that provided a modest means of surviving. However, disability coverage has been available only to people who generally have no viable means of supporting themselves, which has not resolved the issue of survival for individuals with disabling conditions that did not result in a complete loss of functioning in a work context.

One of the more thoughtful contributions to emerge from vocational rehabilitation is Neff's (1985) work. As one of the first psychologists who sought to study working in a manner that is similar to the one I am advocating in this book, Neff adopted psychodynamic and social psychological perspectives to study work and human behavior. (Neff's contributions have been reviewed in chapter 1.) In relation to the study of disabling conditions, Neff focused primarily on the challenges of individuals with long-term psychiatric conditions. Neff argued that psychiatric impairments do not necessarily lead to impairments in the work domain. He proposed that a major goal of psychiatric rehabilitation is to restore the client's ability to work, even if the underlying disorder remains untreated. He also noted that the process of adapting to work involves more than simply the acquisition of specific skills or interpersonal attributes. Neff aptly observed that individuals need to acquire skills, attitudes, and values that are consistent with contemporary working environments. He also acknowledged that not everyone would be able to obtain the requisite skills needed to work in a competitive work context.

One of the hallmarks of the vocational rehabilitation movement has been the exploration of the meaning of working for individuals with disabling conditions (e.g., Black, 1988; Cinamon & Gifsh, 2004; Rubin & Roessler, 1987). For example, a debate has ensued within rehabilitation circles about the extent to which working represents a positive attribute on its own, above and beyond the extrinsic rewards that are available to workers (such as pay, benefits, etc.). Some scholars (e.g., Black, 1988) have argued that working provides a means of connecting an individual to a broader social context and may offer possibilities for feelings of accomplishment. Yet at the same time, other scholars have argued that it is not critical for individuals with pronounced disabling conditions to work, particularly because many of the rote tasks that were delegated to sheltered workshops and other noncompetitive occupational environments are now being accomplished via technology (see Black, 1988, for an overview of this position). Following this argument has been the suggestion that having individuals with disabling conditions working at highly routine tasks may reflect a form of oppression or discrimination. This point is worth exploring, particularly as some individuals are working who have little cognitive means for understanding what they are doing and why they are in fact engaging in selected tasks. For example, requiring that individuals with very minimal intelligence engage in mundane occupational tasks ought to be discussed and debated, particularly if the individuals have no viable means of indicating their feelings and beliefs about working. This debate, which has generated very thoughtful insights into the sociological and philosophical nature of working (Black, 1988; Neff, 1985), has considerable relevance to an inclusive psychology of working. The debate about the meaning of work that is not inherently interesting or rewarding is a critical issue in the psychology of working, as detailed in chapter 5. With technology replacing so many of the rote tasks that have characterized work in the early industrial era, I advocate that we immerse ourselves in the sort of thoughtful dialogue and debates that rehabilitation scholars have contributed to psychological discourse. (See chapter 2 for further discussion of the meaning of work in the face of changing job opportunities.)

Like the other sources of social barriers, the existence of disabling conditions has generally been examined from an experience-distant perspective. Indeed, for those practitioners and scholars without the sort of abling/disabling conditions that might impair functioning, the world of disabling conditions is conveniently placed at a distant pole in our internal psychological maps. I believe that the focus on the inner experience of workers and others who are confronting these social filters is necessary for a fully inclusive psychology of work. In the excerpt that follows, a worker who was born deaf describes her experiences as a merchandise handler in a department store:

I'm forty-eight years old. I was born deaf. And I have a condition called Usher's Syndrome. Most people who have it are born with normal vision and then later on in their lives they develop tunnel vision and then their vision starts to get smaller and smaller. When I was about thirty-seven or thirty-eight, my vision started to get a lot smaller, and it started to get blurrier until it just faded away. So right now, I have no vision whatsoever—well, I can see if somebody might turn on a light maybe. But that's it. So to communicate I'm using tactile signing where I'm actually having to hold on to people's hands when they sign me. So I can feel them making the signs.

I've been working here for two and a half years. It's the first real job I've ever had in my life. Before this, I was a housewife. Things didn't work out with my husband and I—and I was really sad that we got divorced .... My children were getting older, they'd gone off to college. I was by myself. I felt lonely. I couldn't really afford to pay my bills plus food, transportation ....

I really enjoy my job. I like it because it's something that I can do with my hands. It's easy for someone like me to do, and I can do it continuously. It's not complicated. It's not dangerous ....

And the people here are so nice. When I first started, there was one time I got lost, and I was wandering all over the place for a long time, and I kind of yelled out loud and someone came, a salesgirl, and she was able to guide me to where I was going, you know, and I was safe.

It's not like I don't have problems at work, though. I'm not saying that. Most of the time, I'm very organized—everything has its place and I'm used to things being in their place. But it's just nice the way they treat me. They're caring. They're very caring. They just seem sensitive to my needs.

I want to work. I think having a job is good for people—especially someone with a disability. It gives you a goal, something to get up and look forward to in the mornings and it gives you things to do. Without anything to do, I think you get more closed-minded. You feel more and more like there's not anything you can do. It hurts your self-esteem. Working is wonderful for your self-esteem. (Bowe et al., 2000, pp. 84–85)

This vignette describes an account of a woman who has lost two of the most vital senses. Yet, despite these losses, she seems to thrive at work, with the structure of working and the sense of social connection emerging most prominently. Lest we forget about the social stigma of disabling conditions, the next vignette conveys a somewhat less optimistic scenario. In this next contribution, a woman with polio describes an incident during her professional training:

I had applied for an internship and at the end of the interview, [the interviewer] said, 'Well, I've got to admit you know your stuff, but ... you have polio and no matter what I read in the reports about polio, I still think it's neurological, it's brain damage … I can't entrust our clients to a brain-damaged person.' I was really furious and upset and I went to my advisor and the head of the clinical division … and their response was to sort of pat me on the shoulder and say, 'That's really tough, that's not fair, maybe next year you'll get an internship.' They wouldn't go to bat for me, they wouldn't encourage me to fight it or anything. I was very alone. (Noonan et al., 2004, p. 74)

The complexity of working life when one is faced with a disabling condition is one of the more common threads in the material reviewed thus far. In both the theoretical material and in the vignettes, working presents both special challenges and opportunities for people with disabling conditions. For some individuals, working represents a connection to the social world (which is detailed in greater depth in chapter 4) as well as a source of self-esteem. Yet, at the same time, working can systematically expose people to the pain of the stigmatization and denigration that often characterizes the lives of individuals with disabling conditions. Furthermore, we are confronted with many thorny philosophical issues about working when we consider the reality that many individuals with severe cognitive deficits are placed in working contexts, often without their full volition. Thus, exploring the work lives of individuals with disabling conditions offers us a vista into issues about working that are often at the margins of consideration in most accounts of working within psychology. In the development of a psychology of working, I would hope that we would create space for inclusion of individuals with disabling conditions. From a conceptual standpoint, there is much for social and behavioral scientists as well as counselors to learn from our colleagues in the rehabilitation professions. Moreover, as counseling practice, prevention, and policy change emerge from this nascent field, we will need to incorporate tools and methods from rehabilitation counselors and psychologists who have increasingly developed activist roles not only within the professional world, but also within the political arena.

Sexual Orientation Diversity and Heterosexism

The marginalized status of individuals who are not heterosexual comprises a form of social categorization that is often excluded from discussions of human diversity and social justice. However, recent contributions, especially in counseling psychology (e.g., Chung, 2003; Dunkle, 1996; Fassinger, 1996, 2000; Pope, Prince, & Mitchell, 2000) have created a groundswell of interest in the working lives of lesbians, gay men, and individuals with bisexual or transgendered orientations. Lesbian, gay, bisexual, and transgendered (LGBT) individuals have been in the workforce since the advent of working life. However, within the past 30 years, greater attention has been devoted to identifying the challenges and opportunities that LGBT individuals face as they seek to explore viable vocational options and develop a rewarding work life.

Fassinger's (e.g., 1996, 2000) contributions on sexual orientation have helped to elevate awareness about the diverse sources of categorization and stigmatization that LGBT individuals face at work. Fassinger (2000) observed that the actual selection of careers (for those who have some choice in this matter) may be compromised by a number of internal and external factors. For example, some LGBT individuals may not be developmentally ready to make informed choices if they are still in the midst of sorting out their sexual orientation. In addition, some people who are exploring their sexual orientation may purposely select a given career (such as an abstinent religious vocation) as a means of warding off uncomfortable sexual strivings.

Once LGBT individuals move into the workforce, they continue to experience socially determined barriers that may impact their safety, security, and overall comfort in a given occupational context and more generally within their lives. First, given the reality that there is a history of physical abuse emanating from homophobic co-workers or peers, it is important to note that LGBT individuals continue to face potential physical danger as they venture in the workplace. Second, LGBT individuals may face marginalization or termination if they are open about their lifestyles and sexual orientations. Third, LGBT individuals often have to learn how to live two types of lives, one within an accepting community of peers and loved ones and a second within a workplace that may be homophobic or even physically threatening.

The intersection of roles in the lives of LGBT individuals as they relate to working underscores many important points about the psychology of working. The implausibility of circumscribing working from other aspects of life becomes immediately evident when one considers the lived-experience of LGBT workers. The following vignette by Rudel (1995) describes the experiences of an environmental health scientist as she seeks to find a way to be herself in her work life:

> Despite my core sense of my gayness as being okay, I have struggled with the issue of how to be out at work—and have felt very much alone in this endeavor. I am struck by the absence of role models, instruction books, or other resources for figuring out how to manage the process.

My job at the neuroscience research laboratory was particularly pleasant, largely because of the fact that the three professors in the department were women and that most of the students and staff in the lab were women. [This job preceded her current job, which is described next.] Despite the fact that my coworkers were nice, I typically did not bring up the fact that I am gay in general conversation. For example, when I moved in with my lover, I simply noted that I was moving and, if asked, gave her name without describing her as either a friend or a lover. While my coworkers did things outside of work with boyfriends or husbands or friends, I always did things with "friends." And while they talked about new love interests or a hot date or the painful end of a relationship, I was silent about my romantic pursuits. As a result of my reluctance to bring up gay-related parts of my life, I ended up censoring a lot about my life outside of work ....

Just before I left that job [at the neuroscience lab], I promised myself that in my next workplace I would be different. My guiding principle was going to be that I would be just as out about my sexual orientation as straight people were about theirs. I wanted to be myself, sharing what I would have shared had I had been straight. For example, in my new job at Gradient, I would use "we" all the time or say "Lisa did" this or "Lisa said" that without explaining who my partner Lisa was—just the way straight people did in referring to their spouses, who didn't require explanation ....

I soon began to realize that it was impossible for me to be out in the way I intended .... I cannot be myself without making a statement, because being myself means coming out, and coming out means defying the social order to be straight or be quiet. And so, I began to accept that I would often feel as if I was making a statement, and that the price I would pay for not making myself bring up the issue was continued invisibility. (pp. 53–58)

It is important to note as we examine working from a global perspective that many cultures still do not tolerate any variations at all from a sexual orientation that is fully heterosexual. The implications of being LGBT in a culture of this nature are no doubt dramatic and far-reaching, ranging well beyond one's access to work. Yet when we consider that work functions as one of the primary means by which people obtain power to ensure their survival, the stakes of being open in a homophobic work environment become far more potentially devastating for people. As in other sources of social barriers, diversity with respect to sexual orientation functions as a barrier that reduces access to the full array of education and work opportunities that might be available within a given community. In many ways, the struggle for LGBT people to attain equal access to the requisite skills and opportunities for a rewarding work life remains one of the great challenges that face those of us interested in social justice.

Social Barriers and Working in Psychological Treatment

As noted earlier in this volume, issues related to working have not had a clear or explicit place within most theories of psychotherapy. Despite the lack of explicit attention to issues pertaining to working and access to opportunity in clinical contexts, the process of psychotherapy encourages people to open themselves up to the deeply felt experiences that they may face as they struggle to obtain work, sustain themselves economically, and find meaning at work. As I have suggested earlier, the very process of preparing for, engaging in, and negotiating one's work life often embeds people most saliently with the social forces that function to stratify opportunity. In the case that I summarize next, issues pertaining to the role of social barriers in the development of a rewarding work life are presented in the context of a counseling case. (This case is fictional, but is based on themes that have emerged in my own clinical work.)

Mary Jane

Mary Jane was a 31-year-old European American woman who had sought therapy to work on issues related to the recent knowledge that she had been diagnosed with multiple sclerosis. In addition, she reported that she has struggled in some ways with her sexual orientation. Mary Jane presented with considerable depressive affect, anxiety, and interpersonal problems. The initial stages of treatment focused on ameliorating her depressive moods, which had interfered with her daily functioning and her ability to seek a job. Within the first few sessions, I referred Mary Jane to a psychiatrist, who concurred that Mary Jane would be a good candidate for anti-depressant treatment. Within the first two months of treatment, Mary Jane initiated a course of treatment with Zoloft and had begun to feel less depressed and anxious.

In this weekly treatment, which lasted for 18 months, Mary Jane initially worked on issues pertaining to her adjustment to the multiple sclerosis diagnosis. Although the disorder was not yet having a disabling impact upon her life, she was still quite worried about its impact and the potential that existed for more serious health problems. Mary Jane also had initiated a course of the new medication regimen that has been developed for people with multiple sclerosis, which was well tolerated and not causing major side effects. Within the first few months of treatment, Mary Jane discussed her concerns about her sexual orientation and her struggles at work. Since she was an adolescent, Mary Jane realized that she was attracted to women. Indeed, in college, she had initiated a long-term relationship with another woman, which had lasted for several years after college. However, her partner ended this relationship reportedly because her partner had felt that Mary Jane was not able to sustain an intimate relationship. Within the 5-year period since this relationship had ended and Mary Jane had initiated treatment with me, she was not involved in any serious long-term relationships. In fact, she had presented with feelings of loneliness and despair related to her sense of feeling isolated and unloved.

Mary Jane's family had moved to the southwest and she maintained reasonably close connections with them. Although she was "out" about her sexual orientation in her family of origin, the family essentially adopted a "don't ask, don't tell" policy with respect to her lesbian identity. Mary Jane's parents, however, had strongly invested in her achieving success in her career, which was their main focus in conversations with their daughter and their two other children. Mary Jane had strong interests in science and math as a young girl and had continued to pursue these areas, despite some obstacles along the way. Her parents seemed to want her to go into law or business, which were fields that were prevalent in her high-achieving and wealthy family. However, Mary Jane pursued engineering in college and obtained a degree in chemical engineering from a major state university in the mid-Atlantic region.

Once Mary Jane began to work in an engineering firm, she began to experience some hostility from some of her male co-workers, many of whom were not used to working with women as equals. Early in her career, she also was very open about her sexual orientation at work, which evoked additional hostility from her co-workers. She was often the victim of anti-gay and lesbian "jokes," which left her feeling alone and even ashamed of her sexual orientation. Furthermore, Mary Jane felt that she was not being considered for promotions and more challenging assignments, which would have helped to develop a track record for a promotion to a senior position. By the time she began therapy with me, she was feeling isolated at work, although she did have two good friends in the office who were supportive and warm to her. In addition to these friends at work, Mary Jane was connected to other lesbian women in the community.

When considering the stress of her work life, the recent news about her multiple sclerosis diagnosis seemed to add to her feelings of being overwhelmed. The psychological treatment focused on the major barriers she was experiencing as well as helping her to consolidate her strengths. Amidst the pain of her diagnosis and the struggles at work, Mary Jane also demonstrated considerable resilience. For example, she was able to develop connections at work despite the sense of feeling stigmatized and denigrated. Furthermore, she was extraordinarily bright and was able to work at a highly efficient and creative level at her job. Moreover, she was able to handle disappointment in an adaptive way. Yet at the same time, she was facing a difficult point in her life, with the combined effect of her gender, sexual orientation, and disability status interacting in ways that left her feeling far less empowered than she had in most of her life.

Using an integrative approach wherein I balanced work and relationship issues (e.g., Blustein & Spengler, 1995; see chapters 8 and 9 for further details) as well as action-oriented and insight-oriented approaches (e.g., Wachtel, 1993), I worked with Mary Jane to help her identify her strengths and to use her inner resources more adaptively in her current life circumstances. First, she began to feel less overwhelmed by her multiple sclerosis diagnosis by seeking out information from the regional multiple sclerosis society and by joining a support group of men and women with the disease. As she became more informed about multiple sclerosis, she felt more hopeful about her life. At the same time, we explored her feelings of vulnerability and sadness about the unfairness of her contracting this disease.

Another source of Mary Jane's feelings of disempowerment was related to her experiences at work. Her struggle as a lesbian woman in a traditionally male and homophobic organizational culture often left her feeling that she had to be disloyal to a significant aspect of her identity. In this context, I explored her feelings of anger about the unjustness of a culture that tolerated discrimination and prejudice based on one's sexual orientation. Mary Jane made a decision to deal with these issues on two fronts—a personal front and a sociopolitical front. From a personal perspective, Mary Jane was moving toward not tolerating anti-gay and lesbian jokes and comments. Rather than walking away feeling hurt and angry, Mary Jane decided to give voice to her feelings. We explored different scenarios in therapy for her to express her feelings in a way that would be understood by her co-workers. This was a complex and nuanced process in which I affirmed her intense feelings of anger; I also helped her to take a mindfulness approach to these feelings so that she did not feel overwhelmed by them. With the use of a mindfulness approach (Brown & Ryan, 2003), Mary Jane was able to develop a greater sense of resilience in the face of oppressive remarks. It is important to note that a mindfulness approach does not seek to invalidate a feeling state or to have a person feel shame about feelings (Brown & Ryan, 2003; Maske, 2002; Martin, 2002).

From the sociopolitical perspective, Mary Jane became more involved in LGBT activist groups in the community. She joined the Women's Center and volunteered to work with public policy groups in her city that were addressing heterosexism via legislation.

The next few months of therapy was devoted to helping Mary Jane develop more options with respect to work and her relational life. She began to understand that the level of sexism and homophobia was so pronounced at her current job that she might be better off in leaving for another company. As Mary Jane began to think more about her options, she realized that she also had a great deal of interest in teaching and research in chemical engineering. She then decided to explore doctoral programs in her area, which was very enriching for her. During this process, she began to try on the idea of moving to another part of the country and of starting a new educational venture that would enhance her sense of control and power in her life. She was accepted to one of the top programs in the United States with a guarantee for full funding throughout her training. She also chose this particular university because it was closer to her parents and siblings and the city it was located in was known for being particularly gay/lesbian friendly.

Exploring Mary Jane's relational life was actually quite complex and emotionally painful for her at times. Mary Jane acknowledged that she missed her partner and that she yearned to be in love again. She was aware that her previous partner had stated that she was not able to sustain the relationship with her; moreover, she was able to own that she had been ambivalent about the relationship, in part because she felt that her partner was not "perfect." As we explored this notion, it became clear to Mary Jane that she was being unrealistic about her expectations. In addition, she understood that she perhaps used this notion of her partner's lack of perfection as a means of warding off her fears of actually internalizing her lesbian identity. The doubts about her partner, in her recollections, were more prominent when she felt shamed by her colleagues. These insights were very useful to Mary Jane as she began to date a bit more. However, she was not able to connect to anyone with whom she felt that she could develop a long-term, intimate relationship.

By the time she terminated therapy, she was no longer struggling with any of the problems that were so pronounced when she started therapy. In addition, she was not experiencing any multiple sclerosis symptoms, which seemed to be responding well to her treatment regimen.

Discussion

The case of Mary Jane provides more of a "happy ending" than many of the cases presented in this book. Mary Jane faced some complex and challenging social barriers that were related to her sexual orientation, gender, and more recently her potentially disabling condition. Mary Jane's intelligence, ability to connect to others, and her confidence were critical attributes in helping her to overcome very real barriers. Much of the focus in this treatment revolved around themes of power, connection, and self-determination; the natural linkages between these issues flowed to some extent through Mary Jane's work life. In relation to the power issues, Mary Jane was able to negotiate some complex challenges, although the reality is that she was not able to change the climate at her job. One of the advantages that Mary Jane had in relation to some other cases presented in this book is her European American status, which clearly gave her access to privilege in her culture, including access to good schools, decent health care, and continued connection to the powerful majority group (Helms & Cook, 1999; Wilson, 1996). Yet at the same time, Mary Jane faced discrimination because of her gender, sexual orientation, and possibly because of an emerging disabling condition. One of the primary means for Mary Jane to experience her power and agency in her life was through her working life. Despite the obstacle of homophobia, Mary Jane was bright and competent, which was never an issue in her position. Yet she was passed over for promotions, in large part due to her gender and sexual orientation. Thus, the paradox of this case is that it suggests the dialectic that working often offers people. On one hand, it can be the source of empowerment and on the other hand, it can be the source of disappointment and despair.

This case also illustrates the prevailing concerns about social connections that emerged in this treatment. As detailed in chapter 4, the striving for relatedness forms one of the key aspects of human functioning and is evident in a careful analysis of the needs that working can optimally fulfill. Moreover, the linkage between relational functioning outside of work and within an occupational context merits attention in clinical work, as exemplified in the case of Mary Jane. Throughout Mary Jane's life, her connections to her family, friends, and lovers formed a pivotal part of her life space. In this case, the striving for connection alternated between being the "figure" and the "ground" of the treatment process. At times, Mary Jane's sense of aloneness was most apparent at work; however, as she reached out to friends at work and outside of work, she was increasingly capable of responding assertively to the nasty homophobic comments made in her presence. Moreover, the comfort, connection, and relatedness that Mary Jane experienced from the multiple sclerosis support group was important in giving her the ability to explore new work and relationship trajectories in her life.

This case also demonstrated the importance of self-determination in Mary Jane's life. Mary Jane's educational and occupational history reflects considerable access to the pursuit of intrinsically interesting activities, which culminated in her selection of a line of work that was potentially self-determining. However, the context of Mary Jane's life was not as supportive of her active and agentic pursuit of her goals. The prevalence of homophobia and sexism in her work setting, coupled with some relational lapses in her personal life, had led her to feel more isolated at work and not as satisfied. One of the emerging themes in Mary Jane's therapy was the evolution of her sense of autonomy and empowerment. As she began to understand and internalize the depth of her knowledge about chemical engineering, she could in fact view herself as a leading researcher and teacher in this field. The enhanced sense of self-esteem in her working role, which actually reflected an accurate appraisal of her skills, helped Mary Jane to embark on a somewhat different developmental pathway that would ideally yield even more pronounced potential for self-determination in her work life.

Social Barriers and Working: Conclusion

The role of working in providing people with access to power and survival, relational connections, and self-determination has been articulated in the chapters that preceded this one. However, an honest view of the psychology of working necessarily must include a discussion of the social barriers that create inequitable conditions for many people and easy access to wealth and power for some. The existence of social barriers such as racism, sexism, classism, heterosexism, and ableism function to create very disparate conditions that consign many individuals to a life of despair and want. While the perspective that I am developing in this book is not going to cure these social ills with the wave of a magic wand, I do envision scholars, practitioners, and policymakers exploring the interface of work and social oppression in developing arguments for programs and policies that will foster greater equity. The material presented in this chapter has sought to give voice to the voiceless in our field—those whose social status has been denigrated and relegated to marginal places in our discourse. In doing so, I have sought to place access to opportunity as a central issue within the psychology of working. In addition, the discussion of such issues as racism, sexism, ageism, heterosexism, and ableism needs to be explicitly included in subsequent discourse on working. The very powerful roles that these social barriers play in the distribution of resources and supports for people are clearly part of the landscape of the psychology of working. As reflected in this chapter, the psychology of working is a natural ally of feminism, multiculturalism, and other social justice movements that seek to contextualize our understanding of human behavior.

The major themes that have emerged in this chapter are fairly clear. Access to the opportunity structure is far from equal. Moreover, much of this inequality is due to phenotypic attributes that have no bearing on one's ability to profit from training, education, and other opportunities. My hope is that this chapter will generate a body of knowledge that will ultimately inform social policy efforts to reduce and eradicate these pernicious social barriers, thereby enhancing opportunities for people to feel empowered and engaged in their working lives.

CHAPTER 7

Implications of an Inclusive Psychology of Working for Research and Theory

Many people are in dead-end jobs, no-hope jobs. Many people lack the skills and experience to get—or hold—jobs. We talked much of the sausage plant worker; what do we have to say to her or him? We need to keep that in mind. Many people are scared. Many people have given up.

—Hall (1996, p. 343)

I don't think I could have made it [in school] without a job, because that was my inspiration. If I hadn't had a job I don't think I would have went to school or nothing like that. [The fast food restaurant] really helped me out, because you know if you have one thing going for you, you want another thing going for you. And it's … like a chain reaction.

See, when I first started [working], I didn't like to go to school at all. But see, my manager told me, "I wanna see your report card. If you're not doing this or you're not doing that, we don't want you here." They told me just like that. My first period class, I was failing because I was late. My manager told me, "Why are you failing this class?" I told her that I didn't get there on time. She said, "Well, I think that you should cut your hours [at work], 'cause maybe you're not getting enough sleep."

They just pushed me. If I wanted to keep this job, I had to go [to that class]. You know, they really tried hard, 'cause they say, "We don't want you to work here forever. We want you to move on."

—Newman (1999, p. 129)

As these quotes (as well as this entire book) seek to demonstrate, scholarly and clinical interests in working, as well as human reactions to working, vary considerably. Indeed, these quotes attest to highly complex and nuanced aspects of working, which have often been missing from the traditional social and behavioral sciences and mental health considerations of careers and working. In order to understand the full gamut of working experiences, I believe that sustained inquiry is needed to flesh out an inclusive perspective on the psychology of working. To guide these efforts, I outline my thinking in this chapter on the most viable research directions that are needed to construct the foundation for the psychology of working.

The initial section of this chapter presents two meta-perspectives (i.e., social constructionist thought and the emancipatory communitarian perspective) as organizing frameworks for research efforts and theory development within the psychology of working. The second section of the chapter outlines a number of directions for further research, integrating illustrative existing studies and research trajectories that fit with the mission of a psychology of working. The third section examines methodological issues inherent in studying working. The final section reviews the theory development process in relation to the inclusive and contextual nature of the psychology of working.

As the first six chapters of this book convey, considerable research, both quantitative and qualitative, has been conducted from various perspectives, including vocational psychology, I/O psychology, sociology, labor economics, and anthropology, which have sought to explain selected aspects of the experience of working. In my view, many of the observations and conclusions from existing research inform the needed scholarship and theory development efforts in the psychology of working. In this section, I integrate the research findings that have been published in various disciplines to summarize what we know about working. Rather than restating findings that have been presented elsewhere in this book, I have organized this section by a set of themes that reflect the major conceptual areas that are represented to date in the nascent psychology of working. In each of these sections, I also highlight future research directions that are indicated based on my review and the collective input of other scholars and policy analysts. One of the prevailing themes of the research domains that I review in this chapter is that they have the potential to inform counseling practice, public policy on work and family life, educational reform efforts, and labor policies. Given the vast array of fundamental needs that people face with respect to working (such as unemployment, underemployment, dissatisfaction, lack of dignity, exposure to harassment, occupational health and safety challenges), I advocate that researchers initiate projects that will enhance knowledge that, ultimately, can inform efforts to create more equitable and dignified working experiences. In addition, I believe that research that informs the development of a fully inclusive approach to counseling practice is indicated. Ideally, the scholarship that emerges from the psychology-of-working perspective will serve to create the conceptual infrastructure for interventions that help all adults who wish to work with the potential to find meaning and dignity in their working lives. In order to create the scaffolding for the necessary research on the psychology of working, I begin initially with a review of two conceptual perspectives that serve to frame the subsequent discussion. The first of these perspectives is social constructionism and the second is the emancipatory communitarian perspective; when considered together, these two frameworks provide important conceptual perspectives for research and practice in the psychology of working.

Singular Versus Multiple Perspectives of Working: Infusing a Social Constructionist Perspective

One of the most prevalent themes in the initial chapters of this book is that working is a complex and individualistic experience that is influenced by culture, politics, and economics, as well as intrapsychic and interpersonal factors. As such, the psychology of working necessarily must embrace the multiple and relativistic nature of human experience in order to develop a sufficiently expansive framework to understand the depth and complexity of the experience of working. The social constructionist perspective, which has emerged as a key element in the critical analysis of contemporary psychological discourse (Burr, 1995; Gergen, 1999), offers a useful lens with which to make sense of the complexity of working. Prior to delineating the role of the social constructionist critique in the psychology of working, I first summarize the major attributes of this epistemological perspective.

The social constructionist perspective actually reflects a critique of the traditional social scientific enterprise (Gergen, 1999). A number of scholars in vocational psychology have described the utility of a social constructionist position in considerations of working and career development (e.g., M. S. Richardson, 1993, 2004; Stead, 2004). Prior to reviewing the advantages of a social constructionist perspective in research and theory on the psychology of working, I first provide a conceptual framework that explains the core element of social constructionist thought:

> Several key assumptions underlie the social constructionist perspective and are central to the position that we are advancing in this article (Burr, 1995). First, a social constructionist position assumes a critical stance toward taken-

for-granted knowledge, or ways of understanding the world and ourselves (Gergen, 1999). It challenges the viewpoint that knowledge is based on objective, unbiased observations, and calls into question positivism and traditional empiricism (Burr, 1995). Alternatively, critical reflection and the questioning of one's beliefs are thought to lead to new ways of knowing and multiple perspectives of knowledge (Gergen, 1999). Second, the social constructionist perspective presumes that one's understanding of the world is historically and culturally embedded. Recognizing knowledge as a product of history and culture acknowledges the legitimacy of historically and culturally embedded traditions. In effect, this perspective ensures that no one person's ways of knowing are considered superior, or closer to the truth, than alternate ways of knowing (Gergen, 1999). Third, knowledge is constructed between people through social interactions and relationships, not from objective observation. Fourth, socially constructed and negotiated views of the world can take a variety of forms and lead to associated patterns of social action. Transformation into social action can emerge from alternative interpretations of the world, and result in generative discourses, or communications that challenge existing traditions of knowledge and suggest new possibilities for action (Gergen, 1999). Thus, from a social constructionist perspective, the focus is on the process and dynamics of social interaction, and not on the structure of individual knowledge or objective truth (Burr, 1995). (Blustein et al., 2004, p. 427)

As this passage suggests, the social constructionist perspective offers a major—indeed, a radical—transformation of our understanding of social scientific discourse. Rather than searching for universal truths that may be observed and tested via objective methods, the social constructionist critique seeks to replace this impossible task with a more manageable and, ideally, more useful approach that is based on the complex and relativistic nature of human experience. The following contribution from an article that my colleagues and I wrote on the social constructionist integration of relational perspectives and working underscores the need for diverse intellectual lenses for the study of working:

(I)n vocational psychology, the focus on an autonomous, vertical progression of paid work in the public sphere has predominated, and has been held as an ultimate model of success and worth (Höpfl & Atkinson, 2000). Notwithstanding, nonpaid work and work in the private or personal sphere or domain has been relegated to "the context of career," and thus marginalized by a society that discredits its worth (M. S. Richardson, 1993; 2000). Moreover, current discourses of career favor those with more privilege and greater access to prevalent models of success (M. S. Richardson, 2000). Consequently, prevailing discourses serve to reinforce existing power structures (Collin & Young, 2000). Such discourses weigh heavily not only in the social constructions of persons and groups, but in the theory, research and practice of vocational psychology. In this light, a social constructionist paradigm is well-suited as a foundation for movement from the traditional study of middle-class careers to a more broadly inclusive study of working across cultures and social classes (cf. Blustein, 2001a; M. S. Richardson, 1993). (Blustein et al., 2004, p. 428)

As reflected in this passage, the application of the social constructionist critique to theory development and empirical research efforts is an ideal fit with the development of the psychology of working. However, rather than adopting a rigid or entrenched social constructionist perspective that would raise questions about the veracity or applicability of every possible inference or assumption, I propose that the social constructionist perspective be used to *inform* subsequent scholarship rather than *constrain* subsequent scholarship. For example, a number of the tenets of the psychology of working, such as the notion that working fulfills some human needs (such as the need for survival, social connection, and self-determination) may have broader relevance across time frames and cultures. Naturally, these ideas require further assessment and inquiry. Yet at the same time, working for many people is directly linked to their cultural experiences, economic circumstances, social relationships, and historical contexts. For example, in research conducted on the school-to-work transition, we found that the adaptive antecedents of an effective transition are not easy to identify across situations (Blustein et al., 2000). There may be some factors (such as relational support and the acquisition of high levels of academic skills) that may be generalizable, but the full picture of an adaptive transition is very likely rooted in the culture and economy of a given community. As I hope to explicate in this chapter, I believe that the social constructionist perspective contains a number of important attributes that will help to advance our knowledge of the psychology of working.

One of the most compelling advantages of the social constructionist perspective for the psychology of working is that by expanding the nature of the discourses away from the traditional focus on people with choices and options, research and theory will have an opportunity to explore the working lives of people who have typically been relegated to the margins. Another asset of the social constructionist perspective is its focus on the importance of understanding the full depth of the inner experiences of people, which fits with many of the core elements of the psychology of working. Given that the social constructionist perspective focuses on the lived experiences of people within cultures and relationships, scholars and counseling/organizational practitioners can begin to chart the complex and richly textured aspects of the psychology of working in different ways and with diverse objectives. In addition, the social constructionist perspective has advocated that social scientists should seek to create theories that are more localized and contextualized as opposed to universal (Gergen, 1999). The prevailing assumption of the social constructionist perspective is that truth is rarely universal and is essentially negotiated in social interactions that are framed by cultural boundaries and interpretations. This point is particularly important for the psychology of working which is rooted in individual experience, cultural meanings, and socioeconomic and historical influences. Furthermore, social constructionist thinking seeks to reduce the artificial boundaries that have been placed around aspects of psychological and social experiences. With respect to psychological analyses of working, the social constructionist critique has already been very helpful in articulating the interconnections between relational functioning and vocational functioning (Blustein et al., 2004). Using the aforementioned rationale regarding the advantages of a social constructionist perspective, I will explore some of the most important directions for research in the psychology of working, with a focus on the development of a relevant, culturally affirmative framework that will yield findings that advance knowledge and enhance the lives of people. Prior to outlining some promising direction for research and theory development on the psychology of working, I introduce another meta-perspective, which, when considered with the social constructionist critique, functions as an important conceptual foundation for an inclusive and socially relevant psychology of working.

The Role of Values in the Psychology of Working: The Emancipatory Communitarian Perspective

The advantage of the social constructionist perspective is its focus on grounding scholarship within the cultural, historical, and social framework of a given community. However, I believe that scholars exploring the psychology of working also need to be mindful of the impact of their work and the values that underlie their research and practice efforts. More precisely, I advocate the inclusion of a conceptual framework that entails careful attention to the explication of one's values with a concomitant examination of the impact that these values have on the life experiences of the targets of our research, theoretical efforts, practice, and policy efforts. The view that most accurately captures my concern about the importance of an honest appraisal of one's values is the emancipatory communitarian perspective that has been articulated by Prilleltensky (1997). Initially, I review the major elements of the emancipatory communitarian (EC) position, followed by a discussion of my personal values with respect to the psychology of working.

(Consistent with the EC position and the social constructionist critique, I do not seek to create hegemony with respect to my values in the study of working; instead, I simply wish to make the implicit values and assumptions of my own scholarly efforts more explicit.)

The EC perspective represents an amalgam of social scientific, political, and epistemological movements that have been integrated by Prilleltensky as a means of offering psychologists a meta-perspective to practice and conduct research. The problem that led Prilleltensky to the EC position stems from the relative neglect of values and morals within much psychological discourse. In short, Prilleltensky argued that psychologists have sought to distance their work from systematic and explicit considerations of moral and ethical values. The main reason for this neglect, according to Prilleltensky (1997), is the concern that "discussing morality may elicit a negative reaction from psychologists who are afraid of dogmatism, fanaticism, and authoritarianism (Fowers & Richardson, 1996; Kane, 1994). After all, previous claims to morality that were based on ethnocentric and androcentric models resulted in discrimination and oppression of powerless groups (Prilleltensky & Gonick, 1994; Sampson, 1993)" (p. 518).

In order for psychologists to respond to the challenge of exploring and identifying their values, Prilleltensky proposed that two criteria had to be fulfilled. The first criterion is that psychologists need to identify their view of the good life and the good society. The second criterion is that psychologists seek to find ways of translating their views on the good life and the good society into action. Prilleltensky is clear that he does not espouse that psychologists need to concur on their beliefs about the good life and good society. Rather, he advocates that psychologists ought to be aware of their values with respect to these fundamental questions.

As a means of generating greater interest in exploring values and morals among psychologists, Prilleltensky proposed a perspective that draws from emancipatory and communitarian perspectives, respectively. Noting the contribution of liberation scholarship (e.g., Freire, 1984; Martín-Baro, 1994), Prilleltensky developed a position that has sought to critique existing social structures as playing an instrumental role in developing and sustaining inequitable contexts. In the following quote, Prilleltensky (1997) describes the core elements of the emancipatory component of the EC perspective.

> The essential contribution of these [emancipatory] theories lies in challenging the belief that our social system, wherever we may be, is not only the best but the only possible one. Once people overcome the myth that existing social arrangements are immutable, they are in a position to question power struc-

tures that interfere with the pursuit of fundamental values for everyone, rather than just for those who benefit from privilege and comfort. A critical analysis of who benefits from current social conditions, and at whose expense, is the first step in overcoming oppression (Korten, 1995; Macedo, 1994). This analysis is highly relevant to psychological well-being, for psychological problems do not exist in isolation from societal structures of power (Gil, 1996; Prilleltensky & Gonick, 1996). (p. 530)

The communitarian aspect of the EC perspective is derived from a fairly diverse array of theoretical and ideological positions, including the work of scholars who have advocated for collaboration and compassion (e.g., Etzioni, 1991) as well as those who advocate for distributive justice (e.g., Frazer & Lacey, 1993). Prilleltensky sought to integrate these perspectives to develop a comprehensive conceptualization of the communitarian framework. It is important to note that Prilleltensky is not necessarily advocating a specific political ideology here; indeed, he noted that communitarian ideologies have been advanced within progressive and conservative forums. The passage that follows describes how the communitarian perspective can be manifested in psychological research and practice:

A blueprint for a communitarian psychology may contain the following aspects. Community members, clients, and psychologists would collaborate in setting the agenda for personal or social change, and interventions would be primarily proactive and directed at social systems (Gil, 1996). Local and grounded knowledge would help assess the needs and goals of communities. Perhaps more than other approaches, communitarian practice would emphasize collaboration and power sharing. Groups who are served would be enabled to negotiate the contents, procedures, processes, and ethical parameters of psychological interventions, a practice that is lacking in other modalities (Prilleltensky, Rossiter, & Walsh-Bowers, 1996; Serrano-García, 1994). (Prilleltensky, 1997, p. 529)

Prilleltensky noted that the emancipatory and communitarian perspectives, in and of themselves, have significant shortcomings that can be redressed if they are used in tandem. The EC approach, therefore, seeks to blend important aspects of the emancipatory and communitarian positions, thereby constructing an integrative perspective, which I believe coheres effectively. In a recent article that applied the EC approach to vocational development theory and practice, my colleagues and I (Blustein et al., 2005) described the EC perspective as follows:

(A)n EC approach defines the self primarily from an interpersonal and sociopolitical frame of reference. As such, the targets of intervention are both individual problems as well as problems residing in social systems. The term "communitarian" refers to the emphases on compassion, social obligation, and mutual-determination. Human rights and responsibilities are balanced in such a way that the principles of justice, human diversity, collaboration, caring, and self-determination complement rather than compete with each other. (p. 150)

In order to frame the EC perspective in light of existing psychological traditions, Prilleltensky assessed various meta-perspectives with the goal of defining the values, assumptions, practices, potential benefits, and potential risks of each psychological approach. The four approaches include traditional approaches, empowering approaches, postmodern approaches, and emancipatory communitarian approaches. Table 7.1 provides an excellent comparison of the four approaches. It is important to note that Prilleltensky honestly critiques his own EC perspective, noting that there is a possibility of denying individuality at the expense of the greater community.

The EC perspective has considerable potential to inform research and theory development in the psychology of working. First, the EC perspective encourages scholars to make their values explicit, while also acknowledging that social scientific research is inherently value-laden. In advocating for an explicit statement of one's values, especially with respect to how one defines the good life and the good society, the EC perspective provides a framework for elaborating one's assumptions in the design of studies, theoretical efforts, and practice interventions. Thus, rather than assuming that studies conducted on college students or well-educated corporate managers are sufficient to construct theories and interventions for the modal worker in North America (or anywhere else), the EC perspective would provide the balance that is needed to maintain honesty and openness in such appraisals. Second, the EC perspective endorses a view of human behavior that is deliberately framed by the knowledge that individual efforts are both constrained and facilitated by structural forces (such as racism, sexism, economic factors, and heterosexism). In this context, the EC view fits well with the extensive literature that has been cited earlier in this book about the impact of social filters and barriers on one's access to a meaningful and rewarding working life. Third, the EC perspective values knowledge that can help to eradicate structural and social forces that constrain psychological growth and development. As such, the EC framework has the potential to be highly informative in creating research agendas and practice efforts that seek to change public policies about education, work, labor economics, training, and counseling. (See Blustein et al., 2005, for a detailed discussion of the potential of the EC perspective to inform important gains in the study of working.)

TABLE 7.1

Summary of Values, Assumptions, and Practices in Four Psychological Approaches

Domain	Traditional approaches	Empowering approaches	Postmodern approaches	Emancipatory communitarian approaches
Values	Promote caring and self-determination of individuals but neglect distributive justice. Major emphasis on helping individuals, not communities.	Promote human diversity and self-determination of individuals and of marginalized groups.	Promote human diversity and self-determination of individuals. Also concerned with collaboration and participation but have equivocal stance with respect to distributive justice.	Promote balance between self-determination and distributive justice. High degree of concern for well-being of individuals and communities.
Assumptions	Based on scientistic assumptions about knowledge. Good life and good society are based on value-free liberalism, individualism, and meritocracy.	View knowledge as tool for action research. Good life is based on ideas of personal control. Good society is based on rights and entitlements.	Emphasize epistemological relativism and moral skepticism. Good life is associated with pursuit of identity. Assumptions informed by social constructionism.	Promote grounded knowledge at the service of moral values. Good life and good society are based on mutuality, social obligations, and the removal of oppression.
Practices	Problems defined in asocial and deficit-oriented terms. Interventions are reactive. Problems defined in terms of risk and disempowering conditions. Interventions are reactive and proactive.	Problems defined in terms of clients' constructions of their own circumstances. Clients encouraged to pursue their own identity.	Problems defined primarily in terms of interpersonal and social oppression. Interventions seek to change individuals as well as social systems.	
Potential benefits	Preserve values of individuality and freedom.	Address sources of personal and collective disempowerment.	Value the importance of identity, context, and diversity and challenge dogmatic discourses.	Promote sense of community and emancipation of every member of society.
Potential risks	Victim-blaming and tacit support for unjust social structures.	Social fragmentation through pursuit of own empowerment at expense of others.	Social and political retreatism. Skepticism and lack of moral vision.	Denial of individuality and sacrifice of personal uniqueness for the good of the community.

Note: From Values, Assumptions, and Practices: Assessing the Moral Implications of Psychological Discourse and Action by I. Prilleltensky. Copyright © 1997 by the American Psychological Association. Adapted with permission.

Prior to identifying promising research agendas, I would like to explore the complexities in using such broad-based meta-perspectives in informing the psychology of working. One issue that merits attention is the possibility of creating an intellectual amalgam of ideas that are somehow incompatible or, even more disconcerting, overly rigid or ideological. Prilleltensky noted that the post-modern approach (which shares many of the assumptions of social constructionism) has a number of limitations with respect to the issues that he raised about the importance of values and morality in psychological discourse. Prilleltensky cites the post-modern approaches as one of the traditions that the EC perspective seeks to supplant or at least inform (see Table 7.1). The Prilleltensky critique of post-modern thinking is informative and relevant to my position that both the EC and social constructionist perspectives frame subsequent inquiry in the psychology of working. In short, Prilleltensky (1997) views social constructionism as espousing a highly relativistic perspective with respect to morality and ethical behavior. In addition, he cited an extensive literature from a group he calls skeptical social constructionists, who advocate a form of "political retreatism," which explains "why there is not a strong voice advocating social change" (p. 528). In my view, this is a very valuable criticism of the social constructionist perspective, which clearly merits our consideration in this discussion. Similarly, the point that Prilleltensky raised about the EC perspective regarding its potential to inhibit individual self-determination and volition is certainly noteworthy. I believe that the way out of this dilemma is by explicitly integrating the needs of a psychology of working with salient aspects and assumptions of both the social constructionist and EC perspectives. In doing so, I propose that we can create a pathway that adopts conceptually congruent aspects of both perspectives that will inform scholarship on the psychology of working.

Mapping the Pathway for Research on the Psychology of Working

When considered collectively, the social constructionist and EC perspectives offer some valuable markers as we chart the relatively unexplored terrain of the psychological nature of working. Prior to delineating the marker points, I would like to state my own assumptions about how these two perspectives can be used. First and foremost, I am not advocating either framework as a panacea or as dogma that must necessarily inform our scholarship. To the contrary, I view the social constructionist and EC frameworks as meta-perspectives that have the potential to shape an engaged and relevant body of knowledge about work and working. Indeed, these perspectives share substantial common assumptions and values, as well as some notable differences. Both of these perspectives critique traditional psychological research and practice (see Table 7.1), which has been characterized by an overly decontextualized view of human behavior. In that light, the social constructionist and EC perspectives move us out of the individualistic assumptions of traditional scholarship, which has tended to view human problems and challenges in a relatively insulated fashion. In addition, the traditional psychological framework (which has informed the vast majority of vocational psychology and I/O psychology) has been entrenched in a view that diminishes the role of values and morals. Both social constructionism and the EC perspective grapple with morality, although they yield very different positions about how to incorporate the moral dimension into psychological discourse. One of the notable differences that Prilleltensky pointed out between these two viewpoints is that social constructionism tends to assume an overly relativistic position about morals, with the very real possibility that social injustices can be ignored or sustained. However, Prilleltensky also noted that the notion of moral relativism is not central in all social constructionist ideologies. I believe that, provided that one is distanced from the moral retreatist or skeptical views of some social constructionist perspectives (see Prilleltensky, 1997, for a review of the distinctions within social constructionist thought), sufficient shared values and assumptions exist to create a meaningful rapprochement between these perspectives.

My position is that social constructionism and the EC perspective can be used, either in tandem or individually, as a means of furnishing guidance to scholarship emerging from the psychology of working. The shared assumptions of these perspectives revolve around a number of salient points. First, both social constructionist and EC thought endorse the notion that culture, relationships, and social structures play a major role in human development and in psychological functioning. Second, EC and social constructionist views both endorse the position that traditional social scientific approaches limit the growth of knowledge by constraining the methods used in exploring psychological phenomenon. Third, both approaches are rooted in philosophical perspectives that have been instrumental in critiquing existing power structures in the social sciences, public policy, and mental health communities.

There are, however, notable differences between the EC and social constructionist perspectives that merit discussion here. One such distinction is that client problems are conceived as a manifestation of individual constructions in social constructionist thought and as a manifestation of interpersonal and social oppression in the EC approach. Another notable difference between these two approaches is their views of morality and values. The social constructionist framework seeks to adopt a more relativistic stance with respect to distributive justice. In Prilleltensky's terms, distributive justice is the fair distribution of social and economic resources so that greater balance is achieved within a given culture or society. Other differences pertain to distinctions in how self-determination is viewed. In the social constructionist view, self-determination is valued highly, whereas in the EC approach, self-determination is balanced with a focus on distributive justice. My position is that the social constructionist and EC perspectives can function to generate a discussion in the psychology of working about morality, values, truth, and social barriers. I believe that the social constructionist and EC frameworks, when considered in tandem, are instrumental in forcing us to contend with these very challenging issues.

The major applications of the social constructionist and EC perspectives to the present discussion are summarized in the following points:

- Given the contextualized nature of the psychology of working, it would be difficult to imagine that highly generalizable inferences can be developed, aside perhaps from studies that examine the utility of the basic needs that working ostensibly fulfills and other very general inferences that have been derived to date.
- Both the social constructionist and EC perspectives advocate for an open and honest agenda on the part of researchers; the notion that science can be value free is thoughtfully critiqued in both perspectives.
- The two perspectives, taken together, offer scholars options with respect to the issue of research that informs social justice. For scholars interested in advocating structural change to create more equitable systems in society, the EC perspective provides important conceptual tools to help scholars examine the impact of diverse and often subtle social forces in developing and sustaining inequitable opportunity structures. In addition, the social constructionist perspective provides a conceptual framework that immerses researchers and theorists into the cultural and social fabric of people's lives. In this manner, the emerging conclusions and recommendations are more likely to relate to issues of power and access to opportunity.
- The EC and social constructionist perspectives are both overtly rooted in a cultural framework that places the context of individual functioning into the same field of view as individual experience. As such, ensuing studies and theoretical developments on the psychology of working will have an advantage of placing the figure and ground on the same visual plane.

In keeping with the commitments of the EC perspective, which argues assertively for an explicit discussion of one's values and moral position, I review the central assumptions that guide my own views regarding the directions for research and theory development that are outlined in this chapter:

- As readers have no doubt discerned at this point in the book, I value scholarship that can lead to greater equity and social justice. The suggestions that follow, for the most part, are clearly rooted in an agenda that seeks to identify social structures that sustain inequity and to create the knowledge base to reduce unequal access to the resources needed for a meaningful work life.

- In addition, I value self-determination, but not at the expense of the greater good. In a sense, my views here parallel the ethical aspirations of the counseling and psychology professions (American Counseling Association, 2005; American Psychological Association, 2002), which have placed nonmalificence as the key ethical principle. As such, I endorse self-determination as long as others are not hurt in the process. I realize, naturally, the notion of who is "hurt" in a given set of circumstances is not always easy to discern and would involve careful deliberation and reflection.

- I also value research that informs policy and practice. Although I do value scholarship that seeks to explore the nuances and subtleties of working behavior, I believe that with limited time and resources, research should endeavor to make life better for people.

- I affirm both qualitative and quantitative methods as viable and important methodological approaches to studying working. I do not have rigid epistemological ideologies that would place one set of methods as developmentally or morally superior to the other.

- I strongly endorse a view that seeks to identify how social and cultural forces influence work-related behavior and access to opportunity. More precisely, rather than using social class as the "primary" designation of marginalization or race as the "primary" index, I would argue that these social barriers (along with sexism, ableism, ageism, heterosexism) are each problematic, both singularly and in combination.

- I value interdisciplinary and interprofessional collaboration (cf. Brabeck, Walsh, Kenny, & Comaling, 1997). Indeed, I believe that the most imaginative and important bodies of work in the next generation of scholarship on working will include scholars from diverse fields (such as economics, sociology, psychology) working in tandem on the most pressing social issues of the day.

The final point that merits attention here is that I strongly affirm the right of researchers to engage in scholarship that is meaningful and important to them and their constituents. Rather than presenting my values as the "gold standard," I hope that the psychology of working will attract adherents as well as critics who have differing values and beliefs. However, I do endorse Prilleltensky's (1997) view that scholarship in psychology is necessarily rooted in a moral and value-laden context. To operate in an artificial "value-vacuum" does not serve our field well and would inhibit the sort of creative scholarship that is needed to address the complex and challenging problems that exist as people interact with their work contexts.

In the following section, I outline some directions for research that have been suggested by my own experience and by the reading and reflection that this book project has engendered. Naturally, this summary is necessarily constrained by space and by the reality of my own experiences. I also encourage readers to generate their own agendas and critique the agenda that is outlined here.

Promising Directions for Research on the Psychology of Working

In identifying avenues for future scholarship, I have sought to identify themes and patterns from the literature that seem to cohere and that would function to generate subsequent theory and research development efforts, while informing public policy. The material that is outlined in this section represents only some of the specific issues that merit attention. My expectation is that the input of more scholars in this area, coupled with expected and unexpected changes in the world of work, will further shape the agenda for this line of scholarship.

The Role of Work in Psychological and Social Functioning

One of the assumptions of much of the literature reviewed in this volume (e.g., Flum, 2004; Neff, 1985; Newman, 1999; O'Brien, 1986; Wilson, 1996) is that working is fundamentally important to psychological and social functioning. For example, considerable evidence exists suggesting that working, when associated with stress, physical strain, and tedium, may in fact negatively impact upon an individual's overall level of functioning and satisfaction with life (e.g., Blustein & Spengler, 1995; Powell, 1999; E. J. Smith, 1983). That work varies in its manifestations in our lives is obvious; however, what is not obvious or clear is the identification of the range of factors that impact the way that people experience work. Moreover, the reciprocal relationships that exist between working and other aspects of psychological functioning are also well documented (Betz & Corning, 1993; Blustein & Spengler, 1995; Lofquist & Dawis, 1984). However, much of the research conducted in this area has been with individuals who have exercised considerable volition in their choices about work (e.g., dual career literature; see, e.g., Gilbert, 1994).

The existing research literature conducted on those fortunate workers who can make conscious, volitional choices about their work options suggests that a good person–environment fit and job satisfaction will enhance the quality of one's working life, with a positive halo effect impacting upon selected aspects of psychological and social functioning (e.g., Holland, 1997; Landy, 1989; W. B. Walsh, 2003). Moreover, a relatively extensive body of research exists detailing how stress from one sector of life (either work or relationships) can impact the other sector of life (Googins, 1991; Hall, 1996; Landy, 1989). However, once we move beyond the life experiences of people who have some choice and volition in their working lives, the degree of knowledge and theory to inform our understanding of the role of work in psychosocial functioning is far less evident or certain.

One of the quotes from the outset of this chapter, taken from Newman's (1999) study of adolescent and young adult workers in a fast-food restaurant, describes an experience in which work functions to provide the protagonist with emotional and instrumental strength to pursue an education. Using the social constructionist lens, it is possible to infer that within some cultural contexts, work can furnish people with valuable connections to important role models and supportive people who will help to foster positive gains in collateral aspects of life. Yet one can also describe periods of history in which work has been associated with hardship, pain, and trauma (such as indentured servants, slaves, prisoners, mine workers, and sex workers). These arduous work experiences could easily generate even further despair in one's psychological and social contexts. Thus, the reality of theory development in the psychology of working necessarily must invoke some of the relativism of social constructionism. While the direction and strength of relationships between working and psychosocial functioning is difficult to predict in a highly generalizable fashion for a broad range of people, the wealth of social scientific literature coupled with the vastly informative narratives produced by authors, poets, songwriters, playwrights, and ordinary workers suggests that this area is rich in insights and importance. In short, working very likely has a powerful and pervasive impact on the nature of life experiences; the direction and strength of this impact, naturally, is difficult to predict for aggregate groups. Yet, the evidence presented thus far in this book underscores the sort of conclusions that scholars such as Gini (2000), Newman (1999), Wilson (1996), M. S. Richardson (1993), and others have generated: Working is a core aspect of life with enormous potential to provide rewards and/or pain for individuals and communities.

The insights that can be gleaned from explorations of the impact of work on psychological and social functioning will be very relevant in the clinical and counseling applications of the psychology of working. For example, rather than developing linear or simplistic notions about how working impacts the lives of people, an experience-near approach to research can help to map the space shared by work and relationships. (An experience-near approach to research refers to the use of empathic introspection as a means of connecting to and defining the issues and people who are grappling with a given set of issues or problems. This point is explored in further depth toward the end of this chapter.) The literature that was presented in chapter 4, coupled with the emergence of the relational perspective of the psychology of working (e.g., Blustein et al., 2004; Flum, 2001; Schultheiss, 2003), attests to the complexity of exploring the relationships between work and psychosocial functioning. (Further ideas about the clinical applications of the psychology of working are presented in chapters 8 and 9.)

The importance of this line of work is critical. That the world of work is changing is fundamentally clear to scholars and to nearly all of the citizens of this planet (e.g., Arthur & Rousseau, 1996; Collin & Young, 2000; Santos, Ferreira, & Chaves, 2001). Without an understanding of the depth, nature, and consequences of the impact of work on psychological and social functioning, we are left with little knowledge to inform counseling practice and public policy. Perhaps the most compelling challenge that psychologists interested in working face is to chart the role of the lack of dignified and consistent work in relation to the full gamut of psychological and interpersonal functioning. This line of inquiry ought not to focus solely on giving voice to people who are impacted so profoundly by the changes in the workforce. Rather, our responsibility is to detail the connections with empirical evidence and with the compelling arguments that such evidence supports. My position is that there are multiple pathways to the presentation of empirical evidence (see later in the chapter). With the empirical data that social scientists can muster, we can develop arguments that, like Wilson's (1996) contribution, provide clear evidence that working is not simply a means to an end. Working is a natural part of human life, and to lose the opportunity to engage in this critical component of being alive, we risk losses that we can only dimly contemplate at this point in time. Indeed, the losses that accrue to individuals and their communities can be explored in further detail in research on unemployment and underemployment, which is described next.

Unemployment and Underemployment

Scholarship on unemployment and underemployment has a rich and extensive history in psychology and related social sciences (e.g., Amundson, Borgen, Jordan, & Erlebach, 2004; Borgen & Amundson, 1984; O'Brien, 1986; A. C. Petersen & Mortimer, 1994). In fact, as I detail later in this section, some of this scholarship fits well within the purview of the psychology of working. However, for the most part, the study of unemployment has typically been considered from a macro-level, often with informative statistical analyses of employment and unemployment trends presented at the aggregate level (e.g., Ellwood et al., 2000; Jaeger & Stevens, 2000). In my view, the psychology of working offers a critically important opportunity to move social scientific discourse about unemployment to the individual psychological level, where numbers and names can become embodied into full and rich narratives and psychological insights. These narratives can then be interpreted to derive new insights into the experience of being without work, looking for work, and working in a job that does not provide the basic needs to survive.

The psychological study of unemployment has represented only a modest research line within vocational psychology (e.g., Herr, Cramer, & Niles, 2004; Super, 1957) and a somewhat more extensive line of work within organizational psychology (e.g., Arthur et al., 1989; Furnham, 2000; O'Brien, 1986; Waters & Moore, 2002). However, it is striking that so little effort has been devoted to the plight of unemployed people in the traditional homes of the psychology of career development and organizational functioning. One of the more compelling and increasingly relevant aspects of traditional psychological research on unemployment has been the examination of the relationship between unemployment and various mental and physical health problems. The review by Herr et al. revealed that unemployment has been associated with digestive dysfunctions, irritability, depression, anxiety, and interpersonal relationship problems. In addition, Herr and his colleagues described the evolution of social exclusion, which can then lead to significant levels of alienation. Social exclusion refers to the sense of isolation and alienation which results from having no structured connection to the labor market and the broader social context. That unemployment is a social and economic burden in our culture is not controversial; indeed, few scholars or policy analysts would disagree with this appraisal (e.g., Bynner & Parsons, 2002; Hanisch, 1999; Meeus, Dekovic, & Iedema, 1997; Wanburg, 1995). However, within the social sciences, the vast majority of research on unemployment has been conducted by economists and other macro-level social scientists (e.g., Mishel & Bernstein, 1994), without the concerted contributions of psychologists who may be able to advance our thinking into new and potentially innovative directions.

Further insights into the broader social and community-based consequences of unemployment have been detailed in sociology and anthropology. The contributions of Wilson (1996) have been cited in depth previously in this book; in short, Wilson has charted the aversive consequences that have been associated with the loss of employment opportunities within a given urban community. Newman's (1999) anthropological analysis of the benefits of working for urban youth further affirms the results of Wilson's studies. Working in a job that has some level of dignity and social connection can provide a powerful resource for many people to remain engaged in their lives, communities, personal welfare, and other adaptive citizenship roles.

Another related problem that often is discussed in conjunction with unemployment is underemployment. As defined by Herr et al. (2004, p. 98), "(u)nderemployment is frequently characterized by part-time rather than full-time work or work which only partially provides an outlet for the range of talents an individual can bring to the workplace or provides very low pay." For example, a former computer programmer who needs to locate employment with health benefits settles for a job as a security guard, which is very likely not a viable fit with this individual's talents, skills, and experiences. The experience of underemployment is often understood as a closely linked phenomenon to unemployment. Many people who find themselves underemployed may be seeking to avoid unemployment, often at any cost, including the obvious consequences of lower pay, less interesting work, and a corresponding loss of social and economic status. In an economic analysis of underemployment, Mishel and Bernstein (1994) reported that underemployment is related closely to economic cycles, with the proportion increasing during economic downturns. They also described the growth of underemployment in that many people who prefer to work full-time have had to settle for part-time work. The importance of considering underemployment in tandem with considerations of employment is clearly evident in a close examination of the data presented in the Mishel and Bernstein analysis. Policymakers and government officials often try to camouflage stagnant employment trends by neglecting to include workers who have had to take jobs that provide far less than they are capable of achieving, in terms of personal satisfaction and financial rewards.

While the issue of unemployment has captured a great deal of attention in this book as well as in the popular media, psychologists who study working would benefit from an examination of global trends. The International Labour Organization (ILO), which is sponsored by the United Nations, has provided information and policy advice, much of which is freely available on the Internet (http://www.ilo.org). The 2003 report revealed that global unemployment is escalating, with 185.9 million people looking for work, representing about 6.2% of the total labor force (http://www.ilo.org/public/english/bureau/inf/pr/2004/1.htm). This report also indicated that the level of unemployment for youth between 15 and 24 includes about 14.4% of this age cohort, representing 88.2 million people. In addition, the ILO report stated that the "informal economy" consisting of workers without a specific job in the formal labor market is growing in poor countries, resulting in a large number of working poor, reflecting an estimated 550 million people. Thus, the existing data on unemployment and underemployment (which certainly may include many of the working poor) point to a sizable proportion of people around the globe who are not working or who are working in a highly marginal fashion.

Given these data and the pervasiveness of the aforementioned findings regarding the social and psychological consequences of unemployment, what, then, can a psychology of working offer scholars and practitioners? In my view, the perspective offered by the psychology of working has the potential to help place the *human dimensions* of unemployment and underemployment onto the agendas of policymakers and government officials. The vast majority of research on unemployment has not sufficiently or explicitly given voice to the individual experience of losing a job and of struggling to find a means of supporting one's family. Of course, there are many exceptions to this trend, including Wilson's (1996) book, the contributions of Rubin (1994), and others who have collected the narratives of workers (e.g., Bowe et al., 2000; Newman, 1988; Terkel, 1974). Ideally, research from the psychology-of-working perspective would provide unemployed workers with an opportunity to speak their minds as well as furnishing a means of documenting the consequences to the individual, the family, and one's community. Moreover, research using the psychology-of-working framework might allow for a greater understanding of the factors that help people to maintain their dignity and resilience in the face of unemployment. In addition, research is needed to identify the most effective systemic interventions that help people to gain employment, including the development of effective and flexible retraining plans, the use of career interventions to help people focus their job searches, and identifying the role of support systems in an individual's proximal context. In addition, the psychology-of-working perspective ideally may yield the development of interprofessional and interdisciplinary research teams that can address the broad, systemic sort of changes in the structure of work and the labor market that can create new work opportunities.

One of the most important needs for further research on unemployment at this point is for psychologists to provide empirical support for the proposition that working is part of a natural human striving and that to limit or circumscribe this experience can lead to significant, long-range problems that are difficult to manage, both individually and systemically. In addition, scholars need to find ways of developing the infrastructure within poor communities that will break the cycle of poverty and unemployment that transcends generations and economic trends. For too long, traditional scholars of careers and organizations have neglected very poor citizens within impoverished communities that exist in cities, suburbs, and rural settings, who often have eked out an existence without the stability and security that work provides. In addition, the role of retraining and retooling, which often receives so much attention in the academic literature and popular press (e.g., Cappelli, 2004; Tango & Kolodinsky, 2004; Winefield et al., 2002) needs to be explored and explicated. For example, to what extent should the traditional tenets of a good person–environment fit guide decisions about retraining? How can we help individuals move into new fields that are not interesting to them, but that may still provide a viable source of income? To what extent is the Deci and Ryan (1985) model of self-determination useful in informing interventions for workers who need to be retrained?

Research that can inform public policymakers of the critical importance of work in people's lives is fundamentally needed. Perhaps the infusion of studies from various communities and cultures documenting the domino-like effects of aversive consequences that are associated with unemployment will place this issue on the front burner for policymakers and government leaders (cf. Dooley, 2003; Hanisch, 1999; Kates, Greiff, & Hagen, 2003; Wanberg, 1995; Wilson, 1996). By exploring the impact of losing one's job with respect to the three sets of needs that working fulfills, I believe that it will be possible to present compelling arguments, buttressed by empirical data and observations, which would help to advance policy initiatives to create more meaningful employment opportunities. Moreover, as I detail later in the chapter, the development of interprofessional teams of scholars and policy analysts interested in working issues will have the potential to have a major impact on the broad economic and social policies that affect the distribution of educational and vocational opportunities.

Work-Based Transitions

Scholars in education, sociology, psychology, counseling, and labor economics have sought to understand the complexities of the school-to-work transition, which is particularly challenging for youth who do not attend college (e.g., Blustein et al., 2000; Glover & Marshall, 1993; Wilson, 1996; Worthington & Juntunen, 1997). In brief, the challenge that has been attracting so much interest and energy among scholars, practitioners, and government leaders is that the non-college graduating youth in the United States (as well as in many other Western countries) have had a difficult time in negotiating the transition from high school to a meaningful and productive working life. The problem has been described from both moral and economic considerations. From a moral vantage point, there is a notable lack of equity in the services and resources provided to poor and working class youth in comparison to students from affluent and educated backgrounds in helping them to prepare for their entry to the adult working force. Moreover, non-college-educated youth have often spent their early years in the labor market floundering in jobs that are typically associated with the adolescent workforce (e.g., fast-food restaurants, store clerks, etc.) (Blustein et al., 2000; Wilson, 1996). For the most part, these jobs offer little training, minimal contact with other adults (who can serve as role models), and few, if any, opportunities for advancement. Thus, the school-to-work transition for non-college-bound youth functions as yet another structural barrier that further reduces social mobility based on social class, race, ethnicity, and a host of other factors (Blustein et al., 2000). From an economic vantage point, the lack of coherence in the school-to-work transition has left the United States with a notable disadvantage in the competition for industries and jobs (Marshall & Tucker, 1992; Reich, 1991). Another key issue in the school-to-work transition is that students who do not know where they are going in terms of their working lives often struggle to see the utility in their academic work, thereby reducing their ability to acquire the skills that are so central to success in adult life (e.g., Baker & Taylor, 1998; Bynner, Ferri, & Shepherd, 1997; Evans & Burck, 1992). Indeed, this line of inquiry and the accompanying interest in developing broad and systematic policies and interventions to redress these problems foreshadows the sort of research/public policy linkage that I think can be established by a fully engaged psychology of working.

The interest in the school-to-work transition for non-college-bound youth has also fostered a greater interest in the nature of work-based transitions in general. (In fact, the focus on the school-to-work transition in the 1990s also may have been instrumental in helping psychologists to take note of the entire spectrum of people who work.) When considering the changing nature of the working world in light of the growing knowledge base on the school-to-work transition, I believe that a critical line of research will be needed on work-based transitions across the life span, including, of course, continued scholarship devoted to the school-to-work transition for the non-college bound. As we are beginning to observe currently in the workforce, people of all ages are increasingly faced with more transitions (Arthur & Rousseau, 1996; Collin & Young, 2000; Rifkin, 1995), and often highly challenging transitions. In contrast to the "mid-life crisis" that has received so much attention in the popular press in recent decades (which often involved people *wanting* to reinvent themselves in middle age; Cochran, 2001; Levinson, 1978; Schlossberg, 1995), the changes that are occurring currently very often involve adjustments to rapid shifts in working options and conditions that are not under our control. From my perspective, focusing on transitions has the potential of providing psychologists, counselors, and policy analysts with a tangible process that is amenable to scholarship and interventions. In effect, if we can develop models and methods that explicate the nature of adjustment to unplanned transitions, we will be able to design more effective counseling and systemic interventions as well as provide more informative advice to policymakers and government officials.

In examining the landscape of work-based transitions, it might be useful to invoke Super's (1980) life-span, life-space taxonomy, which offers a means of expanding our thinking about transitions. People transition both longitudinally (life span) and latitudinally (life space). The longitudinal dimension generally encompasses the typical definition of transitions; this dimension entails moving from school to work, job to job, shifting occupational fields, as well as transitions between working and not working (e.g., unemployment and retirement). In effect, the longitudinal dimension encompasses the life-span developmental trajectory. However, transitions also occur among life roles, underscoring Super's important contributions about the need to examine the full array of social roles that we occupy, many of which are linked to the worker role. For example, a stay-at-home father in his mid-30s may wish to shift to a more active working role as his children enter high school, thereby requiring a transition that impacts on his working life as well as his related life roles.

The infusion of the psychology-of-working perspective into the study of work-based transitions offers a number of viable pathways for informative and policy-oriented research. Following Super's (1980; Super et al., 1996) comprehensive conceptual framework, the psychology of working would encourage scholars to examine the full range of life roles that are associated with working. However, unlike Super's work, which has tended to focus on those with access to the "grand career narratives" of the mid- to late part of the 20th century, the psychology-of-working perspective would necessitate a more inclusive scope. Given the arguments that I have advanced in this book, work-based transitions are relevant to all people who work, not just to those with options and choices.

I envision the development of work-based transition models as perhaps a prototype of the sort of contributions that a psychology-of-working research program can make. First, one of the attributes of the next generation of research on work-based transitions ideally would be the development of localized models that are relevant to a given population at a given time in history. One of the lessons of the school-to-work literature is the observation of considerable variation in the needs, assets, and cultural attributes of specific populations (e.g., Blustein et al., 2000). The complexity of the working world, which is replete with rapid changes in economic conditions, educational and training resources, and cultural transformations, suggests the utility of a more relativistic approach to theory and research on work-based transitions (as suggested by a social constructionist perspective). For example, the array of predictors that my colleagues and I identified in the review of the school-to-work literature seems viable for many, but certainly not all, communities within the United States and other highly industrialized countries at this point in time (Blustein et al., 2000). It is likely that a different array of factors might be identified in other settings. While there very well may be some predictors that are very common across communities (such as relational resources and effective basic academic skills), other attributes of an adaptive transition may be more specific to given cultural contexts. The result of theory-building and research on the school-to-work transition, however, does not need to conclude with a chaotic set of ideas and principles. Rather, it may be possible to derive some common factors as well as more localized factors, thereby yielding flexible models that can be adapted to specific contexts and circumstances.

Another important line of inquiry with respect to work-based transitions is to identify the role of retraining and retooling in the process of transitioning into different work roles. This issue is already attracting considerable attention in the labor economics and sociological literatures (Cappelli, 2004; Robson, 2001; Wolf-Powers, 2001). I believe that research emanating from the psychology of working can have a major impact on this issue. One of the challenges that many people face when they have been laid off from jobs that they have enjoyed is the consideration of the need to begin a new trajectory in their working lives by pursuing a field that is outside of their traditional area of skills and interests. Given the trends that I detailed in chapter 2, it seems clear that many workers will need to return to school or training programs in order to update their skills and become more competitive in the labor market. The issues that are engendered in this process are highly complex and not well understood. The literature on adult unemployment is replete with examples of the struggles that people face in transitioning from one field to another, especially when additional schooling is required (e.g., Capelli, 2004; Robson, 2001). Certainly, there are considerable external barriers that make the transition process very difficult. For example, in the United States, very little, if any, external financial support is available for adults who would like to pursue full-time training in another field. By exploring the external and internal resources and barriers that play a role in the decisions that people make to attempt retraining, we may have far more relevant information to share with policymakers, counselors, higher education professionals, and training specialists. In my view, the need to identify the factors that help people move adaptively into new training programs is critical in developing a useful and effective retraining policy.

In a broader sense, research is needed that would help to understand how the experience of control and volition affects people's decisions to engage in retraining. As I have proposed in this book, one of the key elements in the psychology of working is the inclusion of people who have constrained volition or no real choice in their decisions about what sort of work to pursue. Research that can delineate how the variations in access to choices influence the way in which people explore and engage in training options would be very helpful in advancing scholarship in the psychology of working. By infusing a wide array of conceptual influences and problems into considerations of work-based transitions, the psychology-of-working perspective may help to produce models and programs that will be maximally useful to the countless workers who will be faced with unexpected transitions and transitions that ideally will yield desirable outcomes.

Social Filters and Working: Exploring New Vistas in the Interface of Social Access and Opportunity

As reflected in chapter 6, considerable research has been conducted on the impact of sexism, racism, heterosexism, and classism in relation to career development and organizational life. In this section, I describe the sorts of questions that a psychology-of-working analysis can furnish in understanding the nature of social filters in relation to working experiences. The literature presented in chapter 6 on the impact of sexism, racism, heterosexism, and classism also serves to foreshadow the potential of the psychology of working. The theoretical efforts of Helms and Cook (1999), Carter and Cook (1992), Liu (2001, 2002), Fassinger (1996, 2000), and Betz and Fitzgerald (1987), among others, have created the scaffolding for a study of working that seeks to be inclusive. However, much more research is needed to create an informative knowledge base that will facilitate policies leading to greater equity in preparing for meaningful work, locating jobs, and in adjusting to work. In this section, I review some of the more compelling issues that merit further study.

Fitzgerald (2003) has presented compelling evidence that our society has not created safe working environments for women. It is clear that further research is needed on the impact of sexual harassment, particularly for women who have fewer options and resources in life. One of the common themes of the literature on sexual harassment is the abuse of the power differential in working environments (Hotelling, 1991; Malamut & Offerman, 2000). Using a psychology-of-working perspective, we may be able to obtain experience-near accounts of the experience of harassment from women who are on the front lines day after day. Moreover, the findings from a psychology-of-working perspective may be particularly informative in discerning the nature of the abuse, the degree to which organizational climates contribute to abusive situations, and the extent of the psychological trauma that follows abusive interactions. In addition, examining the full context of the harassment process may help to identify systemic interventions that can be used to prevent the emergence of this painful phenomenon. For example, by identifying the complex and often subtle manifestations of power within the workplace, we may be able to identify mechanisms that reduce the enactment of harassment in the workplace.

Another critical issue that will likely require concerted research is the challenge of reducing gender-based stereotypes, especially for poor and working class individuals. Considerable research has been conducted to date on the nature of gender-based stereotypes and the impact of these biases on educational performance (Hackett & Betz, 1981; Hackett, Betz, Casas, & Rocha-Singh, 1992; McWhirter, Hawley, Hackett, & Bandalos, 1998) as well as vocational choices (Betz & Fitzgerald, 1987; Hackett & Lonborg, 1993). Yet considerably more work still needs to be conducted in order to reduce the impact of gender-based stereotyping. Two specific areas in particular seem promising. First, the continued existence of biases in the educational system merits attention and systematic research. For example, students of color and girls/women are still receiving less encouragement and less attention in many aspects of their academic work, particularly in the science, technology, and mathematical areas (Brown & Josephs, 1999; Heilman, Wallen, Fuchs, &

Tamkins, 2004; Yelland, 1998). From the perspective of the psychology of working, the focus would necessitate a broad and inclusive view, encompassing all students and adults who often have to face environments that can be discouraging and denigrating. Second, the vast majority of the literature on gender-based stereotyping has, appropriately, focused on the experiences of women, who have confronted (and continue to face) harsh and aversive messages about the occupations that may be suitable for them (e.g., Betz, 1989). Yet, men also face gender-based stereotypes, which often function to reduce the degree to which they can explore the full gamut of the occupational world (L. Gottfredson, 2002). For example, nursing programs and other helping professions are increasingly finding it difficult to attract men, which has likely contributed to labor shortages in selected fields. Moreover, this phenomenon curtails the possibility that men who are oriented toward caregiving would be able to find meaningful outlets for their work.

While sexual harassment has appropriately received attention in psychological research, there is comparatively little research on the overt or covert expression of racism at work. A number of recent initiatives have documented such phenomena as "ethnic bullying" (Fox & Stallworth, 2004), racism at work (Banks, 2002), and minority perceptions of institutional racism (Jeanquart-Barone & Sekaran, 1996). While these recent efforts reflect an admirable beginning, a number of questions emerge when considering the complexity and challenges of racism within the work context. First, like sexual harassment, it is likely that the people within occupational settings who have less conferred power would be more likely to be prone to harassment due to their racial and ethnic characteristics. As such, the psychology-of-working perspective might be particularly well suited as an organizing framework for the study of racism in the workplace. Second, the psychology of working would encourage us to learn more about racism at work in an empathic and experience-near fashion. Rather than approaching this problem from the distance of broad macro-level investigations, I recommend that qualitative research be used initially to document the existence and impact of racism in the workplace. Third, the degree to which others within organizations and occupational settings collude to foster a climate that tolerates racism can be ascertained and reported, thereby giving voice to a process that has been rarely explored in the psychological literature (with some notable exceptions, including Carter & Cook, 1992; Helms & Cook, 1999).

Research on the role of classism in relation to working also is a viable and necessary area for the psychology of working. The contributions of Liu (2001, 2002, 2004; Liu et al., 2004) have attested to the powerful role that social class plays in psychological discourse. The nascent scholarship on social class is highly relevant to the next generation of research on the psychology of working. A number of questions merit further attention in this area. There is a significant need to understand how people experience their own social class. As Fouad and Brown (2000) have argued, the experience of social class may be particularly profound for people who feel marginalized. The degree to which internalized impressions of social class are intertwined with one's experience of power and authority at work would be a very informative line of inquiry with clear ramifications for counseling practice and organizational interventions. Furthermore, the model developed by Liu and his colleagues (Liu et al., 2004) offers great potential to the study of social class and classism. In addition, the impact of classism at all stages of the job search, adjustment to work, and satisfaction with work processes represents a critically needed line of research.

Another social filter that has had a profound impact on the lives of workers across the economic and cultural spectrum is oppression and discrimination based on sexual orientation. Following the literature that was reviewed in chapter 6, we know that considerable discrimination has existed against lesbian, gay, bisexual, and transgendered (LGBT) individuals in a wide array of work settings. What is not known, however, is the role of power differentials among workers in the expression and manifestation of oppression and abuse. In addition, the struggles of LGBT workers in positions where the expression of social distance and prejudice is less overt, yet still pernicious, are not well documented in the literature. For example, what inferences are made within work settings about LGBT workers? Furthermore, how does the expression of sexual orientation at work differ among heterosexual and LGBT individuals? Research that explores the full range of experiences that occur as LGBT individuals confront often unfriendly and perhaps even dangerous work settings is clearly indicated. The psychology-of-working perspective, while not offering panaceas, would support the sustained exploration of complex issues such as LGBT orientations and the impact of these sources of diversity on other workers within one's social space.

As we have observed in the literatures on culture, race, gender, and sexual orientation, scholars and practitioners have struggled with creative ways of integrating understandings of human diversity into their conceptualizations (e.g., Arbona, 1995; Betz & Fitzgerald, 1987; Leong, 1995). Consequently, the next generation of research would benefit from tackling the question of the interface of the social filters in an overt and intentional fashion. Thus, rather than focusing on one source of diversity and controlling for (or acknowledging) the existence of other forms of human variability, I recommend that sophisticated methods be employed to explore the *space* shared by the various social barriers that so profoundly influence one's access to work and one's experience in the work setting. Some of these methods (which are explored in greater depth toward the end of the chapter) include both qualitative and quantitative approaches as well as combinations of these modalities. For example, the use of discovery-oriented and theory-developing qualitative methods (e.g., Hill, Thompson, & Williams, 1997; Strauss & Corbin, 1990) would be highly informative in exploring the intersection of sources of social oppression. In the quantitative realm, numerous options exist that would be informative in the exploration of complex social forces and multiple identities. For example, structural equation modeling (Fassinger, 1987) offers considerable advantages for researchers who are interested in infusing a causal model onto cross-sectional and non-experimental data. However, amidst the recent press toward the use of modeling approaches, there has been a tendency to neglect the role of more exploratory studies using quantitative data. As an example, canonical correlation analysis, which represents a subset of multivariate analysis of variance, is very helpful in examining the impact of multiple predictors and outcome variables, which ostensibly function in tandem. In addition, the use of moderator and mediator variables, which was described by Frazier, Tix, and Barron (2004), offers scholars with a potent tool to examine psychological and social variables that interact in complex ways. I review these and other potential methodological innovations in greater depth toward the end of this chapter. While research examining multiple sets of variables simultaneously is indeed challenging, the greater risk is in ignoring the interaction of the social barriers. One of the most troublesome consequences of the treatment of singular sources of prejudice and discrimination is the inadvertent competition that occasionally emerges among scholars and practitioners who are invested in one set of issues as the core source of social and economic oppression. My view is that inequity has many antecedents and that, regrettably, the sole cohering factor seems to be the human tendency to create stratification and categories based on irrelevant demographic or phenotypic characteristics (cf. Devine, 1995).

Role of Basic Skills in Work

A major trend of the school-to-work movement in the United States has been the growing awareness that basic skills in literacy, quantitative reasoning, and interpersonal skills are critical to a successful adjustment to the world of work (Blustein et al., 2000; Marshall & Tucker, 1992; Worthington & Juntunen, 1997). For the most part, attention to basic skills has not been a significant part of the discourse in vocational psychology and I/O psychology. In some ways, the relative avoidance of basic skills was consistent with the development of vocational and I/O psychology, which tended to focus on areas of particular significance to each respective discipline. There was, however, attention devoted to intellectual aptitudes, and to a lesser extent, basic academic skills, in the beginning and middle of the 20th century within vocational psychology (e.g., Super, 1957). For the most part, the focus on aptitudes has tended to cluster around the use of tests to predict performance in the future, which created a host of problems with respect to biases in the testing process (Greenfield, 1998; Helms, 1992; Helms & Cook, 1999; Helms et al., 2005). Unfortunately, the focus on aptitudes took precedence over considerations of basic academic skills, which, until recently, resulted in diminished interest in the role of basic skills in the transition from school to working and adult life.

I believe that the psychology of working needs to explicitly incorporate attention to basic skills for a number of reasons. First, the acquisition of basic skills in literacy, quantitative reasoning, and interpersonal relationship skills has been consistently associated with positive vocational outcomes, including an adaptive transition to the world of work from adolescence (Blustein et al., 2000) and the development of a more engaged connection to the labor market (Bynner et al., 1997; Bynner & Parsons, 2002). Second, as I have argued, one of the most effective ways to empower people is by helping them to obtain access to the world of work, particularly jobs that confer social and economic power. Following this observation, the need for individuals to develop their basic cognitive skills to their maximum potential emerges as a clear means of empowering the marginalized within society. Thus, if the psychology of working is to be useful in the generation of scholarship, policy recommendations, and practice implications, it is critical that an explicit discussion of basic skills become part of the research mission. Third, the connection between basic skills acquisition (or lack thereof) and other aspects of working, outside of the connection to the need for survival and power, is not well understood. For example, to what extent can the acquisition of basic skills in childhood and adolescence predict greater access to volition in one's working life? Similarly, how do basic skills interface with the development of adaptive interpersonal and social skills? Also, how effective is educational reform in raising basic skills? In that light, what are the public's obligations and commitments to students and workers whose skills are attenuated by learning difficulties, developmental delays, and inadequate environmental resources (such as health care, decent housing, and effective schools)?

A key assumption about the optimal means of enhancing the employment opportunities of a community or nation is to develop a highly skilled work force (e.g., Herr et al., 2004; Marshall & Tucker, 1992; Reich, 1991; Wilson, 1996). Naturally, testing this assumption is a complex macro-level challenge; however, there are elements of this assumption that can and ought to be examined in light of the psychology-of-working perspective. A critically important line of research is needed on the exploration of the impact of basic skills training with adults who have been out of the work force for an extensive period of time (e.g., individuals who have been disabled, people who have been on public assistance or welfare).

Another research direction that would be fruitful is the development of a broader understanding of how students and workers can be motivated to enhance their basic skills. It is clear that the acquisition of basic skills ideally occurs most optimally in childhood and adolescence. However, for the vast numbers of people who have not had access to the cultural and economic resources of good schools and neighborhoods, learning basic skills is more of a challenge. This dilemma is highly pronounced in urban schools and poor rural schools (Ascher, 1998; Beloin & Peterson, 2000; Dowrick et al., 2001), in which students often feel disengaged at the outset of their academic experiences (Fredricks, Blumenfeld, & Paris, 2004). In my view, the study of how work-based learning and career development education can enhance motivation to learn basic skills is needed as so many nations grapple with growing achievement gaps based on race and social class (R. Johnson, 2002; Orr, 2003).

The Role of Volition and Self-Determination in Working

A core issue in this book is that considerable variation exists in the level of volition that people experience in deciding on the line of work they would like to pursue, their actual choices about jobs, and their decisions about how to integrate their working lives with the rest of their life experiences. Indeed, the motivational perspective outlined in chapter 5 is premised on the fact that many activities that are important in our lives are not necessarily intrinsically interesting (Deci & Ryan, 1985; Flum & Blustein, 2000; Ryan & Deci, 2000). As such, a major research agenda is needed to explore how volition is experienced within the working context and to identify how volition can be enhanced.

Following on the experience-near perspective that also has defined a major theme of this book, I recommend that we initially strive to understand how people understand and experience issues pertaining to choice and volition in their working lives. An assumption that I have made here, based in part on my own background, values, and experience as a researcher and practitioner, is that the experience of volition is a positive attribute within the greater social and economic world. I also value the notion of work providing people with the means for a satisfying and rewarding life. It would be particularly revealing to examine the extent to which this view is culturally encapsulated. In addition, qualitative studies exploring how workers across the economic spectrum understand and describe issues of choice and volition would be very informative. Furthermore, once a sufficient body of knowledge is accrued about volition via qualitative and narrative studies, it may be possible to develop meaningful quantitative measures that may have relevance as larger scale studies are initiated.

In a related vein, the ideas proposed in chapter 5 regarding the utility of self-determination theory (Ryan & Deci, 2000) as an explanatory tool within the psychology of working need to be assessed empirically. One such project that is important is the assessment of the developmental stages of internalization in relation to the working context for people whose jobs are primarily extrinsically motivating (cf. Flum & Blustein, 2000). In addition, the inference that extrinsically motivating jobs can actually become self-regulating, and hence more meaningful, requires careful investigation. I recommend, for example, studies that examine how variations in motivation are defined by people across a wide spectrum of cultural and social contexts. In the United States, self-determination theory would be an illuminating theoretical lens with which to explore the welfare-to-work transition, which has challenged policymakers and social service workers. In a general sense, the loss of control, which is a hallmark of the current labor market era (Sennett, 1998), may in fact strike at the heart of the self-determination process. Indeed, the degree to which the loss of employment opportunities may result in an overall reduction of one's experience of volition and hope needs to be assessed. These sorts of studies have very important ramifications for public policy (which is discussed in chapter 10). As indicated earlier in this chapter, the large pockets of unemployment around the globe represent numbers and statistics to many government officials and social and behavioral scientists. Yet, as the psychology of working seeks to push the envelope on issues of choice, volition, self-regulation, unemployment, mental health, and power (and the lack thereof), it may be possible to chart a new course for our field that can have a major impact on how we view work in people's lives.

The Role of Working in Psychotherapy and Counseling

Although I discuss the psychotherapeutic implications of the psychology of working in greater depth in the following two chapters, I have several ideas about needed scholarship in the counseling context. One of the central reasons for this book is my observation that work issues have not been accorded the appropriate level of attention in traditional (or even nontraditional) approaches to psychotherapy. This observation is buttressed by research that has documented the existence of diagnostic overshadowing problems in the collateral consideration of vocational and nonvocational problems (Spengler et al., 1990). In addition, research has demonstrated that counseling psychologists (who are the only doctoral-level specialists trained to intervene on the individual level within the career realm) do not devote as much attention to vocational cases at intake (Blustein & Spengler, 1995). In addition, the overall lack of attention to work-related issues in psychotherapy continues to be noteworthy, relegating a substantial part of our lives to the margins of psychotherapeutic discourse (Blustein, 2001b).

One of the goals of the psychology of working is the development of a knowledge base that would encompass work-related problems in counseling and psychotherapy. While some scholars and clinicians have sought to establish taxonomies or conceptual frameworks of work-related clinical issues (e.g., Axelrod, 1999; Lowman, 1993), this literature has tended to focus on the experiences of people who have access to the grand career narrative. For others who are working primarily as a means of survival, the psychotherapy literature offers little informed scholarship to guide practice. The needs in this line of work are extensive and compelling. One of the primary issues meriting attention is the need to understand how work-related issues are understood by psychotherapists; in other words, to what extent are the work-related issues viewed within a framework that dignifies the experiences that people have at work? This question is particularly pertinent given that some of the literature that has explored work-related issues in treatment has tended to view these issues as manifestations of unresolved family dramas or as tangential issues that are less relevant to the overall treatment process (e.g., Chusid & Cochran, 1989). The application of the rich counseling process research methodologies to the questions raised here would be very helpful and informative (Hill & Williams, 2000).

One of the most disconcerting aspects of contemporary counseling and psychotherapy is the lack of coherent theoretical models with which to understand work-related issues that arise in treatment (Blustein, 2001b). Given the lack of inclusive and integrative theories with which to understand work-related issues in counseling and psychotherapy, I suggest that a key scholarly task is to integrate theories derived from vocational psychology and the psychology of working with existing psychotherapy models. Although the psychology of working is directed toward a broader set of issues, I propose that the ideas and goals of this perspective would have direct relevance to theory-building efforts that effectively integrate work-related issues. For example, understanding the fundamental need that people have to earn a living, above and beyond any of the psychological needs that work fulfills, places work-related issues into a very realistic and accessible framework. In addition, considering the reality that work connects people to the broader social milieu would help clinicians integrate work-related issues with other relational issues that may emerge in treatment (cf. Flum, 2001; Schultheiss, 2003). Furthermore, the application of Deci and Ryan's (1985) contributions to our understanding of work-related issues in psychotherapy would be richly informative and would ideally link to other efforts underway that have integrated self-determination theory with psychological treatments (Sheldon et al., 2003).

Another approach to integrating work-related issues into psychotherapy would be for adherents of the major theoretical models to consider working more explicitly in their theory construction efforts. For example, it would be helpful if psychologists and counselors with an interest in cognitive-behavioral therapy would consider systematic ways of integrating work-related issues into the assumptions, methods, and evaluation criteria of this treatment modality. Similar efforts from followers of relationally oriented psychoanalytic theories, existential-humanistic theories, traditional psychoanalysis, and other major therapy models would furnish our field with critically needed theoretical frameworks. My personal hope is that efforts from various sectors of mental health and vocational counseling will function to reduce the tendency to deny, denigrate, reframe, or simply ignore the diversity of work-related issues that clients bring to counseling and therapy sessions. By explicitly examining how work-related concerns can be integrated in a meaningful and affirming way within the major schools of psychotherapy and counseling, we will have a greater opportunity to influence training and research within the prevailing perspectives.

Research is also needed on the impact of the psychology of working in relation to traditional career counseling and career development interventions. For the purposes of this book, I consider career interventions to be counseling interventions and psychoeducational programs that are designed to help people consider, select, explore, decide, and adjust to vocational options. (While I do not subscribe to the notion that career counseling and psychotherapy are inherently different as processes, I am focusing on these modalities in somewhat discrete ways in order to highlight the challenges that exist as we seek to expand these services to encompass the psychology of working.) As S. D. Brown and Krane (2000) noted in their review of the literature, career interventions have demonstrated efficaciousness across a range of client problems and populations. However, a review of the Brown and Krane chapter, along with other reviews of the career intervention literature (e.g., Sexton & Whiston, 1994), suggests that the vast majority of career counseling and intervention studies have been conducted on college students or other similar populations, whose needs, while clearly prominent and valid, are not necessarily analogous to the needs of the vast majority of adolescents and adults who do not have access to the grand career narrative. Clearly, many questions and unresolved issues exist as we consider traditional career counseling in light of the psychology of working. In short, these issues relate to the way in which counseling services can be delivered to the full gamut of people who struggle with work-related issues, which will be explored in greater depth in the next two chapters.

Research is needed, for example, in assessing the degree to which traditional career counseling interventions can be used with clients who do not have access to extensive supports in their educational, relational, and economic contexts. While it is ideal, naturally, to help clients strive for the sort of work life that provides meaning and satisfaction, clients with the short-term pressure of needing to obtain work immediately often require a different set of interventions. As such, empirically supported interventions that are effective in providing clients with the means for meeting their short-term, medium-term, and long-term objectives are needed. While some of these interventions can be culled from the existing career counseling and job placement literatures (as detailed in the next two chapters), further research on the attributes of adaptive and satisfying working may help to generate additional insights about effective work-based psychological interventions.

Methodological Issues and Research on the Psychology of Working

The methodological approaches that would be optimal in studying the psychology of working have been foreshadowed throughout this chapter and, indeed, throughout this book. As the social sciences currently sort out the epistemological fault lines among the logical positivist, post-positivist, and post-modern positions (cf. Lincoln & Guba, 2000; Morrow & Smith, 2000; Prilleltensky, 1997), workers and potential workers struggle every day to find work, maintain their dignity at work, and to sustain a stable working life to support themselves and families. As such, my overriding value here is on scholarship that will help to make a difference in people's lives. Yet, at the same time, I am deeply invested in research that is integrated within a broader conceptual rubric, thereby allowing for the development of a coherent body of work that may inform counseling and psychotherapy practice as well as educational and public policies.

Using the social constructionist and emancipatory communitarian (EC) perspectives to guide the development of research methods in the psychology of working offers both challenges and opportunities. One of the major challenges is in dealing with the somewhat incongruent aspects of social constructionist and EC thought. As I indicated earlier, my approach to finding a rapprochement between these conceptual frameworks is to avoid the moral retreatism and skepticism of the more radical social constructionists. Another challenge is in ensuring that the research that is conducted is in fact embedded in the culture, historical period, and social milieu of a given population. Furthermore, the notion of developing a seemingly infinite array of models and perspectives for each cultural context seems daunting. However, the alternative is to go back to a period in which theory, research, and practice was based on a privileged group of people with little applicability to the modal individual who faces a working life that has little in common with the people who inhabited the grand career narrative of late 20th-century scholarship in vocational and organizational psychology. As such, we have little choice, in my view, but to immerse ourselves into the muddy waters of a social constructionist perspective with its obvious complications and limitations.

A key opportunity presented by the conjoint reliance on social constructionist thought and the EC perspective is that scholars of the psychology of working have an opportunity to employ ideas and research models that are consistent with the inclusionary framework of the psychology of working. Moreover, the social constructionist and EC perspectives, when considered collectively, seek to place the context of individual behavior into a clear and visible light, thereby reducing psychology's historic preoccupation with individual attributes to the detriment of our consideration of culture, social factors, and political forces, as well as more proximal factors like community and family influences. Furthermore, the EC perspective argues compellingly for research that will help to reduce inequity; in my view, these are values that are central in the psychology of working. With these epistemological lenses in mind, the next step is to highlight promising social scientific methods that can be used to explore the nature of contemporary working experiences.

Discovery-Oriented Research

One of the primary methods that I propose as a means of understanding the psychology of working is discovery-oriented research (Mahrer, 1996; Mahrer & Boulet, 1999). While discovery-oriented research is generally qualitative in nature (e.g., Morrow & Smith, 2000), I also describe some exploratory methods that are associated with the quantitative traditions. In the qualitative realm, the use of personal narratives to understand the psychological experience of working, which has been one of the primary methods used in this book, represents one approach to charting new conceptual terrain. One of the limitations in using this approach is the lack of representativeness in using vignettes that were not obtained in a random or systematic way. However, in keeping with an approach that is quite viable within many schools of qualitative methodology, the use of more evocative cases can be very informative in understanding the full range of a psychological or social phenomenon (Stake, 2000). In addition to obtaining new ideas about a given phenomenon, the use of vignettes from the voice of the people we wish to study offers an opportunity for scholars to develop more empathy for their participants and problems that are under investigation. (This issue is explored at the conclusion of this chapter.)

In addition to using published or pre-existing vignettes, scholars of the psychology of working can explore new domains of inquiry by talking with and interviewing workers and potential workers. Thus, more traditional qualitative methods can be used in which extensive interviews are conducted with people who are facing a particular aspect of working that is not well understood (Denzin & Lincoln, 2000; Fontana & Frey, 2000; Morrow & Smith, 2000). The advantage of using qualitative methods is that we have an opportunity to learn about new concepts and experiences in relation to working that are above and beyond what we already know.

Given the dearth of direct knowledge about working, I would encourage the use of interviews and other observational and ethnographic methods as a means of charting the complexity and cultural embeddedness of working (Angrosino & Mays de Pérez, 2000; Tedlock, 2000). For example, studies of workers in shantytowns outside of large cities in South America and Africa are needed if we are to understand how to provide coherent services and public policies to this nearly forgotten population. Similarly, the work experience of prisoners, which is also not well researched, has enormous potential in developing more effective rehabilitation services in our prisons. The work experiences of unemployed management and professional workers whose jobs have been outsourced also would be very influential in developing interventions for this cohort of people who have been so traumatized by losing their jobs. In addition, the work lives of small business owners, who represent a diverse and growing population in many nations, requires careful investigation. The struggles of small business owners are particularly noteworthy given that many of these individuals are immigrants and face multiple challenges simultaneously.

One possible trajectory for research within the psychology of working context is to use qualitative methods to generate ideas about a given phenomenon and then to use exploratory or theory-building quantitative methods to explicate the relationships that have been observed in the initial set of studies. For example, a researcher who is exploring the impact of unemployment on low-skilled workers in an inner city context might use interviews and observations to chart the psychological and social consequences of not working. In addition, this line of research optimally would detail the impact of lack of work within a community, much as Wilson did in his 1996 study. Once inferences were developed from these qualitative data, it might be possible for research to examine the nature and extent of the putative relationships by using exploratory quantitative methods. As I indicated earlier, one of the most viable tools for continuing a discovery-oriented approach within the quantitative framework is canonical correlation and its univariate cousin, multiple regression. Canonical correlation is used when investigating the relationships among a group of predictor variables and a group of criterion variables (B. Thompson, 2000). As opposed to such methods as structural equation modeling, which is based on the delineation of an a priori theoretical model to guide the analysis of the data, canonical correlation simply provides a means of exploring the extent and nature of the relationships among a set of variables.

The question of moving from exploratory qualitative research to exploratory quantitative research has not been well documented in the literature. However, the underlying exploratory or discovery-oriented objectives of a given line of inquiry would suggest the following steps. Once qualitative research had identified some promising relationships and constructs in a given setting or population, additional studies could be conducted to examine the generalizability of the findings across cultural contexts. Assuming that meaningful measures of the constructs identified in the interviews were available (either via the research literature or developed by the research team), the next step would be to explore the set of relationships that exists among a given set of variables within a specific context. In addition, the researcher could use either multiple regression or canonical correlation to explore the relationships in greater depth. One study that is an exemplar of this approach is the Kenny, Blustein, Chaves, Grossman, and Gallagher (2003) investigation, which explored the relationships between perceived barriers and relational supports on one hand, and school engagement and career adaptability on the other hand, in a population of urban high school students. While the relationships examined were in fact suggested by the theoretical literature as well as the authors' experiences working with urban high school students, the actual study adopted a more exploratory tone in examining the constructs of school engagement and career adaptability within the framework of youth of color living in the urban core of a large northeastern city. By exploring the relationships among these variables without the imposition of an a priori theoretical framework, it was possible to generate a number of viable and culturally affirming hypotheses about urban youth.

One of the inherent limitations in quantitative research is in the generalizability of the findings. As such, quantitative findings that seem robust at a given point in time and place may in fact not be as viable if examined in different contexts and in different time frames. One example, which was detailed in chapter 4, is the finding by Phillips and her colleagues (e.g., Phillips et al., 2001) that consultative decision making is very likely quite adaptive for use with working class and poor individuals. This finding contrasted sharply with the prevailing notion that consultative or dependent approaches to career decision making were, in fact, maladaptive (e.g., Harren, 1979). The issue of the adaptiveness of a given modality of decision making, while at one time examined almost exclusively via quantitative methodologies (e.g., Blustein, 1987), requires integrative approaches, as Phillips and her colleagues have provided. This point is explored in greater depth in the following section on the role of relativism in psychology-of-working scholarship.

Infusing Relativism Into Psychology of Working Research

Considering the traditional repertoire of research methods in psychology in light of the social constructionist perspective presented earlier in this chapter creates considerable challenges for researchers. However, assuming a less radical view of social constructionist thinking allows for a middle ground that is potentially instructive. In this section, I explore viable ideas for infusing relativism into scholarly efforts on working, with the goal of embedding the cultural, historical, political, and economic contexts into relevant analyses. As indicated earlier, the social constructionist perspective critiques the social sciences along many dimensions (Gergen, 1999; Stead, 2004); however, for the purposes of the present discussion, the most pertinent critique pertains to the notion that social scientific observations and inferences can be easily generalized across different cultural, historical, and social milieus. Given the reality that knowledge is constructed within a cultural context that defines to a large extent the meaning of experiences and relationships, the notion of designing a study that will yield a new overarching principle or assumption about human behavior is nearly impossible. One might argue that this conundrum results in a state of paralysis in which future research is almost exclusively "local," pertaining to a circumscribed time and place.

One of the most viable means of avoiding retreating into this paralytic stance that would immobilize researchers is to develop studies and ideas that are carefully rooted in a given cultural and historical context. In a sense, this movement is already underway, although it is not often framed as a social constructionist paradigm. A review of counseling and vocational psychology journals would reveal numerous articles that seek to explore the cultural context of the participants and that limit the discussion of results to the population under investigation (e.g., Chaves et al., 2004; Juntunen et al., 2001; Kenny et al., 2003). However, in moving beyond the notion of simply acknowledging the cultural background of a population, I believe that we need to place the culture and time period into the full light of our vision so that the findings from a study are carefully assessed and integrated into our analyses. An example of a study that has some of these attributes is the study by Chaves et al. (2004) that examines urban students' conceptions of working. This study, which emerged from a lesson in a psychosocial and career intervention known as Tools for Tomorrow (TFT), sought to explore and document ninth-grade urban students' views of working. The students' conceptions of working were generated from a worksheet used in the TFT lesson on the world of work. As such, the data emerged out of a natural, organic process, representing a traditional educational assignment that occurred within the context of a social interaction between the teachers and students. Moreover, Chaves et al. were very careful to examine the findings within the local reality of urban education during the early part of the 21st century. Furthermore, the findings, which indicated that many inner city youth do not view work as a means of self-determination or self-concept implementation, contrasted sharply with the assumptions about working that prevail in the dominant discourse within vocational and organizational psychology.

Thus, the social constructionist perspective that I advocate here is designed to embed scholarship in the local communities in which it emerges. Rather than casting aside all that is known about psychological research, I urge caution in deriving inferences. Moreover, I would like to embed research on working into the natural, lived experiences of the people we seek to study as opposed to beginning the scholarly journey from our own unique, and often highly privileged, positions. The social constructionist view that I advocate, therefore, builds on the natural framework of exploratory and discovery-oriented scholarship that is carefully embedded into the cultural and historical framework of the problems that are examined.

Infusing Emancipatory Communitarian Ideas Into Psychology-of-Working Research

By adopting an EC approach, researchers of the psychology of working are encouraged to examine issues pertaining to distributive justice, social oppression, and systemic influences. For many psychologists, integrating these notions into the research enterprise is daunting and may even be overwhelming. As I indicated earlier in the chapter, the first step for a researcher or theorist is to be clear about his or her values, particularly with respect to the goals of research and in relation to the issues under investigation. Once one's values are clearly delineated, the next task would involve framing the given set of problems into a clear political and social context. In other words, rather than focusing solely on individual variables or the more proximal contextual variables (such as access to adequate schools, availability of relational resources), the researcher must examine the social and systemic forces that serve to sustain oppressive conditions. Indeed, it may be that the purpose of the research is to identify these systemic factors.

Moving from the conceptual or ideological standpoint of the EC perspective to the realities of theory construction and empirical research represents a major challenge. In this section, I identify the challenges and discuss some possible resolutions. One of the most obvious dilemmas is in identifying, studying, and demonstrating the impact of oppressive forces in people's working lives. Another difficult challenge is in getting research out of journals and conferences and into public policy debates. However, our colleagues in community psychology and in sociology as well as social work have been examining these issues for decades (e.g., Maton, 2000; Pinderhughes, 1983; Riley, 1997). When considering the literatures in community and critical psychology (e.g., Prilleltensky & Nelson, 2002), coupled with other relevant initiatives in the social sciences and education (e.g., Fine, 2003; Solomon, 1987), a number of viable and practical ideas emerge.

One of the key issues in adopting an EC perspective is in locating the most pervasive array of social forces that function to create unfair contextual conditions for people in their educational and vocational trajectories. Identifying these factors from the comfort of one's own study or office is, naturally, not as challenging as is going into a community and asking hard questions of individuals who vary along the powerless–privileged continuum. A number of ideas for identifying the etiological factors underlying unequal access to education and work, naturally, have been identified in a host of fields and disciplines. In our application of the EC perspective to vocational development, my colleagues and I identified lack of access to reasonable health care and inadequate schools as two key factors that function to create and sustain inequality (Blustein et al., 2005). We adopted the EC perspective along with the liberation psychology underpinnings in our analysis, underscoring the distributive justice component of an EC framework. Other factors include poor housing (Wilson, 1996), lack of access to mental health care (Thompson & Neville, 1999), racism (Carter & Cook, 1992; Helms & Cook, 1999), classism (Liu, Ali, et al., 2004; Lott, 2002), and the other social barriers identified in chapter 6.

The methodological approaches best suited to studying these contexts present additional challenges. For the most part, sociologists, anthropologists, and other social scientists who have explored social behavior at the macro level have the most experience in examining these issues. In this context, I advise the use of interdisciplinary research teams that would provide some of the unique methodological skills that are particularly useful in examining macro-level variables. Moreover, a number of psychological disciplines have made significant progress in explicating broader contextual factors. One of the best exemplars of this approach is the developmental contextual and development systems views advanced by Lerner and his associates (e.g., Ford & Lerner, 1992; Lerner, 2002). The developmental contextual framework and the research that has emerged from that perspective have provided some illuminating lessons about social and political conditions that influence development. One study of particular relevance for this discussion is the Silbereisen, Vondracek, and Berg (1997) investigation, which compared the vocational planning and exploration attributes of youth from the former East Germany with a similar cohort from West Germany. The results revealed that the political context of the communist system in East Germany and the free market context of West Germany had major influences on the nature of the youth's vocational development. While this study is naturally hard to replicate given that it took place at a very unique period of time, it does offer some insights into the explanatory power that can be obtained by exploring systemic and political social systems.

Other means of identifying the social context of individual work-related behaviors and experiences include the use of qualitative methods that can help to illuminate and give voice to sources of oppression. (The need to understand the nature of oppression from the perspective of the person who experiences it is a wonderful case in point for the utility of integrating aspects of the EC and social constructionist perspectives as a conceptual framework for the psychology of working.) In effect, identifying the sources of oppressive conditions may be constrained by the limitation of the researchers' own life conditions. As such, using ethnographic, observational, and narrative analyses can be very informative in understanding the impact of oppression in our working lives (cf. Juntunen et al., 2001; Wilson, 1996).

In closing, the most appropriate methodologies for studies on the psychology of working will naturally take on different shapes and forms depending on the goals of a project and the questions that are being raised. In my view, there should be no specific dogma with respect to the use of qualitative or quantitative methods when studying working. I do, however, want to underscore the importance of theory in the psychology of working. Recent criticisms of traditional psychological research have centered in many ways on the hegemony of theories that are derived from the experiences of the researchers or the privileged (Gergen, 1999; Prilleltensky, 1997; Sloan, 2000). I concur with this critique, which has had particular relevance in the study of working, which has been dominated by a discourse that has focused on the working lives of the well educated. However, this critique does not intend to diminish the role of theory in subsequent scholarship on the psychology of working. While I realize that it will be difficult to develop highly generalizable theories given the culturally embedded nature of working across the globe, I believe that theoretical propositions are central to the scholarly enterprise. As I have indicated in this chapter, the types of theories that may be most viable are localized theories that are relevant for a given time and place. Ideally, the social constructionist and EC perspectives, along with the more specific methodological suggestions identified in this section, will provide the road map for the next generation of scholars of the psychology of working.

Experience-Near Research on the Psychology of Working: Closing the Gap Between Researcher and Participant

One of the key attributes of this book has been my attempt to move the reader to a position of deep and genuine empathy with respect to both the pain and satisfaction that can emerge from working. In considering methodological issues with respect to work, I believe that it is important to conclude with some ideas about bridging the gap between the researcher and participant. As I indicated in chapters 1 and 2, the movement toward an experience-near approach to research parallels analogous trends in the psychotherapy community (Bohart & Greenberg, 1997; Jordan et al., 1991; Kohut, 1977). In short, the notion that underlies many of the clinical advances in empathy is the growing awareness of how powerful empathic introspection can be in connecting to clients and in understanding their issues and concerns. (See Bohart &

Greenberg, 1997, for a detailed overview of recent advances in empathy in psychotherapy theory, research, and practice.)

Bohart and Greenberg (1997) examined the role of empathy across a broad spectrum of psychological thought and concluded that empathy is differentially understood and can be categorized as follows:

■ Empathic rapport: In this context, "empathy is primarily kindliness, global understanding, and tolerant acceptance of the client's feelings and frame of reference. The therapist shows that he or she recognizes what the client is feeling .... However, this understanding is at a general level, in which the therapist applies his or her knowledge of human experience to 'understand' that it makes sense that if the client feels rejected he or she will feel sad, or if the client feels neglected he or she will feel angry and so on." (p. 13)

■ Experience-near understanding of the client's world: This notion, which is similar to the view that I am advancing, is based on an attempt "to grasp the whole of the client's perceived situation. The therapist wants to empathically understand what it is like to be this client based on knowing about the client's perceived world—what it is like to have the problems the client has, to live in the life situation the client lives in, and so on." (p. 14)

■ Communicative attunement: This category, which is emphasized by client-centered therapists, "involves moment-by-moment attunement and frequent understanding responses. The therapist tries to put himself or herself in the clients' shoes at the moment, to grasp what they are consciously trying to communicate at that moment, and what they are experiencing at that moment." (p. 14)

As reflected in these views of empathy, multiple ways exist with which to bridge the gap between therapists and clients. In a similar vein, social psychologists and developmental psychologists have studied empathy in natural interactions among people (Duan & Hill, 1996; Feshbach, 1997; Gladstein, 1983). For example, Feshbach observed that empathy is a natural aspect of social discourse and that it has its roots in our early development. Building on scholarship in social and developmental psychology, Feshbach suggested that empathy is an outgrowth of early evolutionary processes in which our forebears may have developed distress responses to others of their cohort who were in danger. In contemporary human interactions, Feshbach described empathy as having its roots in some automatic responses; however, for the most part, the empirical research has indicated that empathy is a consequence of external socialization and learning (Aronfreed, 1970; M. H. Davis, 1983).

In the research realm, empathy has been discussed generally within the qualitative tradition and within the feminist literature (Campbell, 2003; Grossman, Kruger, & Moore, 1999). The researchers explore issues related to empathy and intimacy to better understand phenomenon related to equality, gender issues, and power structures. Following this rich tradition, I am advising that researchers seek to use a variety of means to enhance their empathic clarity. One method, which has been used extensively in this book, is the use of narratives, vignettes, archival data, and other expressions of individual experience as a tool in enhancing one's connection to the people and problems that one is studying. However, rather than simply reading the text of an interview, tabulating the results of quantitative questionnaires, or observing a group of workers at a job completing a task, I believe that a fully embraced affirmation of the psychology of working would entail careful empathic understanding. Using the terminology noted earlier by Bohart and Greenberg (1997), I suggest that scholars find ways of developing an experience-near connection to the people and problems that they seek to study. Prior to outlining some of the ways of enhancing the experience-near connection, I first will respond to the expected critique of this approach that suggests that it blurs the lines between subjectivity and objectivity. The fact that an explicit focus on empathic understanding may reduce the objectivity of a research team, in my view, simply makes an implicit aspect of our work more explicit. Consistent with the social constructionist and EC perspectives that I have outlined earlier in this chapter, I believe that researchers' values are embedded in the work that they do (Gergen, 1999; Prilleltensky, 1997). The role of empathic understanding would not inherently confound a researchers' objectivity any more than any other aspect of the scholarly enterprise. Every decision that a scholar makes about a study, beginning with the literature reviewed, the choices of approaches to study a given problem, and the data analytic method, is framed by hypotheses, beliefs, and values. In my view, empathic introspection offers a means of reducing a critical gap in existing psychological research pertaining to the distance that we create between our clients and research participants and ourselves. Ideally, empathic understanding can help researchers to make their values more explicit as they are exposed to aspects of participants' lives that may have been inaccessible or inadequately understood.

Some of the approaches to enhancing empathy have actually been used in this book. One of the intentions in using vignettes from workers has been to help readers obtain an experience-near connection to the lives of workers who face hardship, struggles, and denigration (as well as joy, satisfaction, and a sense of accomplishment). Because vocational psychology and I/O psychology have tended to focus on the lives of individuals with some degree of volition in their work lives, I have sought to bring readers closer to the emotional and psychological worlds of workers across a wider spectrum. In addition to using narratives of workers, I suggest that researchers consider the following ideas as they explore the complex nature of working.

One idea that has merit is to develop interdisciplinary teams that include representatives from the population that is the target of inquiry. While it may not be practical or productive to include representatives of the target population in all of the meetings and activities, some representation at the beginning of a project may be helpful in enhancing empathy and deepening one's understanding of the problem under investigation. Another idea is to expose oneself to the cultural artifacts of a given population. As an example, if a researcher is interested in studying the working lives of African American young adults, it may be helpful to learn about the cultural influences within the community, including exposure to music, films, and other forms of cultural expression. I also would suggest that investigators and theorists explore the wider world of artistic statements about working. For example, I have been moved by the photographs of Salgado (1993), whose collection of photos of workers in poor countries not only enhanced my empathy for aspects of working that I had not considered so overtly, but also taught me about working conditions that I would not have ordinarily observed. Clearly, I am not advocating that observing photos would, in of itself, construct the essence of a research project; however, it may be a start in a process of expanding one's horizons.

Aside from increasing our sensitivity to the struggles of workers across the globe, questions may be raised about the precise value that an experience-near approach to research empathy adds to the scholarly enterprise. In my view, attempting to cross the gulf that exists between researchers and theorists and the phenomena that we seek to understand is a complex process, one that can offer important assets to our work. First, I would suggest that by reducing the gaps that exist in our social discourse, we have a greater opportunity to understand the nature of poverty, unemployment, harsh working conditions, and the like. By understanding the *human* costs of these pervasive social problems, I would argue that we will be able to mobilize greater action in advancing a socially engaged research program. Second, I believe that an experience-near approach is helpful in expanding the array of ideas and constructs that we consider in our work. For example, the interviews that I have conducted with participants in the school-to-work studies that I cited earlier in this chapter (e.g., Blustein et al., 1997; Phillips et al., 2002) have been instrumental in giving me ideas that may not have been easily discernible in traditional reviews of social science literature. By delving deeply into the conversations that my colleagues and I had with our participants, we were able to infer that relational and instrumental support were critical, not just peripheral elements in an adaptive work-based transition. Third, the experience-near approach will help to connect research more overtly with counseling and clinical practice, which is detailed in the following two chapters. By moving beyond the scope of traditional vocational and I/O psychology, it may be possible to develop a truly affirming view of working within psychotherapeutic discourse.

Conclusion

The material that I have presented in this chapter is designed to initiate conversations, critical comments, and future research. Therefore, I would like to underscore that the directions that I have mapped out in this chapter are not designed to be the only path to explicating the psychology of working. In addition, because of space limitations, I have not been able to cover all the potential issues of relevance to psychologists interested in working. I hope that future scholars and practitioners will be able to critique and extend my positions and recommendations, and develop alternative pathways for the psychological study of working.

Embedded within this chapter is a rather dramatic shift in epistemology for the study of working within psychology. Rather than approaching the infusion of social constructionist and emancipatory communitarian thought as the new dogma, I have sought to present these ideas as a means of loosening up the increasingly constricted positivist paradigm, which has functioned well within the scope of traditional vocational and I/O psychology. The critical point, in my view, for the next generation of theory and research on the psychology of working, is that we confront many of the seemingly intractable problems that face workers across the globe. As I have detailed in chapter 4, the relational connections that are formed within the working context are critical to our well-being. In the case of scholars who are devoted to working, I would suggest that forming supportive research teams, including people outside of our discipline and perhaps including the targets of our effort, will help to ensure that our efforts are effective in meeting a wider array of problems related to working. While my road map may be overly optimistic in its endorsement of the power and potential for psychology to shape public policy and the lived experiences of people, I am hopeful that by attracting others to this pursuit, we will be able to chart our way through the muddy waters of working in the 21st century.

CHAPTER 8

Implications of an Inclusive Psychology of Working for Practice: Counseling and Psychotherapy

The fact that, with few exceptions (e.g., Axelrod, 1999; Lowman, 1993), work issues are still marginalized in most psychotherapeutic theory and practice affirms the reality that existing methods and ideas are not sufficient to convey the richness and depth of the space shared by work and relationships. In addition, empirical research has indicated that counseling psychologists exhibit a bias against work-related issues in treatment and assessment concerns (e.g., Spengler, Blustein, & Strohmer, 1990). (Of course, one can only wonder how powerful this bias may be in other practitioners such as clinical psychologists, social workers, and psychiatrists, who have not had formal exposure to a body of knowledge about the psychological aspects of work.) Furthermore, with some notable exceptions, particularly within vocational psychology and industrial/organizational psychology, much of the psychological world functions as if work-related issues were either non-existent or inconsequential.

—Blustein (2001b, p. 184)

I believe that there is a need to move beyond career development to a broader emphasis on fostering the development of individuals considered as whole persons in relation to the work in their lives. I no longer believe it is tenable to separate the study of career from the multiple and interacting strands and trajectories of development that make up the texture of lives over the life span. Work is embedded in family and personal lives, as well as in paid employment. In any one case, this work may contribute to or impede development or well-being. A privileging of any one of the developmental strands relating to work in a person's life would necessarily distort and limit an understanding of that person.

—Richardson (1993, p. 431)

The material presented thus far in this book, coupled with the quotes that lead off this chapter, underscore the centrality of work in people's lives. My position about the critical nature of working, which echoes similar ideas in the literature (e.g., Betz, 1993; N. Peterson & González, 2005), forms a major theme within this chapter and the next. In the material that follows, I explore the implications of a fully inclusive psychology of working in relation to counseling, psychotherapy, psychoeducational interventions, and the broader world of mental health practice. The clinical material presented here, coupled with the theoretical and research contributions from previous chapters, creates the conceptual infrastructure for the inclusive psychological practice perspective that is presented in chapter 9.

Historical, Definitional, and Conceptual Framework

The framework for an inclusive and integrative mode of psychological practice that builds on the psychology-of-working perspective is best constructed by exploring two branches of the helping professions—one devoted to vocational counseling and the other devoted to psychotherapy. In this section, I explore the existing conceptual frameworks in vocational counseling and psychotherapy, noting the important contributions and inherent limitations of each discipline.

Vocational Counseling: An Historical and Contemporary Overview

The history of vocational psychology and counseling psychology is inextricably woven with the history of vocational counseling (Whitely, 1980). As detailed in chapter 1, the earliest beginnings of vocational counseling are typically traced to the contributions of Parsons (1909), who started the Vocation Bureau that served primarily working class immigrants in Boston's North End. The growth of vocational counseling as a helping profession was further fueled by advances in psychometrics, theoretical developments in counseling, and the increasing need for assistance in choosing jobs and training opportunities as the labor market became more complex and varied (Herr et al., 2004; Pope, 2000). At the outset of the development of the vocational guidance movement, counseling services primarily were available within high schools and some post-secondary institutions. In addition, a number of non-profit agencies in large cities offered vocational counseling to adults who were interested in exploring their options (e.g., Federation of Guidance Services in New

York City; Jewish Vocational Services; some YMCA offices in large cities). Furthermore, the United States Department of Labor, under the rubric of the Job Service (now generally known as One-Stop Career Centers), offered counseling and assessment to adults, many of whom were unemployed or struggling to find stable sources of employment. (See Herr et al., 2004, and Pope, 2000, for excellent overviews of the history of career counseling in the United States.)

I enter the literature of counseling practice with the knowledge that the language used to describe our work varies, often dramatically. Rather than reviewing the wide array of definitions that exist, I have sought to integrate existing perspectives from diverse sources (e.g., Gysbers et al., 2003; Hall, 1996; Herr et al., 2004; Lapan, 2004) to develop operational definitions for this discussion. The primary term that I use to refer to counseling in the work domain is *vocational counseling*. While the term "career counseling" is used more commonly in the literature, the elitist nature of the career concept, as detailed in previous chapters, may result in practitioners continuing with the circumscribed focus that is characterizing much (but clearly not all) of our current practice efforts. In my view, vocational counseling refers to psychological interventions, delivered individually or in groups, which seek to help clients explore their options, values, and abilities with respect to work. Moreover, vocational counseling includes activities designed to help people access greater opportunities to enhance their options (such as the exploration and acquisition of training and education) as well as interventions designed to empower clients to increase their self-regulation and self-determination at work. Vocational counseling also includes exploration of work-related adjustment issues. Furthermore, the expanded vision of vocational counseling that is articulated in this chapter includes psychoeducational efforts that help clients understand the social and economic influences that are responsible for disparities in access to opportunities (cf. Blustein et al., 2005; Freire, 1970/1993; Martín-Baro, 1994; Solberg, Howard, Blustein, & Close, 2002). (I provide definitions of psychotherapy and integrative treatments later in this chapter.)

It is important to note, however, that my use of the term *vocational counseling* differs from the traditional views of vocation, which has two diverse meanings in our work. On one hand, vocation has been used to denote the sense of "calling" that is often most profoundly experienced by religious clergy or spiritually minded individuals (Bloch, 2004; Bogart, 1994). In addition, vocation is typically understood in the United States as a shorthand term to designate occupations that do not require much higher education; in effect, a vocation has emerged as a term that refers to blue-collar or pink-collar jobs. My use of the term *vocational counseling* seeks to circumvent the problems inherent in the continued use of "career" as a descriptor of our work. However, I would like to underscore that the ideal evolution of work would involve far greater expansion of volition in the choices that people have in making decisions about education and work.

The question of assessing the effectiveness of vocational counseling, as it has been practiced in the later part of the 20th century, has attracted considerable attention among researchers. For the most part, the literature has demonstrated that vocational counseling is effective (e.g., S. D. Brown & Krane, 2000; Swanson, 1995; Whiston, Sexton, & Lasoff, 1998); however, consistent with the Brown and Krane focus, the bulk of the literature examining the impact of vocational counseling has assessed the effectiveness of interventions directed toward helping clients make career choices. Despite the limitations of the vocational counseling outcome literature, many of the practices and policies may be relevant to a more inclusive mode of psychological practice that seeks to explicitly affirm and explore the role of work in life experience.

As I convey throughout this chapter, the objective of a psychology-of-working perspective for counseling and psychotherapy practice revolves around the notion of inclusion. The most apparent manifestation of inclusion is evident in my concern that all workers and potential workers receive the benefits of our efforts as psychological researchers and practitioners. The vast majority of theories in vocational psychology and counseling have been constructed around the notion that people have choices with respect to education and work and that their task is to sort through their options (see D. Brown, 2002a, for a review of the major theories). While this is indeed an admirable objective (and indeed one that I encourage scholars of the psychology of working to advance), the reality is that the theories that have informed vocational counseling and career development education have been framed around the rather circumscribed context of counseling people who are experiencing decisional dilemmas. A close examination of the counseling literature reveals a number of bodies of work that are relevant to developing an expanded conceptual framework for vocational counseling (e.g., Lapan, 2004; N. Peterson & González, 2005; M. S. Richardson, 1993, 1996; Savickas, 1993). My position is that the best potential for effective interventions involves further inclusiveness across a number of dimensions. One level of the inclusiveness entails an incorporation of nonvocational aspects of life. The second level of inclusiveness involves interventions that are designed to alter social systems. (This issue is reviewed later in this chapter and in chapter 10.) The third level of inclusiveness pertains to the need to develop an effective, moral, and engaged modality of vocational counseling that will help all citizens find meaning and satisfaction in their working lives. In other words, the view of vocational counseling that I advocate herein is designed to be useful for all workers and potential workers. Ideally, as systems and structures improve to expand access to opportunity, the notion of counseling people to help define and attain their ideal fit in the working world—the notion that inspired Parsons (1909) a century ago—will increasingly define the specialty of vocational counseling. However, as I propose later in the chapter, helping professionals still ought to provide constructive, effective, and empowering services to all potential workers across the socioeconomic spectrum.

The literature in vocational counseling reveals that the framework for an engaged and inclusive mode of practice does exist, often in the margins of the literature. For example, the literature from such diverse areas as vocational rehabilitation (e.g., Szymanski & Parker, 2003), working with at-risk youth (e.g., Blustein et al., 2000), working with clients of color (e.g., Carter & Cook, 1992; Helms & Cook, 1999), as well as working with unemployed workers (e.g., Amundson et al., 2004) has the potential to inform practice of an expanded vocational counseling. Indeed, the literature from vocational counseling that has explored the challenges of "nontraditional clients" (which actually may represent the modal worker and potential worker across the globe) provides the basis for an expanded vision of vocational counseling.

As I have argued in this book, the experience of working involves so much more than selecting a field of interest and locating training and work in that area. Indeed, the passages that I have included in this volume, ranging from Arthur Miller to Bruce Springsteen, have collectively underscored the complex intersection of relationships, emotional functioning, and working. One of the goals of the psychology of working is to provide the framework for a thoughtful and inclusive infusion of work-related issues into the framework of psychotherapeutic theory and practice. As the quote from one of my earlier articles (Blustein, 2001b) that leads this chapter reveals, the vast majority of the psychotherapy literature has tended to neglect or diminish the impact of working in human life and in psychological treatment.

Psychotherapy: An Historical and Contemporary Overview

The history of psychotherapy, naturally, is difficult to summarize in a limited space. In fact, entire books have been devoted to delineating the complex history of psychotherapeutic practice (Bankart, 1997; Freedheim, 1992). However, scholars and practitioners (e.g., Betz & Corning, 1993; Blustein & Spengler, 1995) have observed that the vast majority of theoretical formulations in psychotherapy have tended to ignore issues pertaining to work. Of course, some notable exceptions exist. As I indicated in chapter 1, Freud observed that mental health could be best understood as the ability to love and work. Also, Erikson's (1968) influential theory of psychosocial development, which has had a notable impact in psychotherapy (e.g., Shore & Massimo, 1979; Smelser & Erikson, 1980), includes attention to working, particularly in the description of the identity formation process.

Like vocational counseling, psychotherapy has been defined in different ways, often reflecting the assumptions and objectives of a specified theoretical orientation. From my perspective, psychotherapy represents the application of psychological research and theory to the task of helping individuals deal with problems of a diverse nature, including but not limited to physical health, mood, interpersonal problems, psychiatric illnesses, family concerns and conflicts, adjustments to trauma, work-related problems, and related mental health issues. Others define psychotherapy in more limited ways. For example, Zeig and Munion (1990) suggested that "psychotherapy is a change-oriented process that occurs in the context of a contractual, empowering, and empathic professional relationship. Its rationale explicitly or implicitly focuses on the personality of the client(s), the technique of psychotherapy, or both. Durable change is affected on multiple aspects of clients' lives. The process is idiosyncratic and determined by the interaction of the patients' and therapists' preconceived positions" (p. 14). In the same volume, Gladfelter (1990) defined psychotherapy as "the bringing about of change in both the internal and social psychological processes of the individual" (p. 338). Wolberg (1977) presented the following definition: "Psychotherapy is the treatment, by psychological means, of problems of an emotional nature in which a trained person deliberately establishes a professional relationship with the patient with the object of (1) removing, modifying, or retarding existing symptoms, (2) mediating disturbed patterns of behavior, and (3) promoting positive personality growth and development" [p. 3]. When considered collectively, these definitions, as well as others (see Zeig & Munion, 1990), suggest that psychotherapy is a modality of treatment that is best delivered via "talk therapy," with adherents from the full range of psychological and personality theories each espousing their particular view as the prototype or ideal. For the most part, the empirical literature in mental health has determined that psychotherapy is indeed effective for a wide array of clients and problems (e.g., Barlow, 2004; Wampold, 2001). However, while I included a focus on work-related issues in my own definition in the Zeig and Munion volume, the vast majority of approaches and definitions in psychotherapy theory, research, and practice do not include a specific reference to work, careers, occupations, or the like.

Despite the relative lack of attention to work-related issues in psychotherapy, some recent efforts from traditional psychotherapy theorists and practitioners (e.g., Axelrod, 1999; Lowman, 1993; Socarides & Kramer, 1997) have sought to address work-related issues in explicit and often very thoughtful ways. The contribution by Lowman used the traditional approach of focusing on psychopathology to examine the nature of work dysfunctions and their impact on people's lives. While Lowman's book is to be commended for placing work on the radar screen of traditional clinicians (including clinical psychologists, social workers, and psychiatrists), the scope of this contribution is rather limited. For example, much of the Lowman book explores the work lives of people with choices and volition. A similar critique can be invoked in the Axelrod and Socarides and Kramer books, respectively. While these contributions are evocative and creative in their application of relationally oriented and psychodynamic theories to various aspects of working, they also focus, for the most part, on relatively affluent and well-educated clients living in urban Western cultures.

One specialty that has sought to include workers from across the gamut of the labor market is occupational psychiatry and the related employee assistance programs (e.g., Berridge, 1999; A. Kahn, 1993; Oher, 1999). Occupational psychiatry has carved a niche within organizations in which employees can seek out assistance for work-related stress and other psychological problems. Similarly, employee assistance programs (EAPs), which are generally staffed by social workers and other Master's level clinicians, provide support in terms of both referrals and short-term counseling for employees, often at the worksite (Herr et al., 2004; Oher, 1999). These efforts are notable and are clearly relevant to the development of effective practice within the scope of the psychology of working. One of the admirable aspects of these efforts is that they have included non-managerial workers, particularly municipal workers such as firefighters and police officers. (At their best, in-house mental health agencies at the workplace can function as a critical resource for workers, helping to furnish employees with accessible and competent mental health professionals. However, EAPs and occupational psychiatry programs are not universally available to workers. Moreover, given the lack of much formal training in the mental health world on workplace issues in treatment, it is likely that many of the problems that emerge from the working context of individuals lives (i.e., the specific nature of workers' tasks, struggles pertaining to the rigidity of hierarchical relationships, the impact of the increasing instability in the world of work, inadequate person–environment fit) may not be well understood or effectively integrated into the preventive and intervention modalities. Ideally, the psychology of working will produce a body of research and theory that will be informative in the continued development and expansion of EAPs so that far greater inclusiveness and sensitivity to work-related issues increasingly characterizes best practices within organizational settings. Furthermore, it would seem particularly useful for unemployed workers to have access to services that integrate vocational counseling and psychotherapeutic efforts. In addition, workers who are struggling with specific supervisors would benefit from having an opportunity to explore the nature, antecedents, and consequences of the conflict. Also, workers who may not find their assignments and tasks interesting or consistent with their values would find EAPs to be helpful, particularly if other options may exist within a given occupational setting that may provide a better fit for the worker and a more productive employee for the organization.

The relative absence of any sustained discourse about the role of work in people's lives within the vast majority of psychotherapy theory and research (cf. Zeig & Munion, 1990), with the exceptions noted previously, is quite disconcerting. Many counseling psychologists have bemoaned this particular observation (e.g., Betz, 1993; Blustein, 2001b; M. S. Richardson, 1993, 1996), noting that this neglect leaves a vast majority of people's lives unexamined, or even worse, denigrated. As I indicated in an earlier contribution (Blustein, 2001b), a number of reasons for this absence can be inferred from the literature. Clearly, many scholars, practitioners, and theorists find it easier to compartmentalize life issues into neat and tidy boxes. Regrettably, these boxes are not as coherent in real life as they are on the written page, as life issues from one aspect of our lives tend to spill over into other life domains (Blustein, 2001b; Cinamon & Rich, 2002; Flum, 2001).

A review of many of the most prominent career counseling textbooks reveals that the majority of emphasis is on the tasks of specifying, crystallizing, and entering an occupation that is a good match for one's personality, abilities, and values (e.g., Brown, 2002a; Herr et al., 2004; Issacson, 2003; Sharf, 2000). While these books are conceptually rich and highly relevant to the needs of students and clients who are facing the challenging dilemmas of making educational and vocational decisions, they do not fully encompass the needs of the vast majority of workers. For example, it is notable that so little attention has been devoted to people who are unemployed or who have had to take jobs that are overwhelmingly unsatisfying. (Two noteworthy exceptions to this trend are the Gysbers, Heppner, & Johnston, 2003, and Herr et al., 2004, texts, which weave in the struggles of adult workers, including unemployed clients in their discussions.) As such, the traditional career development theories may not be viewed as easily applicable to the conceptual framework of mental health interventions. For example, the prevailing career choice and development theories explore the antecedents of adaptive decisions, which may not be that relevant to clients struggling with abusive supervisors, lack of employment opportunities, and the existence of external barriers to achievement and satisfaction. Moreover, while many psychotherapy practices consist of the "worried well," a significant proportion of clients in psychotherapy are more impaired by their illnesses and need to focus on work in a very different way than the traditional vocational counseling client who often has considerable choice in his or her world. A client, for instance, with bipolar disorder, may need to locate work that provides the consistent structure and predictable social demands that are so important in regulating this challenging mood disorder (S. Jones, 2004; Zaretsky, 2003).

In addition, the lack of interest in work-related issues is related, to some extent, to the marketplace demands of psychotherapy. With the advent of third-party payments in the United States and the struggles to have psychotherapy included in national health services in many other nations, the psychological treatment field has had to befriend the medical model in an overt manner (Barlow, 2004). By linking so closely to the medical model, the psychotherapeutic world has increasingly focused on internal and interpersonal problems, which are generally well understood within existing taxonomies and diagnostic systems. An additional reason for the lack of interest in work-related issues in psychotherapy may be related to the lack of inclusion of work as a relevant domain of life experience within most theories of personality and psychopathology. For the most part, the family and other relationships are seen as the crucible of both mental health and mental illness (e.g., Bowlby, 1988; Kohut, 1977; Wachtel, 1993). While the important role of relational and family factors is not in doubt here, the lack of attention to the full context of people's lives, which clearly includes working, is not entirely consistent with the reality that most people face.

Another possible reason for the relative neglect of work-related issues in psychotherapy theory, research, and practice relates to the point raised by M. S. Richardson (1993) in the quote that opened this chapter. As Richardson noted, the absence of an explicit discussion of work in psychotherapeutic discourse offers the field a way of avoiding the harsh realities of inequity, which are often most pronounced in the working context. In effect, by taking work out of the conceptual framework, psychotherapists maintain a fairly narrow view of life, with a corresponding focus on inner cognitions, emotions, and biological bases of human functioning. I would like to note here that the internal factors that have been the focus of the vast majority of psychotherapeutic theories are indeed very important in determining the state of our emotional, interpersonal, and, indeed, our working lives. However, with the infusion of critical psychology, multicultural theory, and feminism into the mental health literature (e.g., Doherty, 1995; Fox & Prilleltensky, 1997; Helms & Cook, 1999; Prilleltensky, 1997; Willkinson, 1997), the social and economic context, with its disparities in opportunities, is increasingly acknowledged, although its impact is not always well understood. As noted in chapter 7, I view many of the tenets of the critical psychology movement, particularly the emancipatory communitarian approach of Prilleltensky (1997), to be highly relevant to the psychology of working. Moreover, the contributions from the multicultural and feminist perspectives have influenced my thinking and the work of others who are seeking to carve out a broader niche in the understanding of the psychological nature of working (Betz & Fitzgerald, 1987; Fassinger, 2000; N. Peterson & González, 2005; M. S. Richardson, 1993, 1996). An intentional infusion of a psychology-of-working perspective into the psychotherapy literature has the potential to help shape a more vigorous and relevant body of work that can address many of the concerns raised by scholars such as Doherty, Prilleltensky, and others. For example, Doherty has argued that psychotherapists need to understand and attend to the moral and ethical issues that are inherent in the lives of our clients and in our own lives. In my view, Doherty's concern about the relative neglect of moral and ethical issues, which has been echoed by others throughout the past few years (e.g., Goodman et al., 2004; Prilleltensky, 1997; Vera & Speight, 2003), may be effectively responded to as work-related issues are more explicitly linked to psychotherapeutic theory and practice. In order to construct the conceptual infrastructure for an inclusive psychological practice, I next summarize the growing literature on integrating psychotherapy and vocational counseling.

Integrating Vocational Counseling and Psychotherapy: An Historical and Contemporary Overview

The preceding discussion conveys a view of vocational counseling and psychotherapy as essentially discrete enterprises with little, if any, overlap. In actuality, a number of scholars and practitioners have considered the potential opportunities and pitfalls of careful integration of treatment modalities. For example, Super (1955) made a case for vocational counseling providing a means of personality integration for clients. Moreover, the development of the counseling psychology specialty directly after World War II facilitated the potential for integrative treatments (Whitely, 1980). However, as I detailed earlier in this chapter, there were many social, economic, and intellectual pressures that offered a counterbalance to any natural tendency to integrate vocational and psychological counseling.

Despite the rise of a relatively discrete set of theories and research studies within vocational psychology and vocational counseling, parallels in the counseling process that exist in vocational and personal counseling have been documented, which has underscored the connection and overlap between these two modalities (e.g., Heppner & Heppner, 2003; Swanson, 1995). In addition, a number of scholars and practitioners have noted the strong parallels in the therapeutic factors in vocational counseling and personal counseling (e.g., Blustein & Spengler, 1995; Holland, Magoon, & Spokane, 1981; Kirschner, Hoffman, & Hill, 1994). Furthermore, practitioners in both vocational and personal counseling have thoughtfully highlighted parallels that have emerged in their practices and thinking (e.g., Manuele-Adkins, 1992; Savickas, 1993). The essence of this argument, as detailed in these contributions, is as follows:

- The distinctions between vocational and personal counseling are an artifact of language and do not conform to the realities of people's lives.
- Vocational problems have often been misconstrued as somehow less important or painful than relationship problems.
- Vocational counseling is as complex and challenging as is personal counseling.
- The process of human change across the various contexts of life contains many parallels and few distinctions.

Despite the compelling nature of the view that considers vocational and personal counseling as strongly analogous, alternative arguments can also be invoked to maintain the distinctions. First, the reality of vocational counseling is that it requires additional skills in comparison to personal counseling. In short, a competent vocational counselor needs to be a skilled mental health counselor or psychotherapist as well as a skilled counselor within the working context. Second, the strong focus on the parallels between vocational and personal counseling might lead to the sort of thinking that has unfortunately prevailed in contemporary mental health practice—that is, that work-related problems are primarily the manifestation of inner psychological struggles, unresolved family issues, or other relational problems. While these inferences may in fact be sufficiently explanatory in some cases, it is hard to imagine that the decontextualized view that has prevailed in clinical circles would be entirely accurate for the full range of issues that confront workers and potential workers. Indeed, these types of explanations, while often compelling and evocative, risk denigrating a client's experience and may in fact offer a means of colluding with inequitable systems that deny access to opportunity based on arbitrary factors (like race, ethnicity, age, gender, etc.). Another important issue to consider with respect to the integration of treatment modalities is the conclusion of researchers who have explored the overlap of vocational and psychological functioning (e.g., Barkham & Shapiro, 1990; Shore & Massimo, 1979). After reviewing this literature, a colleague and I (Blustein & Spengler, 1995) concluded as follows:

> When considered collectively, the literature reviewed in this section points to the tendency for a given intervention to foster a modest, yet discernible, positive effect (or spillover) on collateral domains of functioning. Of course, the spillover of outcomes from an intervention in one domain to another [from the vocational to personal and vice versa] is not always uniform or consistent. Yet the prevalent findings in this review suggest that interventions in both the career and noncareer domains as well as integrative treatments have the potential for a relatively broad scope of influence. The fact that the scope tends to embrace both career and noncareer domains in generally predictable ways supports the assumption of meaningful interconnections between these aspects of psychological functioning. (p. 308)

The Domain-Sensitive Approach

We (i.e., Blustein & Spengler, 1995) concluded our review of the interconnections of vocational and personal counseling with a meta-perspective known as the domain-sensitive approach. The initial statement of the domain-sensitive approach describes a modality that fits well with the objectives of the psychology of working:

> A domain-sensitive approach refers to a way of intervening with clients such that the full array of human experiences is encompassed. The goals of such an intervention are to improve adjustment and facilitate developmental progress in both the career and noncareer domains. The term *domain* pertains to the scope of the client's psychological experiences, encompassing both career and noncareer settings. By following *domain* with the term *sensitive* [italics in original], we are attempting to capture counselors' inherent openness, empathy, and interest with respect to both the career and noncareer domains and their ability to shift between these content domains effectively. In effect, a domain-sensitive approach is characterized by the counselor's concerted interest in and awareness of all possible ramifications of a client's psychological experience and its behavioral expression. In this approach, the counselor clearly values the client's experiences in both the career and noncareer domains. The counselor bases a decision about where to intervene on informed judgments

about where the problem originated and where it is most accessible for intervention. (1995, p. 317)

Other important attributes of the domain-sensitive approach include the clear statement that work-related problems are real and merit the full attention in the psychological treatment process. While we cautioned therapists that immediate mental health problems and crises always take priority, we also sought to provide some structure for the affirmation and effective treatment of work-related issues in mental health practice. Moreover, we advised vocational counselors to attend to mental health issues as well in their work. However, the prevailing message of the domain-sensitive approach is that work-related issues need to be validated in counseling. The case that follows provides an illustration of how work-related problems can be viewed in different ways in a counseling context.

Nathan

Nathan is a computer specialist with a medium-sized consulting company who seeks out treatment to help him deal with his increasing level of suspiciousness regarding his job security. He is also experiencing rather marked outbursts of anger, most of which are evoked by events that had been innocuous in the past (such as traffic jams; disagreements with people at work, etc.). Nathan, who is a 36-year-old European American man with a college degree in computer science, has found that he is becoming very concerned with the security of his job. While there have not been many layoffs in his firm, he has heard rumors that the management has been flying to India and Pakistan to explore outsourcing of programming work. His level of suspiciousness has also affected his relationships with his partner, a 42-year-old man, with whom Nathan has lived for the past 10 years. (Nathan is "out" with respect to his sexual orientation with his family and friends, although he is rather discrete about his personal life in general, particularly at work.) Nathan is reporting increasing tension in his relationship with Mark. He is not clear about the nature or etiology of the conflict; however, he is clear that he is reacting much more strongly, with greater anger than he had prior to the stress that he feels in his work life.

A brief psychosocial history that is obtained in the first session reveals that Nathan has had no history of major mental illness. However, his father suffered from major depression throughout his life, which was treated with reasonable effectiveness with medication and therapy. His mother was a rather reclusive woman, with few friends and little opportunities for social connection. Nathan indicated that his mother did not experience any evident mental health problems. Nathan has an older brother, who is married and has three children. His brother lives in another part of the country and he is not very close to him or his family. Nathan reported that his childhood was "awkward" in that he was aware that he was not similar to other boys, especially with regards to the prevailing leisure activities which typically revolved around sports. Nathan enjoyed reading and working on puzzles and other challenging tasks, often in isolation from others. His parents, on the other hand, encouraged him to make friends, which he did throughout his life. Often his friends also were children or adolescents who felt as "outsiders."

Nathan stated that he was not as depressed or anxious in college or in his 20s. He became increasingly comfortable with his sexual orientation in college, and connected to an active gay community in his urban community. He met Mark when he was 26 and they moved in together when he turned 28. Nathan's rather rich social life began to diminish once he and Mark moved in together. At this point, Nathan reports that he has few close friends who live in his area. He is friends with some of his former college classmates and he speaks to a few of these people every few months.

Nathan's major presenting concerns center on his anxiety about his working life. Nathan had a deep interest in computer science in college and was an excellent student in his university. He also enjoyed the challenges of programming and debugging programs, which fit his interests and abilities. Nathan was very committed to his career and sought to keep up with changes that occurred in the field by learning new programming languages after he graduated from college. Over the past few years, he has been following the trend of large organizations and programming consulting firms to outsource their work to less expensive settings. A number of his former college classmates who majored in computer science recently lost their jobs, leading him to worry about his own job security. He observed that few of these programmers were able to locate a job that offered the similar sort of intellectual challenges and financial rewards.

In the first few sessions, Nathan shared that he has had trouble sleeping and that he is feeling more depressed. He did not report suicidal ideation nor has he experienced any suicidal thoughts in the past. However, Nathan has been feeling increasingly angry at the management of his company; in fact, he has fantasized about finding ways to "hurt them back" if they outsource jobs to India and Pakistan. He is not able to articulate what he means by this phrase and says that he is just saying things off the top of his head and that it is no "big deal."

Discussion

One of the main themes of the domain-sensitive approach is that each context of life experience is real and valid. In contrast, some of the traditional approaches to psychotherapy might explore Nathan's issues without a clear understanding of the work-related problems. While most therapists would be empathic with Nathan's worries about his job, the concern that I have is that the case might be conceptualized in a manner wherein the work-related issues become the "ground" to the "figure" of unresolved family issues, conceptualizations that are exclusively biological in nature, or intrapsychic conflicts, or some combination thereof. The domain-sensitive approach seeks to find balance in the conceptualizations and in the treatment strategies. A key element of the domain-sensitive approach is that work-related issues do not systematically become transformed into a psychotherapeutic or family systems framework that fit with existing theories or models. Although such conceptualizations might be indicated in given contexts, their utility would need to be weighed against other, more parsimonious conceptualizations.

A traditional approach to treating Nathan might focus on the possibility that his anger is a manifestation of a biologically based depression that is emerging at this point in his life, perhaps evoked by the stress he faces. Moreover, a traditional clinician might view Nathan's worries as a displacement of anger and anxiety about other issues, perhaps related to his interpersonal conflicts, social isolation, or his family-of-origin. Another view that may be articulated in Nathan's case is that his anxiety about his job is a more tolerable manifestation of his anxiety about other uncertainties in his life, perhaps relating to his sense of safety as a gay man or his fear of a relationship breakup. While each of these ideas may be used within a domain-sensitive framework, the major distinction is that the therapist would clearly validate Nathan's worries about his job and help him explore ways to cope with this potential loss. With knowledge of the world of work and with the knowledge that Nathan's current job is an ideal fit with his abilities, interests, and personality attributes, a domain-sensitive therapist's appreciation of vocational counseling would support an integrative approach that does not either implicitly or explicitly denigrate any aspect of his psychological experiences. Indeed, a close examination of these various conceptualizations reveals that they are not necessarily mutually exclusive.

One of the first tasks for a domain-sensitive therapist is to review all treatment decisions with the client. The therapist would share his or her impression that the issues that are presented are intertwined and would be optimally explored and treated conjointly. (It is important to note that the standard ethical guidelines and principles are relevant in the design and delivery of counseling and psychotherapy interventions. Specifically, therapists should only practice within their areas of expertise; as such, the domain-sensitive approach is primarily of relevance to therapists who have training in both vocational and personal counseling.) The next step would be to assess the nature of Nathan's strengths as well as his areas of struggle and pain. In relation to Nathan's case, it would be useful to acknowledge the real possibility that his job could be outsourced. At the same time, the therapist ought to assess the level of depression, anxiety, and related symptoms of each client, exploring the possibility that a more pronounced mental health problem is emerging.

Once a careful assessment has been conducted, the treatment would commence. Ideally, therapists may find it preferable to work in the domain that seems to be the most resilient and open to exploration. In the case of Nathan, it might be helpful to explore his anger and disappointments in his relational contexts first, which seemed less vulnerable from his initial presentations. As these issues were explored and processed, the therapist and Nathan might concur that the current set of relational struggles is not critical in creating the psychic disturbances that Nathan faces. The therapist and Nathan would then explore his feelings about the emerging sense of job insecurity; at this point, it would likely become clear that the diminishment of stability in the work context is evoking considerable anxiety and tension. One of the tasks of the domain-sensitive treatment, therefore, would be to give these feelings a voice in treatment, with the careful validation and empathy that is so critical to effective psychotherapy (Bohart & Greenberg, 1997). While the therapist could not easily reframe this anxiety as its cause is based on potentially accurate perceptions of the world of work, a number of alternative actions could be explored that may help to reduce the sense of despair that Nathan is experiencing.

One option might be to help Nathan develop back-up plans that will function to empower him in the event that he does lose his job. This could include a transferable skills assessment (see, e.g., the *Quick Job-Hunting Map* from Bolles & Bolles, 2005). This sort of intervention conceivably could help Nathan to explore some options that would build on his interests and skills, while also reducing his sense of helplessness in the face of events over which he has little control. A second option is for Nathan to become more knowledgeable about globalization. By becoming more aware of the impact of globalization, Nathan can become more active in the social and political discourse of his community. At the same time, Nathan may find it helpful to develop a support group of other computer workers in his community who may be able to brainstorm some ideas about new directions for their skills and talents. Although these initiatives all sound quite relevant and potentially useful, it would be important to not diminish Nathan's sense of indignation and anger about his situation. By exploring the intense affect that the potential job loss evokes, the therapist might be able to sort through a number of interrelated issues that are related to conflicts in both the past and present. A key aspect of the domain-sensitive approach is that one set of issues does not need to overshadow another set of issues. With the infusion of the psychology-of-working perspective, I hope to enhance the vividness of work-related issues; however, the precise etiology of each client's set of concerns is naturally quite unique and may point to a complex interaction of relevant personal and contextual factors.

The case of Nathan illustrates one direction for the use of the domain-sensitive approach in a clinical context. While the literatures within vocational counseling and psychotherapy are rich with theories and intervention strategies that are useful in cases where people have access to financial and relational resources (e.g., D. Brown, 2002a; Sharf, 2000), far less is known about the lives of poor and working class clients and populations. By exploring current efforts that have been developed for clients who are generally on the margins of our work, I believe that it is possible to sketch the framework for an inclusive and affirming practice that explicitly includes attention to work, power, relationships, and self-determination.

Integrating the Voices and Practices from the Margins of Psychotherapeutic Discourse

As indicated earlier, the history of vocational counseling emerged in the early part of the 20th century as workers were faced with increasing numbers of choices and options (Pope, 2000). The early 20th century also was characterized by the trend toward occupational stability as workers in both manufacturing and professional fields tended to prefer to stay with an employer or a line of work for much of their adult lives, with obvious exceptions based on economic shifts, pay, working conditions, and geographic moves. Moreover, for the vast proportion of workers in industrialized and agrarian countries, choice was typically not available for most decisions related to school and work. As such, there is little literature that directly describes the best ways to help people negotiate work-related problems, such as unemployment, unsteady employment, unsatisfying work, oppressive conditions at work, harassment at work, and the like. My view is that the structural aspects of practices directed toward the vast array of work-related issues may be inferred from existing practice guidelines and recommendations that have emerged in working with clients who have been on the margins of traditional vocational counseling. Accordingly, I present brief overviews of contemporary practices with clients with disabling conditions, at-risk youth, unemployed adults, and clients of color. When considered collectively, these bodies of work generate fruitful directions for psychological practice within the working context.

Working With Clients With Disabling Conditions

One of the most important professions that has contributed to the health and vigor of vocational counseling is rehabilitation counseling (Chan, Berven, & Thomas, 2004; Riggar & Maki, 2004). Rehabilitation counseling, which was originally known as vocational rehabilitation counseling, has been committed to helping clients with disabling conditions adjust to their life tasks, with a particular focus on work-related issues (Gilbride & Stensrud, 2003). In addition to the general vocational counseling goals that I articulated earlier in this chapter, rehabilitation counseling has historically included a focus on job placement and adjustment to the work context (Szymanski & Parker, 2003). Prior to reviewing relevant practice implications, the disability construct, which is so central to the vibrant practice modality of rehabilitation counseling, is explored in further depth. According to Szymanski and Parker (2003), the concept of disability has the following attributes:

- The experience of disability is not a constant; the definition changes in relation to historical changes and cultural influences as well in relation to the challenges of the current context of individual's lives.
- People with disabilities make up the largest minority group in the United States.
- Recent data reported by Szymanski et al. indicate that 15% of the non-institutionalized adults in the United States have limitations in their functioning that inhibit their overall activity level in their lives.
- A very strong correlation exists between disabling conditions and poverty; for example, only 29% of adults with disabilities reported employment in the labor market.

Taken together, these attributes of disability suggest that the problems that exist are extensive and are closely linked with working and access to the opportunity structure. Given the compelling nature of these data, it is increasingly clear why vocational counseling has become such an important aspect of the professional identity of rehabilitation counseling. In addition, the challenges faced by clients with disabling conditions may point to some important and more general insights about the potential of counseling as a support for the full gamut of people who struggle with work-related problems. A review of the edited text by Szymanski and Parker (2003) reveals a number of themes that are relevant to the task of creating an inclusive mode of practice for the vast majority of people who struggle with work-related issues and challenges. One prominent theme, articulated by Hershenson and Liesener (2003), is that vocational counseling with individuals with disabling conditions entails a considerable degree of uncertainty, which is suggested by both the labor market and the shifting needs and conditions of clients. Another relevant theme is that clients benefit from assistance in job development and the job search (Hagner, 2003). This aspect of rehabilitation counseling has an historic and contemporary role in the profession; however, traditional vocational counselors and psychologists have generally shied away from job-development and job-search activities. The importance of work in the lives of individuals with disabling conditions is underscored by the prevalence of supported employment, which functions to provide important connections and activities for many individuals whose ability status inhibits their capacity to work in a competitive context (Hanley-Maxwell, Owens-Johnson, & Fabian, 2003).

Other relevant features in the rehabilitation field include the use of job clubs. Job clubs provide support and behavioral counseling designed to enhance motivation, job-seeking skills, and the social networks of unemployed adults (Gilbride & Stensrud, 2003). Originally developed by Azrin and Philips (1979), job clubs have demonstrated success in helping individuals with disabling conditions locate stable employment. Another trend in rehabilitation counseling is the explicit attention that is devoted to working with employers. For many clients, rehabilitation counselors have sought to develop relationships with employers that will allow for modifications and adjustments based on the needs of workers. One of the outcomes of this role has been the advent of employer consulting (Gilbride & Stensrud, 2003) and job coaching (Hershenson & Liesener, 2003). Both of these roles involve active engagement with employers, with the intention of creating supportive conditions for the new workers, many of whom may have little experience in a work setting.

While it may seem that the client is passive as the counselor actively helps to create equitable working conditions and search for employment, the reality of the disabled community is that clients are increasingly seeking out and obtaining political power. A vivid example of this power is the passage of the Americans with Disabilities Act (ADA, 1990). This act, which followed considerable lobbying on the part of the disabled community, represents an exemplar of policy change that was steered in large measure by many of the formerly disempowered clients who struggled to achieve equitable working conditions (Shapiro, 1994).

When considered collectively, the themes that emerge from this brief overview of counseling clients with disabling conditions are of clear relevance to the increasing demands of expanding counseling services to encompass all potential workers. One prominent theme is the central role of an activist stance on the part of the counselor. Rather than working primarily from the comfort of a consulting office in an agency, the rehabilitation counselor is often actively engaged in the broad context of the client's life. For example, the use of job clubs provides relational connections that may serve to help clients deal with the often unpredictable vicissitudes of looking for and adjusting to a job (Bond & Boyer, 1988). In addition, the counselor is able to effectively work with employers in helping to set up jobs and in creating supportive conditions for employees. Another key element of the practices of rehabilitation counseling is the clear intention of empowering clients. One of the means of empowering clients is to connect them to the competitive labor market. A second means has been to provide clients with the tools for engaging in the public policy arena, which reflects some of the key elements of Prilleltensky's (1997) emancipatory communitarian approach. Finally, the expansion of the counseling role beyond the traditional realms of vocational and/or personal counseling is a major theme, one that will continue to emerge in exploring other marginalized populations and is further examined in chapter 9.

Working With At-Risk Youth

Over the past two decades, the struggles of at-risk adolescents and young adults have entered into the discourse on vocational counseling and psychotherapy (Blustein et al., 2000; Vera & Reese, 2000). The definition of "at-risk," naturally, is beset with ambiguity. At-risk youth may include adolescents who face considerable challenges in accessing education and vocational opportunities, such as poor urban students and poor rural students (Bloch, 1991). In addition, at-risk youth may often encompass adolescents who are struggling with behavioral and emotional issues. For the purposes of this chapter, I focus on the former cohort of youth, who represent a core, and often neglected population within our society and in most other cultures.

The literature on the school-to-work transition (e.g., Blustein et al., 2000; Worthington & Juntunen, 1997) is of particular relevance to the current discussion. For the most part, interest in the school-to-work (STW) transition has focused on the difficulties that non-college-bound youth face as they move from high school to the world of work. Moreover, the U.S. has been characterized by the lack of a coherent or structured process that would serve to facilitate the transition from school to work for non-college-bound youth. As such, the population of youth who do not move directly into full-time college attendance face the sorts of obstacles that likely characterize the population of adults who also struggle to locate work that will lead to stability and dignity.

The review of the STW literature conducted by my colleagues and I (Blustein et al., 2000) identified the antecedents, characteristics, and consequences of an adaptive transition from school to work. Noting the diversity of definitions of an adaptive transition, we observed that the meaning of "adaptive" often varied in relation to the sociopolitical objectives of the researchers. Thus, for those who did not endorse governmental intervention in structuring the school-to-work transition, some degree of floundering (wherein young people drift from job to job, often without any explicit plan for further training or education) is viewed as part of the emerging adult years of occupational entry (Heckman, 1994). On the other hand, scholars who view the prevalence of floundering as problematic for the young people who are often trapped in low-paying jobs tend to view an adaptive transition as a more orderly movement from school to work with corresponding growth in the individual's skills and options (Bynner et al., 1997; Way & Rossman, 1996a, 1996b). Consistent with the latter view, we (Blustein et al., 2000) defined an adaptive transition as including the following attributes:

1. Subjective indices of the individual's level of satisfaction with work and nonwork roles and responsibilities.
2. Objective indices of the individual's access to growth, training, further education, and other forms of skill advancement.
3. Access to economic rewards and job stability.

When considered collectively, these attributes suggest that an adaptive transition has numerous qualities, both internal and external to the individual. The STW literature also offers important hints of the sorts of factors that support an adaptive transition. In our review, four specific sets of individual and contextual factors were identified as playing a role in helping youth to move adaptively into a sustainable and growth-oriented work role:

1. Clear competencies in basic academic skills and in more vocationally focused skills.
2. Self-initiated motivation, flexibility, and planfulness.

3. Engaged and accessible relational support system, including family members, peers, teachers and related educators, counselors, job supervisors, and co-workers.
4. An educational environment that offers rigorous connection to work-based learning and that emphasizes school and work linkages.

When considering these four factors in tandem, a counseling approach emerges that is both focused on individual client issues and on broader contextual issues. One of the key findings in our review is the critical role of basic academic skills, which often form the basis for the acquisition of vocationally relevant skills. The barriers in helping at-risk youth obtain the necessary skills that are required by the labor market involve both internal issues as well as external issues. In addition to the development of cognitive skills, we identified the role of an agentic and engaged psychological stance, including planfulness, flexibility, and self-determination. Thus, one of the inferences that can be derived from the literature on at-risk youth is the importance of helping clients become empowered via the maximal development of their talents and abilities as well as their natural strivings for self-determination.

Another theme that has emerged in the literature on at-risk youth is the significant role that an active and engaged relational support system can play in the lives of adolescents and emerging adults (Phillips et al., 2001). A closer look at this literature in relation to counseling practice suggests that the nature of the support encompasses emotional support and overt instrumental assistance in negotiating educational and vocational tasks. Moving beyond the proximal context to more distal contexts suggests that at-risk youth also benefit from engaged educational and vocational environments that help young people learn about the interpersonal demands of work and also about the role of continual education and training. In sum, the sort of counseling interventions that would be most viable for at-risk youth would include some of the traditional elements of effective vocational counseling (S. D. Brown & Kane, 2000) along with integrative interventions that will help young people to engage in systematic emotional growth, ideally culminating in a more internalized sense of agency and assertiveness. The literature on at-risk youth also suggests that the relational context and the broader educational and vocational context can play critical roles in supporting and nourishing the development of a meaningful working life. Thus, systemic interventions that can expand opportunities and supportive conditions for at-risk youth would be helpful in changing the opportunity structure. (Further details on the sort of changes that would be optimal are presented in chapter 10.)

Working With Lesbian, Gay, Bisexual, and Transgendered Clients

One of the most invisible minority groups is the lesbian, gay, bisexual, and transgendered community (Boatwright, Gilbert, Forrest, & Ketzenberger, 1996; Chung, 2001, 2003; Dunkle, 1996; Fassinger, 1996, 2000). For those LGBT individuals who have access to the opportunity structure, the task of selecting occupational options is complicated by the fact that significant prejudice, and indeed hatred, exists in many workplaces and educational settings (Chung, 2001). For those LGBT individuals without access to education and training that would foster greater volition and self-determination, the challenges posed in their working lives are even more pronounced (Boatwright et al., 1996; Chung, 2001, 2003).

A core theme within the LGBT literature is the reality that the establishment of a meaningful working plan involves far more complexity than it would for heterosexual individuals (Chung, 2003; Fassinger, 1996). This complexity has engendered the development of a broader and more integrative approach to vocational counseling. For example, research has indicated that LGBT young adults are often delayed in crystallizing their career plans because of the psychological effort involved in dealing with their sexual orientation in a society that stigmatizes all but heterosexual orientations (e.g., Boatwright et al., 1996). The LGBT movement, like the multicultural, feminist, and disability movements, has helped to contextualize vocational counseling practice. The contextualization process has further fueled the development of a mode of practice that seeks to help clients handle multiple issues at the same time (Croteau & Bieschke, 1996; Dunkle, 1996). The following excerpt from a participant in the Boatwright et al. study provides important insights into the complex nature of establishing and adjusting to one's work life:

> Everything really got disrupted when I came out because I was spending a tremendous amount of energy analyzing the propriety of it ... and getting beyond stereotypes to what it [lesbian identity] really was, so I could analyze it fairly, and reject it or accept it in my own mind. I was exploring all kinds of other issues with regards to intimacy which certainly took energy away from the career plans I had. I had to find out what was more important: passing the bar exam, or finding out who the hell I was. (p. 218)

In addition, the LGBT literature on vocational counseling has helped to explore the role of discrimination and stigma in the psychological experience of one's working life (Chung, 2001). The nature of vocational and personal counseling for LGBT clients with work-related issues naturally includes a focus on the social consequences of coming out to one's colleagues as well as the consequences of maintaining anonymity with respect to sexual orientation (Chung, 2001; Croteau & Bieschke, 1996). Thus, the process of counseling necessarily entails a focus on the broader social and political climate that frames a given community's views about diversity with respect to sexual orientation.

The two lessons that are derived from this brief overview of vocational counseling with LGBT clients focus on themes that are prevalent throughout this chapter. First, the nature of the relationship between sexual orientation and the working world demands a broadened focus, one that does not create arbitrary boundaries between personal and vocational issues. Second, the question of determining how people adjust to the stigmatization of sexual orientation ideally needs to encompass a discussion of how certain groups are marginalized and how other groups are in the position of determining the mores and values for an entire community. Consistent with Prilleltensky's (1997) position presented in chapter 7, a viable goal in working with LGBT clients (and other marginalized clients) may optimally include a focus on liberation and social change. In other words, it makes just as much sense (if not more sense) for counselors to work on changing the underlying values that inherently privilege heterosexuals over non-heterosexuals as it does to work solely with LGBT clients to adapt to a heterosexist world.

Working With Unemployed Clients

The task of helping unemployed people across the life span locate sustainable work has presented a major challenge to vocational counseling since the inception of the field. Indeed, the relative lack of attention to the unemployed in both the vocational psychology and psychotherapy literatures is noteworthy. Unemployment is a persistent and growing problem in many Western nations (Herr et al., 2004). The consequences of unemployment range from modest emotional upset to more substantive psychological problems (e.g., A. Kahn, 1993; Price, Choi, & Vinokur, 2002; Vinokur, Schul, Vuori, & Price, 2000), impacting on the proximal context of one's family and the more distal context of an entire community and nation.

The struggle for unemployed people to find work in many ways parallels the counseling challenges that are derived from an inclusive psychology of working. Clearly, it would be ideal if unemployed individuals could obtain an ideal fit between their personality attributes, values, and abilities and the demands of the labor market. However, the reality is that many unemployed individuals strive primarily to obtain stable and financially secure work, with the goal of achieving a solid person–environment fit (P-E fit) moving to a secondary or tertiary level (Blustein et al., 2002; Herr et al., 2004). The need for survival among the unemployed, particularly those without financial supports, naturally will overshadow the idealized P-E fit concept that has characterized contemporary vocational counseling practice and theory to date.

One of the most popular means for unemployed adults to re-enter the working world can be found in the Bolles and Bolles (2005) classic work, entitled "What Color Is Your Parachute?" While this book also is recommended for adults transitioning from one job to another, both counselors and clients have found the Bolles and Bolles recommendations to be quite useful in negotiating a transition back to employment from a period of unemployment. (It is important to note that the Bolles and Bolles volume is oriented toward relatively well-educated workers, thereby circumscribing its potential utility for an inclusive psychological practice.) A key problem faced by many unemployed individuals is the mismatch between the clients' skills and the available options in the labor market (H. Kahn, 2004; Rankin, 2003). As such, unemployed individuals often need to consider a wider array of possibilities, sometimes well outside of their comfort zones. The Quick Job-Hunting Map includes a Transferable Skills Inventory that provides a number of important sources of information for clients. The Transferable Skills Inventory requires that the client write seven brief essays on achievements and accomplishments in any domain of life, including, but not limited to, the work domain. Once these vignettes are constructed, the client then maps the skills that were manifested in each accomplishment onto a chart that encompasses some broad thematic areas representing a wide array of occupationally related skills. Clients are then asked to underline or circle the skills that they find interesting. Once the skills map is completed, it provides clients with a visual schema of accomplishments, which can be translated easily into skills. Ideally, clients, with the help of counselors, can then explore how these skills can be used in different fields. This process can be very helpful in facilitating a client's move from one area of interest to one that may offer more opportunities. Moreover, a latent effect of the Transferable Skills Inventory is that it can help to bolster the self-efficacy of clients, many of whom may be particularly vulnerable to losses in self-confidence and self-efficacy after losing a job.

While the Bolles and Bolles (2005) process of identifying alternative interests and outlets for skills represents one well-known system for dealing with unemployment, pervasive challenges remain for unemployed clients (p. 287). One of the most common findings in the literature on unemployment is the rise in mental health problems as a result of a job loss (Diener & Seligman, 2004; Herr et al., 2004; Price et al., 2002). Given the important role that work plays in many clients' sense of identity and self-worth (Mallinckrodt & Bennett, 1992), the loss of one's employment may lead to a more pervasive sense of loss that can evoke depression and other psychological problems (Herr et al., 2004). As such, working with unemployed clients very often necessitates a careful and comprehensive mental health examination to rule out risk of suicide or other forms of self-injury. Moreover, the challenge of obtaining new sources of employment creates a great deal of stress, particularly in light of rapidly changing demands within the labor market. As such, one of the key ingredients in effective counseling for unemployed individuals is a thoughtful and individually tailored synthesis of treatments that is centered on a systematic integration of vocational counseling with psychotherapy and perhaps psychopharmacology (as indicated by the client's symptoms).

One of the most prominent interventions that has been developed for unemployed adults is the JOBS program (Vinokur & Schul, 1997; Vinokur et al., 2000). The JOBS program is a short-term intervention designed to provide the participants with skills in managing the job search and with inoculation strategies to reduce the aversive impact of setbacks in the reemployment process. The program is generally delivered over a 1-week period in an intensive fashion (five sessions consisting of 4 hours of psychoeducation each day). The empirical findings from evaluations of the JOBS program 2 years after the interventions indicated that the participants had greater success in their job searches and also experienced fewer depressive symptoms than nonparticipants (Vinokur et al., 2000). The strength of these findings suggests that psychological interventions have a clear and instrumental role in the lives of unemployed individuals.

Similar to the Vinokur et al. (2000) contributions on the JOBS program, the literature on counseling unemployed individuals has also suggested the importance of social learning principles as a means of enhancing the confidence and behavioral effectiveness of job seekers (Sterrett, 1998). The use of behavioral and social learning ideas in working with unemployed clients is generally associated with the contributions of Azrin and his associates (e.g., Azrin, Phillip, Thienes-Hontos, & Besalel, 1981); in a series of studies in the 1970s and early 1980s, Azrin et al. developed a group intervention for the unemployed that is known as the job club. Job clubs, which were established on an explicit application of social learning principles (e.g., Bandura, 1986), sought to use behavioral training, social reinforcement, and group support to enhance the job-seeking behavior of a wide array of populations (Azrin et al., 1981; Sterrett, 1998). In a recent analysis of job club methods, Sterrett argued that the effectiveness of job clubs could be explained via Bandura's social cognitive theory. While Sterrett's study is limited by a very small sample, her conceptual analysis of the job club methodology from a social cognitive perspective was compelling, suggesting the importance of further work in this area. Sterrett's argument that job clubs are appropriately geared to enhance self-efficacy with respect to the job search, is consistent with the focus of such efforts on the development of enhanced skills and the rehearsal of adaptive behaviors.

The contribution by Herr et al. (2004) provides a comprehensive treatment of "best practices" that were derived from their review of the literature. Herr and his colleagues identified three broad principles that can guide counseling interventions for unemployed clients:

1. Counselors need to help clients explore the interconnections between job loss and the psychological consequences of the transition to joblessness.

2. Counselors also would benefit from helping clients to connect to the full array of community resources that can provide emotional and instrumental assistance during a period of unemployment. This recommendation includes the important role of social support during unemployment, which can help to ward off some of the more extreme mental health consequences (Mallinckrodt & Bennett, 1992).

3. The third recommendation, which is a critical point in the unemployment literature, is the need for counselors to provide more than solely social and emotional support. Often, unemployed clients will have multiple issues to contend with, such as lack of basic skills, transportation hurdles, racial discrimination, family discord, and the like. Herr et al. clearly state that counselors ought to help clients deal effectively with these problems. Moreover, the Herr et al. focus on the need for greater skill development is particularly noteworthy given the parallels that exist with the at-risk literature.

When considered collectively, the various strands of literature reviewed thus far suggest that the process of providing assistance to unemployed individuals ideally would require a multidimensional approach. One dimension would clearly involve a focus on the individual's psychological construction of the job loss. Rather than assuming that the job loss will have a predictable impact on an individual's psychological functioning, counselors would benefit from exploring the unique meaning that the client attributes to the job loss. A second dimension pertains to the need for clients to develop their skills, both in vocationally relevant areas (Herr et al., 2004) and in conducting the job search (Azrin et al., 1981; Vinokur et al., 2000). A third dimension entails the development of supportive and engaged social, economic, and educational systems that will furnish needed resources for unemployed individuals (Herr et al., 2004). These services would range from financial support during periods of unemployment to the provision of child care services, further education and vocational training, and enhancing the availability of jobs (Wilson, 1996).

Working With Clients of Color

As I detailed in chapter 6, the discrimination and racism that exists in many contexts clearly disadvantages people of color in relation to the resources needed to develop a meaningful working life (Carter & Cook, 1992; Fouad & Bingham, 1995; Helms & Cook, 1999). The literature on vocational counseling interventions with clients of color offers a number of important suggestions for our efforts to construct an inclusive approach to psychological interventions for the full gamut of people who work or wish to work (e.g., Carter & Cook, 1992; Helms & Cook, 1999; Leong, 1995). A careful analysis of the literature in this area suggests the critical importance of the role of culture in the construction and delivery of vocational interventions and the need for systemic and activist approaches that will redress structural barriers to meaningful employment (Leong & Hartung, 2000; Walsh et al., 2001).

The role of culture in career counseling has been a core element in the models proposed by Carter and Cook (1992), Helms and Cook (1999), Fouad and Bingham (1995), Gysbers et al. (2003), and N. Peterson and González (2005). An integrative view of these perspectives reveals a number of prominent themes, which are summarized below:

1. Counselors need to carefully explore the cultural experience of their clients. This process of exploration involves not just understanding the broad overtones of a given culture, but a thorough examination of the client's unique experiences and constructions that are framed by cultural meanings and influences.

2. In addition to understanding the cultural context of a given client, relevant individual difference factors need to be understood and affirmed. Gysbers et al. proposed that the client's worldview, racial identity status, and level of acculturation are important person-centered variables that need to be explored in the counseling relationship. The worldview refers to the "frame of reference through which one experiences life. It is the foundation of values, attitudes, and relations" (Fouad & Bingham, 1995, p. 335). Racial identity, which was described in further detail in chapter 6, refers to "a complex psychosocial process that encompasses race or ethnic re-

lated attitudes, beliefs, and behaviors" with a focus on "… understanding oneself within a racially oppressive environment" (Gysbers et al., 2003, p. 64). Acculturation refers to the capacity to maintain dual or multiple cultural identities, resulting in an individual having the ability to maintain connection to the culture of one's family and background while also demonstrating the ability to relate to a new culture.

3. Careful attention to the role of culture in the development and expression of vocational attitudes, beliefs, and interests is advised throughout the process of assessment and counseling (Carter & Cook, 1992; Fouad & Bingham, 1995). For example, the models proposed by Fouad and Bingham as well as Carter and Cook are based on the systematic and deliberate infusion of affirming views of cultural diversity throughout the entire counseling process, from intake to the final termination phase.

4. A clear convergence of opinion by major scholars in multicultural counseling implicates structural barriers, such as poor educational opportunities, continued existence of racism, inadequate housing, and unsafe living conditions (e.g., Arbona, 2000; Carter & Cook, 1992; Helms & Cook, 1999) as playing a critical role in the overwhelming array of barriers that people of color face as they seek to enter the world of work (cf. McWhirter, Crothers, & Rasheed, 2000).

The final point raised here regarding the structural barriers that unfairly affect people of color leads to the next major theme that has emerged in the multicultural vocational counseling literature, pertaining to the pervasive role of structural social and economic barriers. In short, structural barriers exist that profoundly reduce opportunities for people of color in the United States and a number of other Western nations (e.g., Carter & Cook, 1992; Sue, 2004; Wilson, 1996). As the counseling profession has increasingly sought to understand the nature and impact of these inequities, greater advocacy efforts have emerged that have challenged the existence of structural barriers in education (e.g., Fine, 2004), in vocational opportunities (e.g., Carter & Cook, 1992; Wilson, 1996), and in access to health care and other attributes of a resource-rich life (e.g., Riley, 1997). A number of options exist with respect to working with clients in light of the structural barriers that continue to reduce access to opportunity. First, counselors have been encouraged to leave the confines of their counseling offices and practices to become more involved in social change and political advocacy work directed to reducing structural barriers (e.g., Goodman et al., 2004; Vera & Speight, 2003). (These recommendations are discussed further in chapter 10.) Second, counselors have explored the possibilities of enhancing the critical consciousness of clients of color (Goodman et al., 2004; Helms & Cook, 1999), which represents a potentially important direction for psychological practice that is affirming of work-related experiences.

The idea of counselors working with systems as well as individual clients, naturally, has a long history in our field (e.g., Carter & Cook, 1992; Kiselica & Robinson, 2001). In relation to the challenges that people of color face as they negotiate the world of training, education, and employment, it seems clear that effective counseling needs to include a focus on helping to reduce discrimination, racism, and other social barriers that collude with racism to reduce opportunities (cf. Carter & Cook, 1992). The difficulties in finding the means for counselors to move into social advocacy roles also have been detailed extensively in recent contributions (e.g., Goodman et al., 2004; Helms, 2003). Nevertheless, despite these obstacles, including resolving the question of who will pay counselors for engaging in social advocacy, the reality is that social changes are needed to create more equity in education and work for people of color. (As I detail in chapter 10, I believe that the psychology of working can be very instrumental in helping counselors and other mental health professionals find ways of enhancing their impact in relation to the systems that frame individual working experiences, such as education, training, employment, support in transitioning between employment roles, and enhancing dignity at work).

The notion of enhancing critical consciousness has its roots in education and liberation theology (e.g., Friere, 1970/1993; Martín-Baró, 1994). Critical consciousness refers to the process of learning "to perceive the social, political, and economic contradictions, and to take action against the oppressive elements of reality" (Freire, 1970/1993, p. 17). For example, enhancing critical consciousness would entail helping clients to understand, both emotionally and intellectually, the implications of slavery and racism, with the goal of helping students of color and European American students to learn about the nature of contemporary racism and its impact on the current occupational landscape. By enhancing critical consciousness, it may be possible for clients and students to become more engaged in political activities that will help to reduce inequities. For example, rather than internalizing a sense of powerless in the face of reducing opportunities in urban communities in the United States, a critical consciousness approach would entail the use of diverse art forms and cultural means (such as hip hop music; paintings within urban landscapes) as well as social advocacy to detail the consequences of reduced opportunities in the lived experiences of people of color. It is important to note here, though, that I do not advocate for solely a critical consciousness approach, as the process of fostering change should not be left to those who are most overtly marginalized.

As reflected in chapter 6 and in many other resources (e.g., Fouad & Bingham, 1995; Helms & Cook, 1999), explorations of the impact of race and racism in vocational psychology have played and will continue to play a major role in informing the psychology of working. In relation to counseling practice, multicultural scholars and practitioners have taught clinicians important lessons that are very relevant to the present discussion. First, racism and other forms of ethnically based prejudice are very real and serious barriers that are not solely historical artifacts (e.g., Helms & Cook, 1999; Sue, 2004; Wachtel, 1999). Indeed, racism lingers in many corners of the occupational world and often moves beyond those corners into center stage (e.g., Leong, 1995; Walsh et al., 2001). Second, the task of helping a client locate a meaningful line of work is often not the major objective for people whose rates of unemployment and underemployment have consistently been elevated in comparison to European Americans. Often the need for work that will fulfill survival needs takes precedence over seeking out an optimal person–environment fit. As many scholars have noted (e.g., Arbona, 1995; Carter & Cook, 1992; Smith, 1983), the work experiences of African Americans and Latinos in the United States has often denigrated their self-concept as opposed to providing an outlet for their interests and talents. In effect, the psychology of working is an outgrowth of this literature in that it seeks to develop a means of understanding and intervening in the world of all people who work, including the vast numbers of people of color who often toil in jobs that are not fulfilling (Helms & Cook, 1999; Smith, 1983). Consistent with the position that I have been advocating throughout this book, the psychology of working seeks to carve out a space within the critical psychological discourse that will help to change structural barriers so that options for meaningful work are increasingly available for all people, regardless of their backgrounds.

The Psychology of Working and Psychological Practice: Conclusion

This review of the current status of vocational counseling and psychotherapy has revealed a number of important ideas and themes that are highly relevant in developing a viable mode of practice derived from the psychology of working. One of the themes is that working is a central aspect of life and that its centrality ought to be no less apparent in psychotherapeutic theory and practice. In addition, integrating vocational and nonvocational issues in counseling and psychotherapy seems to be a logically compelling idea for clients who present with work-related issues in tandem with psychosocial challenges. Furthermore, the guideposts for the development of a fully inclusive approach to psychological practice that affirms and dignifies working are clearly evident in the treatment recommendations emerging from client populations who have been marginalized in psychotherapy theory and research. These guideposts are further explored in the next chapter, which seeks to map the next generation of psychotherapeutic practice that will be maximally inclusive of the full range of clients' experiences and life circumstances.

CHAPTER 9

Toward an Inclusive Psychological Practice

What is of particular interest here is the extent to which ignoring work and work-related issues in the enterprise of counseling and psychotherapy may function to help maintain the blindness of our theories and models of therapeutic intervention to socially structured inequities such as gender, race, and class. These inequities have powerful effects on the opportunities and resources available through work in the occupational structure. Not attending to the significance of work and work-related issues as central to therapeutic practice may essentially insulate practitioners from these uncomfortable realities.

—M. S. Richardson (1996, p. 357)

Finally, and on a more informal note, we can consider the inseparability of the "career" and the "personal" in our own lives. How many of us, for example, would easily sustain loss of or failure in our career without some threat to our level of self-esteem, life satisfaction, and psychological well being? How many of us will painlessly make the transition to retirement from our careers? How many of us could provide easy answers to the dilemmas of spouse partner geographic mobility?

—Betz & Corning (1993, p. 142)

As the literature reviewed thus far, and in particular in chapter 8, suggests, a relevant body of knowledge does indeed exist on the margins of vocational and psychotherapeutic practice, which has the potential to inform an inclusive psychological practice that effectively embraces work-related issues. In this chapter, I seek to develop a comprehensive mode of psychological practice that will fully embrace the working aspects of life as well as the nonworking aspects. In addition, I present two cases that illuminate the inclusive counseling perspective that flows logically from the literature on the psychology of working. To underscore the importance of systemic as well as individual interventions, I also highlight some implications for public policy advocacy and social change that emerge from these two cases.

The question of how to refer to psychological practice in the working realm has already generated a thoughtful debate. M. S. Richardson (1996) developed an argument for the use of the term "counseling/psychotherapy and work, jobs, and careers" (p. 355) as a result of her insightful critique of contemporary career counseling and psychotherapy. This term is certainly descriptive and comes close to the goals that I outline here. However, my position is that any clinician or therapist who seeks to engage in a comprehensive and empathic treatment of individuals or groups will need to understand the importance and complexity of working in people's lives. As such, I use the term "inclusive psychological practice" to refer to the integrative counseling and psychotherapy approach that is advanced in the forthcoming sections of this chapter. The use of this umbrella term allows for those who are focusing more on the vocational and/or nonvocational aspects of treatment to find a welcome space within this evolving perspective. Thus, there may be times when the clinical work is more similar to traditional vocational counseling, with a focus on decision making and vocational exploration tasks. In addition, inclusive psychological practice may be analogous to longer term, insight-oriented psychotherapy or a more focused cognitive-behavioral or solution-focused treatment. The consistent element of an inclusive psychological practice is an explicit and affirming view of the importance of working and the role that work plays in the full spectrum of human life (including fulfilling needs for survival, social/economic power, relational connections, and self-determination).

Creating the Space for Work-Related Issues in Psychological Practice

One of the first tasks for therapists and counselors is to create space for clients to express their work-related concerns in treatment. In the traditional modality of vocational counseling, naturally, this task is inherent to the process. However, in the more traditional forms of mental health practice, including psychodynamically oriented therapy, cognitive-behavioral treatment, and in the vast array of treatments that characterize contemporary psychotherapy, the task of opening up the space for work-related issues may be more difficult. As I have indicated throughout this book, a key issue for therapists is to validate and dignify clients' issues about working. Of course, there may be occasions when the work-related issues do in fact represent an unresolved family drama or pervasive unresolved authority issues; however, the essence of the material presented in this book is that work-related problems and concerns are very real and merit our full attention as clinicians.

Assessing Work-Related Challenges and Strengths

How, then, does a therapist convey this concern to clients in a manner that is authentic? One option would be to include questions about a client's work history in an intake or initial assessment. In my experience, a client's work history offers considerable insights into the nature of an individual's capacity to effectively negotiate with the external world and to manage one's inner life. Moreover, data derived from an individual's work history may convey aspects of strength and vigor, which may be helpful to highlight in light of current struggles and symptoms. The types of questions that may be fruitful in an intake include the following:

1. How would you describe your current working life?
   a. To what extent are you happy and/or content at work?
   b. How would you like to change your working life, if at all?
   c. How effectively is work meeting your needs for survival?
   d. How effectively is work meeting your relational and social needs?
   e. To what extent do you believe that you can determine your future in your working life? In other words, how much choice or control do you exercise in the type of work you do?
2. Tell me the story of how you moved from school to your current working life.
3. How do you define or construct the concept of work?
4. What are your strengths in your working life?
5. What sort of struggles and psychological pain do you experience at work?
6. How do you balance your family and caregiving responsibilities with work in the paid labor market?

In my view, raising questions early on in the therapeutic process may send clear signals to clients that work-related issues are part of the terrain of psychotherapy. Furthermore, as M. S. Richardson (1996) suggested, by including an explicit focus on working, therapists are conveying to clients that issues pertaining to the broader social, economic, and political context are viable pathways for psychotherapeutic discourse. Moreover, therapists need to be able to explore the psychological complexity of work. Recent psychodynamically oriented considerations of work in psychotherapy by Axelrod (1999) and Socarides and Kramer (1997) attest to the potential richness of work-related issues in psychological practice. In short, when clients bring up work-related issues in psychotherapy, therapists need to treat the material with the same degree of gravity and depth as they would any other domain of life experience. Conveying this attitude consistently in the therapy process will provide a strong platform for an informed, validating, and, ultimately, effective treatment of the entire fabric of a client's life.

Articulating the Goals of Inclusive Psychological Practice

Once space has been created for an inclusive approach to psychological practice, the therapist and client need to mutually concur on the goals for comprehensive treatment. Similar to the domain-sensitive approach (Blustein & Spengler, 1995), I advocate that the goals and therapeutic modalities of an inclusive psychological practice be consensually agreed upon by the therapist and client. Naturally, the goals need to encompass any outstanding mental health issues, such as major depression, the advent of a biologically oriented disorder (e.g., schizophrenia), and suicidal risk. As I have stated in chapter 8 and elsewhere (e.g., Blustein & Spengler, 1995), issues relating to the client's welfare and safety need to take precedence in an inclusive psychological practice.

Empowerment. One of the key goals in an inclusive mode of practice is to help enhance a client's sense of empowerment (cf. M. S. Richardson, 2000). While empowerment as a goal in treatment has a rich history in feminist thought (e.g., L. Brooks & Forrest, 1994) as well as in counseling practice (e.g., McWhirter, 1994), empowerment, in of itself, does not fully embrace the scope of the problems faced by people as they attempt to fulfill their work-related needs. For example, being empowered may not help an individual create a job where none exists or may not help when racism is pervasive. Nevertheless, given that the focus of this chapter is on individual interventions, a discussion of empowerment as a goal of inclusive psychological practice seems warranted. In short, empowerment refers to the development of goal-directed behaviors that also lead to mastery within relevant domains (Richardson). More precisely, the goal-directed aspects of empowerment, according to Richardson, are critical in providing individuals with a clear sense of where they are going in their lives. Richardson proposes that the goal-directed aspects of empowerment are still relevant, if not even more important, in light of the post-modern assumptions of constant change and flux. However, she notes that the nature of goal identification may need to reflect the mutability of contemporary life and particularly the mutability of the working context.

The second aspect of empowerment in M. S. Richardson's (2000) framework pertains to the development of the skills, competencies, and attributes that will result in effective and agentic engagement with the world. When considering the skill-building aspect of empowerment in the Richardson contribution in light of the literature reviewed earlier in this chapter, it becomes clear that an inclusive psychological practice needs to focus on helping clients to develop their talents and abilities to their fullest. Moreover, the facilitation of cognitively based skills ought to be complemented by an equal focus on psychological and interpersonal skills needed by the world of work in the 21st century.

One of the clearest trends noted in this book and in others (e.g., Rifkin, 1995; Wilson, 1996) is the need for a highly skilled workforce. The nature of these skills, of course, varies. However, the prevailing wisdom is that workers need to be able to read well and understand verbal and written communication in a highly literate fashion. In addition, workers need to exercise competence in quantitative reasoning and in writing (Bynner et al., 1997; Marshall & Tucker, 1992). Given the importance of skills across the full spectrum of the labor market (Rose, 2004), counseling efforts may optimally focus on enhancing clients' sense of power and competence by helping them to acquire high levels of basic skills.

The reality of much psychological practice is that many clinicians work on their own or work in small cohorts of practitioners who are often not highly engaged in the support services of a given community. One means of combating this isolation (which is a major challenge for many therapists and counselors) is to establish professional relationships with programs in one's community that provide opportunities for basic skills development. Adult learning centers, many of which are located in high schools, represent one viable option. I also suggest that counselors connect with local colleges and universities, especially community colleges, which provide numerous opportunities for skills development for young learners as well as older learners. Dealing with client resistance to retraining and retooling is another major challenge, one that I identified in chapter 7 as an important research agenda for the psychology of working. In my view, clients who are faced with the need to retool and retrain represent a growing proportion of people who will be seeking out services in the coming decades. Obviously, there are no easy answers in helping clients to face a reality of ongoing education and training, especially in light of the fact that there are no guarantees that skills building will necessarily yield uniformly positive outcomes. (The case of Bill, described later in this chapter, explores some ways of dealing with this resistance in treatment.)

Other aspects of skill building need to encompass the noncognitive array of factors that have been associated with adaptive transitions to working (e.g., Blustein et al., 2000). The consensus of opinion among scholars studying workforce development is that interpersonal skills and the capacity to function effectively in small groups is one of the key ingredients to a successful worker (Blustein et al., 2000; Marshall & Tucker, 1992). Therapists can work with clients in a number of creative ways that may help to enhance their ability to function well in an interpersonally demanding work environment. For example, for clients who report difficulties in their interpersonal relationships at work, it is important to explore these issues in depth, observing for in-session experiences that parallel the client's presenting concerns. Once these relationship patterns emerge in treatment, I would suggest a cautious exploration of the here-and-now interactions in which these interpersonal problems have become evident, following Wachtel's (1993) recommendations on how to communicate about potentially painful issues in treatment. Other viable recommendations would be the use of group treatments to explore the impact of various client behaviors in interpersonal settings. Indeed, the critical role of interpersonal skills in the working world of the 21st century provides a viable role for group work in an inclusive psychological practice.

Fostering Critical Consciousness.   A major theme of the psychology of working is that changes are needed throughout the broader social and political world to reduce inequities that are most evident in education, training, and working. Therefore, another viable goal for counselors and therapists would be to develop clients' critical consciousness. As Freire (1993) advocated in his contributions on the role of education as a means of liberation, critical consciousness encompasses individuals' ability to reflect upon the broad structural aspects of the world and to take action on these observations. The structural aspects of the social world that are inherent in critical consciousness include the economic, historical, political structures, and cultural aspects of human experience that often intersect in unique ways to maintain a given status quo. The status quo very often will privilege some groups over other groups, based on demographic attributes, immigrant status, or other superficial qualities. A critical consciousness view of outsourcing computer jobs to India, for example, would encompass knowledge about the impact of global capitalism coupled with the reality that many workers experience diminished power in the face of competing for jobs. One outcome of critical consciousness, for example, may be for workers to form unions or professional associations to represent their interests in a collective fashion. For urban youth living in inner cities, critical consciousness may be reflected in less self-blame, greater strength in the face of racism, and engagement in political activities designed to empower disenfranchised communities (Watts, Abdul-Adil, & Pratt, 2002).

The question of how to foster critical consciousness in the process of counseling is a complex issue, one that in many ways brings us to the crux of a dilemma about the nature of psychological interventions. On one hand, many counselors might find it difficult to infuse such an explicit political focus in their work. One of the arguments advanced by those questioning the critical consciousness perspective is that such a movement reduces the extent to which the counseling process can be value-neutral (Robinson, 1984). In contrast to this position, the emancipatory communitarian approach (Prilleltensky, 1997) is based on the premise that values are inherent in psychological work of all sorts, including counseling and psychotherapy. My position here is aligned with Prilleltensky's in that the counseling process is inherently laden with values. That some therapists would advocate that their clients enhance their critical consciousness is not necessarily problematic in my view. I do not believe, however, that counseling ought to turn into an exclusively political discourse that would obviate the client's individual concerns and individual constructions of relevant issues. Rather, I propose a process of helping clients to become increasingly knowledgeable about the sociopolitical structures that influence their lives—and particularly their working lives—in a manner that is thoughtfully weaved into the counseling experience.

A logical consideration that might arise here is how critical consciousness might actually help a given client. An enhanced level of critical consciousness would ideally help clients to engage in less self-blame with respect to struggles in locating and sustaining meaningful work. In addition, critical consciousness may serve as a buffer against some of the stark blows to one's self-esteem that characterize many contemporary workplaces (Sennett, 1998; Wilson, 1996). Furthermore, growth in critical consciousness would help clients to organize their efforts to advocate for political and economic changes that support the very human need to work.

Given these two broad goals for inclusive psychological practice, therapists can then construct more individualized goals that are tailored around the client's specific goals. As I have indicated earlier, these goals need not exclusively focus on the working context. Indeed, one of the themes of this book is that working is embedded in the full texture of people's lives, thereby suggesting that counseling and psychotherapy in the working domain would not always have consistent thematic elements. In addition to this discussion of the content of an inclusive psychological practice, a full appreciation of this perspective necessarily includes a focus on the process of therapeutic change, which is explored next.

The Process of Inclusive Psychological Practice

Considerations of counseling and psychotherapeutic process have long been part of the intellectual research agenda of counseling psychology (e.g., Heppner & Heppner, 2003; Hill & Williams, 2000). The major questions that have been raised in the process literature have focused on identifying the change elements that are responsible for positive outcomes in counseling and psychotherapy (Hill & Williams, 2000). In the working domain, my definition of process is similar to the one proposed by Heppner and Heppner in their description of process as "the overt and covert thoughts, feelings, and behaviors of both client and counselor during a career counseling session" (2003, pp. 430–431). Examining the process elements of an inclusive psychological practice would encompass relevant contributions from the psychotherapy and vocational counseling literatures along with some observations inferred based on the analyses conducted in preparing this book.

Potential Core Elements of Inclusive Psychological Practice. Without an empirical and theoretical road map, it is perhaps a bit premature to discuss core elements of any particular therapeutic concept emerging from the psychology of working. However, given that the essence of intervening effectively with clients will be similar, although clearly not identical across content domains (Blustein & Spengler, 1995; Heppner & Heppner, 2003; Swanson, 1995), it would seem logical to expect that the same sets of qualities would be important in an inclusive psychological practice. Several core elements emerge when integrating the Hill and Williams analysis on general psychotherapy process research, the Heppner and Heppner analysis of career counseling, and other contributions from the psychotherapy literature (e.g., Teyber & McClure, 2000; Wachtel, 1993; Wampold, 2001). I list these below with an infusion of a psychology-of-working perspective, which will connect these concepts clearly to the agenda I am advocating in this book:

1. *Working Alliance:* The importance of the working alliance (also known as a therapeutic alliance) has an historic place in both psychotherapy (Bordin, 1979) and career counseling (Meara & Patton, 1994). The working alliance refers to the development of a complex and affirming relationship between therapist and client that is characterized by the capacity to take the necessary level of perspective needed for the treatment to advance (Meara & Patton). In addition, "a good initial therapeutic alliance provides the context within which the therapist can use other interventions to achieve therapeutic effect" (Bohart & Greenberg, 1997, p. 13). In the context of an inclusive psychological practice, the working alliance is considered to be very important for effective treatment to ensue. The nature of an inclusive psychological practice is constructed around a sound and flexible working alliance that will allow for needed explorations of the therapeutic relationship and for the discussion of painful material as well as material that is ultimately empowering.

2. *Interpretation:* As in most modes of psychotherapy, the role of interpretation is likely to remain paramount in an inclusive psychological practice (Heppner & Heppner, 2003; Wachtel, 1993). In relation to the psychology of working, interpretation may assume the traditional psychoanalytic direction of exploring the intrapsychic basis for a given set of experiences or reactions. In the language and methodology of the newer analytic approaches based on self psychology and intersubjectivity (Stolorow & Atwood, 1997; Atwood, Orange, & Stolorow, 2002), interpretation can also be instrumental in helping a client reintegrate previously disavowed affect. In a similar vein, a cognitive-behavioral stance may yield an equally intrapsychic interpretation, with a focus on cognitions as opposed to disavowed affect or unconscious drives. However, interpretations might also encompass a focus on sociopolitical circumstances, thereby helping clients to understand the broader structural aspects of life experience that play a role in a person's life. The manifestation of interpretation in the psychology of working may entail a wide range of issues, including such standard vocational treatments as an analysis of interest inventory returns in light of a given client's aspirations or an exploration of a client's resistance to committing to a decision. In addition, psychological interpretation may include examining the meaning of intense feelings of hurt and anger in relation to supervisory feedback at work as well as in relation to the sociopolitical causes of diminishing job opportunities in a previously flush labor market.

3. *Exploring Discrepant Beliefs and Behaviors:* In contrast to the Hill and Williams (2000) and Heppner and Heppner (2003) positions that describe

confrontation as a process component, I prefer to use Wachtel's (1993) conceptualization (and corresponding terminology) to convey the importance of exploring discrepant beliefs and behaviors. The provision of feedback or input to a client that differs from a client's core understanding of a given set of beliefs, feelings, and reactions to events forms a key element in the psychotherapy change process. Following the recommendations of Wachtel, I view the careful and empathic articulation of alternatives to prevailing client intrapsychic constructions as a major source of therapeutic change. The key difference between confrontation and the more exploratory tone that I adopt here is based on the notion that therapists and clients are mutually discovering the lived experience of a client (Stolorow & Atwood, 1997; Wachtel, 1993). Given the advances in social constructionist thought (cf. Gergen, 1999), I believe that confrontation, which assumes a reality defined by the therapist, is generally not helpful. (Of course, there are exceptions as there are to most inferences in psychological discourse. In this case, confrontation is useful when clients are abusing drugs, abusing others, or otherwise depriving themselves and others of their basic human rights.) In the psychology-of-working realm, providing discrepant information can help clients to face their underlying, and often disavowed, feelings about the ways in which the opportunity structure and racism have colluded to reduce their options. Initially, a client may respond with feelings of anger or helplessness; however, creatively constructed therapeutic efforts may help to channel this anger into critical consciousness, thereby enhancing the client's overall capacity to read and respond to the social realities. Another example of using discrepant information in therapy is to help clients who may have foreclosed on given choices and options due to sex-role socialization to consider alternatives in areas that had been heretofore dismissed. This process, which is akin to Gottfredson's (2002) ideas about expanding the zone of alternatives, may involve complex sets of issues pertaining to a client's beliefs about social status, gender, and occupational attainment.

4. *Helping Clients Change:* One of Wachtel's (1993) most important contributions is his focus on creating the appropriate conditions for client change. Similarly, Hill and Williams noted the importance of encouraging client action, which Heppner and Heppner (2003) echoed in their contribution on career counseling process. For those of us who have practiced psychotherapy, the struggles of helping clients to move from insight to action is certainly no easy task. An inclusive psychological practice does not offer simple remedies. Yet, at the same time, I believe that a focus on the working context brings clients closer to the real-life experiences that they

face outside of the consulting office, and therefore may offer some useful means of rooting therapeutic efforts in an action-oriented framework. As M. S. Richardson (1996) noted, by including work-related issues in the discourse of psychotherapy, clinicians are confronted with social inequities, racism, sexism, classism, and heterosexism in a manner that may have felt abstract within a more circumscribed interpersonal and intrapersonal framework. Some examples of helping clients to change were foreshadowed earlier in the discussion of the importance of enhancing both basic skills and vocationally relevant skills among our clients. Improving a client's skills set can have dramatic effects on self-esteem (Creed, Bloxsome, & Johnston, 2001; Creed, Hicks, & Machin, 1998) as well as on a client's ability to negotiate a rapidly changing world of work. Furthermore, helping clients to become more assertive in the face of abusive supervisors can lead to changes in the working environment that can have a ripple-like effect throughout the various domains of life.

When considered collectively, these four change elements place an inclusive psychological practice into the conceptual rubric of well-established psychological interventions. However, I would like to underscore the tentative nature of my analysis given that the perspective I am advancing is novel and has not been explored empirically. Ideally, as counselors and therapists begin to expand their practices to fully embrace the full scope of contemporary life including working, it will be possible to revisit this brief list of change factors to assess their veracity in light of empirical evidence and clinical experiences.

The Role of Assessment in Inclusive Psychological Practice

Within traditional vocational counseling, assessment has played, and no doubt will continue to play, a major role in psychological interventions. Indeed, the reviews by Brown and colleagues (Brown & Ryan, 2003; Brown & Krane, 2000) along with the review by Whiston, Breicheisen, and Stephens (2003) point to the consistent role of vocational appraisal (generally of interests or personality type) in vocational counseling. Consistent with the goals of the psychology-of-working initiative, I seek to construct a perspective and a practice modality that will be far more inclusive than the traditional modalities of vocational counseling and psychotherapy to date. So, one might wonder, how would assessment fare in this new, expanded field?

Given that my objective is not to supplant existing modalities of intervention, but to enhance, enrich, and ultimately create different modes of practice for clients who had not been previously served in traditional treatment modalities, I would envision a healthy future for vocational appraisal. Naturally, when clients enter counseling with questions related to decisional dilemmas and the need to expand one's array of considerations, vocational interest tests and other measures may be helpful. However, as the work of counselors expands beyond the middle-class, European-American realm, it is critically important to construct measures that are relevant and informative to a wider array of client populations. As such, the normative groups that are used to validate tests need to be expanded so that the true scope of a given population is represented. In addition, I support the calls for culturally framed interpretations of tests (e.g., Fouad & Walker, 2005; Helms & Cook, 1999), which insist that test results be viewed from an explicit cultural framework in which the meaning of the items and the nature of the scores is embedded within the cultural understandings of the client's life space and worldview.

In my view, vocational appraisal has the potential to function as both a social barrier and social resource. As detailed in the debates on the use of Holland's (1994) Self-Directed Search (Spokane, Luchetta, & Richwine, 2002), scores can be used to describe the status quo with respect to the distribution of personality types in relation to sex and/or racial group. Alternately, some argue (e.g., Fouad & Spreda, 1995; Prediger & Swaney, 1995) that test scores can be configured in a way that will enhance clients' options without distorting their meaning or validity. For example, many women will score higher on the areas of an interest inventory that reflect their own experiences, such as working in nurturing roles and working in clerical tasks, which are embedded within contemporary socialization processes. These sorts of responses, however, will enhance their scores on the personality types (such as Conventional or Social) that are not associated with more prestige and power in the contemporary social and economic world. This debate has evoked a complex discussion about the use of norm-referenced scores for each sex, which is beyond the scope of this book (see Betz, 1993, and Zunker & Osborn, 2002, for informative reviews of this debate). However, in accordance with the social change mission of the psychology of working, I advocate that test developers and psychologists who work with such developers appreciate how powerful test results can be in people's lives. Given psychology's role in the use of intellectual testing as a means of controlling access to schools and opportunities (Helms et al., 2005; Marshall & Tucker, 1992), our field needs to be particularly careful in the design and use of testing materials. (I refer interested readers to Helms et al., 2005, for a further discussion of the complexities of intellectual assessment and social change.) When constructed in light of needs of clients and students, testing has the capacity to provide individuals with important information that can help identify untapped talents. Yet, at the same time, testing can be used to sort people into categories that further reify differences based on demographics, ethnicity, and other irrelevant attributes of individuals.

Moving beyond the realm of traditional vocational counseling to the inclusive psychological practice that is advanced herein, I do envision an important role for testing in the design and delivery of counseling services. For counseling issues that revolve around person–environment fit issues, the traditional tripartite mode of assessment of interests, personality, and abilities/achievements can be informative. However, given the problems with assessing and interpreting measures based on the "g" factor (cf. Eisner, 2004; Helms et al., 2005; W. Johnson, Bouchard, Krueger, McGue, & Gottesman, 2004), I advise that counselors explore other, less traditional means of assessing abilities and achievements. For those clients who have some experience in the working world, I suggest the use of the Transferable Skills Inventory (Bolles & Bolles, 2005), which I reviewed in chapter 8. Similarly, I hope that greater efforts will be devoted to designing personality assessments that are based on meaningful and culturally embedded taxonomies, which are relevant for each group of clients.

In addition to revisions needed for existing assessment practice, I believe that an expanded net of tools can be useful in an inclusive psychological practice. For example, recent research has revealed that considerable differences exist in how people construct work, school, vocational training, and education (Chaves et al., 2004; Cinnamon & Gifsch, 2004). Initial qualitative research in this area has revealed some notable distinctions that would very likely affect how counselors would optimally discuss work-related issues in treatment (Chaves et al., 2004). Given the strong trends identified in this research, I believe that a need exists for a user-friendly quantitative measure of constructions of work that may have informative implications for practitioners. In addition, given that the psychology of working moves beyond the scope of vocational interests and job matching that has defined traditional vocational counseling to date, I believe that assessment tools that can identify the values of both individuals and work environments may be quite useful (cf. D. Brown, 2002b). Furthermore, measures that assess variations in motivational orientations with respect to working environments will be helpful in an inclusive psychological practice. For example, assessing the extent to which clients are able to internalize their extrinsically motivated experiences and construct self-regulating activities in relation to working would be quite informative at various phases of the counseling process.

In sum, the role of assessment in the psychology of working has the potential to have an equally important role as it has in traditional vocational counseling and I/O psychology. With the increased knowledge of how tests function in the broader social context (Helms et al., 2005), it is now possible to develop measures that will have greater local relevance for given groups of clients. My preference for the role of tests, as implied thus far, is in the realm of explanation and exploration as opposed to prediction. Given the expanded range of issues and concerns that exist in an inclusive psychological practice, I believe that a significant role for a revitalized and culturally sensitive assessment process exists in expanding the reach and impact of our collective efforts.

The Psychology of Working and Challenging Therapeutic Relationship Issues

The inclusive psychological practice perspective advanced here offers some unique challenges and opportunities with respect to the therapeutic relationship. The contributions of Axelrod (1999) and Socarides and Kramer (1997) underscore the potential richness that can be achieved in insight-oriented explorations of working. However, the movement toward a more affirming understanding of working in counseling evokes the potential for some complications in the therapeutic relationship as well as creative responses that can help advance the clinical applications of the psychology of working.

The Role of Empathy

Empathy serves as a key element in helping therapists to connect to their clients, understand their life experiences, and, in many cases, in facilitate therapeutic gains (Bohart & Greenberg, 1997). One of the challenges that an affirmative approach to working presents in psychotherapy is in finding ways to truly connect with clients whose working experiences may be dramatically different from our own. As detailed in chapter 7, empathy functions in a number of ways in the psychotherapeutic process, with significant implications for research and scholarly endeavors. In the clinical context, I envision that empathy will provide both a challenge and opportunity for therapists who wish to fully include the psychological experiences of working in their clinical efforts. For example, a therapist who is working with a migrant farmer in a community agency may not understand even the most superficial aspects of the client's working life. The lack of knowledge, however, does not need to function as a barrier. In this context, the therapist's desire to understand the full scope of the client's life can provide a means for an emotional exploration of the client's working experiences.

The following passage, constructed from an amalgam of previous clinical work, describes how the process of enhancing empathy can be powerfully beneficial for clients and therapists:

> **Therapist:** Marcus, I understand that you're feeling very depressed now and that you're not clear about how this depression arose. You have been quite open and clear about your family life and relationships, which as you indicate, are going well. I would like to ask you more about your life working in the textile plant.
>
> **Marcus:** I actually don't really like the job, but it's a paycheck, you know? I just feel a bit scared right now as the company is starting to lay off workers. I have seniority, but I'm not sure how long it will last. I have two kids who are getting close to college age; I'm just not sure what I am going to do if I lose my job.
>
> **Therapist:** Marcus, I can sense your feeling of vulnerability as you speak. It seems as if the world that you have known is no longer feeling secure.
>
> **Marcus:** That is exactly it. You have hit the nail on the head! I feel so scared these days. I'm not used to feeling this way and I just don't know what to do.
>
> **Therapist:** How depressed are you feeling now as we speak?
>
> **Marcus:** I still feel depressed, but I'm now aware that I am also feeling frightened and a bit helpless.
>
> **Therapist:** Okay, this is really helpful. Now you are putting some words to the feelings that have been haunting you for months. With this clearer sense of your own experience, it may be possible for you and I to work on some ways for you to become less helpless in your working life. This may actually help to reduce your feelings of depression. Now, let me see if I can understand more about your working life. Tell me what you have felt as you've entered the plant in recent days ….

As this brief interchange suggests, the therapist followed the empathic trail, which led to fruitful emotional experiences that seemed to underlie at least some of the depressive mood. Naturally, the depression that Marcus reports here may have a multifaceted etiology; however, the difficulties that Marcus reports in feeling safe and secure in a world with no guarantees is clearly contributing to the emergence of the depressive symptoms. By seeking to learn more about Marcus' working life, which represents a very different world for this therapist (and for many others as well), the empathic connection becomes stronger, leading to greater emotional awareness (Bohart & Greenberg, 1997).

Countertransference Challenges

Countertransference represents another source of both challenge and opportunity for therapists who wish to incorporate the psychology of working into their practice. Hill and Williams (2000) noted that two definitions of countertransference exist. One definition is derived from a strict interpretation of Freud's (1910/1959) work and encompasses the therapist's unconscious and distorted reactions to therapeutic material and relationship issues. The second definition, which is derived from the ego psychological contributions of Fromm-Reichman (1950), consists of the full array of therapist reactions to clients. As Hill and Williams noted, considerable disagreement exists with respect to these two positions. For the present discussion, I concur with the latter definition, which provides a rubric for understanding the reality that therapists are human and that they react to clients both professionally and from a more individualistic and emotional perspective. Ideally, the professional reactions will remain in control, which is, thankfully, the case with the vast majority of clinicians. However, for many therapists who have developed a modicum of self-knowledge, the emotional reactions that clients' material evokes in us often may stimulate further "grist" for the therapeutic mill.

For the most part, discussions of countertransference tend to focus on such feelings as anger, attraction, frustration, and admiration with respect to a given client (Mills, 2004). In the psychology-of-working realm, countertransference can take on new meanings. As we embrace the importance of working in our clients' lives, therapists will increasingly need to confront their own issues about their working lives. For example, a therapist may find herself or himself feeling envious of a given client's wealth, which may have been obtained without much effort. The feelings of envy, if not acknowledged and attended to, could in fact defuse therapeutically important explorations of the meaning of money in a client's life. An additional example would be a case in which a client presents concerns about starting a new business, which may parallel the therapist's own entry into private practice. The therapist's anxiety about the unknowns of private practice may function to limit a productive exploration of the meaning of the client's new business endeavor.

My concern with work-related countertransference is that many therapists have little exposure to their own inner life with respect to working. Inherent in clinical discussions of working are concerns about equity, fairness, access to opportunity, parental expectations for achievement, as well as the entire spectrum of issues pertaining to race, gender, social class, sexual orientation, and ableism (Blustein, 2001b; Flum, 2001; M. S. Richardson, 1996). As the knowledge base grows in the psychology of working, one would expect that clinicians, scholars, and others will develop a language for exploring these issues clinically. In the meantime, I urge therapists who take on the full spectrum of work-related issues to take note of their countertransference and to contribute to the professional discourse by sharing their observations in conferences, journals, and books.

Case Explorations of an Inclusive Psychological Practice

With the goal of helping to illustrate the clinical attributes of an inclusive psychological practice, I offer two cases, each representing amalgams of my previous clinical work. The two cases each reflect distinct aspects of the sort of clinical work that can emerge as work-related issues are fully and openly accepted into the realm of counseling and psychotherapy. Naturally, these two cases do not cover the full scope of the material presented thus far; however, they ideally provide readers with ideas about how to implement the inclusiveness and affirmation of work-related issues into the natural rhythm of counseling.

Chrissie

Chrissie is a 20-year-old woman who has recently immigrated to the United States from Jamaica in search of more employment opportunities and to get away from a stressful family situation in her home back on the island. Chrissie graduated from high school in an urban community in Jamaica; she developed excellent skills in typing and other clerical duties, which allowed her to obtain a job in a doctor's office near her family's home. She was also involved in a romantic relationship with a man that culminated in an unplanned pregnancy. Unfortunately, once her boyfriend heard about the pregnancy, he backed off from his commitment to Chrissie and soon thereafter, broke off the relationship. Chrissie's parents were very upset that she was pregnant and that she did not have an opportunity to marry the father of the baby. Both of her parents were quite religious and felt that Chrissie shamed the family. As such, the family climate soon disintegrated into a highly conflictual state, leaving Chrissie feeling depressed and overwhelmed.

Chrissie contacted a cousin living the United States and arranged to emigrate to the small urban city where her cousin and her cousin's family lived. (Chrissie's cousin was a teacher and her cousin's husband was an auto mechanic; they had two children, ages 7 and 10 as well as a nice home.) Chrissie arrived in the United States about 8 months prior to her contact with the therapist. During that time, she struggled to find employment, moving from job to job, in fields ranging from caring for the elderly to working in a department store. In each of these jobs, she struggled to make ends meet. She did not make enough money to support the expensive child care that was available in her community. In addition, Chrissie continued to struggle with depression, which was associated with an increasingly isolated social life with little contact with friends or relatives (aside from her cousin and her family). She also blamed herself for the difficulties that she experienced in obtaining a job and further education and training. She convinced herself that she was useless and that she had nothing to contribute to the world, aside from being a mother. In this context, Chrissie reported feeling good about her parenting; she also indicated that she was close with her cousin, who became an important friend and mentor to her since her arrival in the United States.

Chrissie's family in the United States suggested that she consider psychotherapy to deal with her depression and her isolation. She concurred and began treatment, with most of her concerns focusing on her depressed mood, struggle to find employment, low self-esteem, and ambivalence about being a single parent. She did not report suicidal ideation; moreover, her depression fit into a dysthymic diagnosis as opposed to a major depression. Chrissie indicated that she really needed someone to talk with, as her parent's disapproval of her coupled with her struggles in the United States had left her feeling sad. She did, however, maintain some hope that a good job or training opportunity might help her to feel more optimistic. She also was very much interested in meeting new people and expanding her social connections. Chrissie indicated that she did not understand the American educational system; she did not view herself as a good student and was unclear about what she would like to do.

During the course of the 9 months of treatment, Chrissie began to feel more hopeful and was increasingly engaged in exploring options and making new friends. She was able to project herself into a future that involved greater self-determination in her work life and in her relationships.

Discussion

As the therapist in this case, I initially offered Chrissie a treatment plan consisting of a synthesis of traditional psychotherapy and vocational counseling, culminating in an integrative and inclusive mode of treatment. As such, an assessment about the potential of suicidal ideation or intent coupled with a consideration of the use of psychotropic medications (which were not indicated) provided useful starting points after the initial intake sessions. In addition, the domain-sensitive approach, detailed in the previous chapter, provided guidance about ways of integrating the vocational and nonvocational themes. However, Chrissie's case includes numerous other issues and factors that suggest a broader array of therapeutic influences and objectives.

One of the notable factors in Chrissie's case is her sense of isolation and lack of interpersonal support. Consistent with the relationally oriented views of working (Flum, 2001; Schultheiss, 2003) and the literature on work-based transitions (Blustein et al., 2000), it seems clear that Chrissie would benefit from far greater social support and intimacy in her life. Exploring Chrissie's feelings about her family's rejection of her parenting status emerged as a very useful issue to examine in the early stages of treatment. One plausible inference is that Chrissie has internalized negative views of herself, which made it harder for her to take risks in interpersonal relationships. In addition, the reality of immigration needs to be examined in treatment. Specifically, given the very real challenges of moving to a new country and learning new social and cultural mores, the immigration experience often leaves people feeling very disengaged and alienated (Suarez-Orozco, 2004). Furthermore, interventions designed to help Chrissie feel more engaged and agentic in her life, which are described shortly, were used as a central aspect of the therapeutic work. Yet at the same time, I acknowledged the very real challenges that face Chrissie, especially in immigrating to a country where little opportunity awaits those without high levels of skill, which is further complicated by racism and sexism.

The predictors of an adaptive school-to-work transition that my colleagues and I identified (Blustein et al., 2000) also furnished useful conceptual ideas for the counseling efforts with Chrissie. Clearly, the role of relational support is important for both Chrissie's mental health as well as her capacity to locate a more rewarding working life. In addition, the consistent observation that adaptive transitions are associated with the acquisition of competent basic skills and relevant vocational skills would suggest that some discussion ensue about Chrissie's skill level and openness to further education and training. Like many clients who feel depressed and/or who suffer from low self-esteem, it is often difficult to internalize their positive attributes. Helping Chrissie to see herself via affirming mirroring experiences (Tolpin, 1983; Wolf, 1980) may be instrumental in helping her to own her resilience, flexibility, and agentic stance in life. Certainly, Chrissie's transition from Jamaica to the United States reflects a level of initiative that she may have lost touch with since her move. The importance of a supportive relational context, particularly in the education and/or training realm, is often overlooked in traditional vocational counseling and in many types of psychotherapy. In the approach suggested by the psychology of working, clear attention to the clients' context is indicated, including but not limited to relational support.

The counseling approach for Chrissie entailed a complex yet integrated approach to exploring her strengths, resources, and barriers. In my work with Chrissie, I initially sought to provide some positive mirroring experiences for her, exploring and affirming the overt and more subtle aspects of her personality and character that have been diminished by her depressive mood. One particularly useful means of enhancing self-esteem and consolidating self-cohesion is to use the Quick Job-Hunting Map and the Transferable Skills Inventory (Bolles & Bolles, 2005); this task can be very affirming for clients and was quite beneficial for Chrissie.

The integrative nature of Chrissie's issues suggested the importance of explicitly highlighting the embedded nature of her presenting problems. Given that Chrissie understood the linkage between her sense of loneliness, pessimism about the future, family relationships, and interpersonal alienation, I asked her to identify how her life can be improved. In doing so, I encouraged Chrissie to dream more openly about a working life and interpersonal relationships that would be more rewarding. To help Chrissie dream, I asked her to complete an interest inventory, specifically, the Strong Interest Inventory (Harmon, Hansen, Borgen, & Hammer, 1994). One of the implicit goals of this work was to help Chrissie feel more hopeful about her life, which was helpful in reducing her depressive mood. Once Chrissie was able to connect the dots in her picture of herself, I worked on helping her to engage in active, exploratory behavior, which also functioned to get her out of her home more and into the community. For example, helping Chrissie to access financial aid and linking her to a community college was very helpful in mobilizing her adaptive skills and in reducing her sense of helplessness. Chrissie ended treatment by starting community college; once she entered the community college, she then began to join groups and organizations that functioned to enhance her social supports.

While many of the features of this approach are consistent with best practices in working with immigrant youth or single parents (e.g., Blustein et al., 2000; Falk, 1993; Riala, Isohanni, Jokelainen, Jones, & Isohanni, 2003), there are a number of ways in which the work with Chrissie conveyed salient elements of the psychology-of-working aspects of an inclusive psychological practice. First, the narrative that was used with Chrissie in helping her to understand her problems was framed to reduce her sense of self-blame. In particular, Chrissie's difficulty in understanding her struggle to obtain work and training was reframed within a broader discussion of the changing world of work and of the importance of basic skills and vocationally relevant skills.

This discussion functioned to help Chrissie feel more empowered as well as less prone to negative self-statements, which are associated with depressive moods (Beck, 1987).

Second, the work with Chrissie helped her to enhance her critical consciousness, which yielded both greater levels of energy from Chrissie and the emergence of social activism. Naturally, the process of exploring the broader social, economic, and political framework of Chrissie's life served to move the treatment into an overly intellectual space that, at times, was not entirely productive in exploring her emotional life. In my work with Chrissie, I sought to find natural linkages between her own personal narrative and the exploration of contextual factors that were contributing to her struggles. For example, in describing her movement from Jamaica to the United States, Chrissie noted that she experienced far more racism in the United States due to the fact that people of color are a minority in this country. This discussion evoked greater openness about Chrissie's ambivalence about moving to a primarily European American culture and also helped her to explore how racism plays a role in the maldistribution of resources in her community. The struggle here was to enhance Chrissie's sense of agency in the face of this racism as opposed to enhancing her sense of helplessness.

As in the domain-sensitive approach, I also sought out an area of Chrissie's life wherein she demonstrated greater resilience. In this case, Chrissie was increasingly comfortable with her parenting and her relationship with her cousin. This suggests that she has solid interpersonal skills, which may function as a source of resilience in her life. As such, the treatment benefited considerably from exploring ways for Chrissie to expand her social network. Once a broader social support system was identified and cultivated, it was possible to explore the more tender issues related to Chrissie's self-esteem as a worker and her relationship with her parents.

The case of Chrissie provides some texture and depth to the clinical implications of the psychology of working that have been presented thus far in this chapter. While the specific treatment interventions are all consistent with existing practices, the integrative nature of the counseling process and the tightly weaved context in which work and nonwork issues were explored represent new vistas in psychotherapeutic practice.

Bill

Bill is a 27-year-old African American man who presented for treatment due to problems in dealing with supervisors at work and his fears of a layoff (which were soon confirmed). He was urged to seek out therapy by his Employee Assistance Program counselor at the state agency where he worked in a shop repairing computers. Bill also reported increasing problems in sleeping and in modulating his overall level of anxiety. During the course of the 11 months of treatment, Bill was ultimately laid off due to the fact that the state agency no longer invested in repairing computers given that the desktop computers were increasingly less costly and that they were being updated and replaced periodically. The few computers that would be repaired would be outsourced to a local shop.

Early in the treatment, Bill presented as passive and anxious, particularly with respect to his work-related issues. In fact, he reported that his relationship with his fiancée, Sandra, was excellent; they were living together and enjoying the process of creating a romantic partnership. However, once Bill received notice that he was being laid off because his unit in the state agency was being severely downsized, he became enraged and began drinking more regularly. Bill was prone to outbursts of anger in the various domains of his life, including but not limited to his job. He reported that his fiancée was becoming more inpatient with his dark moods. Bill also acknowledged that he was using alcohol and, when available, marijuana to cope with his deep sense of disappointment.

Bill is the youngest son in a working-class family; he has two other siblings (a brother and sister), both of whom also worked for the state government. Bill's father was a salesman at a local department store and his mother worked for a local hotel chain. Both of his parents struggled in obtaining steady employment. Bill's father, in particular, had numerous periods of unemployment and underemployment (part-time jobs without benefits), which were profoundly painful events in his childhood and adolescence. He indicated that he had good relationships with his parents. He sometimes argued with his parents about curfews in adolescence, but he recalls that they were generally supportive of him. Bill described himself as "an average student" in high school. After his high school graduation, he went to the local community college and majored in data processing and computer repair. Bill does not recall making a conscious decision about his choice of major in college. He indicated that he pursued this area because it seemed to offer the most secure job openings in his community.

Bill reported that he had never considered counseling before. He indicated that he was reasonably content in his life until the recent episodes at work which resulted in this referral. (The incident that evoked the referral involved a shouting match that he engaged in with his boss. Bill was upset by his own lack of control and sought out the input of the Employee Assistance counselor in his agency, who then recommended psychotherapy.) He did not necessarily enjoy his working tasks; he did, however, dislike his boss a great deal. Bill indicated that his boss reminded him of a supervisor he had had when he was 18 and worked in a department store in shipping and receiving. His supervisor at that time was described as a sadistic man who liked to humiliate his subordinates with insults, profanity, and manipulation. Bill reported that his supervisor in the department store often called him "a moron" in front of other workers and stated that he would be a failure in his life. At times, the supervisor threw boxes at him and called him "college boy" (as he was attending community college full-time while he worked part-time). Bill also felt that the supervisor was racist, as he treated the European American staff members with greater respect. Bill very much wanted to walk out of this job, but his father worked in the same store and he did not want to embarrass his father by either leaving the job or arguing back to the supervisor. He ended up leaving the job when he was 20, after receiving his Associate's degree. He received a job offer from a computer repair shop that provided him with a full-time job and an opportunity to learn more about his trade. A few years later, Bill was hired by the state agency to work in their computer repair shop.

Early in the counseling process (before he was laid off), Bill was not very verbal in sessions. He was not sure how to engage in therapy and seemed to struggle with how to talk about his feelings. After his layoff, he became much more verbal, particularly in relation to his anger. He was able to connect his anxiety with his boss from his job with the state to his fears of his supervisor at the department store job. Bill also explored issues pertaining to the institutional racism in his agency, which was manifested by both overt acts of hostility and covert acts of neglect. Bill's supervisor at the state agency would often make nasty comments about Affirmative Action hires, while looking directly at him. The more subtle acts of racism involved providing other workers (from European American backgrounds) with opportunities for training and development, which were not generally available to Bill. He continued to feel angry throughout the sessions, but was able to contain the anger more effectively as the therapy winded down. Bill reported that his relationship with his fiancée improved and they set a date for a wedding. Also, Bill returned to college to continue his studies in graphic design, and was working part-time in computer-based graphics when he elected to terminate treatment.

Discussion

While this case ends seemingly "happily-ever-after," there were many bumps along the therapeutic journey that reflect some of the important aspects of inclusive psychological practice. Bill's case reflects some of the most salient aspects of the psychology of working in a clinical context. The fact that Bill was reserved early in the process of therapy is actually consistent with some of the challenges in counseling men and particularly men of color (G. Brooks & Good, 2001; Hayes & Mahalik, 2000; Levant, 2000). As Mahalik (1999), G. Brooks (2001), and Levant (2000) have discussed, counseling men often entails a wide array of complexities and nuances related to the impact of gender-based socialization. In short, Bill's reticence to present in therapy, rather than reflecting resistance, may be a function of growing up as an African American man in contemporary U.S. culture.

By reaching out to Bill in ways that he was able to relate to, which naturally included his working life, I was able to establish a solid and flexible therapeutic alliance. Indeed, focusing on his work life, while beset with pain and disappointments, provided Bill and me with a means of exploring many aspects of his emotional life in depth. For example, I was able to learn more about his sense of vulnerability at work, which was initially connected to the traumatic experiences he faced while working in the shipping and receiving department of the department store. His sense of vulnerability also was connected to his experience as person of color in an agency where the staff and supervisors were primarily European American. As we explored these issues in greater depth, it became clear that his father's struggles to locate work that helped the family to survive and thrive played a major role in his anxiety about work in general. By talking about working, Bill was able to open up to his own sense of vulnerability, which was manifested early in the treatment by his anxiety and later in the treatment by his anger.

The second part of the case emerged around halfway through the 8-month period when Bill received notification that he was going to be laid off indefinitely. This experience stirred up deep levels of fear, which Bill could not give voice to easily. He became much more reactive and angry, with increasing outbursts directed at his family members and friends. I encouraged Bill to monitor his angry feelings and to take notice of them rather than attempt to act on them. In fact, using some of the approaches suggested by Eastern traditions (K. Brown & Ryan, 2003; Linehan, 1993; Masske, 2002), I explored with Bill ways of attending to his anger, carefully, intensively, and without judgment or interpretation. By using his anger as a signal from his inner life to take notice of his emotional state, Bill began to develop more diverse responses to anger, which resulted in a marked decrease of outbursts and tantrums. At the same time as we focused on developing new coping skills, I worked with Bill to explore the anger to see where it led us. Bill was clearly angry at the supervisor at his state job, who he felt had sabotaged his department. He also had considerable anger related to the trauma he experienced in his job at the department store.

While Bill was able to reduce his anger and anxiety, he struggled considerably in moving to the next step, which involved preparing for the working world that existed in his community rather than the one he wished existed. For a number of months, Bill steadfastly refused to consider returning to school. He reported that he hated school and that he was not going to be "a newly married husband (and father, hopefully) attending college with a bunch of kids." He also indicated that he did not do well in college and that he was going to try to get his job back with the state. During this time period, I used the Transferable Skills Inventory (Bolles & Bolles, 2005) and the Strong Interest Inventory (Harmon et al., 1994) with Bill. One of the interesting findings from both assessment tools was an interest in academic pursuits and the recognition that he enjoyed art and graphic design. Some of the vignettes that Bill prepared in the Transferable Skills Inventory were particularly evocative of successful experiences at community college, including his art courses. Bill then discussed how he felt very ambivalent about moving into a 4-year college as he somehow thought that this would be disloyal to his family. Bill's family and siblings were not college educated and tended to feel a bit alienated from the world of professionals. Discussing the meaning of success for Bill naturally encompassed deep feelings of empathy for his father who had struggled so much in finding work. Indeed, during this phase of treatment, Bill was able to cry as he recalled how hurt he felt when his father was home all day long, waiting for calls from prospective employers that never came.

Bill also reflected on racism in the United States and was able to explore his own racial identity in counseling. He increasingly demonstrated a growing critical consciousness that allowed him to understand the broader social and political forces that colluded to keep him and others from his community from reaching their goals.

Bill explored the option of graphic design tentatively at first, by taking a course at the local community college. However, once he entered this course, there was no looking back. His graphic design instructor loved his work and he began to feel powerfully mirrored and affirmed (Kohut, 1977), which helped him to explore programs in 4-year colleges. During this period of treatment, we also explored his substance use in greater depth. A careful analysis revealed that he was prone to alcohol abuse, although I made him aware that abuse could quickly emerge as dependence. He also gave up his episodic use of marijuana, which he associated with the potential for birth defects in his future offspring. Thus, as treatment ended, Bill was enrolled full-time in a graphic design program and was working part-time at a printing shop which gave him some experience in graphic design.

Concluding Comments

Both of these cases reflect some, but clearly not all, of the features and nuances of an inclusive psychological practice. The common themes in these two cases are the integrative focus on work and nonwork issues, the explicit focus on affirming work-related issues in treatment, and the use of the domain-sensitive approach as the organizing meta-perspective in the treatment. In both cases, I worked with the clients' strengths, consolidating internal and external resources prior to moving to the more painful and vulnerable aspects of their functioning. Moreover, both cases dealt with clients who initially did not experience much choice in their working lives; through the treatment process, we were able to expand their volition by helping them to develop their skills and their access to resources.

Evaluation Issues

In the current era in psychotherapy and counseling, it seems disingenuous to write about clinical issues without reference to evaluation and empirically supported treatments. Mental health practitioners of all stripes (i.e., social workers, mental health counselors, psychologists, psychiatrists) need to deal with managed care, empirically supported treatment protocols, and evaluation issues (Wampold, 2001). The two cases presented here reflect the flexibility that exists in the pages of a book wherein one does not have to answer to treatment limitations imposed by circumscribed health care resources.

In evaluating these cases, one can explore a host of viable outcome variables that would have currency in the managed care and insurance worlds. For example, the reduction in symptoms reported by both Chrissie and Bill is certainly affirming. In addition, I would argue that the development of meaningful work-related plans for both of these clients represents an important index of return to full functioning (Shore, 1998; Shore & Massimo, 1963). Furthermore, the fact that these treatments were with clients with diagnosable conditions suggests that inclusive psychological practice would in fact meet the criteria for third-party reimbursements. Indeed, I would argue that the focus on work-related issues in both of these cases is not a luxury, but is the most appropriate ethical and professional treatment decision.

The question of developing empirically supported treatments for work-related issues is clearly premature. Far more research and clinical work is needed prior to exploring this issue in depth. I am also concerned with the development of highly structured treatment protocols that are not sufficiently flexible to adapt to cultural and historical changes. Despite my concerns, the movement toward the use of empirically supported treatments is clearly advancing (Barlow, 2004) and will merit the full attention of practitioners engaged in work-related treatments. I also would argue that existing empirically supported treatments need to be reviewed in depth to determine the degree to which they adequately deal with working. This issue represents a critical research endeavor that would illuminate the psychotherapy literature immeasurably.

Conclusion

This chapter has sought to present some preliminary ideas about the clinical and counseling applications derived from the psychology of working. The map that I have drawn here was intended to provide a sketch for future journeys into this rich and exciting area rather than furnishing a specific set of instructions or treatment recommendations. As the psychotherapy and counseling fields move further into the 21st century, the challenges that emerge from work-related issues that our clients bring into treatment will become increasingly complex. As in other areas of complexity, it may be that the movement to embrace the work-related domains of life experience will, in fact, serve as a means of further enhancing psychotherapeutic efforts. By including the entire spectrum of life domains, my view is that therapists have a far greater chance to build on client strengths, to help clients become more fully empowered, and to help clients develop a critical consciousness about the world we live in.

I also hope that this chapter will evoke further clinical discussions of the therapeutic meaning of working. Ideally, this chapter (and the entire book) can serve as a stimulus for counselors and therapists to listen with an enhanced set of senses to the dreams and disappointments that are evident in their clients' experiences in work-related contexts. By helping our clients to listen to their own voices about work with greater honesty and affirmation, it may be possible to help clients construct lives that provide meaning, strength, and vigor in all domains of human experience.

CHAPTER 10

Conclusion:
The Future of the Psychology of Working

In thinking about constructing the closing chapter for this book, I have focused on preparing one that will serve as a beginning as well as an ending. Throughout this book, I have sought to engage readers in a journey that seeks to explore the richly complex and often bittersweet landscape of the psychology of working. In addition, I have sought to add my voice to those who are dedicated to the study of work as a focal point in efforts to reduce inequity and to level the playing field of our lives (e.g., Fassinger, 2000; Fouad & Brown, 2000; M. S. Richardson, 1993; Wilson, 1996). As a means of helping readers to consider the broad implications of the material presented thus far, I have two interrelated objectives for this chapter. First, I discuss the underlying themes that cohere across many of the chapters of this book. Second, I highlight the potential implications of the psychology of working for public policy, encompassing education, mental health, unemployment, and training.

Overriding Themes and Dialectical Conflicts Within the Psychology of Working

The preceding nine chapters have sought to carve the conceptual structure of the psychology of working in a manner relatively consistent with existing psychological discourse. However, in using traditional categories that differentiate among such issues as historical trends, broad social and economic influences, clinical issues, and research and theory implications, some of the underlying themes that transcend these categories may have been diminished or less visible in the preceding chapters. In this section, I examine these issues, which include a number of questions and dialectical conflicts that merit our collective attention as we move forward with the psychology of working.

Need for Inclusiveness in the Study of Working

One of the most prevalent themes in this book has been the need for greater inclusiveness in the psychological study of working. As I conveyed in the first few chapters, the relative absence of attention to those who exercise little to no volition in their choices of jobs and experiences at work is noteworthy in vocational psychology, I/O psychology, and other branches of psychological discourse, including the psychotherapeutic literature. Giving voice to the modal worker across the globe has been a major goal of this book, reflecting a concerted effort to expand the scope and impact of psychological considerations of working. However, other aspects of inclusiveness are relevant to the future of the psychology of working and may have been overshadowed in the material presented thus far.

Working Outside of the Labor Market.   The reality of life for most people is that work does not end when we leave our place of employment. In addition, many people, either out of choice or necessity, devote many of their working hours to caregiving (Barnett & Hyde, 2001; Hesse-Biber & Carter, 2000). Consistent with M. S. Richardson's (1993) position, I believe that the exclusion of caregiving from psychological considerations of working has had a markedly limiting impact on our ability to fully understand the nature of working. I do want to underscore that my commitment to including caregiving is not intended to buttress the notion that women ought to assume the majority of caregiving responsibilities. A fully inclusive psychology of working will need to confront gender-based inequities in caregiving and work within a household. As I have indicated earlier in this book, I endorse the view that preparing for adulthood must include a systematic effort for everyone to enter the paid labor market with the full richness of his or her talents. In this manner, I concur with the position that women who are socialized to focus on caregiving to the exclusion of work in the labor market are essentially being cut off from their rightful place within our society (cf. Fitzgerald & Weitzman, 1992).

With this point in mind, the relative avoidance of family and relationally based work has further bifurcated psychological thinking about working. With the growing life expectancy of many people in Western societies, the complex demands of caregiving will continue to expand across the life span. Certainly, a rich literature exists on family–work interactions within organizational psychology and vocational psychology (e.g., Parasuraman & Greenhaus, 1997; Whiston & Keller, 2004); yet, much more work is needed in this area, particularly with respect to individuals who have little to no access to the "grand career narrative." The emergence of the relational perspectives of working (Blustein, 2001b; Flum, 2001; Schultheiss, 2003) offers important opportunities to explore the complex space shared by work outside the home, work within the home, and caregiving. In addition, the impact of caregiving in relation to the striving for survival, relational connection, and self-determination will need to be explored. As the psychology of working matures, it is critical that we value all modalities of work. In addition, the disparity of social and economic rewards that exist with respect to caregiving and market-based work will need to be revisited in the coming decades. Ideally, the research and public policy that emerge from the psychology of working will prove to be useful as we strive to dignify, and reduce inequities in, all working experiences.

The Psychology of Working for Nonworkers.   A subtle and, at times, more overt theme of this book has been that many of the issues and concerns raised herein are relevant to the unemployed and to those who are preparing for work (e.g., students, young people, adults in training programs). A key asset of vocational psychology is its focus on the continuity between the student role and the worker role (e.g., Blustein et al., 2000; Super, 1980). This point is critical as well in an inclusive psychology of working. As I detail later in this chapter, one of the policy realms in which the psychology of working is likely to have the greatest impact is in educational reform. Consistent with the view of Lapan (e.g., 2004; Lapan & Koscuilek, 2001) as well as others in both education and psychology (see Baker & Taylor, 1998; Blustein et al., 2000; Evans & Burck, 1992), students who are able to internalize the connection between school and work are in a much better position to become engaged in school and develop their basic skills. Moreover, the linkages between the social and economic policies that govern schools are of immediate relevance to the psychology of working. The social justice roots of the psychology of working detailed in this book and elsewhere (e.g., Blustein et al., 2005) include a concerted commitment to reduce inequities in schooling and other social and economic resources that can nourish or impede the development of adaptive levels of basic cognitive skills and work-based attitudes.

Another group of nonworkers are unemployed individuals, who have been significantly neglected in contemporary psychological discourse. As I have detailed at different points throughout this book, lack of employment for those who want to or have to work is a serious psychological issue as well as an economic one. The majority of social scientific research has focused on macro-level analyses (e.g., Neumark, 2000), which regrettably functions to keep the lived experiences of unemployed adults out of our individual and collective consciousness. The focus of the psychology of working on the actual life experiences of people interacting with work-based demands and challenges offers an important remedy to the trend of considering unemployment as a statistic as opposed to acknowledging that the inability to locate work profoundly affects real people.

In addition, individuals with disabling conditions, encompassing physical, psychological, and developmental domains, need to be included in the research, theory development, practice, and public policy efforts of the psychology of working. Thanks to research in rehabilitation counseling in particular (e.g., Neff, 1985; Riggar & Maki, 2004; Szymanski & Parker, 2003), a rich scholarship exists on the interface of work and disability. One of the most complex challenges is that of developing activities for individuals whose disabling conditions do not allow for the sorts of jobs that offer volition about work-related tasks and relationships. Another issue of relevance is in designing work environments that will satisfy the essential needs that working optimally may fulfill and that will be supportive of individuals with disabling conditions. My hope is that future efforts using the ideas presented here and related lines of research will advance theory, research, and policy recommendations that will positively enhance the lives of workers and people who wish to work.

Intellectual Diversity in Research and Theory Development. One of the risks of writing a solo-authored book is that one's individual perspective and values have the potential for assuming an intellectual hegemony within a new field like the psychology of working. I am certainly aware of this risk and the limitations that arise from my vision and agenda. I have sought to counter this possibility by including an expansive body of work that draws from multiple disciplines and conceptual positions. In this context, I would like to underscore that I advise against establishing one particular epistemological position over another. While I have used elements of social constructionist thinking (e.g., Gergen, 1999) as well as the emancipatory communitarian approach (Prilleltensky, 1997), I also have endorsed the use of traditional quantitative and positivist methods as one of many vehicles for exploring the nature of working.

In addition, I have sought to present an open mind with respect to debates about psychodynamic conceptualizations, behavioral explanations, person–environment fit models, and social cognitive theories. In my view, the psychology of working is a field of inquiry that seeks to provide a foundation for subsequent theory development and research. Thus, I envision a broad level of inclusiveness with respect to theoretical ideas and positions within the psychology of working.

Dialectical Struggles

Opening up the vast vistas that exist in working around the globe certainly has been an ambitious agenda that includes many potential pitfalls and challenges. I hope that readers of this book who will have the benefit of some distance from the issues that I have been studying for years, will help to identify these difficulties, many of which are inherent in this sort of endeavor. Some of the challenges, though, that have emerged in my work on this book are summarized next.

The Tension Between the Individual and Context. In preparing the groundwork for this project, I read extensively in sociology, anthropology, fiction, and a host of other fields. One of the objectives of introducing this material has been to provide balance between the inner experience of the individual, which has been the purview of psychology, and the more contextual perspectives that are the province of other social sciences and artistic endeavors. In using such a diverse array of ingredients, I certainly have been aware that the result might be far too multifaceted to have any coherent meaning. At this point in the evolution of these ideas, I now view the amalgam of influences as a necessary by-product of trying to describe the psychology of working in the real world.

In my view, the study of working from a psychological perspective will necessarily involve a tension between the individual's experiences and the context that frames the individual. In giving voice to individuals, I hope that it may be possible to understand the nature of this tension in greater clarity. The actual experience of working brings individuals into direct contact with their contexts, including education, job-search processes, various forms of discrimination, and the wide spectrum of social barriers embedded in occupational contexts that exist around the world. Hence, scholars and practitioners who seek to develop viable research programs culminating in theoretical explanations of working with logically derived policy recommendations need to take notice of this tension. Rather than seeking to avoid the muddiness of trying to understand the individual experience of workers and people who wish to work in the actual context of that experience, I believe that the best scholarship and practice will embrace this tension and learn to explore it, work with it, and ideally help individuals live with the reality that their dreams may not always be fulfilled.

The Tension Between Describing Reality and Accepting Reality. One of the most challenging aspects in writing this book has been my intention to describe the reality of life for most working people in a manner that does not implicitly or explicitly endorse the status quo. For example, in presenting the idea that many people do not have access to work that is consistent with their interests, I am clearly not suggesting that this is an ideal state of affairs. Moreover, in providing less relative space to the topics covered in most career development, industrial/organizational (I/O) psychology, and psychotherapy books, I am not implying that we should abandon the tried-and-true methods of career counseling, organizational development, and psychotherapy. My objective in writing this book has been to give voice to those who have not had much voice in our research, practice, and social change efforts. As such, the lack of attention, for instance, to vocational interest inventories, is not intended to suggest that they are not of use to a wider array of workers. In contrast, I hope that the research and public policy advocacy efforts that arise from this book and related initiatives will result in interest inventories becoming increasingly relevant as more people experience the privilege of making decisions about the sort of work they will pursue.

The challenges that we face in mapping the psychology of working is that much of the terrain remains unexplored to date. Therefore, I have felt compelled to focus on the issues and themes not found in most scholarly contributions. In describing this world, I have sought to understand the fundamental human needs that working fulfills; much of this discussion has explored the lives of the have-nots, who often live in rather under-resourced environments. Entering this uncharted terrain has been challenging; however, I have sought to stress that describing this world does not translate into an endorsement of an increasingly divided society. Indeed, I believe that I have been profoundly transformed by this journey. Reading and researching in this area has inspired me even more fervently to advocate that the multifaceted talent that exists in psychology be applied creatively to the social and economic factors that develop and sustain a world of inequitable resources. The next section of this chapter explores some of the more promising directions for public policy efforts that may help to change the unjust economic and social circumstances that have been described throughout this volume.

Implications for Public Policy

I am aware that it may be premature to offer highly specified public policy suggestions for a field that is still taking shape. However, given the wealth of knowledge reviewed in this book from psychology and related disciplines, some preliminary ideas about the public policy implications from the psychology of working can be inferred. Prior to reviewing these recommendations, I would first like to outline some issues that may help researchers to enhance their impact as they move forward with some of the ideas presented in this book.

As I noted earlier in this book, interdisciplinary teams comprised of scholars from various fields interested in working may provide the optimal framework for effective policy-based research. It is clear that some of the most important research cited here has been produced by scholars outside of psychology (such as Newman, 1999; Wilson, 1996). Moreover, compelling arguments have been developed (cf. Brabeck et al., 1997) to support the importance and potential of interdisciplinary research for dealing with complex social problems. I encourage scholars to seek out colleagues both within psychology and outside of psychology who are invested in issues pertaining to working to form collaborative teams. As noted in the previous section, the individual focus that is so integral to psychology can be powerfully informative to sociologists, economists, and political scientists who tend to adopt more macro-level views.

Educational Reform

The debates and challenges of educational reform have evoked significant political discussions about evidence-based practice, the role of government in dealing with educational problems, and inherent sources of inequity in the U.S. opportunity structure (Hargreaves, 2000; Worthington & Juntunen, 1997). No doubt, similar reform issues are part of the political landscape of other nations, as governments seek to prepare high-quality students who will become an equally high-quality work force (Marshall & Tucker, 1992). Within the past decade or so, counseling psychologists and others who study vocational behavior have entered into this reform effort, primarily focusing on the school-to-work transition for non-college-bound youth (Blustein et al., 2000; Worthington & Juntunen, 1997). Given the fundamental role of education as a training ground for workers and as a powerful means of socialization, it would seem clear that some of the research that is conducted by psychologists who are studying work will have relevance for education, and vice versa. In addition, the pivotal role of education in providing people with the skills and resources needed for meaningful working lives suggests that the education–work linkage will continue to receive the attention that has characterized recent scholarly initiatives (e.g., Blustein et al., 2000; Lapan, 2004).

School-to-Work Transition.   As detailed in chapter 7, research on work-based transitions has provided extensive input on the factors that predict an adaptive transition from high school and college to work (Blustein et al., 2000; Bynner et al., 1997). A close examination of this research reveals particularly important implications for educational policymakers. One of the most important points described in numerous studies and reviews (e.g., Blustein et al., 2000; Lapan, 2004; Wilson, 1996) is that school and work ought to be connected explicitly in academic curriculum, support services, and extra-curricular activities. Thankfully, this is an area where some career development scholars have already carved out an important niche in U.S. federal government circles. For example, the development and revisions of the National Career Development Guidelines reflect the input of several vocational psychologists and counseling professionals (http://www.acrnetwork.org/ncdg.htm). A review of these national guidelines, as well as selected state guidelines (e.g., the Massachusetts Department of Education Career Development Education benchmarks; http://www.doe.mass.edu/cd/resources/), reveals that relevant scholarship has impacted on policy recommendations. For example, the guidelines now detail the need for counselors and educators to help students understand and internalize the connection between school and work.

Another impact that the psychology of working can have in educational policy may be at the level of developing sound arguments to support greater equity in funding the education of children and adolescents. One of the unfortunate aspects of U.S. education is the marked disparity that exists in schools, primarily related to the socioeconomic characteristics and often the racial and ethnic attributes of a given community. While compelling arguments have already been advanced to reduce these "savage inequalities" (Kozol, 1991), evidence developed from psychological studies of the school-to-work transition may help to buttress the existing rationales. For example, research that can chart the precise means by which effective schools help young people to develop the skills and attitudes that will generally predict adaptive work-related behaviors would help to enhance the case for greater equity in educational resources. Given that much of the policy debate in U.S. national and state capitals in recent years is devoted to cutting an ever-shrinking pie of public resources, the nature of the evidence would ideally integrate the psychological and moral consequences of inadequate schools with the economic costs.

Training and Post-Secondary Education. The psychology of working has considerable potential to inform policies that guide training and post-secondary education. The rapid evolution of the labor market is very likely going to lead to even greater job instability as people regularly must confront a reality that certain skills wax and wane in their viability (Hunt, 1995; Rifkin, 1995) with concomitant changes in employment options. The psychology-of-working perspective may offer some critically important ideas that policymakers can use in formulating new training structures and support services.

While the nature of the changes needed in training and post-secondary education are difficult to surmise at this point, some hints can be inferred from recent contributions in the literature (e.g., Collin & Young, 2000; Hunt, 1995). One of the key issues to integrate into future thinking about higher education is the reality that people will increasingly rely on colleges and universities throughout their lives to seek out training (Green & Hill, 2003). Naturally, this is not a new idea; many colleges and universities already offer courses, degree and certificate programs to adults in their communities. Embedding these programs and offerings with insights gleaned from the psychology of working may help to ensure that the programs are relevant and supportive of adults who are often struggling with many complex psychological issues while they seek out retraining.

In addition, the importance of providing training and post-secondary education in a manner that is constructed in conjunction with the prevailing cultural framework of a given community is critical. For example, scholarly efforts devoted to exploring how retraining can be presented in a culturally affirming manner may help to reduce the likely resistance that many adults will experience as they struggle with shifting work options. Another important policy implication that may grow out of psychological analyses of working is the serious consideration of the vast potential of community colleges to become major support systems for adults facing retraining. Given the importance of a supportive context for internalizing self-regulating attributes (Flum & Blustein, 2000; Lapan, 2004; Ryan & Deci, 2000), community colleges as well as traditional universities may benefit from research that delineates how these factors can be enhanced in a training and post-secondary context.

Unemployment Policy

In my view, one of the most promising areas for public policy influence for the psychology of working is in the realm of unemployment policy. The existence (and indeed tolerance) of structural unemployment strikes at the heart of some of the key assumptions of the psychology of working. As I have stated in previous chapters, working has the potential to fulfill a number of fundamental human needs. Empirical research (e.g., Caplan et al., 1997; Mallinckrodt & Bennett, 1992; O'Brien, 1986; Wanberg, 1995; Waters & Moore, 2002), coupled with vignettes scattered throughout this book, underscore the pervasive negative consequences of not being able to locate or sustain regular work. How, then, can the psychology of working impact on this pernicious aspect of life in contemporary market-based economies?

First, the literature reviewed here clearly supports the view that the challenge of unemployment and the potential for periodic or chronic increases in unemployment in the coming decades does have critical psychological consequences. As Rifkin (1995) and Wilson (1996) described in their often-chilling accounts of communities without sufficient connection to work, the inner life of individuals and the overall stability of neighborhoods is adversely impacted by the lack of work. Adding an explicitly psychological analysis of working to our understanding of unemployment may help to place a human face on what is often viewed as a macro-level problem. Thus, one of the key contributions that the psychology of working can make to the public discourse on unemployment is to ensure that the public is aware of the human costs of lack of work. The human costs can be documented using a variety of methods, including traditional quantitative approaches as well as narrative and discovery-oriented approaches.

Second, the psychological study of unemployment and underemployment may help to identify some meaningful ways for counselors, therapists, and others in one's life to help people who have little or no opportunity to obtain work. For example, by studying how people adjust to unemployment, it may be possible to learn more about the nature of resilience and risk in relation to working (Masten & Coatsworth, 1998). The study of resilience among unemployed individuals seeking employment may furnish scholars and policy analysts with important insights on how to structure maximally supportive contexts.

In effect, I envision that the psychology of working may inform policy for government officials and political leaders who face critical decisions about the vexing problem of chronic and acute unemployment. At the same time, the psychology of working may furnish ideas for designing effective and empowering counseling and psychoeducational interventions. As in other areas noted in this chapter (and elsewhere in this book), I encourage collaborations of psychologists and other social scientists in the study of unemployment so that the findings of our efforts are sufficiently embedded in the language and constructs that policymakers use.

I am hopeful that subsequent research on the psychology of working ideally will lead to the development of a coherent rationale supportive of policies directed toward full employment. I realize that the call for full employment may seem outdated or naïve on my part. However, given my reading of the empirical and theoretical literature on working, extensive hours counseling unemployed adults, and reading the evocative accounts of people living without work, I do believe that this objective needs to be revisited. The gradual rise in the "acceptable levels" of unemployment in North America and Europe is quite troublesome, especially given the dramatic human cost that has been detailed in the literature. While it is clearly easier to call for full employment as opposed to creating the structures that will culminate in expanded employment opportunities, the reality is that without the statement of this objective, we ensure that we will not achieve this notable goal. Psychologists studying working will need to collaborate with economists, sociologists, and policy analysts to explore the moral and financial costs of accepting certain levels of chronic unemployment as opposed to seeking innovative solutions that create more opportunities for work. Research and theory emerging from the psychology of working may also be informative about the most optimal means of creating more employment opportunities. In particular, the self-determination literature (Ryan & Deci, 2000) may furnish illuminating ideas about the assets and limitations of government-based employment. At the same time, the psychological costs and benefits of a strict reliance on the market to create jobs can be ascertained.

Mental Health Issues and Working

The role of working in sustaining healthy psychological functioning has been apparent since Freud's (1930) prescient dictum about the importance of work and love. As Shore and Massimo (1979; Shore, 1998) have observed, a considerable body of empirical literature supports the view that a return to work is a highly potent predictor of a successful recovery from a psychological crisis or illness. I believe that subsequent research in the psychological study of working will reveal even more pervasive and complex relationships between working and variations in mental health. Of course, the conditions in which one is working have a considerable impact on one's mental health. Thus, there may be times when having no work may be more facilitative of mental health when compared to work wherein one is exposed to abuse or high levels of stress.

Advances in the psychological study of working may help in the design of employee assistance programs, which have often been developed without much attention to the working context. In addition, the psychology of working may inform policy directed toward the development of less stressful and healthier work environments. However, I believe that one of the most important policy implications may emerge as research reveals the fundamental striving of people to ensure their own survival, develop and sustain relational connections, and establish self-determined conditions in their lives. By providing people with the opportunity to manifest these aspirations, it is likely that people will experience less stress and hence will be less likely to suffer dramatic fluctuations in their mental health. I am not suggesting that improving access to dignified work will radically decrease the prevalence of such illnesses as schizophrenia and bipolar disorders, which are linked to significant genetic and biological factors. However, the reduction of stresses related to locating work and sustaining work may help to diminish the intensity of these painful illnesses and perhaps provide greater resources for more meaningful rehabilitation policies. For less pernicious psychological disorders, I believe that working can provide the potential for the fulfillment of many of our fundamental human needs that would help to reduce or diminish the severity of conditions such as depression, anxiety, and other mental health problems.

The policy implications of the psychological study of working in the mental health field can have dramatic effects for highly marginalized cohorts of our population. As I indicated earlier in this chapter, the questions about the meaning of work for individuals with severely incapacitating conditions need to be explored in light of emerging theory and research on the psychology of working. In addition, exploring the complex space that exists between the context of one's work life and one's inner psychological functioning may help to inform policies on sexual harassment, racism at work, and other forms of social oppression. As I present in the next section of this chapter, the existence of these socially oppressive conditions at work (and in the education and job-selection processes) offers policymakers an opportunity to establish programs and laws that will help to prohibit racism, sexism, homophobia, classism, ageism, and discrimination against individuals with developmental and psychiatric disabling conditions.

Social and Interpersonal Oppression at Work

As I noted in previous chapters, working functions as a focal point for our inter-actions with the social world. As such, individuals are often exposed to very pain-ful interactions wherein racism, sexism, heterosexism, and other forms of social oppression are expressed both explicitly and implicitly. Fitzgerald (e.g., 2003), who has explored the impact of sexual harassment at the workplace, provides an excellent exemplar of how scholarship on the interface of work and social oppres-sion can yield important implications for public policy. Subsequent research on the role of gender, sexual orientation, aging, social class, and ability/disability sta-tus may yield important insights about how the work context serves as a vehicle for the sustenance of inequality. This information can then be transformed in po-sition papers, legislative initiatives, and lobbying efforts directed toward the re-duction and ideally the elimination of social oppression at work.

Another potential policy domain has to do with interpersonal forms of op-pression at work. A number of recent contributions (e.g., Crawford, 1997; Lewis, 2004; Rayner & Keashly, 2005) have explored the phenomenon of bul-lying at work. Further work in this area, informed by the psychology of work-ing, may facilitate the development of work-based policies and governmental regulations that will reduce the incidence of bullying at work. The literature on bullying at work has demonstrated the importance of understanding the psychological attributes of both the individuals and the context of a work-place. Ideally, collaborations with other psychologists and social scientists studying interpersonal and social forms of oppression at work may help to in-form the training efforts and policies needed to establish more humane working environments.

Cultural Knowledge: The Psychology of Working

A related point that may fuel policy implications relates to the growing knowl-edge base about the cultural context that frames our understanding of working. As detailed in previous chapters, the nature of working is very much an inher-ent part of a culture's belief systems and individual worldviews (e.g., Carter & Cook, 1992; Wallman 1979). As the North American and European work forces become increasingly diverse, the knowledge that cultural variations exist and need to be affirmed will ideally grow. Research and practice efforts emerg-ing from the psychology of working have thus far revealed that people construct their working lives and needs in a manner rooted within their culture (Carter & Cook, 1992; Flum & Blustein, 2000; Helms & Cook, 1999; Stead, 2004).

Considering variations in the composition of the work force in tandem with globalization, characterized by growing levels of multinational trade and exchange, may make it possible for people to affirm the diversity that exists across the planet. I realize that my vision here is quite optimistic; however, in keeping with the notion that psychology can be a force for social change, I hope that psychologists and counselors consider providing workshops for young adults and adults, both at work and looking for work, which will highlight the importance of culture and diversity in contemporary working contexts. The policy implications of the changing world of work and the growing diversity of work forces in Europe and North America may help to frame psychoeducational efforts directed toward reducing racism, classism, and other forms of human differences.

Summary of Policy Implications

The policy implications outlined here are limited by my own vision, which is further inhibited by the relatively modest level of research on the psychology of working. I am aware that I have outlined an ambitious agenda that suggests a level of facility with public policy that is not typical among many social and behavioral scientists and counselors. However, the psychology of working is a field that ideally is integrally connected with public policy. By moving our vision beyond the confines of the affluent and privileged, we force ourselves to reckon with a world that generally does not offer many choices with respect to work. In facing this world directly, I believe that we have a valuable opportunity for sustained and positive internal development of our professional identities. In effect, as we move from the inner world of our clients and research participants to a clear focus on their outer world, we will necessarily expand our skill set such that it includes engagement with social justice issues and public policy (cf. Blustein et al., 2005). The foundations for public policy-oriented scholarship are evident throughout the psychological literature (e.g., Fitzgerald, 2003; Helms et al., 2005; Prilleltensky, 2003). These resources provide a road map and the moral rationale that may fuel the design and dissemination of policy-oriented research on the psychology of working.

Conclusion

In this chapter, I have sought to integrate the material presented in this book across several relevant dimensions. First, I have identified themes about the psychology of working that transcend the boundaries of the specific chapters and topics. Second, I have described a number of dialectical issues that underlie many of the concerns that will emerge from the psychology of working. Ideally, knowledge about these inherent tensions will serve to enrich the complexity, depth, and ultimately, the utility, of subsequent research and theory development in the psychology of working.

The third section of this chapter focused on the description of public policy implications that may emerge from the psychology of working. As I have presented, the psychological study of working is inherently linked to broader political, economic, and social contexts. The contributions of psychology to existing debates about the nature of working and the future of working are critical, in my view, to developing policies that build on existing knowledge.

The struggles of people to find meaningful and dignified work, support their families, and connect to the social world have inspired this effort. Indeed, it is these brave souls with whom I have spent countless hours as clients in counseling and as participants in research studies, who have so powerfully affected my work life and worldview. I am hopeful that this book will help all workers and potential workers to receive the best of what psychology has to offer. Ideally, this book will result in an expanded vision for our field, both in terms of breadth and depth. By expanding our vision of the psychological aspects of working, I believe that we are in a much better position to create a fully engaged psychology that supports working as a fundamental human act that is the birthright of each person.

REFERENCES

Aamodt, M. (1996). *Applied industrial/organizational psychology* (2nd ed.). Belmont, CA: Brooks/Cole.

Adams, J. S. (1965). Inequity in social exchange. In L. Berkowitz (Ed.), *Advances in experimental social psychology* (Vol. 2, pp. 528–535). New York: Academic Press.

Ainsworth, M. (1989). Attachments beyond infancy. *American Psychologist, 44,* 709–716.

American Counseling Association. (2005). *ACA Code of Ethics and Standards of Practice.* Retrieved December 26, 2005 from http://www.counseling.org/resources/ethics.htm

American Psychological Association. (2002). *Ethical Principles of Psychologists and Code of Conduct.* Retrieved June 21, 2005 from http://www.apa.org/ethics/code2002.html

Americans with Disabilities Act of 1990. (Pub. L. No. 101–336, §2, 104 Stat. 328).

Amundson, N. E., Borgen, W. A., Jordan, S., & Erlebach, A. C. (2004). Survivors of downsizing: Helpful and hindering experiences. *Career Development Quarterly, 52,* 256–271.

Andersen, M., & Collins, P. (1992). *Race, class, and gender: An anthology.* Belmont, CA: Wadsworth Publishing Company.

Anderson, N., Ones, D. S., Sinangil, H. K., & Viswesvaran, C. (Eds.). (2002). *Handbook of industrial, work and organizational psychology, Vol. 1: Personnel psychology.* Thousand Oaks, CA: Sage Publications.

Angrosino, M. V., & Mays de Pérez, K. A. (2000). Rethinking observation: From method to context. In N. K. Denzin & Y. S. Lincoln (Eds.), *Handbook of qualitative research* (2nd ed., pp. 673–715). Thousand Oaks, CA: Sage.

Applebaum, H. (1984). *Work in non-market and transitional societies.* Albany, NY: State University of New York Press.

Aquino, J., Russell, D., Cutrona, C., & Altmaier, E. (1996). Employment status, social support, and life satisfaction among the elderly. *Journal of Counseling Psychology, 43,* 480–489.

Aronfreed, J. (1970). The socialization of altruistic and sympathetic behavior: Some theoretical and experimental analyses. In J. Macaulay & L. Berkowitz (Eds.), *Altruism and helping behavior* (pp. 103–126). New York: Academic Press.

Arbona, C. (1990). Career counseling research with Hispanics: A review of the literature. *The Counseling Psychologist, 18,* 300–323.

Arbona, C. (1995). Theory and research on racial and ethnic minorities: Hispanic Americans. In F. T. L. Leong (Ed.), *Career development and vocational behavior of racial and ethnic minorities* (pp. 37–66). Hillsdale, NJ: Lawrence Erlbaum Associates.

Arbona, C. (2000). Practice and research in career counseling and development—1999. *Career Development Quarterly, 49,* 98–134.

Aronowitz, S., & Cutler, J. (1998). *Post-work: The wages of cybernation.* New York: Routledge.

Arthur, M. B., Hall, D. T., & Lawrence, B. S. (Eds.). (1989). *Handbook of career theory.* New York: Cambridge University Press.

Arthur, M. B., & Rousseau, D. M. (Eds.). (1996). *The boundaryless career.* New York: Oxford University Press.

Aryee, S., & Chay, Y. (2001). Workplace justice, citizenship behavior, and turnover intentions in a union context: Examining the mediating role of perceived union support and union instrumentality. *Journal of Applied Psychology, 86,* 154–160.

Ascher, C. (1998). Improving the school–home connection for poor and minority urban students. *Urban Review, 20,* 109–123.

Astin, H. (1984). The meaning of work in women's lives: A sociopsychological model of career choice and work behavior. *The Counseling Psychologist, 12,* 117–126.

Atwood, G., Orange, D., & Stolorow, R. (2002). Shattered worlds/psychotic states: A post-Cartesian view of the experience of personal annihilation. *Psychoanalytic Psychology, 19,* 281–306.

Axelrod, S. D. (1999). *Work and the evolving self: Theoretical and clinical considerations.* Hillsdale, NJ: The Analytic Press.

Azrin, N. H., & Philip, R. A. (1979). The job club method for the job-handicapped: A comparative outcome study. *Rehabilitation Counseling Bulletin, 2,* 144–155.

Azrin, N. H., Phillip, R. A., Thienes-Hontos, P., & Besalel, V. A. (1981). Follow-up on welfare bene-fits received by Job Club clients. *Journal of Vocational Behavior, 18,* 253–254.

Bailyn, L. (1989). Understanding individual experience at work: Comments on the theory and prac-tice of careers. In M. B. Arthur & D. T. Hall, (Eds.), *Handbook of career theory* (pp. 477–489). New York, NY: Cambridge University Press.

Baker, S. B., & Taylor, J. G. (1998). Effects of career education interventions: A meta-analysis. *Ca-reer Development Quarterly, 46,* 376–385.

Bamber, G., & Lansbury, R. (1998). *International and comparative employment relations: A study of industrialized market economies.* London: Sage Publications.

Bandura, A. (1986). *Social foundations of thought and action: A social cognitive theory.* Englewood Cliffs, NJ: Prentice Hall.

Bankart, P. (1997). *Talking cures: A history of Western and Eastern psychotherapies.* Pacific Grove, CA: Brooks/Cole.

Banks, N. (2002). Counseling Black employees facing racism and discrimination. In S. Palmer (Ed.), *Multicultural counseling: A reader* (pp. 82–91). Thousand Oaks, CA: Sage Publications.

Barkham, M., & Shapiro, D. (1990). Brief psychotherapeutic interventions for job-related distress: A pilot study of prescriptive and exploratory therapy. *Counseling Psychology Quarterly, 3,* 133–147.

Barling, J., & Griffiths, A. (2003). A history of occupational health psychology. In J. C. Quick & L. E. Tetrick (Eds.), *Handbook of occupational health psychology* (pp. 19–31). Washington, DC: Amer-ican Psychological Association.

Barlow, D. (2004). Psychological treatments. *American Psychologist, 59,* 869–878.

Barnett, R. C., & Hyde, J. S. (2001). Women, men, work, and family: An expansionist theory. *Ameri-can Psychologist, 56,* 781–796.

Barrios de Chungara, D. (1978). *Let me speak: Testimony of Domitila, a woman of the Bolivian mines.* New York: Monthly Review Press.

Beck, A. (1987). Cognitive models of depression. *Journal of Cognitive Psychotherapy, 1,* 5–37.

Bell, H. M. (1938). *Youth tell their story.* Washington, DC: American Council on Education.

Belion, K., & Peterson, M. (2000). For richer or poorer: Building inclusive schools in poor urban and rural communities. *International Journal of Disability, Development & Education, 47,* 15–24.

Bergin, A., & Garfield, S. (1994). *Handbook of psychotherapy and behavior change.* Oxford: John Wiley & Sons.

Bergman, S. J. (1995). Men's psychological development: A relational perspective. In R. F. Levant & W. S. Pollack (Eds.), *A new psychology of men* (pp. 68–90). New York: Basic Books.

Berridge, J. (1999). Employee assistance programs and stress counseling: At a crossroads. In C. Feltham (Ed.), *Controversies in psychotherapy and counseling* (pp. 252–268). London: Sage Publications.

Bettenson, H. S. (1947). *Documents of the Christian Church.* New York: Oxford University Press.

Betz, N. E. (1989). Implications of the null hypothesis for women's career development and for counseling psychology. *The Counseling Psychologist, 17,* 136–144.

Betz, N. E. (1992). Counseling uses of self-efficacy theory. *Career Development Quarterly, 41,* 22–26.

Betz, N. E. (1993). Toward the integration of multicultural and career psychology. *Career Develop-ment Quarterly, 42,* 53–55.

Betz, N. E., & Corning, A. F. (1993). The inseparability of career and personal counseling. *The Career Development Quarterly, 42,* 137–142.

Betz, N. E., & Fitzgerald, L. (1987). *The career psychology of women.* Orlando, FL: Academic Press.

Betz, N. E., & Hackett, G. (1981). The relationship of career-related self-efficacy expectations to perceived career options in college women and men. *Journal of Counseling Psychology, 28,* 399–410.

Black, B. (1988). *Work and mental illness: Transitions to employment. The Johns Hopkins series in con-temporary medicine and public health.* Baltimore, MD: Johns Hopkins University Press.

Bladassarri, M., & Paganetto, L. (1996). *The 1990s slump: Causes and cures.* New York: St. Martin's Press.

Bloch, D. P. (1991). Missing measures of the who and why of school dropouts: Implications for policy and research. *Career Development Quarterly, 40,* 36–47.

Bloch, D. P. (2004). Spirituality, complexity, and career counseling. *Professional School Counseling, 7,* 343–350.

Blos, P. (1962). *On adolescence: A psychoanalytic interpretation.* Oxford: Free Press of Glencoe.

Blustein, D. L. (1987). Integrating career counseling and psychotherapy: A comprehensive treatment strategy. *Psychotherapy: Theory, Research, Practice, and Training, 24,* 794–799.

Blustein, D. L. (1989). The role of goal instability and career self-efficacy in the career exploration process. *Journal of Vocational Behavior, 35,* 194–203.

Blustein, D. L. (1994). The question of "Who am I?": A cross-theoretical analysis. In M. L. Savickas & R. W. Lent (Eds.), *Convergence in career development theories: Implications for science and practice* (pp. 134–154). Palo Alto, CA: Consulting Psychologist Press.

Blustein, D. L. (2001a). Extending the reach of vocational psychology: Toward an inclusive and integrative psychology of working. *Journal of Vocational Behavior, 59,* 171–182.

Blustein, D. L. (2001b). The interface of work and relationships: A critical knowledge base for 21st century psychology. *The Counseling Psychologist, 29,* 179–192.

Blustein, D. L., Chaves, A. P., Diemer, M. A., Gallagher, L. A., Marshall, K. G., Sirin, S., & Bhati, K. S. (2002). Voices of the forgotten half: The role of social class in the school-to-work transition. *Journal of Counseling Psychology, 49,* 311–323.

Blustein, D. L., Fama, L. D., White, S. F., Ketterson, T. U., Schaefer, B. M., Schwam, M. F., Sirin, S. R., & Skau, M. (2001). A qualitative analysis of counseling case material: Listening to our clients. *The Counseling Psychologist, 29,* 240–258.

Blustein, D. L., & Flum, H. (1999). A self-determination perspective of exploration and interests in career development. In M. L. Savickas & A. Spokane (Eds.), *Vocational interests: Their meaning, measurement, and use in counseling.* Palo Alto, CA: Davies-Black Publishing.

Blustein, D. L., Juntunen, C. L., & Worthington, R. L. (2000). The school-to-work transition: Adjustment challenges of the forgotten half. In S. D. Brown & R. W. Lent (Eds.), *Handbook of counseling psychology* (3rd. ed., pp. 435–470). New York: Wiley.

Blustein, D. L., McWhirter, E. H., & Perry, J. (2005). An emancipatory communitarian approach to vocational development theory, research, and practice. *The Counseling Psychologist, 33,* 141–179.

Blustein, D. L., & Noumair, D. A. (1996). Self and identity in career development: Implications for theory and practice. *Journal of Counseling and Development, 74,* 433–441.

Blustein, D. L., Phillips, S. D., Jobin-Davis, K., Finkelberg, S. L., & Roarke, A. E. (1997). A theory-building investigation of the school-to-work transition. *The Counseling Psychologist, 25,* 364–402.

Blustein, D. L., Prezioso, M. S., & Schultheiss, D. P. (1995). Attachment theory and career development: Current status and future directions. *The Counseling Psychologist, 23,* 416–432.

Blustein, D. L., Schultheiss, D. E. P., & Flum, H. (2004). Toward a relational perspective of the psychology of careers and working: A social constructionist analysis. *Journal of Vocational Behavior, 64,* 423–440.

Blustein, D. L., & Spengler, P. (1995). Personal adjustment: Career counseling and psychotherapy. In B. Walsh & S. Osipow (Eds.), *Handbook of vocational psychology: Theory, research, and practice* (2nd ed., pp. 295–329). Hillsdale, NJ: Lawrence Erlbaum Associates.

Blustein, D. L., Walbridge, M., Friedlander, M., & Palladino, D. (1991). Contributions of psychological separation and parental attachment to the career development process. *Journal of Counseling Psychology, 38,* 39–50.

Boatwright, K., Gilbert, M., Forrest, L., & Ketzenberger, K. (1996). Impact of identity development upon career trajectory: Listening to the voices of lesbian women. *Journal of Vocational Behavior, 48,* 210–228.

Bohart, A., & Greenberg, L. (1997). *Empathy reconsidered: New directions in psychotherapy.* Washington, DC: American Psychological Association.

Bogart, G. (1994). Finding a life's calling. *Journal of Humanistic Psychology, 34,* 6–37.

Bolles, R. N., & Bolles, M. E. (2005). *What color is your parachute? 2005: A practical manual for job-hunters and career-changers.* Berkeley, CA: Ten Speed Press.

Bond, G., & Boyer, S. (1988). Rehabilitation programs and outcomes. In J. Ciardiello & M. Bell (Eds), *Vocational rehabilitation of persons with prolonged psychiatric disorders.* Baltimore, MD: Johns Hopkins University Press.

Bordin, E. (1979). The generalizability of the psychoanalytic concept of the working alliance. *Psychotherapy: Theory, Research & Practice, 16,* 252–260.

Borgen, W. A., & Amundson, N. E. (1984). *The experience of unemployment*. Toronto, Canada: Nelson.

Borman, K. M. (1991). *The first "real" job: A study of young workers*. Albany, NY: State University of New York Press.

Bowe, J., Bowe, M., & Streeter, S. (2000). *Gig: Americans talk about their jobs*. New York: Three Rivers Press.

Bowen, M. (1978). *Family therapy in clinical practice*. New York: Aronson.

Bowlby, J. (1982). Attachment and loss: Retrospect and prospect. *American Journal of Orthopsychiatry, 52,* 664–678.

Bowlby, J. (1988). *A secure base: Parent–child attachment and healthy human development*. New York: Basic Books.

Boyd, D., & Stevens, G. (2002). *Current readings in lifespan development*. Boston: Allyn & Bacon.

Brabeck, M., & Ting, K. (2000). Feminist ethics: Lenses for examining ethical psychological practice. In. M. E. Brabeck (Ed.), *Practicing feminist ethics in psychology* (pp. 17–35). Washington, DC: American Psychological Association.

Brabeck, M., Walsh, M., Kenny, M., & Comilang, K. (1997). Interprofessional collaboration for children and families: Opportunities for counseling psychology in the 21st century. *The Counseling Psychologist, 25,* 615–636.

Brockner, J. (1988). Self-esteem at work: Research, theory, and practice. *Issues in organization and management series*. Lexington, MA: Lexington Books/D. C. Heath.

Brodsky, A. (2003). *With all of our strength: The revolutionary association of the women of Afghanistan*. New York: Routledge.

Brooks, L., & Forrest, L. (1994). Feminism and career counseling. In W. B. Walsh & S. H. Osipow (Eds.), *Career counseling for women* (pp. 878–134). Hillsdale, NJ: Lawrence Erlbaum Associates.

Brooks, G. (2001). Masculinity and men's mental health. *Journal of American College Health, 49,* 285–297.

Brooks, G., & Good, G. (2001). *The new handbook of psychotherapy and counseling with men: A comprehensive guide to settings, problems, and treatment approaches* (Vols. 1 & 2). San Francisco: Jossey-Bass.

Brown, D. (Ed.). (2002a). *Career choice and development* (4th ed.). San Francisco: Jossey Bass.

Brown, D. (2002b). The role of work and cultural values in occupational choice, satisfaction, and success: A theoretical statement. *Journal of Counseling & Development, 80,* 48–56.

Brown, K., & Ryan, R. (2003). The benefits of being present: Mindfulness and its role in psychological well-being. *Journal of Personality and Social Psychology, 84,* 822–848.

Brown, M. T., Fukunaga, C., Umemoto, D., & Wicker, L. (1996). Annual review 1990–1996: Social class, work, and retirement behavior. *Journal of Vocational Behavior, 49,* 159–189.

Brown, M. T., & Pinterits, E. J. (2001). Basic issues in the career counseling of African Americans. In W. B. Walsh, R. P. Bingham, M. T. Brown, & C. M. Ward (Eds.), *Career counseling for African Americans* (pp. 1–25). Mahwah, NJ: Lawrence Erlbaum Associates.

Brown, R., & Josephs, R. (1999). A burden of proof: Stereotype relevance and gender differences in math performance. *Journal of Personality and Social Psychology, 76,* 246–257.

Brown, S. D., & Lent, R. W. (1996). A social cognitive framework for career choice counseling. *Career Development Quarterly, 44,* 354–366.

Brown, S. D., & Lent, R. W. (Eds.). (2005). *Career development and counseling: Putting theory and research to work*. Hoboken, NJ: John Wiley & Sons.

Brown, S. D., & Krane, N. E. R. (2000). Four (or five) sessions and a cloud of dust: Old assumptions and new observations about career counseling. In S. D. Brown & R. W. Lent (Eds.), *Handbook of counseling psychology* (3rd ed., pp. 740–766). New York: Wiley.

Brownlee, W. (1974). *Dynamics of ascent: A history of the American economy*. Santa Barbara: Alfred A. Knopf, Inc.

Burr, V. (1995). *An introduction to social constructionism*. Florence, KY: Taylor & Frances/ Routledge.

Bynner, J., Ferri, E., & Shepherd, P. (Eds.). (1997). *Twenty-something in the 1990s: Getting on, getting by, getting nowhere*. Brookfield, VT: Ashgate Publishing Company.

Bynner, J., & Parsons, S. (2002). Social exclusion and the transition from school to work: The Case of young people not in education, employment, or training (NEET). *Journal of Vocational Behavior, 60,* 289–309.

Campbell, E. (2003). Interviewing men in uniform: A feminist approach? *International Journal of Social Research Methodology: Theory and Practice, 4,* 285–304.

Caplan, R. D., Vinokur, A. D., & Price, R. H. (1997). From job loss to reemployment: Field experiments in prevention-focused coping. In G. W. Albee & T. P. Gulotta (Eds.), *Primary prevention works: Vol. 6. Issues in children's and families' lives* (pp. 314–380). Thousand Oaks, CA: Sage.

Cappelli, P. (2004). Why do employers retrain at-risk workers? The role of social capital. *Industrial Relations, 43*, 421–427.

Carter, R. T., & Cook, D. A. (1992). A culturally relevant perspective for understanding the career paths of visible racial/ethnic group people. In H. D. Lea & Z. B. Leibowitz (Eds.), *Adult career development: Concepts, issues, and practice* (pp. 192–217). Alexandria, VA: National Career Development Association.

Cartwright, D., & Zander, A. (1968). *Group dynamics*. Oxford: Harper and Row.

Chan, F., Berven, N., & Thomas, K. (2004). *Counseling theories and techniques for rehabilitation health professionals*. New York: Springer.

Chaves, A., Diemer, M., Blustein, D., Gallagher, L., DeVoy, J., Casares, M., & Perry, J. (2004). Conceptions of work: The view from urban youth. *Journal of Counseling Psychology, 51*, 275–286.

Chun, C., & Sue, S. (1998). Mental health issues concerning Asian Pacific American children. In V. O. Pang & L. L. Cheng (Eds.), *Struggling to be heard: The unmet needs of Asian Pacific American children* (pp. 75–88). New York: State University of New York Press.

Chung, B. (2001). Work discrimination and coping strategies: Conceptual frameworks for counseling lesbian, gay, and bisexual clients. *Career Development Quarterly, 50*, 33–44.

Chung, B. (2003). Career counseling with lesbian, gay, bisexual, and transgendered persons: The next decade. *Career Development Quarterly, 52*, 78–85.

Chusid, H., & Cochran, L. (1989). Meaning of career change from the perspective of family roles and dramas. *Journal of Counseling Psychology, 36*, 34–41.

Cinamon, R. G., & Gifsh, L. (2004). Conceptions of work among adolescents and young adults with mental retardation. *Career Development Quarterly, 52*, 212–224.

Cinamon, R. G., & Rich, Y. (2002). Profiles of attribution of importance to life roles and their implications for the work-family conflict. *Journal of Counseling Psychology, 49*, 212–220.

Clark, R., Anderson, N. B., Clark, V. R., & Williams, D. R. (1999). Racism as a stressor for African Americans: A biopsychosocial model. *American Psychologist, 54*, 805–816.

Clawson, D., & Clawson, M. A. (1999). What has happened to the U.S. labor movement? Union decline and renewal. *Annual Review of Sociology, 25*, 95–119.

Cochran, S. (2001). Psychotherapy with men navigating midlife terrain. In G. Brooks & G. Good (Eds.), *The new handbook of psychotherapy and counseling with men: A comprehensive guide to settings, problems, and treatment approaches* (Vol. 1, pp. 444–463). San Francisco: Jossey-Bass.

Cohen, R., & Swerdlik, M. (2002). *Psychological testing and assessment: An introduction to test and measurement*. New York: McGraw-Hill.

Cohn, J. (1997). The effects of racial and ethnic discrimination on the career development of minority persons. In H. S. Farmer (Ed.), *Diversity & women's career development: From adolescence to adulthood* (pp. 161–171). Thousand Oaks, CA: Sage Publications.

Cole, T., & Stevenson, D. (1999). The meaning of age and the future of social security. In D. Boyd & G. Stevens (Eds.), *Current readings in lifespan development* (pp. 72–76). Boston: Allyn & Bacon.

Collin, A., & Young, R. A. (Eds.). (2000). *The future of career*. Cambridge, UK: Cambridge University Press.

Cooper, C., & Lewis, S. (1999). Gender and the changing nature of work. In G. N. Powell (Ed.), *Handbook of gender and work* (pp. 37–46). Thousand Oaks, CA: Sage Publications.

Crawford, N. (1997). Bullying at work: A psychoanalytic perspective. *Journal of Community & Applied Social Psychology, 7*, 219–225.

Creed, P. A., Hicks, R. E., & Machin, M. A. (1998). Behavioral plasticity and mental health outcomes for long-term unemployed attending occupational training programs. *Journal of Occupational & Organizational Psychology, 71*, 171–191.

Creed, P. A., Bloxsome, T., & Johnston, K. (2001). Self-esteem and self-efficacy outcomes for unemployed individuals attending occupational skills training programs. *Community, Work & Family, 4*, 285–303.

Croteau, J., & Bieschke, K. (1996). Beyond pioneering: An introduction to the special issue on the vocational issues of lesbian women and gay men. *Journal of Vocational Behavior, 48*, 119–124.

Dalla, R. L. (2002). Night moves: A qualitative investigation of street-level sex work. *Psychology of Women Quarterly, 26*, 63–73.

Danziger, S. H., & Haveman, R. H. (Eds.). (2001). *Understanding poverty*. Cambridge, MA: Harvard University Press.

Davidson, M., & Fielden, S. (1999). Stress and the working woman. In G. Powell (Ed.), *Handbook of gender and work* (pp. 413–426). California: Sage Publications.

Davis, H. V. (1969). *Frank Parsons: Prophet, innovator, counselor.* Carbondale: University of Southern Illinois Press.

Davis, M. H. (1983). Measuring individual differences in empathy: Evidence for a multidimensional approach. *Journal of Personality and Social Psychology, 44,* 113–126.

Dawis, R. V. (2002). Person–environment correspondence theory. In D. Brown (Ed.), *Career choice and development* (pp. 427–464). San Francisco: Jossey-Bass.

Dearborn, W. E., & Rothney, J. W. (1938). *Scholastic, economic, and social backgrounds of unemployed youth.* Cambridge, MA: Harvard University Press.

Deci, E. L. (1975). *Intrinsic motivation.* New York: Plenum.

Deci, E. L., & Ryan, R. M. (1985). *Intrinsic motivation and self-determination in human behavior.* New York: Plenum.

Deci, E. L., & Ryan, R. M. (2000). The "what" and "why" of goal pursuits: Human needs and self-determination of behavior. *Psychological Inquiry, 11,* 227–268.

De la Peña, T. (1995). Fiction into fact. In R. A. Rasi & L. Roddriguez-Nogues (Eds.), *Out in the workplace: The pleasures and perils of coming out on the job* (pp. 24–30). Los Angeles, CA: Alyson Publications.

Denzin, N., & Lincoln, Y. (2000). *Handbook of qualitative research.* Thousand Oaks, CA: Sage Publications.

Devine, P. G. (1995). Prejudice and out-group perception. In A. Tesser (Ed.), *Advanced social psychology* (pp. 467–524). Boston: McGraw-Hill.

Diamond, J. (1999). *Guns, germs, and steel: The fates of human societies.* New York, NY: W. W. Norton & Company.

Diener, E., & Seligman, M. (2004). Beyond money: Toward an economy of well-being. *Psychological Science in the Public Interest, 5,* 1–31.

Doherty, W. (1995). *Soul searching: Why psychotherapy must promote moral responsibility.* New York: Basic Books.

Dooley, D. (2003). Unemployment, underemployment, and mental health: Conceptualizing employment status as a continuum. *American Journal of Community Psychology, 32,* 9–21.

Donkin, R. (2001). *Blood, sweat, & tears: The evolution of work.* New York: Texere.

Dowrick, P., Power, T., Manz, P., Ginsberg-Block, M., Leff, S., & Kim-Rupnow, S. (2001). Community responsiveness: Examples from under-resourced urban schools. *Journal of Prevention & Intervention in the Community, 21,* 71–90.

Drenth, P., Thierry, H., & Wolff, C. de (1998). *Handbook of work and organizational psychology: Vol. 1. Introduction to work and organizational psychology* (2nd ed.). Hove, England: Psychology Press/Taylor & Francis.

Drucker, P. (1999). *Management challenges for the 21st century.* New York: Harper Business.

Duan, C., & Hill, C. (1996). The current state of empathy research. *Journal of Counseling Psychology, 43,* 261–274.

Dunkle, J. H. (1996). Toward an integration of gay and lesbian identity development and Super's life-span approach. *Journal of Vocational Behavior, 48,* 149–159.

Edwards, R. (1993). *Rights at work.* Washington, DC: Brookings Institution.

Educational Health and Welfare Department. (1973). *Work in America: Report of a special task force to the U.S. Department of Health, Education, and Welfare.* Boston: The MIT Press.

Eisner, E. (2004). Multiple intelligences: Its tensions and possibilities. *Teachers College Record, 106,* 31–39.

Ellwood, D. T., Blank, R. M., Blasi, J., Kruse, D., Niskanen, W. A., & Lynn-Dyson, K. (2000). *A working nation: Workers, work, and government in the new economy.* New York: Russell Sage Foundation.

Epstein, M. (1995). *Thoughts without a thinker: Psychoanalysis from a Buddhist perspective.* New York: Basic Books.

Erikson, E. (1950). *Childhood and society.* Oxford, England: Norton & Co.

Erikson, E. (1968). *Identity: Youth and crisis.* Oxford, England: Norton & Co.

Etzioni, A. (1991). *A responsive society.* San Francisco: Jossey-Bass.

Evans, J. H., & Burck, H. D. (1992). The effects of career education interventions on academic achievement: A meta-analysis. *Journal of Counseling & Development, 71,* 63–68.

Falk, A. (1993). Immigrant settlement: Health and social supports. In R. Masi & L. Mensah (Eds.), *Health and cultures: Programs, services, and care* (pp. 307–329). Buffalo, NY: Mosaic Press.

Farmer, H. S. (1985). Model of career and achievement motivation for women and men. *Journal of Counseling Psychology, 32,* 363–390.

Farmer, H. S. (Ed.). (1997). *Diversity & women's career development: From adolescence to adulthood.* Thousand Oaks, CA: Sage Publications.

Fassinger, R. (1987). Use of structural equation modeling in counseling psychology research. *Journal of Counseling Psychology, 34,* 425–436.

Fassinger, R. E. (1996). Notes from the margins: Integrating lesbian experiences into the vocational psychology of women. *Journal of Vocational Behavior, 48,* 160–175.

Fassinger, R. E. (2000). Gender and sexuality in human development: Implications for prevention and advocacy in counseling psychology. In S. D. Brown & R. W. Lent (Eds.), *Handbook of counseling psychology* (3rd ed., pp. 345–378). New York: Wiley.

Feeney, J., & Noller, P. (1990). Attachment style as a predictor of adult romantic relationships. *Journal of Personality and Social Psychology, 58,* 281–291.

Ferrie, J. E. (2001). Is job insecurity harmful to health? *Journal Royal Society Medicine, 94,* 71–76.

Feshbach, D. L. (1997). Empathy: The formative years—Implications for clinical practice. In A. C. Bohart & L. S. Greenberg (Eds.), *Empathy reconsidered: New directions in psychotherapy* (pp. 33–59). Washington, DC: American Psychological Association.

Festinger, L. (1957). *A theory of cognitive dissonance.* Evanston, IL: Row, Peterson.

Fine, M. (2003). Silencing and nurturing voice in an improbable context: Urban adolescents in public school. In M. Fine & L. Weis (Eds.), *Silenced voices and extraordinary conversations: Re-imagining schools* (pp. 13–37). New York: Teachers College Press.

Fine, M. (2004). The power of the *Brown v. Board of Education* decision: Theorizing threats to sustainability. *American Psychologist, 59,* 502–510.

Fineman, S. (1983). *White collar unemployment.* Chichester, England: Wiley.

Firth, R. (1979). Work and value: Reflections on Karl Marx. In S. Wallman (Ed.), *Social anthropology of work* (pp. 177–206). London: Academic Press.

Fischer, W. (2001). Poverty in history. In *International Encyclopedia of the Social & Behavioral Sciences* (25, pp. 11907–11911). Amsterdam, Netherlands: Elsevier.

Fitzgerald, L. F. (2003). Sexual harassment and social justice: Reflections on the distance yet to go. *American Psychologist, 58,* 915–924.

Fitzgerald, L. F. (1993). *The last great open secret: The sexual harassment of women in academia and the workplace.* Washington DC: Federation of Behavioral, Psychological, and Cognitive Sciences.

Fitzgerald, L. F., & Rounds, J. (1994). Women and work: Theory encounters reality. In W. B. Walsh & S. H. Osipow (Eds.), *Career counseling for women. Contemporary topics in vocational psychology* (pp. 327–353). Hillsdale, NJ: Lawrence Erlbaum Associates.

Fitzgerald, L. F., & Weitzman, L. M. (1992). Women's career development: Theory and practice from a feminist perspective. In H. D. Lea & Z. B. Leibowitz (Eds.), *Adult career development: Concepts, issues, and practice* (pp. 124–160). Alexandria, VA: National Career Development Association.

Fletcher, J. K. (1996). A relational approach to the protean worker. In D. T. Hall (Ed.), *The career is dead—Long live the career: A relational approach to careers* (pp. 105–131). San Francisco: Jossey-Bass.

Fletcher, J. K., & Bailyn, L. (1996). Challenging the last boundary: Reconnecting work and family. In M. B. Arthur & D. M. Rousseau (Eds.), *The boundaryless career* (pp. 236–267). New York: Oxford University Press.

Flum, H. (2001). Relational dimensions in career development. *Journal of Vocational Behavior, 59,* 1–16.

Flum, H. (2004). Lo Sviluppo Dell'identità professionale Negli Adolescenti: Una Prospettiva Psicosociale [Adolescents' development of vocational identity: A psychosocial perspective]. *Gipo Giornale Italiano Di Psicologia Dell'Orientamento, 5,* 3–10.

Flum, H., & Blustein, D. L. (2000). Reinvigorating the study of vocational exploration: A framework for research. *Journal of Vocational Behavior, 56,* 380–404.

Fontana, A., & Frey, J. H. (2000). The interview: From structured questions to negotiated text. In N. K. Denzin & Y. S. Lincoln (Eds.), *Handbook of qualitative research* (2nd ed., pp. 645–672). Thousand Oaks, CA: Sage.

Ford, D., & Lerner, R. (1992). *Developmental systems theory: An integrative approach.* Thousand Oaks, CA: Sage Publications.

Foster, M. (1993). Resisting racism. In L. Weiss & M. Fine (Eds.), *Beyond silenced voices: Class, race, and gender in the United States schools* (pp. 273–288). Albany, NY: State University of New York Press.

Fouad, N. A., & Bingham, R. (1995). Career counseling with racial and ethnic minorities. In W. B. Walsh & S. H. Osipow (Eds.), *Handbook of vocational psychology* (2nd ed., pp. 331–365). Hillsdale, NJ: Lawrence Erlbaum Associates.

Fouad, N. A., & Brown, M. T. (2000). The role of race and class in development: Implications for counseling psychology. In S. D. Brown & R. W. Lent (Eds.), *Handbook of counseling psychology* (3rd ed., pp. 379–408). New York: Wiley.

Fouad, N. A., & Spreda, S. L. (1995). Use of interest inventories with special populations: Women and minority groups. *Journal of Career Assessment, 3*, 453–468.

Fouad, N. A., & Walker, C. (2005). Cultural influences on responses to items on the Strong Interest Inventory. *Journal of Vocational Behavior, 66*, 104–123.

Foucault, M. (1965). *Madness and civilization: A history of insanity in the Age of Reason*. New York: Vintage Books.

Fowers, B., & Richardson, F. (1996). Why is multiculturalism good? *American Psychologist, 51*, 609–621.

Fox, D., & Prilleltensky, I. (1997). *Critical psychology: An introduction*. Thousand Oaks, CA: Sage Publications.

Fox, M. (1994). *The reinvention of work: A new vision of livelihood for our time*. New York: HarperCollins Publishers.

Fox, S., & Stallworth, L. (2005). Racial/ethnic bullying: Exploring links between bullying and racism in the U.S. workplace. *Journal of Vocational Behavior, 66*, 438–456.

Frazer, E., & Lacey, N. (1993). *The politics of community: A feminist critique of the liberal–communitarian debate*. Toronto, ON, Canada: University of Toronto Press.

Frazier, P. A., Tix, A. P., & Barron, K. E. (2004). Testing moderator and mediator effects in counseling psychology research. *Journal of Counseling Psychology, 51*, 115–134.

Fredricks, J. A., Blumenfeld, P. C., & Paris, A. H. (2004). School engagement: Potential of the concept, state of the evidence. *Review of Educational Research, 74*, 59–109.

Fredriksen-Goldsen, K. I., & Scharlach, A. E. (2001). *Families and work: New directions in the twenty-first century*. New York: Oxford University Press.

Freedheim, D. (1992). *History of psychotherapy: A century of change*. Washington DC: American Psychological Association.

Freire, P. (1993). *Pedagogy of the oppressed*. New York: The Continuum Publishing Company. (Original work published 1970)

Freire, P. (1984). Education, liberation and the church. *Religious Education, 79*, 524–545.

Freud, S. (1959). The origin and development of psychoanalysis. *American Journal of Psychology, 21*, 181–218. (Original work published 1910)

Freud, S. (1930). *Civilization and its discontents*. Oxford, England: Hogarth.

Freud, S. (1959). *Collected papers*. Oxford, England: Basic Books.

Friedan, B. (1963). *The feminist mystique*. New York: Norton.

Friedman, S. A. (1996). *Work matters: Women talk about their jobs and their jobs*. New York: Viking.

Friedman, T. L. (1999). *The Lexus and the olive tree: Understanding globalization*. New York: Farrar, Strauss, & Giroux.

Friedman, T. L. (2005). *The world is flat: A brief history of the twenty-first century*. Waterville, ME: Thorndike Press.

Fromm, E. (1947). *Man for himself*. New York: Holt, Rinehart, & Winston.

Fromm-Reichman, F. (1950). *Principles of intensive psychotherapy*. Chicago: University of Chicago Press.

Frone, M. R., Yardley, J. K., & Markel, K. S. (1997). Developing and testing an integrative model of the work–family interface. *Journal of Vocational Behavior, 50*, 145–167.

Furnham, A. (2000). Work in 2020. *Journal of Managerial Psychology, 15*, 242–255.

Gardner, H., Csikszentimihalyi, M., & Damon, W. (2001). *Good work: When excellence and ethics meet*. New York: Basic Books.

Gelatt, H. B. (1989). Positive uncertainty: A new decision making framework for counseling. *Journal of Counseling Psychology, 36*, 252–256.

Gergen, K. (1999). Agency: Social construction and relational action. *Theory & Psychology, 9*, 113–115.

Giddens, A. (1983). *The class structure of the advanced societies*. London: Hutchinson.

Gil, L. (1996). A community's commitment to career planning for all: Clarity and commitment. *Journal of Career Development, 23*, 23–31.

Gilbert, L. (1994). Current perspectives on dual-career families. *Current Directions in Psychological Science, 3*, 101–105.

Gilbride, D., & Stensrud, R. (2003). Job placement and employer consulting: Services and strategies. In E. Szymanski & R. Parker (Eds.), *Work and disability: Issues and strategies in career development and job placement* (2nd ed., pp. 407–439). Austin, TX: PRO-ED, Inc.

Gilligan, C. (1982). *In a different voice: Psychological theory and women's development*. Cambridge, MA: Harvard University Press.

Gini, A. (2000). *My job, my self: Work and the creation of the modern individual*. New York: Routledge.

Gini, A., & Sullivan, T. J. (Eds.). (1989). *It comes with the territory: An inquiry concerning work and the person*. New York: Random House.

Gladfelter, J. H. (1990). Integrated psychotherapy. In J. K. Zeig & W. M. Munion (Eds.), *What is psychotherapy? Contemporary perspectives* (pp. 336–340). San Francisco: Jossey-Bass.

Gladstein, G. (1983). Understanding empathy: Integrating counseling, developmental, and psychology perspectives. *Journal of Counseling Psychology, 30,* 467–482.

Glover, R. W., & Marshall, R. (1993). Improving the school-to-work transition of American adolescents. *Teachers College Record, 94,* 588–610.

Goffman, E. (1961). *Asylums: Essays on the social situation of mental patients and other inmates*. New York: Doubleday Anchor Books.

Goldschmidt, W. (1990). *The human career: The self in the symbolic world*. Cambridge, MA: Basil Blackwell.

Goodman, L., Liang, B., Helms, J., Latta, R., Sparks, E., & Weintraub, S. (2004). Training counseling psychologists as social justice agents: Feminist and multicultural principles in action. *The Counseling Psychologist, 32,* 793–837.

Googins, B. K. (1991). *Work/family conflicts: Private lives—Public responses*. New York: Auburn House.

Gordon, E. E., Morgan, R. R., & Ponticell, J. A. (1994). *Futurework: The revolution reshaping American business*. Westport, CT: Praeger.

Gore, S. (1978). The effects of social support in moderating the health consequences of unemployment. *Journal of Health and Social Behavior, 19,* 157–165.

Gorz, A. (1999). *Reclaiming work*. Cambridge, UK: Polity.

Gottfredson, G. (2002). Interests, aspirations, self-estimates, and the Self-Directed Search. *Journal of Career Assessment, 10,* 200–208.

Gottschalk, P., & Moffitt, R. (2000). Job instability and insecurity of males and females in the 1980s and 1990s. In D. Neumark (Ed.), *On the job: Is long-term employment a thing of the past?* (pp. 142–190). New York: Russell Sage Foundation.

Grantham, C. (2000). *The future of work: The promise of the new digital work society*. New York: McGraw-Hill.

Grayson, J. P. (1989). Reported illness after a CGE closure. *Canadian Journal of Public Health, 80,* 16–19.

Green, R., & Hill, J. (2003). Sex and higher education: Do men and women attend college for different reasons? *College Student Journal, 37,* 557–563.

Greenfield, P. (1998). The cultural evolution of IQ. In U. Neisser (Ed.), *The rising curve: Long-term gains in IQ and related measures* (pp. 81–123). Washington DC: American Psychological Association.

Greenhaus, J., & Beutell, N. (1985). Sources and conflict between work and family roles. *Academy of Management Review, 10,* 6–88.

Greenhaus, J., & Parasuraman, S. (1999). Research on work, family, and gender: Current status and future directions. In G. N. Powell (Ed.), *Handbook of gender and work* (pp. 391–412). Thousand Oaks, CA: Sage Publications.

Greiner, B., Krause, N., Ragland, D., & Fisher, J. (1998). Studies of health outcomes in transit operators: Policy implications of the current scientific database. *Journal of Occupational Health Psychology, 3,* 172–187.

Grossman, F., Kruger, L., & Moore, R. (1999). Reflections on a feminist research project: Subjectivity and the wish for intimacy and equality. *Psychology of Women Quarterly, 23,* 117–135.

Grotevant, H. (1987). Toward a process model of identity formation. *Journal of Adolescent Research, 2,* 203–222.

Grunberg, L., Moore, S., & Greenberg, E. (2001). Differences in psychological and physical health among layoff survivors: The effect of layoff contact. *Journal of Occupational Health Psychology, 6,* 15–25.

Gutek, B. (1987). *Women's career development*. London, UK: Sage.

Gysbers, N., Heppner, M., & Johnston, J. (2003). *Career counseling: Process, issues, and techniques* (2nd ed.). Needham Heights, MA: Allyn & Bacon.

Hackett, G., & Betz, N. (1981). A self-efficacy approach to the career development of women. *Journal of Vocational Behavior, 18,* 326–339.

Hackett, G., Betz, N., Casas, M., & Rocha-Singh, I. (1992). Gender, ethnicity, and social cognitive factors predicting the academic achievement of students in engineering. *Journal of Counseling Psychology, 39,* 527–538.

Hackett, G., & Lonborg, S. (1993). Career assessment for women: Trends and issues. *Journal of Career Assessment, 1,* 197–216.

Hagner, D. (2003). Job development and job search assistance. In E. Szymanski & R. Parker (Eds.), *Work and disability: Issues and strategies in career development and job placement* (2nd ed., pp. 407–439). Austin, TX: PRO-ED, Inc.

Hall, D. T. (1996). *The career is dead—Long live the career: A relational approach to careers.* San Francisco: Jossey-Bass.

Hall, D. T., & Mirvis, P. H. (1996). The new protean career: Psychological success and the path with a heart. In D. T. Hall (Ed.), *The career is dead—Long live the career: A relational approach to careers* (pp. 15–45). San Francisco: Jossey-Bass.

Hall, D. T., & Nougaim, K. E. (1968). An examination of Maslow's need hierarchy in an organizational setting. *Organizational Behavior and Human Performance, 3,* 12–15.

Halle, D. (1984). *America's working man.* Chicago, IL: University of Chicago Press.

Hanisch, K. (1999). Job loss and unemployment research from 1994 to 1998: A review and recommendations for research and intervention. *Journal of Vocational Behavior, 55,* 188–220.

Hanley-Maxwell, C., Owens-Johnson, L., & Fabian, E. (2003). Supported employment: Work and disability: Issues and strategies in career development and job placement. In E. Szymanski & R. Parker (Eds.), *Work and disability: Issues and strategies in career development and job placement* (2nd ed., pp. 407–439). Austin, TX: PRO-ED, Inc.

Hareven, T. K., & Langenbach, R. (1978). *Amoskeag: Life and work in an American factory-city.* Hanover, NH: University Press of New England.

Hargreaves, A. (2000). Mixed emotions: Teachers' perceptions of their interactions with students. *Teaching & Teacher Education, 16,* 811–826.

Harmon, L. W. (1971). The childhood and adolescent career plans of college women. *Journal of Vocational Behavior, 1,* 45–56.

Harmon, L. W. (1972). Variables related to women's persistence in educational plans. *Journal of Vocational Behavior, 2,* 143–153.

Harmon. L. W. (1994). Frustrations, daydreams, and realities of theoretical convergence. In M. L. Savickas & R. W. Lent (Eds.), *Convergence in career development theories* (pp. 226–234). Palo Alto, CA: CPP Books.

Harmon, L. W., & Farmer, H. S. (1983). Current theoretical issues in vocational psychology. In W. B. Walsh & S. H. Osipow (Eds.), *Handbook of vocational psychology* (Vol. 1, pp. 39–77). Hillsdale, NJ: Lawrence Erlbaum Associates.

Harmon, L. W., Hansen, J. C., Borgen, F. H., & Hammer, A. L. (1994). *Strong Interest Inventory: Applications and technical guide.* Stanford CA: Stanford University Press.

Harren, V. (1979). Research with the assessment of career decision making. *Character Potential: A Record of Research, 9,* 63–69.

Hartung, P., & Blustein, D. L. (2002). Reason, intuition, and social justice: Elaborating on Parson's Career Decision-Making Model. *Journal of Counseling & Development, 80,* 41–47.

Hayes, J., & Mahalik, J. (2000). Gender role conflict and psychological distress in male counseling clients. *Psychology of Men & Masculinity, 1,* 116–125.

Heckman, J. (1994). Is job training oversold? *The Public Interest, 115,* 91–115.

Heidegger, M. (1962). *Being and time.* Oxford, England: Basil Blackwell.

Heilbroner, R., & Singer, A. (1984). *The economic transformation of America: 1600 to present.* New York: Harcourt Brace Jovanovich.

Heilman, M., Wallen, A., Fuchs, D., & Tamkins, M. (2004). Penalties for success: Reactions to women who succeed at male gender-typed tasks. *Journal of Applied Psychology, 89,* 416–427.

Helms, J. E. (Ed.). (1990). *Black and white racial identity: Theory, research, and practice.* Eastport, CT: Greenwood.

Helms, J. E. (1992). Why is there no study of cultural equivalence in standardized cognitive ability testing? *American Psychologist, 47,* 1083–1101.

Helms, J. E. (2003). A pragmatic view of social justice. *The Counseling Psychologist, 31,* 305–313.

Helms, J. E., & Cook, D. A. (1999). *Using race and culture in counseling and psychotherapy: Theory and process.* Boston: Allyn & Bacon.

Helms, J. E., Jernigan, M., & Mascher, J. (2005). The meaning of race in psychology and how to change it: A methodological perspective. *American Psychologist, 60,* 27–36.

Helms, J. E., & Piper, R. E. (1994). Implications of racial identity theory for vocational psychology. *Journal of Vocational Behavior, 44,* 124–138.

Heppner, M. J., & Heppner, P. P. (2003). Identifying process variables in career counseling: A research agenda. *Journal of Vocational Behavior, 62,* 429–452.

Herr, E. L., Cramer, S. H., & Niles, S. G. (2004). *Career guidance and counseling through the lifespan: Systematic approaches* (6th ed.). Needham Heights, MA: Allyn & Bacon.

Herriot, P. (2001). *The employment relationship: A psychological perspective.* New York: Taylor & Francis.

Hershenson, D., & Leisener, J. (2003). Career counseling with diverse populations: Models, interventions, and applications. In E. M. Szymanski & R. M. Parker (Eds.), *Work and disability: Issues and strategies in career development and job placement* (2nd ed., pp. 281–316). Austin, TX: PRO-ED, Inc.

Herzberg, F. (1966). *Work and the nature of man.* Cleveland, OH: World Publishing.

Hesse-Biber, S., & Carter, G. L. (2000). *Working women in America: Split dreams.* New York: Oxford University Press.

Hession, C., & Sardy, H. (1969). *Ascent to affluence: A history of American economic development.* Boston: Allyn & Bacon.

Hetherington, M., Bridges, M., & Insabella, G. (1998). What matters? What does not? Five perspectives on the association between marital transitions and children's adjustment. *American Psychologist, 53,* 167–184.

Hill, C. E., Thompson, B. J., & Williams, E. N. (1997). A guide to conducting consensual qualitative research. *The Counseling Psychologist, 25,* 517–572.

Hill, C. E., & Williams, E. N. (2000). The process of individual therapy. In S. D. Brown & R. W. Lent (Eds.), *Handbook of counseling psychology* (3rd ed., pp. 670–710). New York: Wiley.

Holland, J. L., Magoon, T., & Spokane, A. (1981). Counseling psychology: Career interventions, research, and theory. *Annual Review of Psychology, 32,* 279–305.

Holland, J. L. (1958). A personality inventory employing occupational titles. *Journal of Applied Psychology, 42,* 336–342.

Holland, J. L. (1994). *The Self-Directed Search* (SDS). Odessa, FL: Psychological Assessment Resources.

Holland, J. L. (1997). *Making vocational choices: A theory of vocational personalities and work environments* (3rd ed.). Odessa, FL: Psychological Assessment Resources.

Höpfl, H., & Atkinson, P. H. (2000). The future of women's career. In A. Collin & R. A. Young (Eds.), *The future of career* (pp. 130–143). Cambridge: Cambridge University Press.

Hotelling, K. (1991). Sexual harassment: A problem shielded by silence. *Journal of Counseling & Development, 69,* 497–501.

Howell, J., & Dorfman, P. (1986). Leadership and substitutes for leadership among professional and nonprofessional workers. *Journal of Applied Behavioral Science, 22,* 29–46.

Hughes, L. (1965). Sharecroppers. In *Selected Poems* (pp. 165–166). New York: Knopf. (Original work published 1942)

Hulin, C. (2002). Lessons from industrial and organizational psychology. In J. Brett & F. Drasgow (Eds.), *The psychology of work: Theoretically based empirical research* (pp. 3–22). Mahwah, NJ: Lawrence Erlbaum Associates.

Hunt, E. (1995). *Will we be smart enough? A cognitive analysis of the coming workforce.* New York: Russell Sage Foundation.

Ireland, M. (1993). *Reconceiving women: Separating motherhood from female identity.* New York: The Guilford Press.

Issacson, L. (2003). Career counseling with diverse populations: Models, interventions, applications. In E. Szymanski & R. Parker (Eds.), *Work and disability: Issues and strategies in career development and job placement* (2nd ed., pp. 281–316). Austin, TX: PRO-ED, Inc.

Jaeger, D. A., & Stevens, A. H. (2000). Is job stability in the United States falling? Reconciling trends in the current population survey and the panel study of income dynamics. In D. A. Jaeger & A. H. Stevens (Eds.), *On the job: Is long-term employment a thing of the past?* (pp. 31–69). New York: Russell Sage Foundation.

Jain, S., & Reddock, R. (Eds.). (1998). *Women plantation workers: International experience.* New York: Berg.

Jeanquart-Barone, S., & Sekaran, U. (1996). Institutional racism: An empirical study. *Journal of Social Psychology, 136,* 477–482.

Johnson, A. W., & Earle, T. (1987). *The evolution of human societies: From foraging groups to agrarian state.* Stanford, CA: Stanford University Press.

Johnson, M. J., Swartz, J. L., & Martin, W. E. (1995). Applications of psychological theories for career development with Native Americans. In F. T. L. Leong (Ed.), *Career development and vocational behavior of racial and ethnic minorities* (pp. 103–136). Hillsdale, NJ: Lawrence Erlbaum Associates.

Johnson, R. (2002). *Using data to close the achievement gap: How to measure equity in our schools.* Thousand Oaks, CA: Corwin Press, Inc.

Johnson, W., & Johnson, G. (1997). A model of union participation among U.S. blue-collar workers. *Journal of Psychology: Interdisciplinary & Applied, 131,* 661–674.

Johnson, W., Bouchard, T., Krueger, R., McGue, M., & Gottesman, I. (2004). Just one g: Consistent results form three test batteries. *Intelligence, 32,* 95–107.

Jones, S. (2004). Psychotherapy of bipolar disorder: A review. *Journal of Affective Disorders, 80,* 101–114.

Jordan, J., Kaplan, A., Miller, J. B., Stiver, I., & Surrey, J. (1991). *Women's growth in connection: Writings from the Stone Center.* New York: Guilford Press.

Jordaan, J., & Super, D. (1974). The prediction of early adult vocational behavior. In D. Ricks, A. Thomas, & M. Roff (Eds.), *Life history research in psychopathology: III.* Minneapolis: University of Minnesota Press.

Josselson, R. (1992). *The space between us: Exploring the dimensions of human relationships.* San Francisco: Jossey-Bass.

Juntunen, C. L., Barraclough, D. J., Broneck, C. J., Seibel, G. A., Winrow, S. A., & Morin, P. M. (2001). American Indian perspectives on the career journey. *Journal of Counseling Psychology, 48,* 274–285.

Kahn, A. (1993). *The encyclopedia of mental health.* New York: Facts on File.

Kahn, H. (2004). Low-wage single mother families in this jobless recovery: Can improved social policies help? *Analyses of Social Issues & Public Policy, 4,* 47–68.

Kahn, W. A. (1996). Secure base relationships at work. In D. T. Hall (Eds.), *The career is dead—Long live the career: A relational approach to careers* (pp. 158–179). San Francisco: Jossey-Bass Publishers.

Kane, R. (1994). *Through the moral maze: Searching for absolute values in a pluralistic world.* New York: Paragon House.

Kates, N., Greiff, B., & Hagen, D. (2003). Job loss and employment uncertainty. In J. Kahn & A. Langlieb (Eds.), *Mental health and productivity in the workplace: A handbook for organizations and clinicians* (pp. 135–154). San Francisco: Jossey-Bass.

Keister, L. (2000). Race and wealth inequality: The impact of racial differences in asset ownership on the distribution of household wealth. *Social Science Research, 29,* 477–502.

Keller, F. J., & Viteles, M. S. (1937). *Vocational guidance throughout the world.* New York: W. W. Norton & Co, Inc.

Kenny, M. E., Blustein, D. L., Chaves, A., Grossman, J. M., & Gallagher, L. A. (2003). The role of perceived barriers and relational support in the educational and vocational lives of urban high school students. *Journal of Counseling Psychology, 50,* 142–155.

Kidd, J. (1998). Emotion: An absent presence in career theory. *Journal of Vocational Behavior, 52,* 275–288.

Kikoski, J., & Kikoski, C. (1996). *Reflexive communication in the culturally diverse workplace.* Westport, CT: Quorum Books.

Kirschner, T., Hoffman, M., & Hill, C. (1994). Case study of the process and outcome of career counseling. *Journal of Counseling Psychology, 41,* 216–226.

Kiselica, M., & Robinson, M. (2001). Bringing advocacy counseling to life: The history, issues, and human dramas of social justice work in counseling. *Journal of Counseling & Development, 79,* 387–397.

Kliman, J. (1998). Social class as a relationship: Implications for family therapy. In M. McGoldrick (Ed.), *Re-envisioning family therapy: Race, culture, and gender in clinical practice* (pp. 50–61). New York: Guilford Press.

Kohut, H. (1977). *The restoration of self.* New York: International Universities Press.

Kooser, T. (1980). *Sure signs: New and selected poems.* Pittsburgh, PA: University of Pittsburgh Press.

Korten, D. (1995). *When corporations rule the world.* West Hartford, CT: Kumarian Press.

Kozol, J. (1991). *Savage inequalities: Children in America's schools.* New York: Crown.

Kram, K. E. (1996). A relational approach to career development. In D. T. Hall & Associates (Eds.), *The career is dead—Long live the career: A relational approach to careers* (pp. 132–157). San Francisco: Jossey-Bass Publishers.

Kressel, N. (1993). *Political psychology: Classic and contemporary readings*. New York: Paragon House Publishers.

Krugman, P. R. (1993). *What do we need to know about the international monetary system?* Princeton, NJ: Princeton University Press.

Kuhl, J., & Fuhrmann, A. (1998). Decomposing self-regulation and self-control: The Volitional Components Inventory. In J. Heckhausen & C. Dweck (Eds.), *Motivation and self-regulation across the life span* (pp. 15–49). New York: Cambridge University Press.

Kurian, R. (1982). *Women workers in the Sri Lanka plantation sector*. Geneva: International Labour Organization.

LaGuardia, J., Ryan, R., Couchman, C., & Deci, E. (2000). Within-person variation in security of attachment: A self-determination theory perspective on attachment, need fulfillment, and well-being. *Journal of Personality & Social Psychology, 79,* 367–384.

Lamberg, L. (2004). Impact of long working hours explored. *JAMA: Journal of the American Medical Association, 292,* 25–26.

Lamont, M. (2000). *The dignity of working men: Morality and the boundaries of race, class, and immigration*. New York: Russell Sage Foundation.

Landy, F. J. (1989). *The psychology of work behavior* (4th ed.). Belmont, CA: Brooks/Cole.

Lapan, R. (2004). *Career development across the K–16 years: Bridging the present to satisfying and successful futures*. Alexandria, VA: American Counseling Association.

Lapan, R., & Kosciulek, R. (2001). Toward a community career system program evaluation framework. *Journal of Counseling & Development, 79,* 3–15.

Lent, R. W., & Brown, S. D. (1996). Social cognitive approach to career development: An overview. *Career Development Quarterly, 44,* 310–321.

Lent, R. W., Brown, S. D., & Hackett, G. (2002). Social cognitive career theory. In D. Brown (Eds.), *Career choice and development* (pp. 255–311). San Francisco: Jossey-Bass.

Leong, F. (1995). *Career development and vocational behavior of racial and ethnic minorities*. Hillsdale, NJ: Lawrence Erlbaum Associates.

Leong, F., & Hartung, P. (2000). Cross-cultural career assessment: Review and prospects for the new millennium. *Journal of Career Assessment, 8,* 391–401.

Leong, F. T. L., & Serafica, F. C. (1995). Career development of Asian Americans: A research area in search of a good theory. In F. T. L. Leong (Ed.), *Career development and vocational behavior of racial and ethnic minorities* (pp. 67–102). Hillsdale, NJ: Lawrence Erlbaum Associates.

Lerner, R. (2002). *Concepts and theories of human development* (3rd ed.). Mahwah, NJ: Lawrence Erlbaum Associates.

Levant, R. (2000). *Psychology of men*. Washington, DC: American Psychological Association.

Levant, R., & Brooks, G. (1997). *Men and sex: New psychological perspectives*. New York: Wiley.

Levenson, A. R. (2000). Long-run trends in part-time and temporary employment: Toward an understanding. In D. A. Jaeger & A. H. Stevens (Eds.), *On the job: Is long-term employment a thing of the past?* (pp. 335–397). New York: Russell Sage Foundation.

Levinson, D. (1978). *The seasons of a man's life*. New York: Knopf.

Levine, D., Lowe, R., Peterson, B., & Tenorio, R. (1995). *Rethinking schools: An agenda for change*. New York: The New Press.

Lewis, D. (2004). Bullying at work: The impact of shame among university and college lecturers. *British Journal of Guidance & Counseling, 32,* 281–299.

Lewis, O. (1966). *The culture of poverty*. San Francisco: W. H. Freeman.

Liang, C., Li, L., & Kim, B. (2004). The Asian American racism-related stress inventory development, factor analysis, reliability, and validity. *Journal of Counseling Psychology, 51,* 103–114.

Lincoln, Y. S., & Guba, E. G. (2000). Paradigmatic controversies, contradictions, and emerging confluences. In N. K. Denzin & Y. S. Lincoln (Eds.), *Handbook of qualitative research* (2nd ed., pp. 163–188). Thousand Oaks, CA: Sage.

Linehan, M. (1993). *Diagnosis and treatment of mental disorders: Skills training manual for treating borderline personality disorder*. New York: Guilford Press.

Lippmann, W. (1914). *Drift and mastery: An attempt to diagnose the current unrest*. New York: Mitchell Kennerley.

Liu, W. M. (2001). Expanding our understanding of multiculturalism: Developing a social class worldview model. In D. B. Pope-Davis & H. L. K. Coleman (Eds.), *The intersection of race, class, and gender in counseling psychology* (pp. 127–170). Thousand Oaks, CA: Sage Publications.

Liu, W. M. (2002). The social class-related experiences of men: Integrating theory and practice. *Professional Psychology: Research and Practice, 33,* 355–360.

Liu, W. M., Ali, S. R., Soleck, G., Hopps, J., Dunston, K., & Pickett, T. (2004). Using social class in counseling psychology research. *Journal of Counseling Psychology, 51,* 3–18.

Liu, W. M., Soleck, G., Hopps, J., Dunston, K., & Pickett, T. (2004). A new framework to understand social class in counseling: The social class worldview and modern classism theory. *Journal of Multicultural Counseling and Development, 32,* 95–122.

Locke, J. (1975). *An essay concerning human understanding.* In P. Nidditch (Ed.), Oxford: Oxford University Press. (Original work published 1690)

Lofquist, L. H., & Dawis, R. V. (1984). Research on work adjustment and satisfaction: Implications for career counseling. In S. D. Brown & R. W. Lent (Eds.), *Handbook of counseling psychology* (pp. 216–237). New York: Wiley.

Lopez, F., & Andrews, S. (1987). Career indecision: A family systems perspective. *Journal of Counseling & Development, 65,* 304–307.

Lott, B. (2002). Cognitive and behavioral distancing from the poor. *American Psychologist, 57,* 100–110.

Loury, G. (2001). *The anatomy of racial inequality.* Cambridge, MA: Harvard University Press.

Lowman, R. (1993). *Counseling and psychotherapy of work dysfunctions.* Washington, DC: American Psychological Association.

Luckey, E. B. (1974). The family: Perspectives on its role in development and choice. In E. L. Herr (Ed.), *Vocational guidance and human development* (pp. 203–231). Boston: Houghton Mifflin.

MacDonald, C., & Sirianni, C. (1996). *Working in the service society.* Philadelphia, PA: Temple University Press.

Macedo, D. (1994). *Literacies of power: What Americans are not allowed to know.* Boulder, CO: Westview Press.

Mahalik, J. (1999). Interpersonal psychotherapy with men who experience gender role conflict. *Professional Psychology: Research & Practice, 30,* 5–13.

Mahalik, J., & Morrison, J. (in press). Examining masculinity schemas in cognitive therapy to increase father involvement. *Cognitive and Behavioral Practice.*

Mahrer, A. (1996). Discovery-oriented research on how to do psychotherapy. In W. Dryden (Ed.), *Research in counseling and psychotherapy: Practical applications* (pp. 233–258). Thousand Oaks, CA: Sage Publications.

Mahrer, A., & Boulet, D. (1999). How to do discovery-oriented psychotherapy research. *Journal of Clinical Psychology, 55,* 1481–1493.

Malamut, A., & Offerman, L. (2000). Coping with sexual harassment: Personal, environmental, and cognitive determinants. *Journal of Applied Psychology, 86,* 1152–1166.

Malley, J., & Stewart, A. (1988). Women's work and family roles: Sources of stress and sources of strength. In S. Fischer & J. Reason (Eds.), *Handbook of life stress, cognition, and health* (pp. 175–191). Oxford, England: Wiley.

Mallinckrodt, B., & Bennett, J. (1992). Social support and the impact of job loss in dislocated blue-collar workers. *Journal of Counseling Psychology, 39,* 482–489.

Manuele-Adkins, C. (1992). Career counseling is personal counseling. *Career Development Quarterly, 40,* 313–323.

Marshall, R., & Tucker, M. (1992). *Thinking for a living: Education and the wealth of nations.* New York: Basic Books.

Martin, J. (2002). The common factor of mindfulness—An expanding discourse: Comment on Horowitz (2002). *Journal of Psychotherapy Integration, 12,* 139–142.

Martín-Baro, I. (1989). Political violence and war as causes of psychosocial trauma in El Salvador. *International Journal of Mental Health, 18,* 3–20.

Martín-Baro, I. (1994). Writings for a liberation psychology. In A. A. Aron & S. Come (Eds.), *Writings for a liberation psychology.* Cambridge, Harvard University Press.

Martínez, O. J. (1994). *Border people: Life and society in the U.S.–Mexico borderlands.* Tucson, AZ: University of Arizona Press.

Marx, K. (1867). *Das Kapital. Kritik der politischen Okonomie* [Capital: A critique of political economy]. Dietz Verlag, Berlin: Marx-Engels Werke Band 23.

Marx, K. (1844/1988). *The economic and philosophic manuscripts of 1844 and the Communist Manifesto.* Prometheus Books: Amherst, NY.

Marx, K. (1891). *Wage labour and capital.* Germany: Neue Rheinische Zeitung.

Maslow, A. (1968). *Toward a psychology of being* (2nd ed.). New York: Van Nostrand Reinhold Co.

Maslow, A. H. (1943). A theory of human motivation. *Psychological Review, 50,* 370–396.

Masske, J. (2002). Spirituality and mindfulness. *Psychoanalytic Psychology, 19,* 777–781.

Masten, A., & Coatsworth, D. (1998). The development of competence in favorable and unfavorable environments: Lessons from research on successful children. *American Psychologist, 53,* 205–220.

Maton, K. I. (2000). Making a difference: The social ecology of social transformation. *American Journal of Community Psychology, 28,* 25–57.

McDonough, P. M. (1997). *Choosing colleges: How social class and schools structure opportunity.* Albany: State University of New York Press.

McWhirter, E. (1994). *Counseling for empowerment.* Alexandria, VA: American Counseling Association.

McWhirter, E., Hawley, E., Hackett, G., & Bandalos, D. (1998). A causal model of the educational plans and career expectations of Mexican American high school girls. *Journal of Counseling Psychology, 45,* 166–181.

McWhirter, E. H., Crothers, M., & Rasheed, S. (2000). The effects of high school career education on social-cognitive variables. *Journal of Counseling Psychology, 47,* 330–341.

Meara, N. M., & Patton, M. J. (1994). Contributions of the working alliance in the practice of career counseling. *Career Development Quarterly, 43,* 161–177.

Meeus, W., Dekovic, M., & Iedema, J. (1997). Unemployment and identity in adolescence: A social comparison perspective. *Career Development Quarterly, 45,* 369–380.

Menaghan, E. G., & Parcel, T. L. (1990). Parental employment and family life: Research in the 1980s. *Journal of Marriage and Family, 52,* 1079–1098.

Menninger, K. A. (1942). Work as a sublimation. *Bulletin of the Menninger Clinic, 6,* 170–182.

Miller, A. (1949). *Death of a salesman.* New York: Viking Press.

Miller, J. B. (1986). *Toward a new psychology of women* (2nd ed.). Boston: Beacon Press.

Mills, J. (2004). Countertransference revisited. *Psychoanalytic Review, 91,* 467–515.

Milner, A. (1999). *Class.* London: Thousand Oaks.

Miner, J. (1969). *Personnel psychology.* London: Collier-Macmillan Limited.

Mishel, L., & Bernstein, J. (1994). *The state of working America, 1994–95.* Economic Policy Institute Series. Armonk, NY: M. E. Sharpe.

Mitchell, L., & Krumboltz, J. (1990). Social learning approach to career decision making: Krumboltz's theory. In D. Brown & L. Brooks (Eds.), *Career choice and development: Applying contemporary theories to practice* (2nd ed., pp. 145–196). San Francisco: Jossey-Bass.

Mitchell, S. A. (1988). *Relational concepts in psychoanalysis.* Cambridge, MA: Harvard University Press.

Mitchell, S. A. (1997). *Influence and autonomy in psychoanalysis.* Hillsdale, NJ: The Analytic Press.

Moore, M. (1996). *Women in the mines: Stories of life and work.* New York: Twayne Publishing.

Morrow, S., & Smith, M. L. (2000). Qualitative research for counseling psychology. In S. D. Brown & R. W. Lent (Eds.), *Handbook of counseling psychology* (3rd ed., pp. 199–230). New York: Wiley.

Neff, W. S. (1985). *Work and human behavior* (3rd ed.). New York: Aldine Publishing Company.

Neumark, D. (Ed.). (2000). *On the job: Is long-term employment a thing of the past?* New York: Russell Sage Foundation.

Neumark, D., Polsky, D., & Hansen, D. (2000). Has job stability declined yet? New evidence for the 1990s. In D. A. Jaeger & A. H. Stevens (Eds.), *On the job: Is long-term employment a thing of the past?* (pp. 70–110). New York: Russell Sage Foundation.

Newman, K. S. (1988). *Falling from grace: Downward mobility in the age of affluence.* Berkeley, CA: University of California Press.

Newman, K. S. (1999). *No shame in my game.* New York: Vintage.

Niles, S. G., Goodman, J., & Pope, M. (Eds.). (2002). *The career counseling casebook: A resource for practitioners, students, and counselor educators.* Tulsa, OK: National Career Development Association.

Noonan, B., Gallor, S., Hensler-McGinnis, N., Fassinger, R., Wang, S., & Goodman, J. (2004). Challenge and success: A qualitative study of the career development of highly achieving women with physical and sensory disabilities. *Journal of Counseling Psychology, 51,* 68–80.

O'Brien, G. E. (1986). *Psychology of work and unemployment.* New York: Wiley.

Oher, J. (1999). *The employee assistance handbook.* New York: Wiley.

Oresick, P., & Coles, N. (1990). *Working classes: Poems on industrial life.* Urbana, IL: University of Illinois Press.

Orr, A. (2003). Black-White differences in achievement: The importance of wealth. *Sociology of Education, 76,* 281–304.

Parasuraman, S., & Greenhaus, J. H. (Eds.). (1997). *Integrating work and family: Challenges and choices for a changing world.* Westport, CT: Quorum Books.

Parsons, F. (1909). *Choosing a vocation.* Boston: Houghton-Mifflin.

Patton, W., & McMahon, M. (1999). *Career development and systems theory: A new relationship.* Pacific Grove, CA: Brooks/Cole.

Payne, R. L., & Cooper, C. L. (2001). *Emotions at work: Theory, research and applications for management.* Hoboken, NJ: Wiley.

Perry-Jenkins, M., & Gillman, S. (2000). Parental job experiences and children's well-being: The case of two-parent and single-mother working-class families. *Journal of Family and Economic Issues, 21,* 123–147.

Petersen, A. C., & Mortimer, J. T. (Eds.). (1994). *Youth, unemployment, and society.* New York: Cambridge University Press.

Peterson, N., & González, R. C. (2005). *The role of work in people's lives: Applied career counseling and vocational psychology* (2nd ed.). Pacific Grove, CA: Brooks/Cole.

Phelps, R., & Constantine, M. (2001). Hitting the roof: The impact of the glass-ceiling effect on the career development of African Americans. In C. Ward, W. B. Walsh, R. P. Bingham, & M. T. Brown (Eds.), *Career counseling for African Americans* (pp. 161–175). Mahwah, NJ: Lawrence Erlbaum Associates.

Phillips, S. D., Christopher-Sisk, E., & Gravino, K. (2001). Making career decisions in a relational context. *The Counseling Psychologist, 29,* 193–213.

Phillips, S. D., & Imhoff, A. R. (1997). Women and career development: A decade of research. *Annual Review of Psychology, 48,* 31–59.

Phillips, S. D., Blustein, D. L., Jobin-Davis, K., & White, S. F. (2002). Preparations for the school-to-work transition: The views of high school students. *Journal of Vocational Behavior, 61,* 202–216.

Pinderhughes, E. (1983). Empowerment for our clients and for ourselves. *Social Casework, 64,* 331–338.

Pollack, W. (2000). *Real boys' voices.* New York: Random House.

Pope, M. (2000). A brief history of career counseling in the United States. *Career Development Quarterly, 48,* 194–211.

Pope, M., Prince, J., & Mitchell, K. (2000). Responsible career counseling with lesbian and gay students. In D. A. Luzzo (Ed.), *Career counseling of college students: An empirical guide to strategies that work* (pp. 267–282). Washington, DC: American Psychologist Association.

Pope-Davis, D., & Hargrove, B. (2001). Future directions in career counseling theory, research, and practice with African Americans. In C. Ward, B. W. Walsh, R. P. Bingham, & M. T. Brown (Eds.), *Career counseling for African Americans* (pp. 177–192). Mahwah, NJ: Lawrence Erlbaum Associates.

Powell, G. N. (Ed.). (1999). *Handbook of gender and work.* Thousand Oaks, CA: Sage Publications.

Prediger, D. J., & Swaney, K. B. (1995). Using UNIACT in a comprehensive approach to assessment for career planning. *Journal of Career Assessment, 3,* 429–451.

Price, T. D., & Brown, J. A. (1985). *Prehistoric hunter-gatherers: The emergence of cultural complexity.* Beaverton, Oregon: Timber Press.

Price, R., Choi, J., & Vinokur, A. (2002). Links in the chain of adversity following job loss: How financial strain and loss of personal control lead to depression, impaired functioning, and poor health. *Journal of Occupational Health Psychology, 7,* 302–312.

Prilleltensky, I. (1997). Values, assumptions, and practices: Assessing the moral implications of psychological discourse and action. *American Psychologist, 52,* 517–535.

Prilleltensky, I. (2003). Understanding, resisting, and overcoming oppression: Toward psychopolitical validity. *American Journal of Community Psychology, 31,* 195–201.

Prilleltensky, I., & Gonick, L. (1994). The discourse of oppression in the social sciences: Past, present, and future. In E. J. Trickett, R. J. Watts, & D. Birman (Eds.), *Human diversity: Perspectives on people in context* (pp. 145–177). San Francisco: Jossey-Bass.

Prilleltensky, I., & Gonick, L. (1996). Polities change, oppression remains: On the psychology and politics of oppression. *Political Psychology, 17,* 127–148.

Prilleltensky, I., & Nelson, G. (2002). *Doing Psychology: Making a difference in diverse settings.* London: Palgrave.

Prilleltensky, I., Rossiter, A., & Walsh-Bowers, R. (1996). Preventing harm and promoting ethical discourse in the helping professions: Conceptual, research, analytical, and action frameworks. *Ethics & Behavior, 6,* 287–306.

Pritchard, R. D., Hollenback, J., & DeLeo, P. J. (1980). The effects of continuous and partial schedules of reinforcement on effort, performance, and satisfaction. *Organizational Behavior and Human Performance, 25,* 336–353.

Putnam, R. (2000). *Bowling alone: The collapse and revival of American community.* New York: Touchstone Books/Simon & Schuster, Inc.

Quick, J. C., & Tetrick, L. E. (2003). *Handbook of occupational health psychology.* Washington, DC: American Psychological Association.

Rafnsdottir, G., & Gudmundsdottir, M. (2004). New technology and its impact on well being. *Work: Journal of Prevention, Assessment, & Rehabilitation, 22,* 31–39.

Rainey, H. G. (1993). Work motivation. In R. T. Golembiewski (Ed.), *Handbook of organizational behavior* (pp. 19–39). New York: Marcal-Dekker, Inc.

Rankin, B. (2003). How low-income women find jobs and its effects on earnings. *Work & Occupations, 30,* 281–301.

Rau, R. (2004). Job strain or healthy work: A question of task design. *Journal of Occupational Health Psychology, 9,* 322–338.

Rayner, C., & Keashly, L. (2005). Bullying at work: A perspective from Britain and North America. In S. Fox & P. Spector (Eds.), *Counterproductive work behavior: Investigations of actors and targets* (pp. 271–296). Washington, DC: American Psychological Association.

Reich, R. B. (1991). *The work of nations.* New York: Vintage Books.

Reich, R. B. (1999). *The new inequality: Creating solutions for poor America.* Boston: Beacon Press.

Riala, K., Isohanni, I., Jokelainen, J., Jones, P., & Isohanni, M. (2003). The relationship between childhood family background and educational performance, with special reference to single-parent families: A longitudinal study. *Social Psychology of Education, 6,* 349–365.

Richardson, C. (1999). *Batos, Bolillos, Pochos, and Peladas: Class and culture on the south Texas border.* Austin, TX: University of Texas Press.

Richardson, M. S. (1993). Work in people's lives: A location for counseling psychologists. *Journal of Counseling Psychology, 40,* 425–433.

Richardson, M. S. (1996). From career counseling to counseling/psychotherapy and work, jobs, and career. In M. L. Savickas & W. B. Walsh (Eds.), *Handbook of career counseling theory and practice* (pp. 347–360), Palo Alto, CA: Davies-Black Publishing.

Richardson, M. S. (2000). A new perspective for counselors: From career ideologies to empowerment through work and relationships practices. In A. Collin & R. Young (Eds.), *The future of career* (pp. 197–211). New York: Cambridge University Press.

Richardson, M. S. (2004). The emergence of new intentions in subjective experience: A social/personal constructionist and relational understanding. *Journal of Vocational Behavior, 64,* 485–498.

Rifkin, J. (1995). *The end of work: The decline of the global labor market force and the dawn of the post-market era.* New York: Tarcher/Putnam.

Riger, S. (1991). Gender dilemmas in sexual harassment policies and procedures. *American Psychologist, 46,* 497–505.

Riggar, T. F., & Maki, D. (2004). *Handbook of rehabilitation counseling.* New York: Springer.

Riis, J. (1890). *How the other half lives: Studies among the tenements of New York.* New York: Scribner.

Riley, D. (1997). Using local research to change 100 communities for children and families. *American Psychologist, 52,* 424–433.

Riverin-Simard, D. (1991). *Careers and social classes.* Montreal: Meriden Press.

Roberts, K. (1978). *The working class.* London: Longman.

Robinson, D. N. (1984). Ethics and advocacy. *American Psychologist, 39,* 787–793.

Robson, W. (2001). *Aging populations and the workforce: Challenges for employers.* Toronto: British-North American Committee.

Rogers, C. (1995). *On becoming a person: A therapist's view of psychotherapy.* Boston: Houghton Mifflin.

Rose, M. (2004). *The mind at work: Valuing the intelligence of the American worker.* New York: Viking.

Rossides, D. (1990). *Social stratification: The American class system in comparative perspective.* Englewood Cliffs, NJ: Prentice Hall.

Rowe, D. C. (2005). Under the skin: On the impartial treatment of genetic and environmental hypotheses of racial differences. *American Psychologist, 60,* 60–70.

Rubin, L. B. (1994). *Families on the fault line: America's working class speaks about the family, the economy, race, and ethnicity.* New York: HarperCollins.

Rubin, S. E., & Roessler, R. T. (2001). *Foundations of the vocational rehabilitation process.* Austin, TX: PRO-ED, Inc.

Rudel, R. (1995). On visibility. In R. A. Rasi & E. Rodriguez-Nougues (Eds.), *Out in the workplace: The pleasures and perils of coming out on the job* (pp. 52–60). Los Angles, CA: Alyson Publications.

Russell, J. (1994). Career counseling for women in management. In W. B. Walsh & S. H. Osipow (Eds.), *Career counseling for women. Contemporary topics in vocational psychology* (pp. 263–326). Hillsdale, NJ: Lawrence Erlbaum Associates.

Russell, J. (2003). Technology and careers. *Journal of Vocational Behavior, 63*, 153–158.

Ryan, R. M., & Deci, E. L. (2000). Self-determination theory and the facilitation of intrinsic motivation, social development and well-being. *American Psychologist, 55*, 68–78.

Ryan, R. M., Stiller, J., & Lynch, J. H. (1994). Representations of relationships to teachers, parents, and friends as predictors of academic motivation and self-esteem. *Journal of Early Adolescence, 14*, 226–249.

Safran, J. (2003). *Psychoanalysis and Buddhism: An unfolding dialogue.* Boston: Wisdom Publications.

Salgado, S. (1993). *Trabalho.* New York: Aperture Foundation.

Sampson, E. (1993). Identity politics: Challenges to psychology's understanding. *American Psychologist, 48*, 1219–1230.

Sanders, T. (2001). Female street workers, sexual violence, and protection strategies. *Journal of Sexual Aggression, 7*, 5–18.

Sandburg, C. (1994). *Chicago poems.* Mineola, NY: Dover Publications.

Santos, E. J. R., Ferreira, J. A., & Chaves, A. (2001). Implications of the sociopolitical context for career services delivery. *Career Development Quarterly, 50*, 45–56.

Savickas, M. L. (1993). Career counseling in the postmodern era. *Journal of Cognitive Psychotherapy, 7*, 205–215.

Savickas, M. L. (1995). Current theoretical issues in vocational psychology: Convergence, divergence, and schism. In W. B. Walsh & S. H. Osipow (Eds.), *Handbook of vocational psychology* (2nd ed., pp. 1–34). Hillsdale, NJ: Lawrence Erlbaum Associates.

Savickas, M. L. (2002). Career construction: A developmental theory of vocational behavior. In D. Brown (Ed.), *Career choice and development* (pp. 149–205). San Francisco: Jossey-Bass.

Savickas, M. L., & Baker, D. B. (2005). The history of vocational psychology: Antecedents, origin, and early development. In W. B. Walsh & M. L. Savickas (Eds.), *Handbook of vocational psychology* (3rd ed., pp. 15–50). Mahwah, NJ: Lawrence Erlbaum Associates.

Savickas, M. L., & Spokane, A. (1999). *Vocational interests: Meaning, measurement, and counseling use.* Palo Alto, CA: Davies-Black Publishing, Inc.

Schaufeli, W. (2004). The future of occupational health psychology. *Applied Psychology: An International Review, 53*, 502–517.

Schein, E. (1965). *Organizational psychology.* Oxford, England: Prentice-Hall.

Schein, E. (1990). Organizational culture. *American Psychologist, 45*, 109–119.

Schlossberg, N. (1995). *Counseling adults in transition: linking practice with theory.* New York: Springer.

Schor, J. B. (1993). *Overworked American: The unexpected decline of leisure.* New York: Basic Books.

Schultheiss, D. E. P. (2003). A relational approach to career counseling: Theoretical integration and practical application. *Journal of Counseling and Development, 81*, 301–310.

Schultheiss, D. E. P., Kress, H. M., Manzi, A. J., & Jeffrey, J. M. (2001). A qualitative investigation of parental and sibling attachment in career development: A cross-cultural comparison. *The Counseling Psychologist, 29*, 214–239.

Sennett, R. (1998). *The corrosion of character: The personal consequences of work in the new capitalism.* New York: Norton.

Serrano-García, I. (1994). The ethics of the powerful and the power of ethics. *American Journal of Community Psychology, 22*, 1–20.

Sewell, W. H., & Hauser, R. M. (1975). *Education, occupation, and earnings: Achievement in early career.* New York: Academic Press.

Sexton, T., & Whiston, S. (1994). The status of the counseling relationship: An empirical review, theoretical implications, and research directions. *Counseling Psychologist, 22*, 6–78.

Shaffer, J. B. P., & Galinsky, M. D. (1989). *Models of group therapy* (2nd ed.). Englewood Cliffs, NJ: Prentice Hall.

Shapiro, J. (1994). *No pity: People with disabilities forging a new civil rights movement.* New York: Times Books.

Sharf, R. (2000). *Theories of psychotherapy & counseling: Concepts and cases.* Belmont, CA: Brooks/Cole.

Sheldon, K., Williams, G., & Joiner, T. (2003). *Self-determination theory in the clinic.* New Haven, CT: Yale University Press.

Shipler, D. K. (2004). *The working poor: Invisible in America.* New York: Vintage.

Shirk, M., Bennett, N. G., & Aber, J. L. (1999). *Lives on the line: American families and the struggle to make ends meet.* Boulder, CO: Westview Press.

Shore, M. (1998). Beyond self-interest: Professional advocacy and the integration of theory, research, and practice. *American Psychologist, 53*, 474–479.

Shore, M., & Massimo, J. (1963). The effectiveness of a comprehensive, vocationally oriented psychotherapeutic program for adolescent delinquent boys. *American Journal of Orthopsychiatry, 33*, 634–642.

Shore, M., & Massimo, J. (1979). Fifteen years after treatment: A follow-up study of comprehensive vocationally-oriented psychotherapy. *American Journal of Orthopsychiatry, 49*, 240–245.

Silbereisen, R., Vondracek, F., & Berg, L. (1997). Differential timing of initial vocational choice: The influence of early childhood family relocation and parental support behaviors in two cultures. *Journal of Vocational Behavior, 50*, 41–59.

Sillitoe, A. (1958). *Saturday night and Sunday morning*. New York: Alfred Knopf.

Silverstein, L., Auerbach, C., & Levant, R. (2002). Contemporary fathers reconstructing masculinity: Clinical implications of gender role strain. *Professional Psychology: Research and Practice, 33*, 361–369.

Sinclair, U. (1906). *The jungle*. New York: Doubleday, Page, & Company.

Sloan, T. (2000). *Critical psychology: Voices for change*. New York: St. Martin's Press.

Smelser, N. J., & Erikson, E. H. (Eds.). (1980). *Themes of work and love in adulthood*. Cambridge, MA: Harvard University Press.

Smith, E. J. (1983). Issues in racial minorities' career behavior. In W. B. Walsh & S. H. Osipow (Eds.), *Handbook of vocational psychology: Vol. 1. Foundations* (pp. 161–222). Hillsdale, NJ: Lawrence Erlbaum Associates.

Socarides, C. W., & Kramer, S. (1997). *Work and its inhibitions: Psychoanalytic essays*. Madison, CT: International Universities Press.

Solberg, S., Howard, K., Blustein, D., & Close, W. (2002). Career development in the schools: Connecting school-to-work-to-life. *The Counseling Psychologist, 30*, 705–725.

Solomon, B. B. (1987). Empowerment: Social work in oppressed communities. *Journal of Social Work Practice, 2*, 79–91.

Spengler, P., Blustein, D., & Strohmer, D. (1990). Diagnostic and treatment overshadowing of vocational problems by personal problems. *Journal of Counseling Psychology, 37*, 372–381.

Spokane, A. R., Luchetta, E., & Richwine, M. (2002). Holland's theory of personalities in work environments. In D. Brown (Ed.), *Career choice and development* (pp. 149–205). San Francisco: Jossey-Bass.

Springsteen, B. (1998). *Songs*. New York: Avon Books.

Stake, J. (2000). When situations call for instrumentality and expressiveness: Resource appraisal, coping strategy choice, and adjustment. *Sex Roles, 42*, 865–885.

Statt, D. (1994). *Psychology and the world of work*. New York: New York University Press.

Stead, G. B. (2004). Culture and career psychology: A social constructionist perspective. *Journal of Vocational Behavior, 64*, 389–406.

Steinbeck, J. (1939). *The grapes of wrath*. New York: Viking Press.

Sternberg, R., Grigorenko, E., & Kidd, K. (2005). Intelligence, race, and genetics. *American Psychologist, 60*, 46–59.

Sterrett, E. (1998). Use of a job club to increase self-efficacy: A case study of return to work. *Journal of Employment Counseling, 35*, 69–78.

Stockman, N., Bonney, N., & Xuewen, S. (1995). *Women's work in East and West: The dual burden of employment and family life*. London, UK: UCL Press Limited.

Stolorow, R., & Atwood, G. (1997). Deconstructing the myth of the neutral analyst: An alternative from intersubjective systems theory. *Psychoanalytic Quarterly, 66*, 431–449.

Strauss, A., & Corbin, J. (1990). *Basics of qualitative research: Grounded theory procedures and techniques*. Newbury Park, CA: Sage.

Strozier, C. (2001). *Heinz Kohut: The making of a psychoanalyst*. New York: Farrar, Straus and Giroux.

Suarez-Orozco, C. (2004). Formulating identity in a globalized world. In M. Suarez-Orozco & D. Qin-Hilliard (Eds.), *Globalization: Culture and education in the new millennium* (pp. 173–202). Berkeley, CA: University of California Press.

Sue, D. (2004). Whiteness and ethnocentric monoculturalism: Making the "invisible" visible. *American Psychologist, 59*, 761–769.

Super, D. (1955). Personality integration through vocational counseling. *Journal of Counseling Psychology, 2*, 217–226.

Super, D. E. (1957). *The psychology of careers*. New York: Harper & Row.

Super, D. E. (1980). A life-span, life-space, approach to career development. *Journal of Vocational Behavior, 13,* 282–298.

Super, D. E., & Overstreet, P. L. (1960). *The vocational maturity of ninth grade boys.* Oxford, England: Columbia University. Teachers College.

Super, D. E., Starishevsky, R., Matlin, N., & Jordaan, J. (1963). *Career development: Self-concept theory.* New York: College Entrance Examination Board.

Super, D. E., Savickas, M. L., & Super, C. M. (1996). The life-span, life-space approach to careers. In D. Brown & L. Brown (Eds.), *Career choice and development* (3rd ed., pp. 121–178). San Francisco: Jossey-Bass.

Swanson, J. L. (1995). The process and outcome of career counseling. In W. B. Walsh & S. H. Osipow (Eds.), *Handbook of vocational psychology* (2nd ed., pp. 217–259). Hillsdale, NJ: Lawrence Erlbaum Associates.

Szymanski, E. M., Hershenson, D. B., Ettinger, J. M., & Enright, M. S. (1996). Career development interventions for people with disabilities. In E. M. Szymanski & R. M. Parker (Eds.), *Work and disability: Issues and strategies in career development and job placement.* Austin, TX: PRO-ED, Inc.

Szymanski, E. M., & Parker, R. M. (1996). *Work and disability: Issues and strategies in career development and job placement.* Austin, TX: PRO-ED, Inc.

Szymanski, E. M., & Parker, R. M. (2003). *Work and disability: Issues and strategies in career development and job placement* (2nd ed.). Austin, TX: PRO-ED, Inc.

Tan, H., & Aryee, S. (2002). Antecedents and outcomes of union loyalty: A constructive replication and an extension. *Journal of Applied Psychology, 87,* 715–722.

Tango, R., & Kolodinsky, P. (2004). Investigation of placement outcomes 3 years after job skills training program for chronically unemployed adults. *Journal of Employment Counseling, 41,* 80–93.

Tatum, B. D. (1999). *"Why are all the black kids sitting together in the cafeteria?" and other conversations about race.* New York: Basic Books.

Tedlock, B. (2000). Ethnography and ethnographic representation. In N. K. Denzin & Y. S. Lincoln (Eds.), *Handbook of qualitative research* (2nd ed., pp. 455–486). Thousand Oaks, CA: Sage.

Terkel, S. (1974). *Working: People talk about what they do all day and how they feel about what they do.* New York: Pantheon Books.

Terman, L., & Oden, M. (1959). *Genetic studies of genius: Vol. V. The gifted group at mid-life.* Oxford, England: Stanford University Press.

Tesser, A. (1995). *Advanced social psychology.* New York: McGraw-Hill Book Company.

Teyber, E., & McClure, F. (2000). Therapist variables. In C. R. Snyder & R. E. Ingram (Eds.), *Handbook of psychological change: Psychotherapy processes & practices for the 21st century* (pp. 62–87). New York: Wiley.

Thomas, K. (Ed.). (1999). *The Oxford book of work.* Oxford, UK: Oxford University Press.

Thomas, R. J. (1989). Blue collar careers: Meaning and choice in a world of constraints. In M. B. Arthur, D. T. Hall, & B. S. Lawrence (Eds.), *Handbook of career theory* (pp. 354–379). New York: Cambridge University Press.

Thompson, B. (2000). Canonical correlation analysis. In L. G. Grimm & P. R. Yarnold (Eds.), *Reading and understanding MORE multivariate statistics* (pp. 285–316). Washington, DC: American Psychological Association.

Thompson, C. E., & Neville, H. A., (1999). Racism, mental health, and mental health practice. *The Counseling Psychologist, 27,* 153–223.

Tokar, D., Withrow, J., Hall, R., & Moradi, B. (2003). Psychological separation, attachment security, vocational self-concept crystallization, and career indecision: A structural equation analysis. *Journal of Counseling Psychology, 50,* 3–19.

Tolpin, M. (1983). Corrective emotional experience: A self-psychological reevaluation. In A. Goldberg (Ed.), *The future of psychoanalysis* (pp. 255–271). New York: International Universities Press.

Triandis, H. C. (2002). Motivation to work in cross-cultural perspective. In J. M. Brett & F. Drasgow (Eds.), *The psychology of work: Theoretically based empirical research* (pp. 101–117). Mahwah, NJ: Lawrence Erlbaum Associates.

Tucker, M., & Codding, J. (1998). *Standards for our schools: How to set them, measure them, and reach them.* San Francisco: Jossey-Bass.

Ulrich, D. N., & Dunne, H. P. (1986). *To love and work: A systematic interlocking of family, workplace, and career.* New York: Brunner/Mazel.

U.S. Department of Health, Education, and Welfare. (1973). *Work in America.* Cambridge, MA: MIT Press.

U.S. Department of Labor, Bureau of Labor Statistics. (2004). *Occupational outlook handbook*. Retrieved July 8, 2004 from DOL Web site via GPO access: http://www.bls.gov/oco/home.htm

Vera, E., & Reese, L. (2000). Preventive interventions with school-aged youth. In S. D. Brown & R. W. Lent (Eds.), *Handbook of counseling psychology* (3rd ed., pp. 435–470). New York: Wiley.

Vera, E., & Speight, S. (2003). Multicultural competence, social justice, and counseling psychology: Expanding our roles. *The Counseling Psychologist, 31*, 253–272.

Vinokur, A., & Schul, Y. (1997). Mastery and inoculation against setbacks as active ingredients in the JOBS intervention for the unemployed. *Journal of Consulting & Clinical Psychology, 65*, 867–877.

Vinokur, A., Schul, Y., Vuori, J., & Price, R. (2000). Two years after a job loss: Long-term impact of the JOBS program on reemployment and mental health. *Journal of Occupational Health Psychology, 5*, 32–47.

Vondracek, F. W., Lerner, R. M., & Schulenberg, J. E. (1986). *Career development: A life-span developmental approach*. Hillsdale, NJ: Lawrence Erlbaum Associates.

Voydanoff, P. (2004). Implications of work and community demands and resources for work-to-family conflict and facilitation. *Journal of Occupational Health Psychology, 9*, 275–285.

Vroom, V. H. (1964). *Work and motivation*. New York: Wiley.

Wachtel, P. L. (1983). The poverty of affluence. New York: Free Press.

Wachtel, P. L. (1987). *Action and insight*. New York: Guilford.

Wachtel, P. L. (1993). *Therapeutic communication: Principles and effective practice*. New York: Guilford Press.

Wachtel, P. L. (1997). *Psychoanalysis, behavior therapy, and the relational world*. Washington: APA Books.

Wachtel, P. L. (1999). *Race in the mind of America: Breaking the vicious circle between Blacks and Whites*. New York: Routledge.

Wachtel, P. L. (2001). Racism, vicious circles, and the psychoanalytic vision. *Psychoanalytic Review, 88*, 653–672.

Wallman, S. (Ed.). (1979). *Social anthropology of work*. New York: Academic Press.

Walsh, W. B. (2003). Person–environment psychology and well-being. In W. B. Walsh (Ed.), *Counseling psychology and optimal human functioning. Contemporary topics in vocational psychology* (pp. 93–121). Mahwah, NJ: Lawrence Erlbaum Associates.

Walsh, W. B., Bingham, R. P., Brown, M. T., & Ward, C. M. (Eds.). (2001). *Career counseling for African Americans*. Mahwah, NJ: Lawrence Erlbaum Associates.

Walsh, W. B., & Osipow, S. (1994). *Career counseling for women. Contemporary topics in vocational psychology*. Hillsdale, NJ: Lawrence Erlbaum Associates.

Walsh, W. B., & Savickas, M. L. (Eds.). (2005). *Handbook of vocational psychology* (3rd ed.). Mahwah, NJ: Lawrence Erlbaum Associates.

Wampold, B. (2001). *The great psychotherapy debate: Models, methods, and findings*. Mahwah, NJ: Lawrence Erlbaum Associates.

Wanberg, C. (1995). A longitudinal study of the effects of unemployment and quality of reemployment. *Journal of Vocational Behavior, 46*, 40–54.

Warnath, C. (1975). Vocational theories: Direction to nowhere. *Personnel & Guidance Journal, 53*, 422–428.

Waters, L., & Moore, K. (2002). Predicting self-esteem during unemployment: The effect of gender, financial deprivation, alternative roles, and social support. *Journal of Employment Counseling, 39*, 171–190.

Watts, R., Abdul-Adil, J., & Pratt, T. (2002). Enhancing critical consciousness in young African American men: A psychoeducational approach. *Psychology of Men & Masculinity, 3*, 41–50.

Way, W. L., & Rossman, M. M. (1996a). Family contribution to adolescent readiness for school-to-work transition. *Journal of Vocational Education Research, 21*, 5–33.

Way, W. L., & Rossman, M. M. (1996b). *Lessons from life's first teacher: The role of the family in adolescent and adult readiness for school-to-work transition* (MDS-725). Berkeley, CA: National Center for Research in Vocational Education.

Weis, L., & Fine, M. (1993). (Eds.). *Beyond silenced voices: Class, race, and gender in the United States schooling*. Albany, NY: State University of New York Press.

Wester, S., Vogel, D., Page, P., & Heesacker, M. (2002). Sex differences in emotion: A critical review of the literature and implications for counseling psychology. *Counseling Psychologist, 30*, 630–652.

Whiston, S., Breicheisen, B., & Stephens, J. (2003). Does treatment modality affect career counseling effectiveness? *Journal of Vocational Behavior, 62*, 390–410.

Whiston, S., & Keller, B. (2004). The influences of the family of origin on career development: A review and analysis. *The Counseling Psychologist, 32,* 493–568.

Whiston, S., Sexton, T., & Lasoff, D. (1998). Career-intervention outcome: A replication and extension of Oliver and Spokane (1988). *Journal of Counseling Psychology, 45,* 150–165.

White, R. (1959). Motivation reconsidered: The concept of competence. *Psychological Review, 66,* 297–333.

Whitely, J. M. (Ed.). (1980). *The history of counseling psychology.* Monterey, CA: Brooks/Cole.

Wilkinson, S. (1997). Feminist psychology. In D. Fox & I. Prilleltensky (Eds.), *Critical psychology: An introduction* (pp. 247–265). London: Sage Publications.

Willis, P. (1977). *Learning to labor: How working class kids get working class jobs.* New York: Columbia University Press.

Wilson, W. J. (1996). *When work disappears: The world of the new urban poor.* New York: Random House.

Winefield, A. (2002). The psychology of unemployment. In C. Hofsten & L. Backman (Eds.), *Psychology at the turn of the millennium: Vol. 2. Social, developmental, and clinical perspectives* (pp. 393–408). Florence, KY: Taylor & Frances/Routledge.

Winefield, A., Montgomery, B., Gualt, U., Muller, J., O'Gorman, J., Reser, J., & Roland, D. (2002). The psychology of work and unemployment in Australia today: An Australian Psychological Society discussion paper. *Australian Psychologist, 37,* 1–9.

Wolberg, L. R. (1977). *The technique of psychotherapy* (Part 1, 3rd ed.). New York: Grune & Stratton.

Wolf, E. (1980). On the developmental line of self–object relations. In A. Goldberg (Ed.), *Advances in self psychology* (pp. 117–130). New York: International Universities Press.

Wolfe, A. (1998). *One nation, after all: What middle-class Americans really think about God, country, family, racism, welfare, immigration, homosexuality, work, the right, the left, and each other.* New York: Viking.

Wolf-Powers, L. (2001). Information technology and urban labor markets in the United States. *International Journal of Urban and Regional Research, 25,* 427–437.

Worthington, R. L., & Juntunen, C. L. (1997). The vocational development of non-college-bound youth: Counseling psychology and the school-to-work transition movement. *The Counseling Psychologist, 25,* 323–363.

Wright, B. A. (1983). *Physical disability: A psychological approach* (2nd ed.). New York: Harper & Row.

Yelland, N. (1998). *Making sense of gender issues in mathematics and technology.* Florence, KY: Taylor & Frances/Routledge.

Yoder, J. (1999). *Women and gender: Transforming psychology.* Upper Saddle River, NJ: Prentice Hall.

Young, K., & Takeuchi, D. (1998). *Handbook of Asian American psychology.* Thousand Oaks, CA: Sage Publications.

Young, R. A., & Collin, A. (Eds.). (1992). *Interpreting career: Hermeneutical studies of lives in context.* Westport, CT: Praeger.

Young, R. A., Valach, L., & Collin, A. (2002). A contextualist explanation of career. In D. Brown (Ed.), *Career choice and development* (4th ed., pp. 206–252). San Francisco: Jossey-Bass.

Zaretsky, A. (2003). Targeted psychosocial interventions for bipolar disorder. *Bipolar Disorders, 5,* 80–87.

Zeig, J., & Munion, W. M. (1990). *What is psychotherapy? Contemporary perspectives.* San Fancisco: Jossey-Bass Publishers.

Zickar, M. J. (2001). Conquering the next frontier: Modeling personality data with item response theory. In B. Roberts & R. Hogan (Eds.), *Personality psychology in the workplace: Decade of behavior* (pp. 141–160). Washington, DC: American Psychological Association.

Zickar, M. J. (2003). Remembering Arthur Kornhauser: Industrial psychology's advocate for worker well-being. *Journal of Applied Psychology, 88,* 363–369.

Zickar, M. J. (2004). An analysis of industrial-organizational psychology's indifference to labor unions in the United States. *Human Relations, 57,* 145–167.

Zinn, H. (1980). *A people's history of the United States.* New York: Harper & Row.

Zunker, V. G., & Osborn, D. S. (2002). *Using assessment results for career development* (6th ed.). Pacific Grove, CA: Brooks/Cole.

Zytowski, D. (2001). Frank Parsons and the progressive movement. *The Career Development Quarterly, 50,* 57–65.

ACKNOWLEDGMENTS

Preface

Page xi, "*Adam Raised a Cain*" by Bruce Springsteen. Copyright © 1978 Bruce Springsteen (ASCAP). Reprinted by permission. International copyright secured. All rights reserved.

Chapter 1

Page 1: From *It Comes with the Territory: An Inquiry Concerning Work and the Person* by A. Gini & T. J. Sullivan. Copyright © 1989. Reprinted with permission by author.

Page 1: From Lessons from Industrial and Organizational Psychology by C. L. Hulin. In J. M. Brett & F. Drasgow (Eds.), *The Psychology of Work: Theoretically Based Empirical Research*, Copyright © 2002, Lawrence Erlbaum Associates. Reprinted with permission.

Page 3: From *Psychology of Work and Unemployment* by G. E. O'Brien. Copyright © 1986. John Wiley & Sons Limited. Reproduced with permission.

Page 6: "*Booker T. Washington.*" Copyright © 1901, from *The Oxford Book of Work* by Thomas Keith. Copyright © 1999, Oxford University Press. Reprinted with permission.

Pages 6–7: From *The Oxford Book of Work* by Thomas Keith. Copyright © 1999, Oxford University Press. Reprinted with permission.

Page 9: From *Families on the Faultline* by Lillian B. Rubin. Copyright © 1994 by Lillian B. Rubin. Originally published by Harper & Rowe. Reprinted by the permission of Dunham Literary as agent for the author

Page 11: Reprinted from *Journal of Vocational Behavior, Vol. 13*, D. E. Super. A Life Span, Life Space Approach to Career Development, pp. 282–298. Copyright © 1980 with permission from Elsevier.

Page 16: From Remembering Arthur Kornhauser: Industrial Psychology's Advocate for Worker Well-being, by M. J. Zickar, 2003. *Journal of Applied Psychology, 88*, 363–369. Copyright © 2003 by the American Psychological Association. Reprinted with permission.

Pages 18–19, 25: From *Work and the Evolving Self: Theoretical and Clinical Considerations* by Steven Axelrod. Copyright © 1999. The Analytic Press. Reprinted with permission.

Page 20: From *Work and Human Behavior* by W. S. Neff. Copyright © 1985 by Aldine Publishers. Reprinted by permission of Aldine Transaction, a division of Aldine Publishers.

Pages 27–28: From *The Corrosion of Character: The Personal Consequences of Work in the New Capitalism* by R. Sennett, Copyright © 1998. W. W. Norton and Company, Inc. Reprinted with permission.

Chapter 2

Page 27: From *SATURDAY NIGHT AND SUNDAY MORNING* by Alan Sillitoe. Copyright © 1958 by Alan Sillitoe. Used by permission of Alfred A. Knopf, a division of Random House, Inc.

Page 32: From *AMOSKEAG: LIFE AND WORK IN AN AMERICAN FACTORY-CITY* by Tamara K. Hareven. Copyright © 1978 by Tamara K. Hareven & Randolph Langenbach. Photo copyright ©

Chapter 3

Chapter 4

Page 86: From *NO SHAME IN MY GAME* by Katherine S. Newman. Copyright © 1999 by Russell Sage Foundation. Used by permission of Alfred A. Knopf, a division of Random House, Inc.

Page 86: 'A Death at the Office.' From *SURE SIGNS: NEW AND SELECTED POEMS*, by Ted Kooser. Copyright © 1980. Reprinted by permission of the University of Pittsburgh Press.

Page 87: From *THE MIND AT WORK* by Mike Rose, Copyright © 2004 by Mike Rose. Used by permission of Viking Penguin, a division of Penguin Group (USA) Inc.

Pages 90–91: From Women, Men, Work, and Family by R.C. Barnett & J. S. Hyde, 2001. *American Psychologist, 56*, 781–796. Copyright © 2001 by the American Psychological Association. Reprinted with permission.

Page 92: From *WOMEN IN THE MINES*, by M. Moore. Twayne Publishers, Copyright © 1996 Twayne Publishers. Reprinted by permission of The Gale Group.

Pages 92–93: From *Chicago Poems* by Carl Sandburg, Copyright © 1994. Dover Publications.

Page 100: From *Death of a Salesman* by Arthur Miller, Copyright © 1949, renewed © 1977 by Arthur Miller. Used by permission of Viking Penguin, a division of Penguin Group(USA) Inc.

Page 101: From American Indian Perspectives on the Career Journey, by C. L. Juntenen, D. J. Barraclough, C. J. Broneck, G. A. Seibel, S. A. Winrow, & P. M. Morin, 2001. *Journal of Counseling Psychology, 48*, 274–285. Copyright © 2001 by the American Psychological Association. Reprinted with permission.

Page 102: From *Journal of Vocational Behavior, Vol. 61*, No. 2, pp. 202–216. Copyright © 2002. In Preparations for the School-to-work Transition by S. D. Phillips, D. L. Blustein, K. Jobin-Davis, & S. F. White. With permission from Elsevier.

Page 103: From *SATURDAY NIGHT AND SUNDAY MORNING* by Alan Sillitoe. Copyright © 1958 by Alan Sillitoe. Used by permission of Alfred A. Knopf, a division of Random House, Inc.

Page 105: From *Families on the Faultline* by Lillian B. Rubin. Copyright © 1994 by Lillian B. Rubin. Originally published by Harper & Rowe. Reprinted by the permission of Dunham Literary as agent for the author.

Page 110: From Beyond Self-Interest: Professional Advocacy and the Integration of Theory, Research and Practice, by M. Shore, 1998. *American Psychologist, 53*, 474–479. Copyright © 1998 by the American Psychological Association. Reprinted with permission.

Chapter 5

Page 114: From "chapter 14" *THE GRAPES OF WRATH* by John Steinbeck. Copyright © 1939, renewed © 1967 by John Steinbeck. Used by permission of Viking Penguin, a division of Penguin Group (USA) Inc.

Page 115: From *Blood, Sweat & Tears: The Evolution of Work*, 1st ed., by R. Donkin. Copyright © 2001, NY: Texere. Reprinted with permission.

Pages 115, 131, 135, 136, 139, 142–143: From *GIG* by John Bowe, Marisa Bowe, & Sabin Streeter. Copyright © 2000, 2001 by John Bowe, Marisa Bowe, and Sabin Streeter. Used by permission of Crown Publishers, a division of Random House, Inc.

Pages 116, 129: From *Border People* by Oscar Martinez. Copyright © 1994, University of Arizona Press. Reprinted with permission.

Page 118: From *The Psychology of Careers*. Copyright © 1957 by Donald E. Super, Harper & Row.

Page 120: From A Contextualist Explanation of Career by R. A. Young, L. Valach, & A. Collin. In D. Brown & Associates (Eds.), *Career Choice and Development*. Copyright © 2002. Reprinted with permission by John Wiley & Sons.

Page 124: From Motivation to Work in Cross-Cultural Perspective by H. C. Triandis. In *The Psychology of Work: Theoretically Based Empirical Research* by J. M Brett & F. Drasgow (Eds.). Copyright © 2002, Lawrence Erlbaum Associates. Reprinted with permission.

Pages 125–126, 145: From *Self-determination Theory in The Clinic* by K. Sheldon, G. Williams, & T. Joiner. Copyright © 2003, Yale University Press. Reprinted with permission.

Page 130: From *NO SHAME IN MY GAME* by Katherine S. Newman. Copyright © 1999 by Russell Sage Foundation. Used by permission of Alfred A. Knopf, a division of Random House, Inc.

Chapter 6

Pages 187–188: From On Visibility by Ruthann Rudel. In *Out in the Workplace: The Pleasures and Perils of Coming Out on the Job* by R. A. Rasi & L. Rodgriguez-Nogues (Eds.). Alyson Books, LPI Media Inc. Reprinted with permission.

Chapter 7

Page 196: From *NO SHAME IN MY GAME* by Katherine S. Newman., Copyright © 1999 by Russell Sage Foundation. Used by permission of Alfred A. Knopf, a division of Random House, Inc.

Page 196: From *The Career is Dead, Long Live the Career* by D. T. Hall. Copyright © 1996. Reprinted with permission of John Wiley & Sons, Inc.

Pages 198–200, 203–204: From *Journal of Vocational Behavior, Vol. 61*, No. 2, pp. 202–216. Copyright © 2002. Preparations for the School-to-Work Transition by S. D. Phillips, D. L. Blustein, K. Jobin-Davis, & S. F. White, with permission from Elsevier.

Pages 202–204: From *Values, Assumptions, and Practices: Assessing the Moral Implications of Psychological Discourse and Action* by I. Prilleltensky. Copyright © 1997 by the American Psychological Association. Reprinted with permission.

Page 205T: From *Values, Assumptions, and Practices: Assessing the Moral Implications of Psychological Discourse and Action* by I. Prilleltensky. Copyright © 1997 by the American Psychological Association. Reprinted with permission.

Page 214: From *Career Guidance and Counseling Through the Lifespan: Systematic Approaches* (6th ed.) by E. L. Herr, S. H. Cramer, & S. G. Niles. Copyright © 2004 with permission from Allyn & Bacon, a part of Pearson Education.

Page 239: From *Empathy Reconsidered: New Directions in Psychotherapy* by A. Bohart & L. Greenberg. Copyright © 1997 by the American Psychological Association. Reprinted with permission.

Chapter 8

Page 243: From Integrated Psychology by J. H. Gladfelter. In *What is Psychotherapy: Contemporary Perspectives* by J. Zeig & W. M. Munion (Eds.). Copyright © 1990. Reprinted with permission of John Wiley & Sons, Inc.

Page 243: From *The Counseling Psychologist*, by David L. Blustein. Copyright © 2001, Sage Publications. Reprinted with permission.

Page 243: From Work in People's Lives: A Location for Counseling Psychologists by M. S. Richardson, 1993. *Journal of Counseling Psychology, 40*, 425–433. Copyright © 1993 by the American Psychological Association. Reprinted with permission.

Page 248: From *What is Psychotherapy: Contemporary Perspectives* by J. Zeig & W. M. Munion. Copyright © 1990. Reprinted with permission of John Wiley & Sons, Inc.

Page 248: Reprinted from *Technique of Psychotherapy*, 3rd ed., by L. R. Wolberg. Copyright © 1978, with permission from Elsevier.

Page 254: From Beyond Self-Interest: Professional Advocacy and the Integration of Theory, Research and Practice by M. Shore, 1998. *American Psychologist, 53*, 474–479. Copyright © 1998 by the American Psychological Association. Reprinted with permission.

Pages 254–255: From Personal Adjustment: Career Counseling and Psychotherapy by D. L. Blustein & P. M. Spengler. In B. W. Walsh & S. H. Osipow (Eds.), *Handbook of Vocational Psychology: Theory, Research and Practice*, 2nd ed. Copyright © 1995, Lawrence Erlbaum Associates. Reprinted with permission.

Page 265: From *Journal of Vocational Behavior, Vol. 48*, No. 2, pp. 210–228, Copyright © 1996. Impact of Identity by K. Boatwright M. Gilbert, L. Forrest, & K. Ketzenberger. With permission from Elsevier.

Page 270: From Career Counseling with Racial and Ethnic Minorities by N. Fouad & R. Bingham. In *Handbook of Vocational Psychology, Vol. 2* by W. B Walsh & H. Osipow (Eds.). Copyright © 1995. Lawrence Erlbaum Associates. Reprinted with permission.

Chapter 9

Chapter 10

Author Index

Subject Index

A

African American racism, 156–160
affluent population, 7–9, 30, 40, 52, 63, 175, 190
anthropological perspectives of working, 71–73
Asian American racism, 162–163
assessment role, 285–288
at-risk youth, 247, 260, 262–264
　　see also school-to-work transition
autonomy
　　and control, 48–50
　　and empowerment, 194
　　and independence, 64, 97
　　and motivation, 126–128
　　need for, 133–137
　　and relatedness, 140–141
　　and self-expression, 70
　　support for, 145–152
　　see also self-determination theory
awareness (racial identity theory), 158
　　see also racial identity theory

B

balance theory, 122–123
basic skills role, 224–226
bisexual clients, 265–266
"Boss," 179

C

capitalism, 7–8, 43, 49, 98–99, 281
career choices
　　adjusting to, 94
　　and development theories, 115–121, 127, 141–142, 167
　　finding, 11
　　making, 246
　　see also career development

career counseling
　　and changes, 24
　　concept of, 245
　　and conflict, 99–100
　　and culture, 270
　　methods of, 307
　　process of, 282–285
　　and psychotherapy, 229–230, 252–259, 276
　　and social connections, 110–111
　　and vocational psychology, 10–17
　　see also career development, vocational counseling
career development
　　theories, 68–76, 115–121, 250–251
　　assumptions, 71, 107–108, 111–112, 116–121, 157, 168, 229–230, 250–251
　　practice, 73, 76, 204–205, 246, 250–253, 259–260, 294–295
　　see also career counseling, vocational counseling
Career Development Quarterly, 99, 111
Career Is Dead—Long Live the Career: A Relational Approach to Careers, 29, 49
careers
　　birth of, 30–37
　　changing nature of, 27–66
　　counseling, 10–17
　　of today, 54–62
　　see also working
caregiving
　　bonds in, 96
　　changes in, 51–53
　　and gender, 165–166, 303–304
　　and working, 51–53, 96, 104–108, 165–166, 303–304
changing career contract, 46–48
Choosing a Vocation, 117
Civilization and Its Discontents, 69